AF572436

GEORGIA'S LEGACY:
History Charted Through the Arts

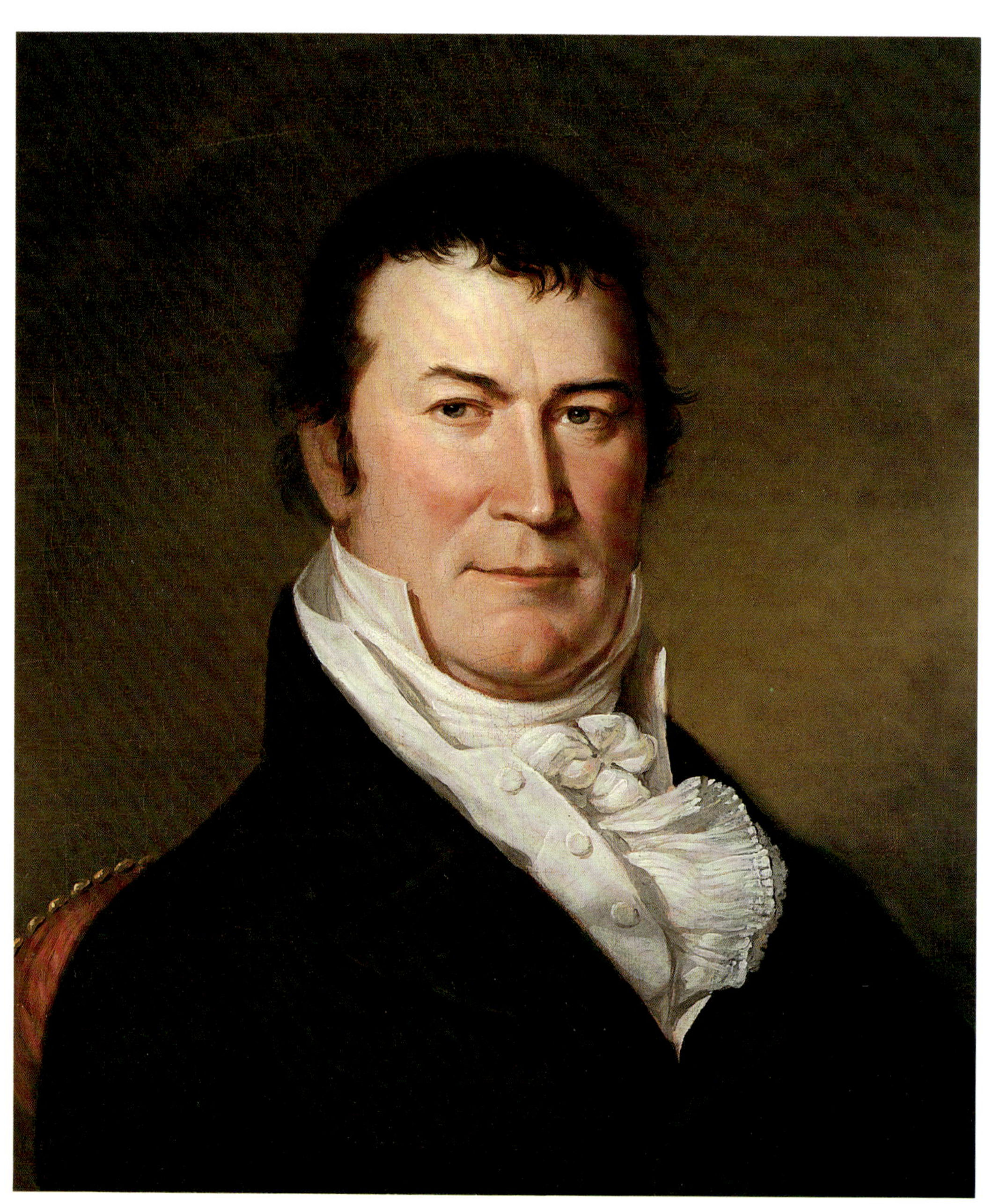

GEORGIA'S LEGACY: *History Charted Through the Arts*

An Exhibition Organized on the Occasion of the Bicentennial of The University of Georgia, 1785–1985

Jane Webb Smith

with additional essays by
Diana Williams Combs
Charles Hudson
B. Phinizy Spalding
Robert M. Willingham, Jr.

edited by
Marianne Doezema

April 25 - September 3, 1985

Georgia Museum of Art
The University of Georgia

This program is supported in part by

National Endowment for the Humanities

Georgia Council for the Arts
through the appropriations of the
Georgia General Assembly and the
National Endowment for the Arts

Office of Bicentennial Planning, The University of Georgia

A-1 Veterans Transfer Company, Athens

In appreciation of his persistent devotion to the preservation of Georgia's legacy, this publication is dedicated to

Henry D. Green

Frontispiece: Charles Willson Peale (1741–1827), *William Harris Crawford*, 1818. Oil on canvas, H. 24", W. 20". High Museum of Art.

Printed in the United States of America

Library of Congress Cataloging in Publication Data

Main entry under title:
Georgia's Legacy

Bibliography: p. 221
1. Material culture—Georgia—Exhibitions. 2. Art, American—Georgia—Exhibitions. 3. Georgia—Industries—Exhibitions. I. Smith, Jane Webb, 1951– . II. Doezema, Marianne, 1950– III. University of Georgia.
F286.G39 1985 975.8 85-8159
ISBN 0-915977-01-X

Photograph credits: Amon Carter Museum, Fort Worth, TX, catalogue no. 56; Armen Photographer, Newark, NJ, catalogue no. 44; Bill Hull, Atlanta Historical Society, GA, catalogue nos. 38, 81, 112, 113, 123, 125–27; Cindy Clarke, Athens, GA, p. 98; Daniel L. Grantham, Savannah, GA, catalogue nos. 49, 124; Department of Library Services, American Museum of Natural History, catalogue nos. 22–25, 28; Georgia Department of Natural Resources, Parks and Historic Sites Division, figure no. 1 (p. 31), catalogue no. 2; Jerome Drown, Atlanta, GA, catalogue nos. 59, 114; Kenneth Kay, Athens, GA, catalogue nos. 50, 75, 82, 83; The Mariner's Museum, Newport News, VA, catalogue no. 40; Museum of Early Southern Decorative Arts, Winston-Salem, NC, figure nos. 2 (p. 55), 4 (p. 62), 7 (p. 68), catalogue nos. 35, 36, 45, 46, 51, 60, 84, 108, 111; Michael McKelvey, Atlanta, GA, figure nos. 1–14 (pp. 38–50), 1 (p. 54), 3 (p. 57), 1–20 (pp. 76–83), catalogue nos. 1, 3–6, 8, 14–21, 26, 27, 29–34, 37, 39, 41–43, 48, 52–55, 57, 58, 61–74, 76–80, 85–89, 91–96, 98–107, 109, 110, 115–22, 128–34, 136–57, pp. 84, 120, 150, 194; Richard Polhemus, figure no. 4 (p. 35); Smithsonian Institution, Washington, DC, figure no. 2 (p. 32), catalogue nos. 7, 9–13, 90, 97; Photographic Services, The University of Georgia Libraries, Athens, GA, figure nos. 5 (p. 66), 6a (p. 67); The Henry Francis du Pont Winterthur Museum, Winterthur, DE, figure no. 6b (p. 67), catalogue no. 135; Yale University Art Gallery, New Haven, CT, catalogue no. 47.

CONTENTS

LENDERS

Mr. and Mrs. Billy F. Allen
Amon Carter Museum, Fort Worth, Texas
Mr. Cecil W. Anderson
Antebellum Plantation, Georgia's Stone Mountain Park
Athens-Clarke Heritage Foundation, Georgia
Mr. and Mrs. Jack P. Atkinson
Atlanta Historical Society, Georgia
Atlanta Masonic Library and Museum Association, Georgia
Mr. William T. Barfield
Mr. and Mrs. Fred D. Bentley, Sr.
Mr. Robert B. Berryman
Dr. and Mrs. J. Turner Bryson
Dr. John A. Burrison
The Columbus Museum of Arts and Science, Georgia
Dr. Diana Williams Combs
Confederate Museum, Alexander Stephens State Park, Crawfordville, Georgia
Mr. and Mrs. Dale C. Critz
Miss Anne Elizabeth Deméré
Department of Anthropology, American Museum of Natural History, New York, New York
Department of Anthropology, The University of Georgia, Athens
Judge and Mrs. Homer Durden, Jr.
Mrs. John Ray Efird
Fulton Federal Savings and Loan, Atlanta, Georgia
Georgia College Foundation, Old Governor's Mansion, Milledgeville
Georgia Department of Natural Resources, Parks and Historic Sites, Atlanta, Georgia
Georgia Historical Society, Savannah
Mr. and Mrs. Henry D. Green
Mr. and Mrs. William W. Griffin
Mr. Steve Cabot Barnes Harvey
Robert M. Hicklin Jr. Inc., Spartanburg, South Carolina
High Museum of Art, Atlanta, Georgia
Mr. and Mrs. Joseph H. Hilsman III
Historic Columbus Foundation, Georgia
Historic Oakland Cemetery, Inc., Atlanta, Georgia
Historic Savannah Foundation, Georgia
Jekyll Island Museum, Georgia
Mr. R. N. Kennedy, Jr.
Mr. Harold King
Kolomoki Mounds Museum, Blakely, Georgia
Mr. F. Clason Kyle and Other Descendants
LaGrange College, Georgia
Mr. and Mrs. L. Milton Leathers III
Madison-Morgan Cultural Center, Georgia

Mrs. Sam McCormick
Montclair Art Museum, New Jersey
Museum of Coastal History, St. Simons Island, Georgia
Museum of Early Southern Decorative Arts, Winston-Salem, North Carolina
National Museum of Natural History, Smithsonian Institution, Washington, D.C.
National Park Service, Fort Frederica National Monument, St. Simons Island, Georgia
National Park Service, Ocmulgee National Monument, Macon, Georgia
National Portrait Gallery, Smithsonian Institution, Washington, D.C.
Mr. Edward W. Neal
Mrs. A. C. Nichols, Jr.
Polk County Historical Society, Cedartown, Georgia
The President of Emory University, Atlanta, Georgia
Private Collections
Mr. and Mrs. Albert Dobbs Sams, Sr.
Ships of the Sea Maritime Museum, Savannah, Georgia
Mr. Howard A. Smith
Mrs. William Tate
Telfair Academy of Arts and Sciences, Savannah, Georgia
Thomas County Historical Society, Thomasville, Georgia
Special Collections, The University of Georgia Libraries, Athens
Special Collections, Robert W. Woodruff Library, Emory University, Atlanta, Georgia
Westville Historic Handicrafts, Inc., Lumpkin, Georgia
Mr. James A. Williams
Mr. Joe Mack Wilson
The Henry Francis du Pont Winterthur Museum, Delaware
Yale University Art Gallery, New Haven, Connecticut
Mrs. William H. Young, Jr. and Mr. William H. Young III

EXHIBITION COMMITTEE

Callie Huger Efird
Katharine G. Farnham
Henry D. Green
William and Florence Griffin
David J. Hally
Frank L. Horton
Charles Hudson
Bradford L. Rauschenberg
Lisa Reynolds
B. Phinizy Spalding
Robert M. Willingham, Jr.

PREFACE

A project of this complexity deserves a statement about its origins and organization. In 1980, a few individuals realized that a very important aspect of Georgia's history, its cultural past, had neither been told nor presented in a comprehensive way. The University of Georgia was then involved in making plans to celebrate its Bicentennial and the founding of this nation's oldest chartered state university. The moment seemed appropriate for an exhibition that would chart the history of the State of Georgia through objects illustrating its cultural achievements prior to the Civil War.

A letter outlining this exhibition was sent to the Bicentennial Planning Committee in July 1980. Shortly thereafter, an ad hoc committee consisting of Mr. Henry Green, Mrs. Albert Jones, Mrs. Emory Thomas, and Professor John Waters met with me to discuss this project. The plan for the exhibition was submitted to and approved first by the university's Bicentennial Cultural Events Committee and then by the Bicentennial Committee under the chairmanship of Professor Thomas Dyer. Subsequent grants from The University of Georgia, through the Bicentennial Office, have assisted in designing and installing the exhibition.

A grant application was submitted in 1983 to the Georgia Council for the Arts and Humanities to support the project's research. The funding enabled the museum to hire Jane Webb Smith as guest curator who would travel throughout the state and Southeast, finding and collecting information about art and decorative objects produced in Georgia before the Civil War. After a year's search, a report on Smith's findings was submitted to the council. A second grant from the council enabled the museum to continue the research and prepare it for publication. Scholars such as B. Phinizy Spalding, Charles Hudson, Robert Willingham, and Diana Combs were invited to contribute articles for the catalogue. Frank Horton, Brad Rauschenberg, Henry Green, Callie Huger Efird, William and Florence Griffin, David Hally, Lisa Reynolds, and Katharine G. Farnham were also called upon to share advice and expertise.

The Georgia Museum of Art also made an application to the National Endowment for the Humanities for an implementation grant. This grant funded an extensive series of lectures to be given in Athens and 17 other cities and towns throughout the state by Miss Smith and Tom Pitts, a University of Georgia Ph.D. candidate. Scholars and experts who will share their knowledge to enhance the scope of this exhibition include John C. Waters, chairman, Historic Preservation Program, School of Environmental Design; William Nathaniel Banks, advisory board member, Georgia Trust for Historic Preservation; Peter H. Wood, associate professor of history, Duke University; David Hurst Thomas, chairman, Department of Anthropology, American Museum of Natural History; and Katharine G. Farnham, adjunct curator of decorative art, High Museum of Art.

Among the individuals and institutions making this exhibition possible through generous loans are the Atlanta Historical Society and the High Museum. Both institutions have lent many works of art that seldom leave their premises. The Telfair Academy of Arts and Sciences in Savannah has permitted us to borrow works of extreme rarity and fragility. The American Museum of Natural History enriched this exhibition with works never before exhibited in Georgia. These were excavated from St. Catherine's Island with funds from the Noble Foundation. This exhibition could not have been realized without the assistance and cooperation of The University of Georgia: extensive loans from special collections, The University of Georgia Libraries, and the anthropology department are just a few examples of the support received from campus colleagues. All the lenders sensed the unique possibilities for this exhibition and willingly cooperated by committing their prized possessions to an extended public display in Athens. The exhibition's long duration, from April through the beginning of September, deprives individuals and institutions of their finest pieces for a protracted period of time. I wish to express the deepest gratitude of university officials and the museum's advisors and officers to all lenders for making possible this special Georgia celebration.

A highly motivated museum staff has participated in all phases of this exhibition. Marianne Doezema, associate director and curator of education, has guided this project since she joined the staff in 1981. She is also due praise for ably managing the editorial tasks of the catalogue with the assistance of registrar Linda Steigleder. For designing the catalogue, recognition goes to Dianne Penny Wilson. Linda Steigleder and secretary Patricia Faerber organized the details of loans, photography, and conservation for the more than 100 objects in this exhibition. Ron Lukasiewicz designed the installation and oversaw the myriad of details necessary to transform the museum's galleries into an appropriate stage for this exhibition. Carol VanSant, museum technician, provided support for these responsibilities. Gratitude goes to the lending institutions' many staff members, who gave valuable time to the research and photographic needs of the exhibition. Appreciation is also due the many other individuals whose help at all stages makes an exhibition of this extent a reality.

Additional professional assistance was also important to the project. Michael McKelvey traveled throughout the state to produce the outstanding photographs in this publication. Editorial suggestions were offered by The Last Word. Brad Sanders assisted with layout and production of the catalogue. Larry Hepburn shared advice and criticism.

This exhibition marks new departures for the Georgia Museum of Art. The originality of presentation, depth of field work, and extent of collaborative efforts make *Georgia's Legacy* an unusual undertaking, a shared venture made by the Georgian community for the public's benefit: it is both ours and yours, reflecting the cultural heritage of this state through the enthusiasms and perspectives of the present.

Richard S. Schneiderman
Director

ACKNOWLEDGEMENTS

Executing a sizable project such as *Georgia's Legacy* within a very tight time schedule requires a great deal of assistance. Fortunately, I was able to find that assistance readily available. The members of my advisory committee are respected scholars in the three areas of the humanities encompassed by *Georgia's Legacy*: historical, cultural, and anthropological/archaeological developments. They include Frank Horton and Brad Rauschenberg of the Museum of Early Southern Decorative Arts in Winston-Salem, North Carolina (MESDA); Phinizy Spalding, Skeet Willingham, Charles Hudson, and David Hally from The University of Georgia; Lisa Reynolds from the Madison-Morgan Cultural Center; Kitty Farnham from the High Museum of Art; and local scholars and collectors of decorative arts including Henry Green, Callie Efird, and Florence and Bill Griffin. They have unselfishly taken time from their own busy schedules to offer advice on everything from the best way to get things accomplished in Georgia to the nineteenth century definition of "beaufet."

Charles Hudson and David Hally have patiently given me a crash course in 2,000 years of Georgia's history before the territory became an English colony. Phinizy and Skeet have supplemented my fifth grade Georgia history deficiency with equal fortitude. Without the foundations created by past exhibitions researched, sponsored, and curated by Henry Green, Kitty Farnham, Callie Efird, Lisa Reynolds, and Bill and Florence Griffin, I could not have developed one of the important concepts of *Georgia's Legacy*, that of getting an overview of Georgia's indigenous craft history by displaying these objects side by side for the first time.

A separate paragraph goes to my friends at MESDA. From the moment I became a field researcher for MESDA in July 1978, Frank and Brad have been a driving force behind my desire to make a substantial contribution to the field of southern decorative arts. Their and their staff's dedication to excellence has been contagious. I feel lucky that they have not only infected me with this enthusiasm for southern decorative arts, but also supported me unwaveringly in every one of my ventures. It is a relationship of which I am very proud. A special thanks to Frank and his staff: Bradford L. Rauschenberg, Luke Beckerdite, Audrey Michie, Sally Gant, Elizabeth Putney, Paula Young, Rosemary Estes, John Bivins, Jr., Sara Lee Frizzell, Wes Stewart, and Carolyn Head.

Other individuals have comprised an "unofficial" committee sharing their expertise in areas unfamiliar to me. These people and their specialties include Billy F. Allen and John Burrison, southern ceramics; Jack Atkinson, textiles; Gwen Cleghorn, grammar and punctuation; Diana Combs, commemorative mourning art; Dale Couch, genealogy; Dick Kennedy, firearms; Edward LaFond, clocks; Dr. Lewis H. Larson, expert on where all Etowah figures have gone; Deanne Levison, Sally Hawkins, Marc Weinberg, experts on "who has what"; and John Ott, moral support expert.

Field work involves getting in a car, driving around the countryside, and going in and out of houses looking for objects to record or exhibit. This past year, my 28,000 miles of field work for *Georgia's Legacy* brought me in contact with many friends, old and new. While I am grateful to all of those who graciously shared their family treasures with me, my great appreciation goes to those who welcomed me into their homes and thus made what can be a lonely process a very rewarding one. These include John and Beth Reiter, Mrs. Lattimore, and Susan Hartridge in Savannah; George and Peggy Burdell Sibley and Harriet and Bryan Haltermann in Augusta; Louise and Buddy Hines in Thomasville; Dorothy and Frank Chandler in Valdosta; Fran and Henry Green on Saint Simons Island. In Athens, my "homes away from home" belonged to Fran, Emory, and Molly Thomas; and Charlotte, John, and Heathcliff Waters. Their support and advice, personal and professional, have been invaluable throughout this project.

The Good Sport Award must go to my traveling companion during the hottest months, photographer Michael McKelvey. Photographing furniture and silver is difficult in a studio environment, much less in living rooms with slippery waxed floors or bedrooms with plush pile carpets. Appreciation for the excellence of Michael's photographs increases in light of some of the conditions under which he good-naturedly labored.

For the busy staff of the Georgia Museum of Art, *Georgia's Legacy* has been an experience from which, I hope, we will all benefit. Much of the research and preparation for the show has occurred away from the museum. With hard work, we have taken the Bicentennial Exhibition from the ground floor, financially and conceptually, and brought it to fruition in a short period of time. Thanks for your help.

Without the 35 individual lenders and 38 institutions listed on page 8, *Georgia's Legacy* could never have taken place. Many people work behind the scenes to orchestrate complex loan transactions; a list alphabetically by institution of many of these people follows: David Hurst Thomas and staff, American Museum of Natural History; Anne Adams, Amon Carter Museum; Shelia Hackney, Athens-Clarke Heritage Foundation; Kathy Dixson, Bill Hull, Elaine Kirkland, and Michael Rose, Atlanta Historical Society; Ira Evans, Atlanta Masonic Museum & Library; Patricia Hall, Chief Vann House; Elizabeth Hodges, City of Savannah; Fred Fussell, Frank Schnell, and Anne King, Columbus Museum of Arts and Sciences; Morton McInvale and Bill Townsend, Department of Natural Resources, Parks and Historic Sites Division; Dolores Proper, Dickey House, Stone Mountain Park; Linda Matthews and Tom Bertrand, Emory University; Phil Noblitt and Curtis Childs, Fort Frederica; Pat Phillips, Georgia Agrirama; Mary Jo Thompson, Georgia College Foundation, Old Governor's Mansion; Barbara Bennett, Georgia Historical Society; Barney Dunbar Lamar, Gertrude Herbert Institute of Art; Bruce Sherwood, Hay House Museum; Donald Peirce, Marge Harvey, and Carol Graham, High Museum of Art; Mrs. Janice Biggers, Historic Columbus Foundation; Kathy Fleming, Historic Savannah; Mimi Henson, Jekyll Island Authority; John Lawrence and Carolyn Burgess, LaGrange College; John O. Sands, Mariners' Museum; Jeff Chapman and Richard Polhemus, McClung Museum; Anne Shelander, Museum of Coastal History; Bruce Smith, National Museum of Natural History; Robert G. Stewart, National Portrait Gallery, Smithsonian Institution; Sibbald Smith and Sylvia Flowers, Ocmulgee National Monument; Jean Lankford, Polk County Historical Society; David Guernsey, Ships of the Sea Museum; Feay Shellman and Elizabeth Shatto, Telfair Academy of Arts and Sciences, Inc.; Tom Hill, Thomas County Historical Society; Mac Moye, Westville Historic Handcrafts, Inc.; and Michael Komanecky, Yale University Art Gallery.

On behalf of the staff of the Georgia Museum of Art, I wish to thank the other individuals who helped in various ways: Mr. and Mrs. Fred Bentley, Mrs. Samuel Burns, Donna Butler, Roy Dickins, Mrs. William Freeman, Eugenia Arnold Friend, Jennifer Goldsborough, Jan Hardy, Dr. George Fenwick Jones, Mrs. Sidney Jones, Mr. and Mrs. Benjamin Levy, Dr. Joe Mahan, Francis McNairy, Dr. John B. Oliver, William A. Parker, Jr., Georgia Patterson, Valerie Aldridge, Susan Rapp, Jill Read, James K. Reap, Louis Schmier, Dr. Samuel Simmons, Mrs. Charlton Theus, and Mr. and Mrs. Carey Williams.

On a personal note, I want to recognize those who have supported me throughout my years of museum traumas and triumphs. First, I must thank my family and my dog, Dewars, for patience and carte-blanche support while I moved from Talbot County, Maryland, to Athens, Georgia. Second, I have counted on my friends all over the country; they have never really understood exactly why I continue to endure the rigors of working in this field but have nevertheless shared my good times as well as bad. Space is limited here, but they know who they are. Last, but by no means least, is my friend Palmer Temple, who has exceeded his part of our "covenant" and has helped me find the necessary strength to persevere and complete this job to the best of my abilities.

Jane Webb Smith
January 1985

INTRODUCTION

Georgia's Legacy: History Charted Through the Arts is just that: an exhibition attempting to show the direct correspondence between historical events in Georgia and the quality and quantity of indigenous decorative arts. *Georgia's Legacy* is a survey spanning Georgia's hesitant beginnings as a new colony to its cultural flowering in the 1850s. Many of these objects have been exhibited before, but always in a specific format rather than in an arrangement pointing to relationships with the overall history of Georgia's craft or fine art production.

Georgia's Legacy is *not* about furniture or folk art, portraits or pots, textiles or silver, although it does represent all these media. Objects were selected as much for their provenance, or history of Georgia ownership, as for their attributes which exemplify uncertain stylistic developments of Georgia's decorative arts. Portraits, particularly, were chosen more for their subject's contribution to the state's political, economic, or educational development than for their inherent value as illustrations of the work of Georgia painters, of whom there were few until the mid-nineteenth century.

An effort has been made to represent every section of the state that had reached a level of economic stability by 1860. Excluded is most of the south central wiregrass region, which remained pine forests with an occasional Carolina turpentiner until after the Civil War. The compilation of objects was easier for the agricultural, coastal, and piedmont areas, which developed during the first 100 years of Georgia's history, than for the later railroad/industrial towns of Atlanta and Columbus.

A fundamental point to remember while assigning these objects a place in Georgia's history is that, excluding portraits and miniatures, they were made to be used. Decorative art is applied art. The earliest Indian pot, the Alonzo Church silver teapot, the Augusta-made secretary bookcase—all were utilitarian objects. The cabinetmaker, silversmith, or potter provided necessary items to a clientele who lived in exquisite Regency houses in Savannah, in white, columned Greek Revival mansions in the piedmont, or in log houses on the western frontier.

The time periods for the galleries were defined by both historical and stylistic guidelines. The maps chosen to chart this history were selected as keys for measuring Georgia's progression towards its present boundaries. These had been reached by 1838 with the final displacement of native Indians.

First considered are objects created by Indians inhabiting Georgia during the Woodland Period (1000 B.C. to A.D. 800). Such things as pipes, pots, and figures reveal both the skills of the creator and the social value placed on these objects. DeSoto's expedition in 1540 brought violence and diseases which gradually unraveled the fragile social fabric of the Mississippian Indians. By the time of English colonization in the mid-eighteenth century, Georgia's native Indian chiefdoms had succumbed to influences of European culture.

Undertaking an intensive search for objects made in eighteenth-century colonial Georgia quickly reveals the extent to which Georgia lagged behind her neighbors. Georgia's founding date, 1733, was considerably later than other southern colonies: Virginia, 1607; Maryland, 1634; and South Carolina, 1670. Furthermore, little progress occurred during the first 20 years of the trusteeship. Laws restricting ownership of slaves, rum, and large land holdings dissuaded new settlers from Georgia.

Few Georgia-made objects dating from 1733–1790 survive. Selection for this second gallery was based on slightly different criteria than those used for later time periods. Chosen objects represent some historical event of the first tumultuous years in Georgia's slow development. Included are portraits executed in Philadelphia, Charleston, and Savannah of an important citizen who helped turn the political and economic tide for the unstable youngest colony; an illustration of scarce eighteenth-century architecture; or one of the few known examples of what are believed to be indigenous decorative arts, so identified by its history and materials. These objects are residuals of an era of repeated frustrations for Georgia's early craftsmen.

Imported goods had been supplementing Georgia's local market since 1759, when the first wharf capable of receiving ocean-going vessels was built. Some of these imported goods came from the continent, but, as early as 1744, New England ships were bringing to southern ports everything from maple syrup to Newport Chippendale furniture. During the war, intercoastal trade ceased, but Georgia's ties with England were only briefly suspended during the first years of fighting, and it is unlikely that foreign-made products were not available for Georgia's Loyalists and British officers in Savannah.

The 40 years following the end of the Revolutionary War were fruitful ones for Georgia's coastal and piedmont areas. Rare examples of coastal furniture dating from this time and place are exhibited for the first time. These pieces, attributed by provenance and use of coastal woods, illustrate the postwar economic recovery. The emerging middle-class, which flowered along with Georgia's rich cotton crop, could afford to enjoy the creations of trained artisans.

Henry Green's 1976 exhibition, *Furniture of the Georgia Piedmont*

Before 1830, brought to light the first evidence of a Georgia regional style developed during these years of prosperity. All of the pieces seen here, excluding one, were included in Green's 1976 show at the High Museum of Art. These choices were made because of the pieces' distinctive inlay designs and construction characteristics, ones that were transplanted to Georgia by Scotch-Irish cabinetmakers traveling south along the Philadelphia Wagon Road. These people settled the Broad River Valley and incorporated their traditions into the furniture of the Georgia piedmont.

By 1830, both Savannah and Augusta had grown into major trading centers, boasting impressive Federal and Regency style homes built by planters and wealthy merchants, and undoubtedly filled with high-style New York or Philadelphia Empire furniture. The upward mobility of Georgia's class structure generated a middle class traditionally supportive of local craftsmen. Why is the furniture attributed to these Georgia craftsmen not more sophisticated, and why is there not more of it? A year and a half of asking these questions has provided several possible explanations.

By the second decade of the nineteenth century, New York/Philadelphia furniture and silver were major sources of competition for local cabinetmakers and silversmiths. That the upper classes preferred these imports could in part account for the paucity of local items. Advertisements and census reports, however, suggest that local shops were providing facsimiles of the Phyfe-style furniture and possibly pewter ware to the growing moneyed working classes. These locally carved examples were less sophisticated and often clumsy. During this period, three highly publicized disasters, two fires in Savannah and a flood in Augusta, undoubtedly destroyed a vast quantity of locally made furniture that would have belonged to those living in middle-class frame houses. Fires constantly threatened Georgians until fire ordinances were enforced. Therefore, the traditional explanation—that Yankee soldiers on Sherman's March to the Sea burned or stole most Georgia-made treasures—seems unlikely. By 1864, what the Union soldiers found was probably either mass-produced Victorian furniture of northern manufacture or plain-style functional chairs or tables of local woods made on the plantations.

Its long history as a trading center suggests that Augusta should have more surviving eighteenth and nineteenth century crafts. A 1926 fire in Augusta no doubt destroyed many significant objects. During the Depression, antique dealers scouring the countryside probably carried away a great number of sideboards, desk-and-bookcases, and other case pieces and sold them elsewhere—misrepresenting their provenances and values.

An entire gallery has been devoted to the special case of metalworking in Georgia before 1860. Silversmiths traditionally produced luxury items, affordable to very few early Georgians. Because these products were in such little demand during Georgia's early years, metalworkers learned to diversify, and repair clocks, watches, guns, and instruments as well as perform other jobs requiring forge work.

By the 1830s, a wealthy planters class arose who could afford silver and who preferred American-made pieces manufactured in northern centers. Local Georgia metal workers in the upcountry produced functional wares at the forge for the local cotton planters.

By the 1840s, mass-produced furniture, textiles, and glassware jeopardized the craftsman's precarious place in the Georgia market. Georgia craftsmen were forced to become businessmen, to function as agents for northern distributors or as assemblers for goods produced in the North but assembled locally. This role is reflected in some of the pieces displayed in this gallery; silver and rifles are marked by both the northern manufacturer and the southern retailer.

Fledgling industries within a largely agrarian economy contributed to social and political dichotomies which became increasingly prominent nationwide after mid-century. Preoccupied with its new wealth, Georgia was existing harmoniously despite these dichotomies and enjoying a false sense of optimism. The state had taken advantage of 70 years of peace to cultivate a successful cotton economy based on the institution of slavery. Georgia's involvement in the Civil War, beginning in 1861, again halted the state's cultural progress.

Jane Webb Smith
Guest Curator

The Development of Material Culture in Antebellum Georgia: An Overview

From its rich prehistory down to its currently envied status in the Sunbelt, Georgia can point to a uniquely varied cultural experience. Yet almost nothing has been done to chronicle or document this unusual story. So little has been written about Georgia's developing material culture that the researcher frequently finds himself trodding dark and untried ways. Almost nothing has been published that marks the state's halting steps toward cultural maturity.

Where, for example, is the permanent record of Georgia's cabinetmakers and ironworkers; its brick masons and architects; its painters and silversmiths? The answer, sadly, is nowhere. Their story has yet to be chronicled or their feats heralded. However, the accomplishments of Georgia artisans and craftsmen are at last coming into their own.

The lush and savage wilderness that became Georgia was crisscrossed by numerous Spanish explorers in the sixteenth and seventeenth centuries. They reported extensively on the Indian tribes found in this rich region—tribes that were more numerous and more independent in action than the Europeanized Indians whom James Edward Oglethorpe met on the banks of the Savannah River in 1733.[1] Full information about the lives and customs of these Indians is lacking, but numerous archaeological finds and the application of advanced anthropological techniques have reconstructed many facets of their civilization.[2]

Spain began its settlements on the Georgia Sea Islands and the adjacent mainland in 1566, and the Spanish friars maintained a presence there for more than a century. Guale—as Georgia was called in the Spanish system—was a pastoral province in which the priests, operating from their missions, taught the natives the settled agricultural ways of the Europeans. At one time Guale actually shipped foodstuffs, including citrus fruit, to other areas of the Spanish Empire in the Caribbean.

This mission area, on the extreme northeastern limit of the empire, was lightly held, never attracting settlers from Spain or from other Spanish controlled areas. Its mission churches were of wattle and daub and its presidios of log. The work of the artisans and craftsmen in Guale remains in obscurity. Recent archaeological excavations on St. Catherine's Island have made it possible to see examples of some of the crockery and religious items that must have been important elements of the lives of the natives and of the priests and soldiers who held so tenaciously to the Georgia coastline.[3]

By the mid 1680s, the Spanish had retreated to the south bank of the St. Mary's River, and the area stretching from that stream to the Savannah came to be called the Debatable Land.[4] James Oglethorpe and his settlers in 1733 ultimately determined that this region would become part of the British Empire.

Georgia's charter gave General Oglethorpe and 20 other Trustees power to set up and run the new colony for a period of 21 years. Oglethorpe, a noted English philanthropist, assumed the primary leadership role. He conceived of Georgia as a colony where certain elements of English and European society might go and prosper. He hoped that the yeoman farmer would be the dominant force in the colony, and to that end land grants were severely limited in size; Negroes and slavery were also forbidden to enter Georgia. The province was expected to be a refuge for persecuted foreign Protestants and a place to which many of London's unemployed laborers and small shopkeepers might relocate. Oglethorpe hoped to create in Georgia a sort of white, middle-class Utopia that would perform a useful mission just as surely as Puritan Massachusetts Bay had done.[5]

The first settlers who came with Oglethorpe on the *Anne* represented a cross-section of eighteenth-century English society—except the debtor element. As a committee of the province's ruling group, the Georgia Trustees excluded debtors. Aboard the *Anne* were carpenters and joiners, peruke makers, a calico printer, a surgeon, merchants, farmers, a clothmaker, a gardener, a heelmaker, a basketmaker and stockingmaker, an apothecary, vintners, and silkmakers—a group from whom one might expect, in a reasonable time, a good deal of creative activity.[6]

Such was not the case. The colony received a severe blow in the summer of 1733 when "the seasoning" first began to take its toll. But perhaps even more important than the appalling death rate were the threats the Spaniards, French, and Indians posed to the colony—threats that made Oglethorpe insist that military considerations come first in the list of his colony's priorities. The colony languished culturally as well as economically, perhaps because many settlers were dissatisfied with the stultifying regulations of the Trustees. When war broke out with the Spanish in 1739, all energies were channeled toward the colony's defense in order to prevent reconquest by Spain. Many people fled; Georgia's development as a creative society was delayed yet again.[7]

In spite of these difficulties, Georgians made some notable strides toward the development of a material culture. Savannah's early housing stock was made up of 20-by-66-foot structures "built of Timber &

Clap board, with Shingled roofs,"[8] and the house Oglethorpe rented when he was in town sported damask curtains. Philip Georg Friedrich von Reck, possessor of "an amazing artistic gift," came to the Salzburgers' settlement at Ebenezer and completed approximately 50 paintings and sketches of the town, the Indians, and Georgia's flora and fauna. His illustrations of the Ebenezer huts and the original shelters the English used in their Frederica settlement afford historians their first actual sketch of building stock outside Savannah.[9]

However, in the Trusteeship period, Georgia was still primarily a frontier society. At the Salzburger settlement of Ebenezer, artisans and craftsmen were actively encouraged—carpenters, blacksmiths, and masons were found there in some number—but such encouragement was the exception. Not surprisingly, the first piece of authenticated Georgia-made furniture came from that community. The Salzburgers' love of music seemed to promise much for the advancement of many of the amenities of life on Georgia's frontier, but instead the Church of England boasted the first organ in the colony. Ebenezer can lay valid claim to Christian Müller, who was probably responsible in part for von Reck's sketches. Müller is given credit for a relatively sophisticated contemporary portrait of Oglethorpe that now hangs in the Chatham Club in Savannah.[10]

The Trustees made serious efforts to encourage the potter Andrew Duché, and they were determined that sericulture would be the rock upon which Georgia's economy would be based. Either development could have triggered the sort of movement necessary to establish a cultural base for the new settlement—but neither bore fruit. Georgia's richest legacy from the Trustees was not in its material culture but in its literature of controversy that swirled about James Oglethorpe and his colonial schemes.[11]

In reality, Georgians were too busy during the 1750s simply trying to stay alive and complete what had to be done. Oglethorpe might have provided Georgia with a cultural push had his colony's location been less open to attack and invasion. He himself had no time for his Greek and Latin interests, nor for history. In a new province, confronted with "the basic problems of life and death," he barely had time for sleep, much less for the luxuries of life.[12]

The Trustees surrendered their charter in 1752, and Georgia became a royal province. With unlimited landholding and slavery now permitted, Georgia began to develop as a plantation-based, staple crop-oriented colony. Capital and new citizens poured in from other provinces and from Great Britain as well. Savannah burgeoned. Sunbury became a second port of entry, reflecting the prosperity and determination of the Dorchester Puritans who moved into Georgia's Midway District even before the Trusteeship period was over. Always a thriving and lusty town geared toward the Indian trade, Augusta sprawled along the banks of the Savannah.

The prosperity that paralleled the development of the plantation regime brought ease, social awareness, and a desire on the part of members of the upper level of society to distinguish themselves from their inferiors. William Gerard De Brahm, a surveyor-cartographer who was intimately familiar with Georgia after 1751, was impressed by the levelheadedness of the people, whose minds were not yet influenced by operas, theatre, or balls. Rather, he found that Georgians were well read and that the province had five "fine Libraries," three in Savannah, one at Ebenezer, and the fifth in Augusta.[13]

As the capital and the center of most of the colony's activities, Savannah reflected the prosperity that swept Georgia in the 1760s and 1770s. The town boasted a good newspaper by 1765 and even held stage presentations. Savannah also had cabinetmaker James Love, who apparently did a thriving business. Upon his death he had for sale "three mahogany desks and two chests of drawers, a high chest of drawers, another desk and bookcase, four beadsteads and the posts for twelve, and he had some coffins." He probably used local woods, such as hickory, pine, oak, walnut, and maple in his craft—"an advantage that accounts in part for the size of his estate," valued at more than £500. Today his work is unknown and unevaluated because "if specimens survive, they have eluded identification."[14] Generally, however, the furniture used by the vast majority of Georgians was either homemade or far more cheaply constructed by builders other than Love.[15]

Had the American Revolution not occurred, Savannah might have developed into another Charleston, with the attendant cultural stranglehold associated with that city's dominance in the history of colonial and antebellum South Carolina. But Savannah was occupied by the British late in 1778 and remained in their hands until the summer of 1782. The pre-Revolutionary political significance of the city declined markedly as the back country assumed the leadership in the fight against England.

In the back areas, Augusta assumed a new importance as the sections to its north and west began to be settled. These sections became more influential when thousands of Carolinians and Virginians poured into upcountry Georgia after 1783. With its nascent culture, inherited at least in part from Charleston, Augusta became the *de facto* capital of Georgia during these years and even claimed the state's first full-fledged academy. Augusta theatres flourished; artists and artisans began to visit or even to settle there.[16] Somewhat later, a group of inspired physicians founded in Augusta the state's first medical college—one of the oldest in the South. Meanwhile, Savannah was recovering nicely from the rigors of the Revolution. The city prided itself on the feats of architect William Jay; rejoiced in William Bulloch Maxwell's drama—"The Mysterious Father"—which was "the first play written and published in the state of Georgia by a native playwright"[17]; and exulted in the transoceanic achievements of the steamship *Savannah*.[18] But it was apparent that Georgia's cultural as well as political leadership had passed to the piedmont.

Post-Yazoo land cessions by the Indians in the early 1800s meant Georgia's population and size doubled. Increased security and profits now assumed dramatic proportions after the invention of Whitney's gin and the consequent increase in cotton production. The stable economy meant a more settled and leisurely existence and a developing awareness of "the good life." Furniture, silver, and books were imported into the state, and the same commodities were produced throughout Georgia as well. The Athens area seems to have been particularly rich in craftsmen, a theory borne out at least in part by a remarkable show of piedmont furniture at Atlanta's High Museum of Art in 1976.[19] Savannah boasted its Jay and Gilbert Butler, but the piedmont had its Daniel Pratt and John Marler. John Abbot, consummate artist and naturalist, chose wiregrass Georgia as his final habitat rather than the low country.[20] Backcountry Georgia also had itinerant artists like George Cooke and innovative southern authors and local colorists like Augustus Baldwin Longstreet, the precursor of Mark Twain and various southern humorists.

Even so, Georgia did not fill its present boundaries until almost 1840—only one brief generation before the outbreak of the Civil War. Throughout the 1820s and 1830s, the state was obsessed with expansion. Only the oldest settled areas produced the kind of material culture that could compare with the achievements of Virginia or the Carolinas. However, recent research into settlement patterns and the cultural attitudes of towns very close to the frontier clearly indicates that these communities had a more varied cultural life and that they encouraged a greater number of creative activities than had been thought in the past.[21]

As in 1775, the outbreak of war in 1861 arrested Georgia's creative development. The state possessed enormous vitality and originality by the mid-nineteenth century, and seemed prepared to embark upon a golden era. It boasted a population in excess of one million, respected colleges, a developing literary awareness, and a promising urban growth. It was a tragedy for the state that it was to enter a vicious civil war from which it has only relatively recently recovered in full. What Georgia's cultural resources might have been will never be known; the state's actual antebellum achievements in material culture are the subjects of this extraordinary exhibition.

B. Phinizy Spalding
Department of History
The University of Georgia

1. On the subject of the Europeanization of the Southeastern Indians, see especially Charles M. Hudson, "The Genesis of Georgia's Indians," in Harvey H. Jackson and Phinizy Spalding, eds., *Forty Years of Diversity, Essays on Colonial Georgia* (Athens, 1984), 25–45.

2. Charles M. Hudson, *The Southeastern Indians* (Knoxville, 1976).

3. John Tate Lanning's *The Spanish Missions of Georgia* (Chapel Hill, 1935) is the best work dealing with this period. For recent finds on St. Catherine's, see *New York Times*, 16 August 1981. This excavation has aroused considerable interest in Georgia. See, for example, *Augusta Chronicle*, 19 December 1982 and *Athens Banner-Herald*, 25 December 1982.

4. See especially "The Debatable Land," written as an introduction to Herbert E. Bolton, ed., *Arrendondo's Historical Proof of*

Spain's Title to Georgia (Berkeley, 1925), 1–110.

5. Phinizy Spalding, "James Edward Oglethorpe's Quest for an American Zion," in Jackson and Spalding, *Forty Years of Diversity*, 60–79.

6. E. Merton Coulter and Albert B. Saye, eds., *A List of the Early Settlers of Georgia* (Athens, 1949), 106–11. Saye has successfully destroyed the debtor colony idea in "Was Georgia a Debtor Colony?" *Georgia Historical Quarterly* (December 1940), 323–32, and *New Viewpoints in Georgia History* (Athens, 1943), 25–26, 31, *et passim*.

7. John Tate Lanning, *The Diplomatic History of Georgia* (Chapel Hill, 1936).

8. Robert G. McPherson, ed., *The Journal of the Earl of Egmont* (Athens, 1962), 44.

9. Kristian Hvidt, ed., *Von Reck's Voyage* (Savannah, 1980), 7.

10. George Fenwick Jones, *The Salzburger Saga* (Athens, 1984), 31–2.

11. Moses Colt Tyler has called Patrick Tailfer's, Hugh Anderson's, and David Douglas's book, *A True and Historical Narrative of the Colony of Georgia*, first published in Charleston in 1741 by the self-proclaimed Georgia exiles, "One of the most expert pieces of writing to be met with in our early literature." See Tyler, *A History of American Literature, 1607–1783*, abridged and edited by Archie H. Jones (Chicago, 1967), 184. For a more extended treatment of this literature which drew much attention on both sides of the Atlantic, see Spalding, "South Carolina and Georgia during the Oglethorpe Period, 1732–1743" (Ph.D. dissertation, University of North Carolina, 1963), 170–80 *et passim*, and Clarence L. Ver Steeg, ed., *A True and Historical Narrative of the Colony of Georgia* (Athens, 1960), xxvii-xxx.

12. Phinizy Spalding, *Oglethorpe in America* (Chicago, 1977), 153.

13. Louis De Vorsey, Jr., ed., *De Brahm's Report of the General Survey in the Southern District of North America* (Columbia, 1971), 44.

14. Harold E. Davis, *The Fledgling Province, Social and Cultural Life in Colonial Georgia, 1733–1776* (Chapel Hill, 1976), 100–01. This volume is far and away the best treatment of Georgia's cultural development for any period of the state's history.

15. Ibid., 63.

16. For the notion that early Augusta is the child of Charleston, see Edward J. Cashin, *The Story of Augusta* (Augusta, 1980). For an excellent thesis on important aspects of the cultural life of Georgia's fall line cities, see Mary Levin Koch, "A History of the Arts in Augusta, Macon, and Columbus, Georgia, 1800–1860" (Master's Thesis, University of Georgia, 1983).

17. Kenneth Coleman and Charles Stephen Gurr, eds., *Dictionary of Georgia Biography*, 2 volumes (Athens, 1983), II, 699–700.

18. Malcolm Bell, Jr., *Savannah, Ahoy!* (Savannah, 1959), 27–49 *et passim*.

19. Henry D. Green, *Furniture of the Georgia Piedmont Before 1830* (Atlanta, 1976).

20. On Abbot, see the exhaustively researched Vivian Jean Rogers, "John Abbot, Naturalist and Artist, 1751–1803" (Master's Thesis, University of Georgia, 1979), and Vivian Rogers-Price and William W. Griffin, "John Abbot: Pioneer Artist-Naturalist of Georgia," *The Magazine Antiques*, October 1983, 768–75. For the craftsman Butler, refer to Mrs. Howard Morrison's typescript at the Georgia Historical Society Library in Savannah. The Scudder brothers—Amos and John—were also prominent artisans in antebellum Savannah. See Saul Jacob Rubin, *Third to None* (Savannah, 1984), 70, 77.

21. For fresh research and new ideas as applied to cultural life on Georgia's frontier, refer to William Lamar Cawthon, "Clinton: County Seat on the Georgia Frontier, 1808–1821" (Master's Thesis, University of Georgia, 1984). This town offered an astonishing number of cultural frontier and creative activities in its infancy. Indications are that it compared favorably in such indices with its counterparts in other sections of the nation.

Aspects of Georgia Indian Art

Thousands of years before Europeans discovered North America, ancestors of Indians migrated from Asia and entered the continent through what is now Alaska and Canada. In time, descendants of these people occupied every part of the land, including what became the State of Georgia. As hunters and gatherers, these people made their living by killing wild animals, some of which are now extinct, and by collecting wild plants, seeds, and fruits. Just as the climate in North America moderated and became similar to what it is today, so did the landscape.

Like adjacent parts of the Southeast, Georgia was a good place for hunters and gatherers to live. As time went on, these hunters and gatherers perfected techniques for gaining their livelihood from the rich array of available wild plants and animals. If these ancient hunters had a rich artistic life, little is known of it, only what can be extracted about it from the material objects they made. Archaeologists happen to have discovered these objects, sometimes little more than some tools and small items for personal adornment, such as shell beads.

Approximately 1000 B.C., the Indians of Georgia, like Indians elsewhere in eastern North America, began to develop a more elaborate ritual life. This time marked the beginning of the Woodland Period. The Indians began expending more effort and care in the burial of their dead, and some individuals began receiving special treatment when they were buried. They were interred not only with weapons, but also with pottery vessels and with objects made from materials that came from a distance—such as conch shells from the Gulf coast, mica from the Carolina piedmont, and copper from the Appalachian mountains and the Lake Superior region. In some cases, these burials were placed in or near small earthen mounds.

In addition to placing increased emphasis on burials and ceremonialism, the Woodland Indians put more effort and care into making expressive objects, such as stone pipes and pottery objects and vessels. Though these objects must constitute only a small sample of the entire range of Woodland art, they nonetheless give us some insight into the world view of the people. Some Woodland designs are so highly conventionalized that one can only guess their meaning. Such is the case with the elaborately carved wooden paddles [1] which made impressions in the soft clay walls of pottery before it was fired. Other Woodland designs in stone and pottery are easily recognizable, and from these it is clear that these people were fundamentally interested in animals.

In their art, the Woodland Indians represented only some of the animals which lived in their territories, and the animals they chose to represent indicate something about their world view. Though these people were basically hunters, they seldom represented the animals they killed. They preferred to depict animals which were themselves hunters. They were particularly fond of predatory birds—especially hawks and falcons. Of the quadrupedal hunters, their favorite was the cougar [3], which once inhabited all of Georgia. This shy, silent cat is a lone hunter, killing by stealth in a lightning attack. The Woodland Indians must have admired all of these qualities.

The Woodland Indians also depicted another hunter—the owl—whose hunting abilities must have seemed preternatural to them [2]. Of all the birds of prey, only the owl can hunt in darkness, killing mammals and birds that are active during daylight. At night, the owl is able to kill even the supreme aerial hunter of the day—the peregrine falcon. It is probable that the Woodland Indians were ambivalent about the owl. As hunters, they admired the bird's ability to kill its prey so easily, but realized that its ability to hunt in darkness gave the owl unfair advantage over its prey. It is likely that the ancient Woodland Indians, like the later Southeastern Indians, associated the owl with witchcraft. Just as an owl had a preternatural advantage over other birds, so did a witch have a similar advantage over humans.

It is reasonable to think that, in using animals as metaphors for humans, the ancient Woodland Indians resembled their descendants in the eighteenth and nineteenth centuries. It seems likely that, in addition to representing mammals and birds in stone and pottery, the Woodland Indians possessed a rich stock of stories and myths involving these creatures. Like later Indians of the South, for example, the Woodland Indians probably told stories about virtuous falcons pitted against nefarious owls, stories that would have been metaphorical expressions of virtue and evil in human affairs.

Approximately A.D. 800, a social and economic transformation began occurring among the Indians of Georgia that affected every aspect of life, including modes and styles of artistic expression. Archaeologists apply "Mississippian" to the cultures this transformation produced, and designate A.D. 800 to the time of earliest European exploration as the Mississippian period.

The Mississippian transformation was set in motion when the Indians changed from hunting and collecting wild foods to becoming more dependent on cultivated foods, particularly corn and beans. As their dependence on corn and beans increased, their dependence on wild foods waned, although such foods still provided part of the In-

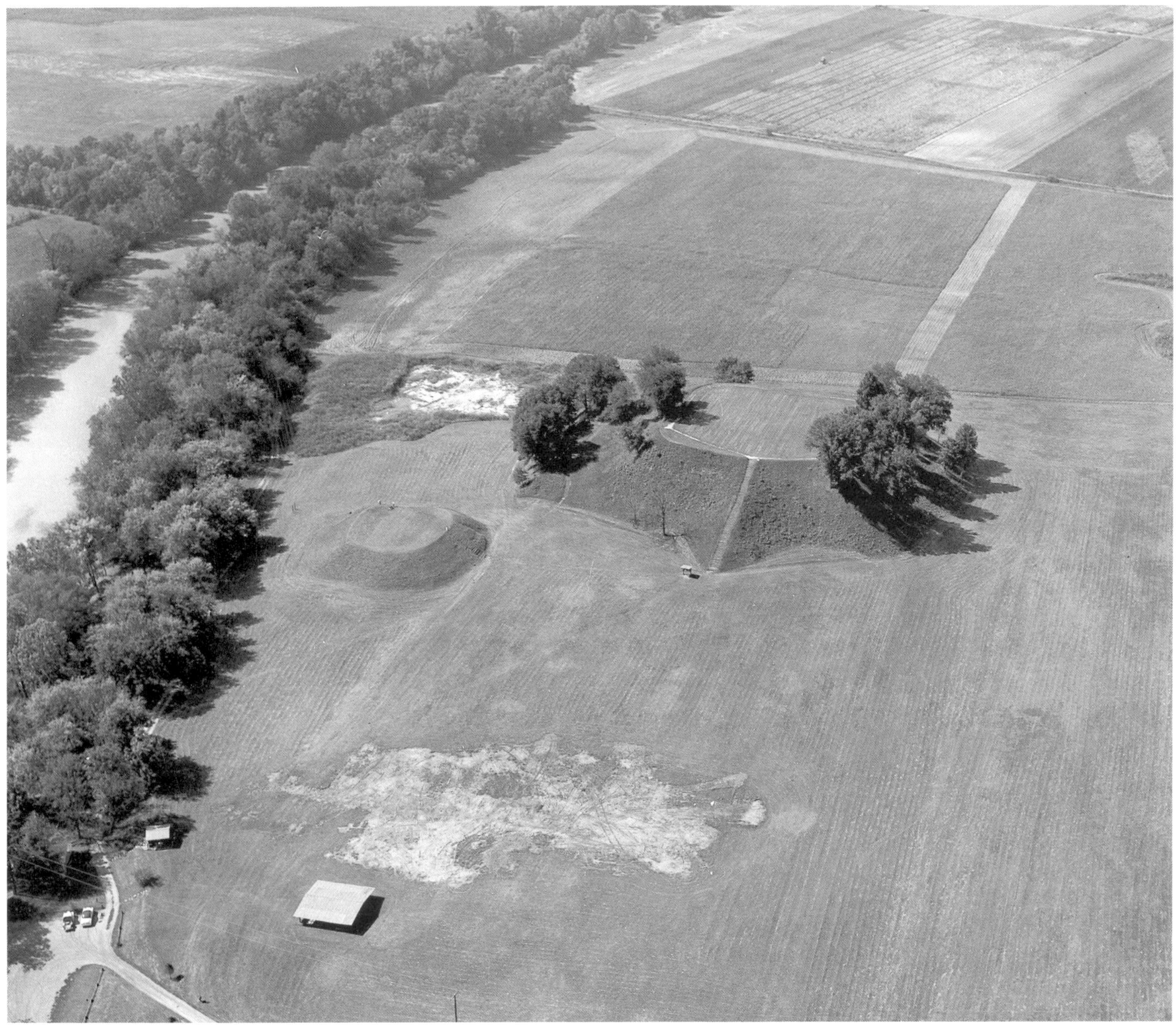

Figure 1. *Etowah Mounds Historic Site,* A.D. 1300–1400. Bartow County, Georgia Department of Natural Resources, Parks and Historic Sites. The Etowah site, near Cartersville, Georgia, was a very large and important Mississippian mound center between about A.D. 1200 and 1400. The people of Etowah built three large temple mounds. By the time of the Hernando de Soto expedition in 1540, Etowah (Itaba) was still an inhabited town, but it was no longer an important center.

dian diet. When they began cultivating corn and beans, the Indians could support a much larger population. Communities became larger, as did the societies to which they belonged.

These Mississippian societies were more centralized and more hierarchical than were societies during the Woodland period. Such societies were chiefdoms, because a chief, set apart from the rest of the people, wielded considerable authority. During this time the great mound centers in Georgia were built—the largest ones being Ocmulgee, Hollywood, and Etowah (figure 1). Each mound center served as the center of a chiefdom, as the site of the most crucial religious rituals and the most influential political decisions.

Even though the Mississippian Indians depended on farming for much of their subsistence, they appear to have been as fascinated with animals as were their Woodland ancestors. Just as in Woodland art, in Mississippian art are representations of cougars, falcons, and owls.

Mississippian art also displays some very important innovations. The Mississippian Indians were perhaps more interested in anomalous animals than the Woodland Indians had been. Anomalous animals were those that behaved in peculiar ways, or ones which were at home in two or more realms. For example, the frog [17] is at home both in water and on land, and the bat is a furry creature that flies. While such creatures are depicted in Woodland art, they seem to have been even more important in Mississippian art.

One indication of this importance is that the Mississippian Indians went a step beyond the anomalies which nature provided. Though perhaps not intentionally, they created several monsters which were animals they believed had the characteristics of two or more different creatures. The most important monster was a serpent with deer teeth or horns. Sometimes it is shown with the wings of a bird. Hence, it was believed to be at home in all three realms—water, earth, and air. There is no question but that this symbolic form was one of the most crucial in Mississippian art (figure 2—Hollywood Bowl). Why the people of the Mississippian period should have been so fascinated with this serpent monster is not clear. Perhaps their fascination is an indication that the evolution of larger and more complicated social systems led them to struggle in new ways to understand the mysteries of existence.

In other ways, their art reflects the more complex social experience of the Mississippian people. The chiefs and their kinsmen of the Mississippian people possessed more social honor than did their subjects. Consistent with this, when these chiefs and their relatives died, they were buried with tokens or markers of their status. The most important of these grave goods were thin sheets of copper embossed with designs and drinking cups and gorgets [19,20] of marine shell engraved with finely wrought designs.

The Indians of Georgia had been making pottery vessels for more

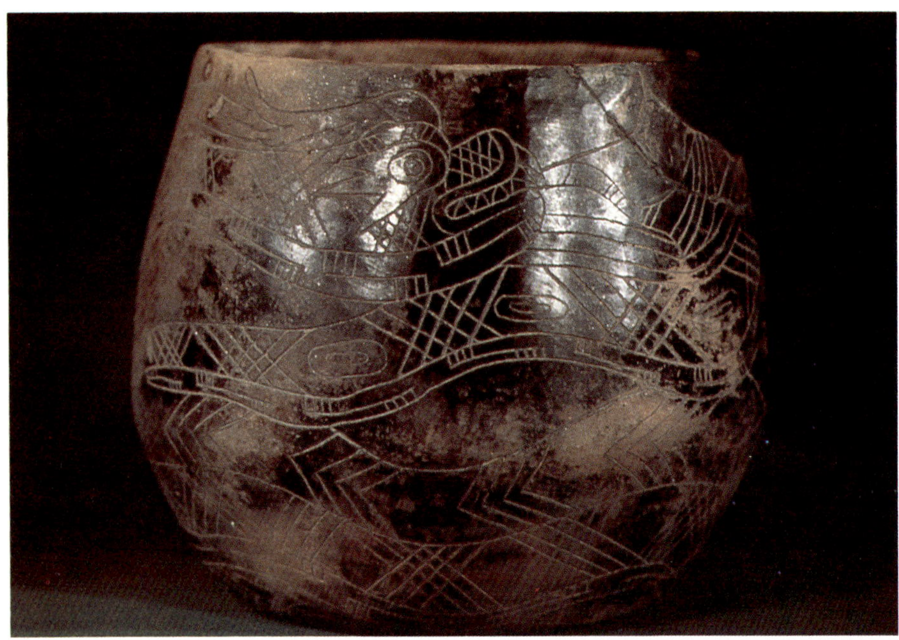

Figure 2. *Serpentine Monster Bowl*, A.D. 1300. Hollywood Mound, Savannah River, Richmond County. Ceramic painted, H. 4", Diam. 5¼". National Museum of Natural History, Smithsonian Institution. Serpentine monsters have antlers and human heads.

than a thousand years before the Mississippian period began. But as in everything else they did, the Mississippian people raised the making of pottery to a higher technical and artistic level than had their predecessors. They never mastered the use of the potter's wheel, but they fashioned excellent vessels using the coiling technique. While most of the pots were for everyday use, some were for restricted use in ritual contexts, such as in grave goods for their honored dead. Perhaps the most elaborate of these goods were bottles shaped like animal and human forms. One of the most enigmatic of these is the so-called "dog pot" [6]—a bottle vaguely resembling a dog, with certain anomalous features. Is it a dog or a mythical monster?

Accompanying an increase in population during the Mississippian period was an increase in social conflict. Much of this conflict is thought to have occurred between chiefdoms that were at odds with each other. Some of it may have been conflict between factions within chiefdoms: Mississippian chiefs wielded more authority than had their Woodland predecessors. When power is wielded in society, people are likely to become resentful or vengeful.

This heightened conflict is clearly reflected in Mississippian art. The bird the Mississippian warriors most admired was the peregrine falcon, the swiftest killer in the sky. The Indians could not have failed to have been impressed by the peregrine speeding through the air, nervously beating its powerful wings, and then hurtling down to kill a bird on the wing. This fierce bird was capable of killing other birds twice its size.

The Indians' regard for the peregrine falcon shows up most clearly on the repoussé copper plates found at Etowah [9, 10]. These plates show warriors dressed as peregrine falcons. They have the V-shaped peregrine eye marking, and they wear capes mimicking the peregrine's wings. Some carry flint daggers and the severed heads of their victims.

Many additional war motifs are evident in the art of these Indians. Ceramic bottles have been found that are adorned with the heads of live people and the skulls of dead people, a depiction of life as opposed to death. The scalp lock is sometimes depicted. Some art objects represent weapons of war, as does the monolithic axe or war club found near Ball Ground, Georgia [13].

In light of this predominant theme of social conflict, these Mississippian societies rose to power and influence, and then, whether because of instability from within or attack from without, or both, they declined and in some cases ceased to exist.

When Hernando de Soto explored Georgia in 1540, the great Ocmulgee mound center at Macon had been abandoned for many years. The Hollywood mound on the Savannah River had also been abandoned. In fact, no people lived on the Savannah River for quite some distance in all directions from the Hollywood mound. De Soto found people still living at the Etowah site, but Etowah at that time had nowhere near the importance it had previously possessed.

Even though these old mound centers were deserted or in decline, there was no dearth of Indians in Georgia in 1540. As Hernando de Soto made his way through Georgia, he entered a series of chiefdoms, both large and small. West of the lower Flint River he came to the chiefdom of Capachequi; on the upper Flint River lay the chiefdom of Toa; Ichisi lay on the upper Ocmulgee River; and Ocute lay on the Oconee River (figure 3—Desoto map).

The largest and most impressive chiefdom de Soto encountered in Georgia was the chiefdom of Coosa. De Soto did not enter the territory of this chiefdom until he crossed the Blue Ridge Mountains, following a trail lying along the French Broad River into the Tennessee Valley. Just on the other side of the mountains, on an island in the river near present-day Dandridge, Tennessee, de Soto came to Chiaha, one of the northernmost towns subject to the grand chief of Coosa. Not until many days later did de Soto meet this Grand Chief in his principal town at the Little Egypt archaeological site near present day Carters, Georgia. From this seat of power, the Grand Chief of Coosa ruled over towns which lay to the southwest, beyond what is now Rome, and he exercised some power or influence over towns that lay far to the south in Alabama.

The people of Coosa made characteristically fine Mississippian pottery, both everyday ware and fancy bottles [16, 18] and ritual vessels. Like other Mississippian peoples, the people of Coosa believed in a serpentine monster. Their own peculiar conceptualization of the

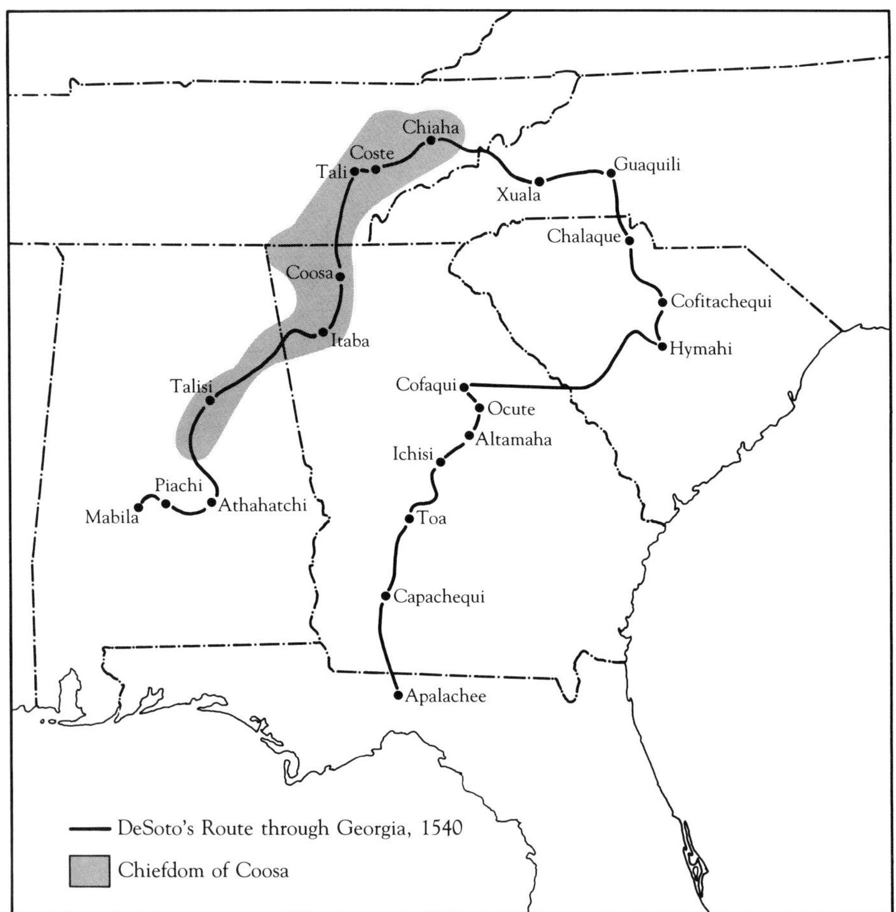

Figure 3. *De Soto's Route Through Georgia, 1540.* The Hernando de Soto expedition entered Georgia twice. In early March 1540, they entered southwestern Georgia and traveled northward and eastward to the vicinity of present Augusta, where they crossed the Savannah River. They again entered Georgia in the middle of July 1540 and spent about a month at the main town of the chiefdom of Coosa, near present Carters, Georgia.

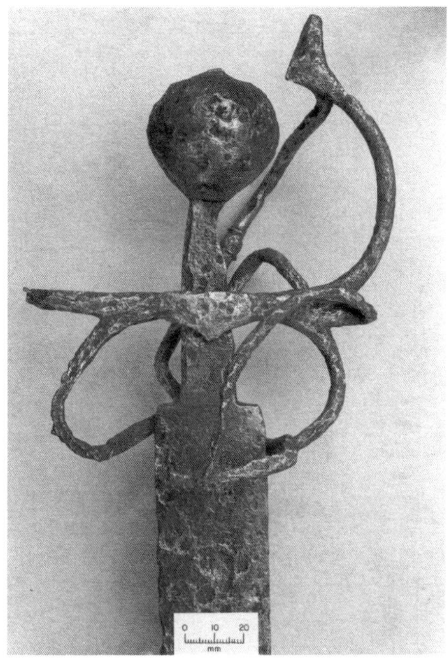

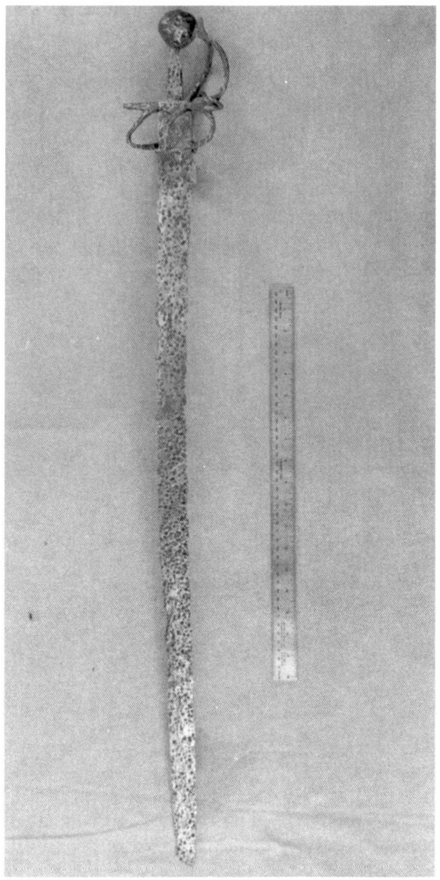

Figure 4. *Sword,* 1500–1600. King Site, Floyd County. Ferrus metal, L. 37". Private Collection, On loan to the Etowah mounds Historic Site, Georgia Department of Natural Resources, Parks and Historic Sites. The King site was probably visited by the Hernando de Soto expedition, and the sword probably belonged to one of de Soto's soldiers.

monster was incised on circular shell gorgets that were worn suspended about their necks [19]. The serpent has a huge eye, usually formed of concentric circles; a huge head, with the teeth of an herbivore; and the body of a serpent coiled around the head, terminating with a rattlesnake's tail. The peculiar decoration about the eye may be an abstract representation of the marking about a peregrine falcon's eye.

Compared to what was in store for them, the conflict and turmoil the Indians of Georgia had experienced before the era of Spanish exploration was nothing. De Soto met relatively little resistance from the Indians as he wound his way through Georgia. But as he traveled down through the territory of Coosa, he began making more and more insistent demands upon the Indians to supply him with burden bearers, and particularly young females. When the Indians of Coosa began trying to escape from de Soto and his men, the Spaniards responded by hunting them down and rounding them up forcibly. From injuries on the bones of burials that were found at the King site (figure 4—sword), just west of present Rome, it is clear that de Soto's men slew a number of the people of Coosa. The only question is whether they were killed in and around the King site, or at a great battle that occurred some weeks later at Mabila, on the Alabama River.

Spanish wardogs, lances, halberds, crossbows, and matchlock guns were undoubtedly horrible for the Indians. More horrible still were the diseases which the Spaniards brought with them. In the last half of the sixteenth century, and throughout the seventeenth century, the loss of life caused by these diseases was almost unimaginable. The great towns de Soto had visited were so depopulated that many of them were abandoned. The temples on the mounds fell into decay. The grand chiefs were no more. And the sumptuary art the chiefs used to validate their status was no longer produced.

After de Soto and his army departed, other Spaniards came to Georgia to establish a system of missions to evangelize the Indians. Primarily built along the coast, missions like Santa Catalina de Guale [22–25] on St. Catherine's Island, found Spanish friars teaching Indians the rudiments of Christianity and sometimes of the Spanish language. The spirits and deities of the Mississippian era gradually gave way to the Judaeo-Christian deity, and the serpent monster gorget gave way to the crucifix and images of the saints. Some of the Indians of the missions began to make pottery in the form of European vessels, such as pitchers [28].

After the great explorations of the sixteenth century, the Spaniards rarely ventured into the interior of Georgia. They did well, in fact, to retain their coastal missions. More than once the Indians rose up in rebellion, killing the friars. The Indians in the missions were so few they could hardly produce enough food to feed the friars and soldiers stationed there.

Though the Spaniards seldom went into the interior, their germs and viruses did. The Indian population continued to fall. Next to nothing is known about what occurred in the Indian societies in the interior of Georgia in the seventeenth century. What little is known has been learned by archaeologists who have excavated sites such as the Joe Bell site on the Oconee River in Morgan County. The people who lived at this site were poor in material possessions, though they still produced pottery that is surprisingly well made [26, 27].

After 1670, English traders from Charleston began to rule the Indians of the Southeast, including those who lived in what is now Georgia. In exchange for Indian slaves and dressed deerskins, they traded guns, shot, powder, woolen cloth, hatchets, knives, and many other items. A major center of this trade was located at Augusta and a minor center near Macon. The Indians who met Oglethorpe at Yamacraw Bluff in 1733 had been involved in this trade for more than half a century. By that time, they were so dependent upon goods manufactured in Europe that they were no longer their own masters [29]. It had been two centuries since de Soto had come through Georgia, but the societies he had encountered no longer existed, not even in the memories of their own descendants.

Charles Hudson
Department of Anthropology
The University of Georgia

The Cartographic Progression of Georgia as Colony and State

Colonization and even exploration of the American Southeast was not immediate after Christopher Columbus set foot upon the "Indies." In fact, quite remote to these earliest explorers was the concept of a great continent waiting behind the string of tiny islands and a huge land mass extending far inland from the coastal dunes.

By 1565, Spain had succeeded in placing a colony at St. Augustine on the Florida peninsula. In 1607, England successfully, if somewhat tenuously, established Jamestown in Virginia. Prior to Jamestown, the Spanish, English, and French attempted to found many other settlements along the southeastern coast, but their efforts were short-lived or abortive endeavors.

However, even though Jamestown was settled, little knowledge of the inland portions of the Southeast had been gained. John Farrer's 1651 "Mapp of Virginia" still promoted the widely held view that the Pacific Ocean lapped the shores just over the Blue Ridge Mountains. By 1670, a young German, John Lederer, was commissioned to explore the interior of "Virginia." In so doing, he became one of the first Europeans to travel the Appalachians and the piedmont area of north Georgia and Carolina. He gained information from the Indians about how to avoid the mountain barrier by following the trading path at the range's southern end in Georgia.

Knowledge of this route became invaluable to English traders in later years because it was the main path into the American heartland. For some misguided reason, Lederer also "confirmed" quite erroneously the existence of a large inland lake in piedmont Carolina which had appeared on southeastern maps from the time of the Mercator-Hondius map of 1606. Probably, he wished merely to exaggerate slightly the extent of his southern journey, hence his fanciful description of "Ushery Lake" with its "brackish water."[1]

Nicolaus Visscher (1649–1709) was a member of a distinguished family of Dutch mapmakers. The 1680 "Insulae Americanae in Oceano Septentrionali ac Regiones Adiacentes, a C. de May usque ad Lineam Æquinoctialem" (figure 1) presented to Europeans a clear picture of the cartographic knowledge of North America in the late seventeenth century. Of particular interest is Visscher's depiction of

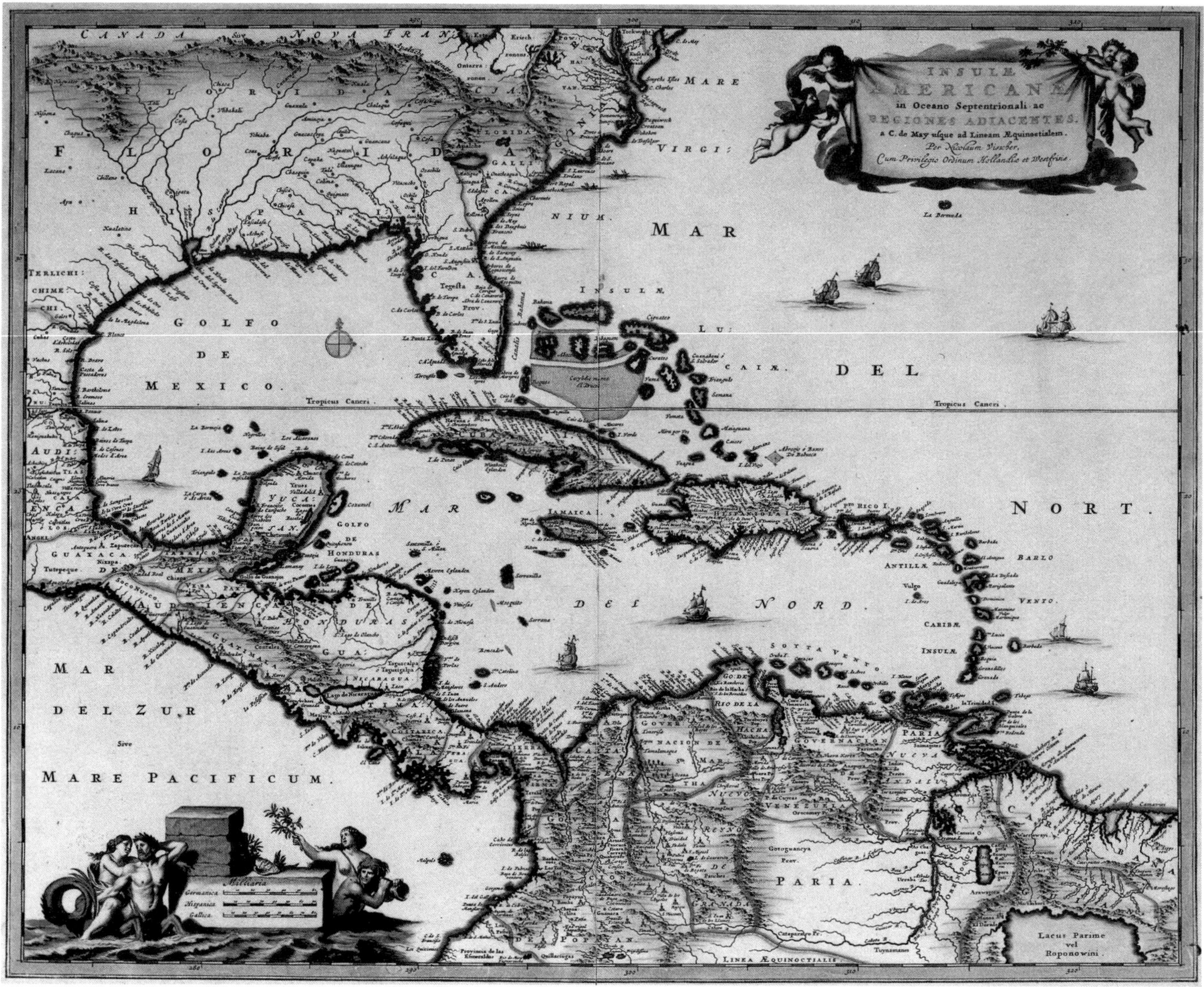

Figure 1. Nicolaus Visscher, *Insulae Americanae in Oceano Septentrionali ac Regiones Adiacentes*, 1680. Amsterdam: Nicolaus Visscher. H. 18½", W. 22½". Special Collections, The University of Georgia Libraries.

the Southeast, no aspect of which reflects either new scholarship or advances in discovery.

Visscher depends most upon the 1656 map of the Southeast by French mapmaker Nicolas Sanson, reproducing the borders of "Florida Gallica" (present Carolina) and the sweeping east-west arc of the "Apalache Montes" from that map. Visscher's simple, almost unindented coastline of modern Georgia-South Carolina is clearly reproduced from a 1640 map by Blaeu. The "R. de May" is still shown as flowing northward into an interior lake. Confused with the Savannah River, this river was actually the St. John's River, discovered by Jean Ribaut on May 1, 1562, and hence called the River May. The St. John's does flow into a body of water but southwestward in Florida. Most of the Indian towns mentioned on Visscher's map, such as "Edelano" and "Cofachiqui," appear on much earlier maps as well.

Dutch mapmakers like Visscher were much more inclined toward commercial artistry than scientific cartography. The unknown lands were more often than not filled with fanciful renderings and conjectures.

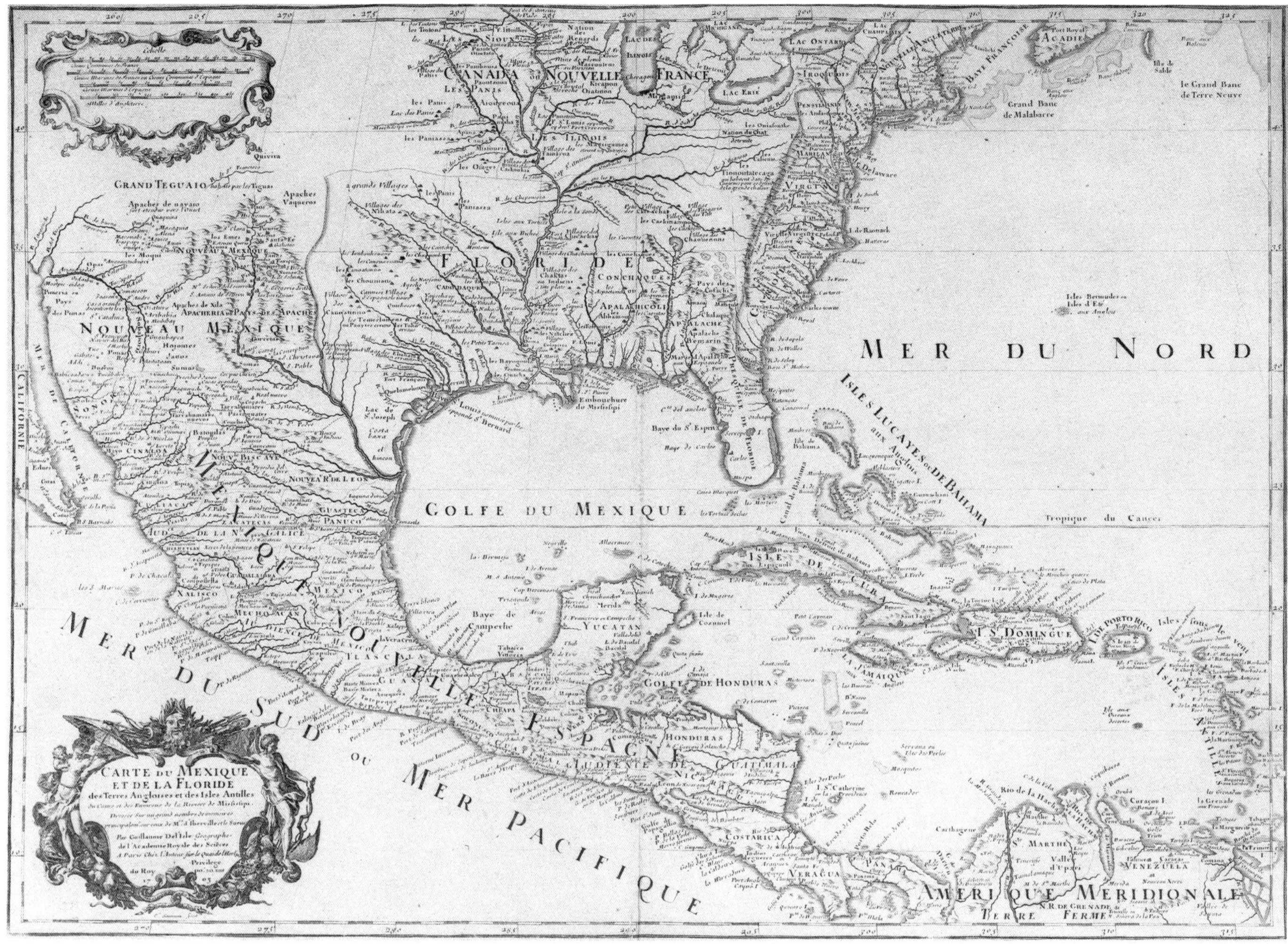

Figure 2. Guillaume Delisle, engraved by C. Simonneau, *Carte du Mexique et de la Floride*, 1703. Paris: Delisle. H. 19¼", W. 26". Special Collections, The University of Georgia Libraries.

With Guillaume Delisle's "Carte de Mexique de la Floride" (1703) (figure 2) came a new realism in cartographic renderings of the Southeast. There are occasional flights of fancy—the legendary Bemarin appears in present southwest Georgia[2], an inland lake remains located in north Georgia, and the Appalachians extend southward toward the Florida peninsula. Delisle nevertheless has advanced considerably from Visscher's copyist technique to actually analyzing the findings of Iberville and Bienville in the Mississippi Valley and using celestial observations to systematize longitude.

Delisle's map also is a clear reminder of the expansionist ideas of the French in the early decades of the eighteenth century. English territory is limited to only a thin stretch along the eastern seaboard. "R. de Sapola," one of the earliest continuous Georgia place names (Sapelo) appears, and Georgia's coastal islands, although unnamed, do begin taking shape. The ancient name of the "golden islands" also is shown as "R. de Wallea" (Guale). The River May does not appear, nor does the Savannah River, with which it was confused. While several unnamed streams flow inward in northerly directions, Delisle obviously had knowledge of neither their sources nor their actual courses.

Robert Montgomery was the original proprietor of lands that later

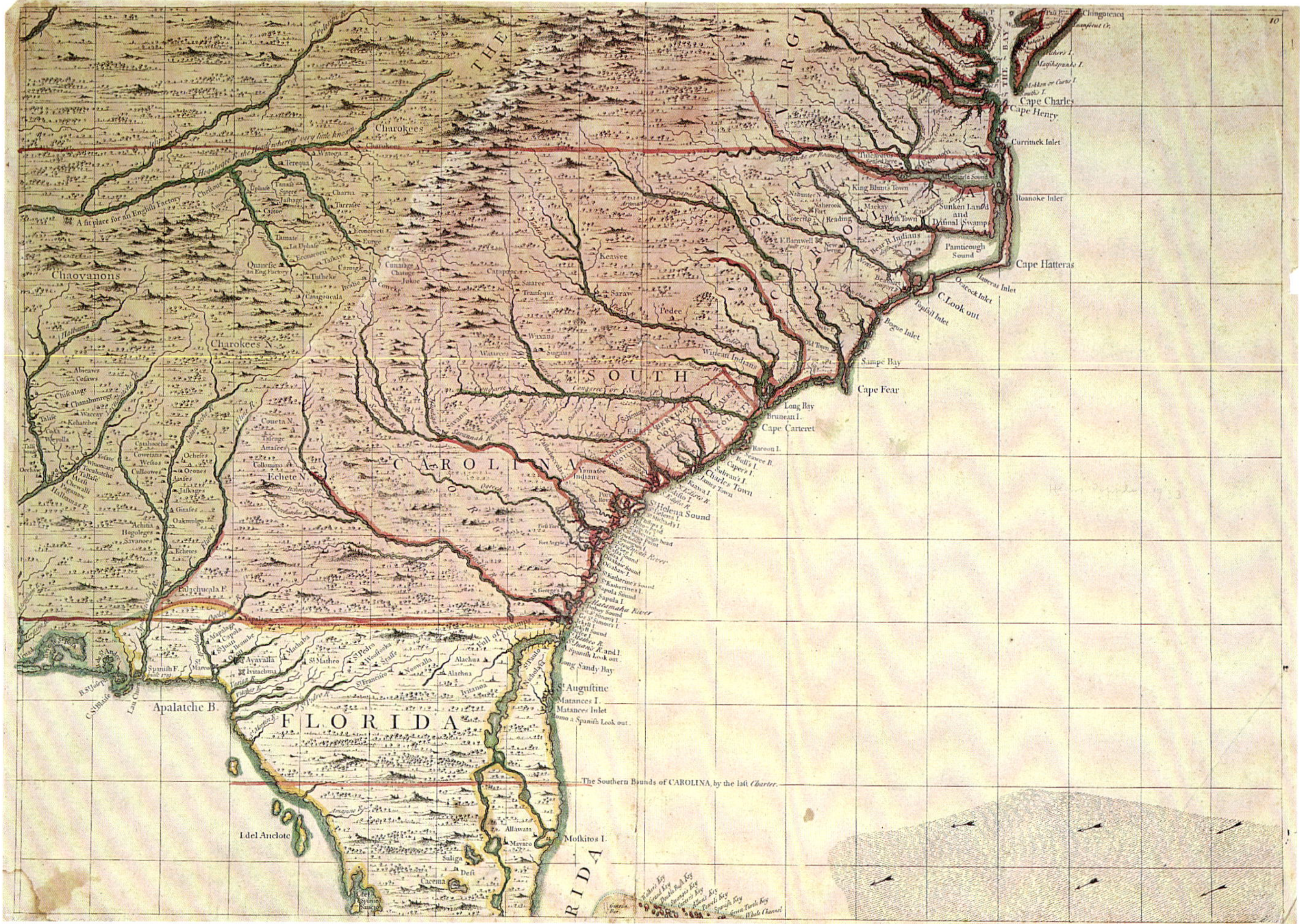

Figure 3. Henry Popple, *A Map of the British Empire in America with the French and Spanish Settlements adjacent thereto*, 1733. London: Henry Popple. One of 20 sheets: H. 19¾", W. 27¼". Special Collections, The University of Georgia Libraries.

became Georgia. Hermann Moll's 1720 map of America placed the "Margravate of Azilia," as Montgomery would have stated, "to the south of Carolina in the most delightful country of the universe." Montgomery was not successful in establishing a colony within the present confines of Georgia. However, 15 years after Montgomery, James Oglethorpe and a group of philanthropic Englishmen did succeed. Chartered in 1732, the colony of Georgia was a reality by the next year with the scattering of settlers on a bluff overlooking the Savannah River.

The first map reflecting this settlement was "A Map of the British Empire in America with the French and Spanish Settlements adjacent thereto," prepared by Henry Popple (London, 1733) (figure 3). Measuring 102 x 104 inches and scaled one inch for 40 miles, Popple's map is "impressive in conception and elaborate in detail, if at times faulty in execution."[3] Printed on 20 sheets, the map vividly portrays the English position in the struggle for domination of the continent. As such, it volleys with the pro-French Delisle maps of 1703 and 1718. The southeastern section maintains the Appalachians as the western boundary of Virginia and North Carolina, but South Carolina's border stretches to the Flint River. Although "Georgia" first appeared on the map published with Benjamin Martyn's *Reasons for Establishing the Colony of Georgia* (London, 1733), the Popple

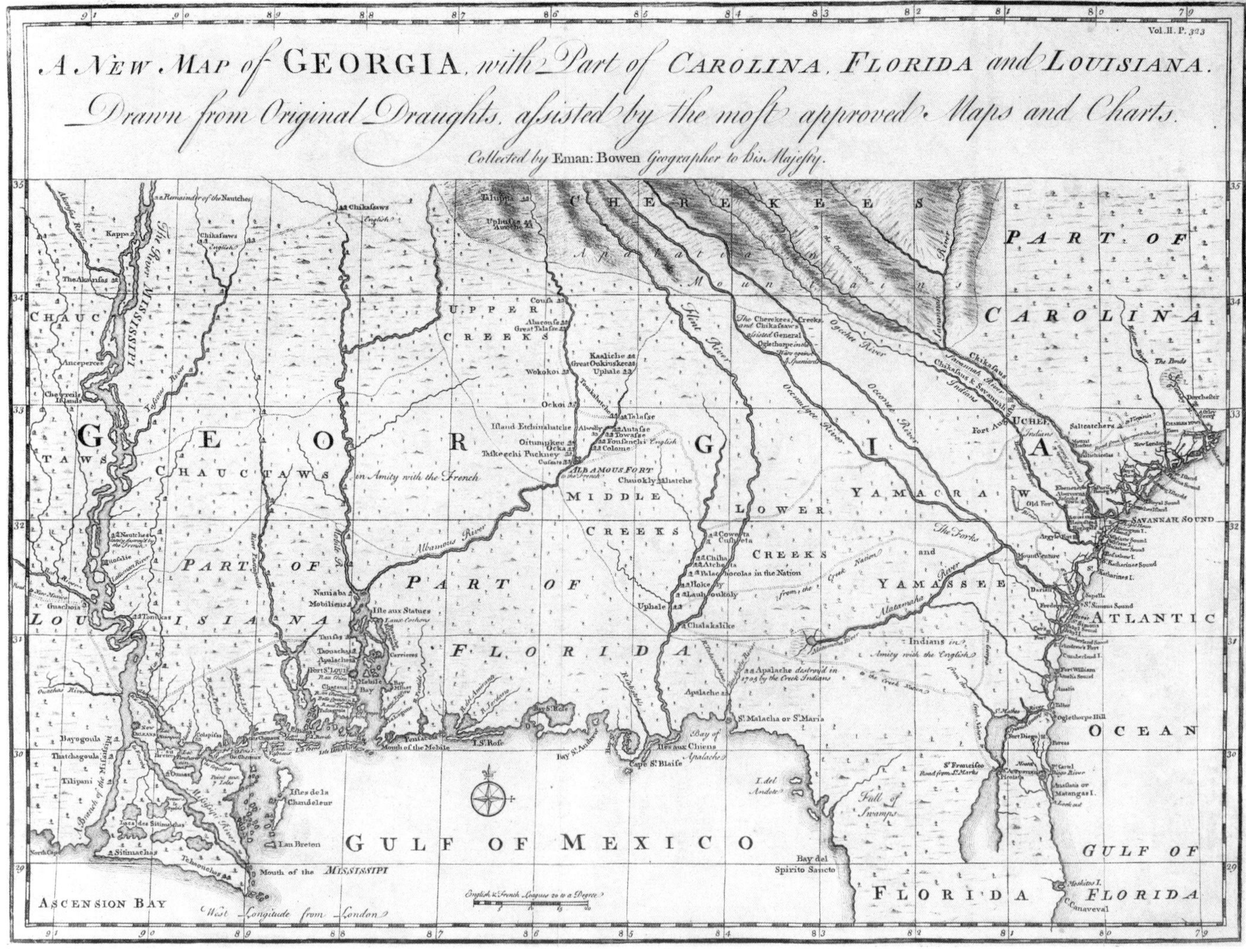

Figure 4. Emanuel Bowen, *A New Map of Georgia, with Part of Carolina, Florida and Louisiana*, 1748. London: John Harris. H. 14⅜", W. 19". Special Collections, The University of Georgia Libraries.

map is the earliest separately printed map bearing the name "Georgia."

On the Popple map, English and Indian place names have replaced the Spanish and French nomenclature from earlier maps for the region. The Georgia coastline is truncated and both the Altamaha and the Savannah rivers are shown pronouncedly flowing eastward to the Atlantic. The "Salwage" (later Broad River) appears with a northerly flow paralleling the "Tugeloo." Georgia's coastal isles are shown in more detail than they are on previous maps and are inscribed with familiar names. Though assigned a 1733 date, this section of the Popple map obviously came a few years later because one can see the presence of a well-defined Savannah, Ebenezer, Joseph's Town, and system of forts, including "Savana F." well inland on the Savannah River on the Carolina side. These developments occurred after 1733. The western reaches of the territory properly place "Coueta" near the Flint and show a relatively accurate course for the "Catahooche R."

Popple has based his rendition on a circa 1722 manuscript map attributed to "Tuscarora Jack" Barnwell, trader, adventurer, and explorer of the Carolina interior. The Popple map gives both the interior

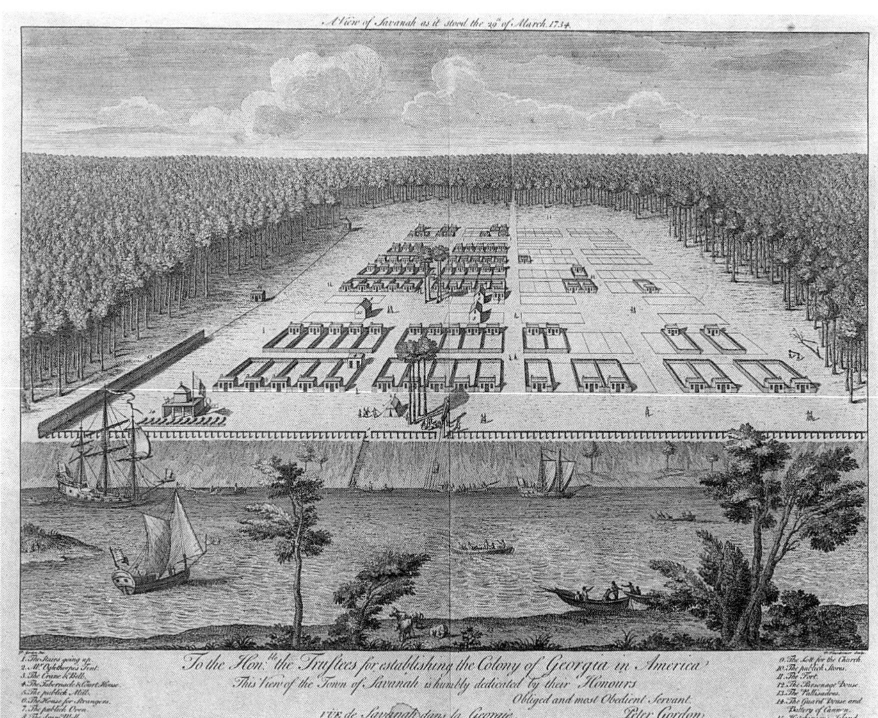

Figure 5. Peter Gordon, engraved by P. Fourdrinier, *A View of Savannah as it stood the 29th of March, 1734*, 1734. London: Gordon. H. 18 1/16", W. 22⅞". Special Collections, The University of Georgia Libraries.

Indian settlements and the coastal names of the region more fully than does any previous printed map.[4]

Popple's map was rapidly disseminated. Within a decade, it had been relied upon heavily by Dutch and French cartographers alike as well as by other English mapmakers such as Emanuel Bowen, whose 1747 map neither enhanced nor altered Popple's original.

The following year, however, Bowen produced for John Harris' *Navigantium atque Itinerantium Bibliotheca* "A New Map of Georgia, with Part of Carolina, Florida and Louisiana" (figure 4). Although still showing some dependence on the Popple map, this map corrects the foreshortened Atlantic coastline of Georgia, improves the course of the Savannah River, and includes numerous trading paths and trails into the interior. The Okefenokee Swamp does not appear by name, but the Alatamaha [sic] River is shown flowing into an inland lake surrounded by marshland. Certain Indian tribes are shown "in amity with" either the English or French. Numerous place names now begin appearing along the Georgia coast and upstream as far as Fort Augusta. A single line of dots paralleling the north bank of the Savannah River is displayed as the boundary line between Georgia and South Carolina, and the line is continued to show separation of the two colonies from the lands of the "Cherekees."[5]

In 1734, Peter Gordon landed in Georgia with the first settlers from the *Anne* and served as the colony's magistrate. He produced "A View of Savanah as it stood the 29th of March, 1734" (figure 5). Gordon produced the work as much for propagandistic purposes—to show the Trustees their success in establishing a new colony—as for historical or geographical wants. The view portrays neat town lots with the Savannah River in the foreground and forests behind stretching to the horizon. Most interesting and informative is the

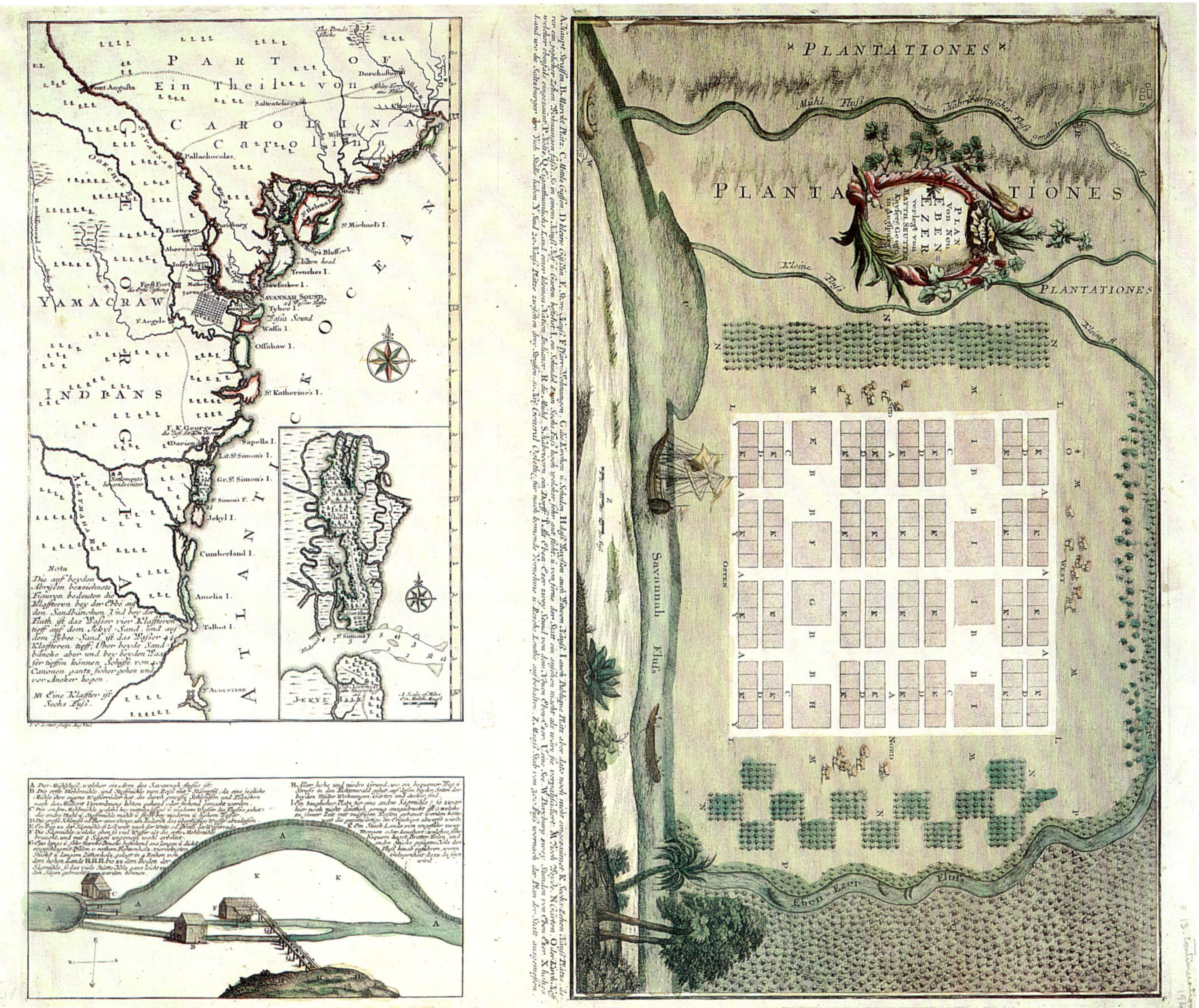

Figure 6. Matthias Seutter, engraved by T. C. Lotter, *Plan Von Neu Eben-Ezer*, 1747. Halle, Germany: Walsenhaus. H. 19½", W. 23". Special Collections, The University of Georgia Libraries.

legend identifying and locating the courthouse, fort, guard house, and other structures in the town.

Also presenting a town plan is Matthias Seutter's "Plan Von Neu Eben-Ezer" (1747) (figure 6), the Salzburger settlement inland from Savannah. In organization it is highly derivative of Oglethorpe's design for Georgia's first city. On the same sheet also is printed an untitled map of Georgia by T. C. Lotter. This map was based on the Robert Seale circa 1741 map published in conjunction with Benjamin Martyn's promotional *An Account Shewing the Progress of the Colony of Georgia* (London, 1741).[6] While Lotter has added notes and legends in German, his map is obviously developed from the rendering. Seale assisted W. H. Toms in the engraving of Popple's map in 1733, and in his own map corrected certain of Popple's misconceptions. This map's influence on Bowen's 1748 revision is unmistakable. An inset of Great St. Simon's is an important contribution because it analyzes this area closely for the first time.

Noble Jones had served an appointment as Oglethorpe's surveyor

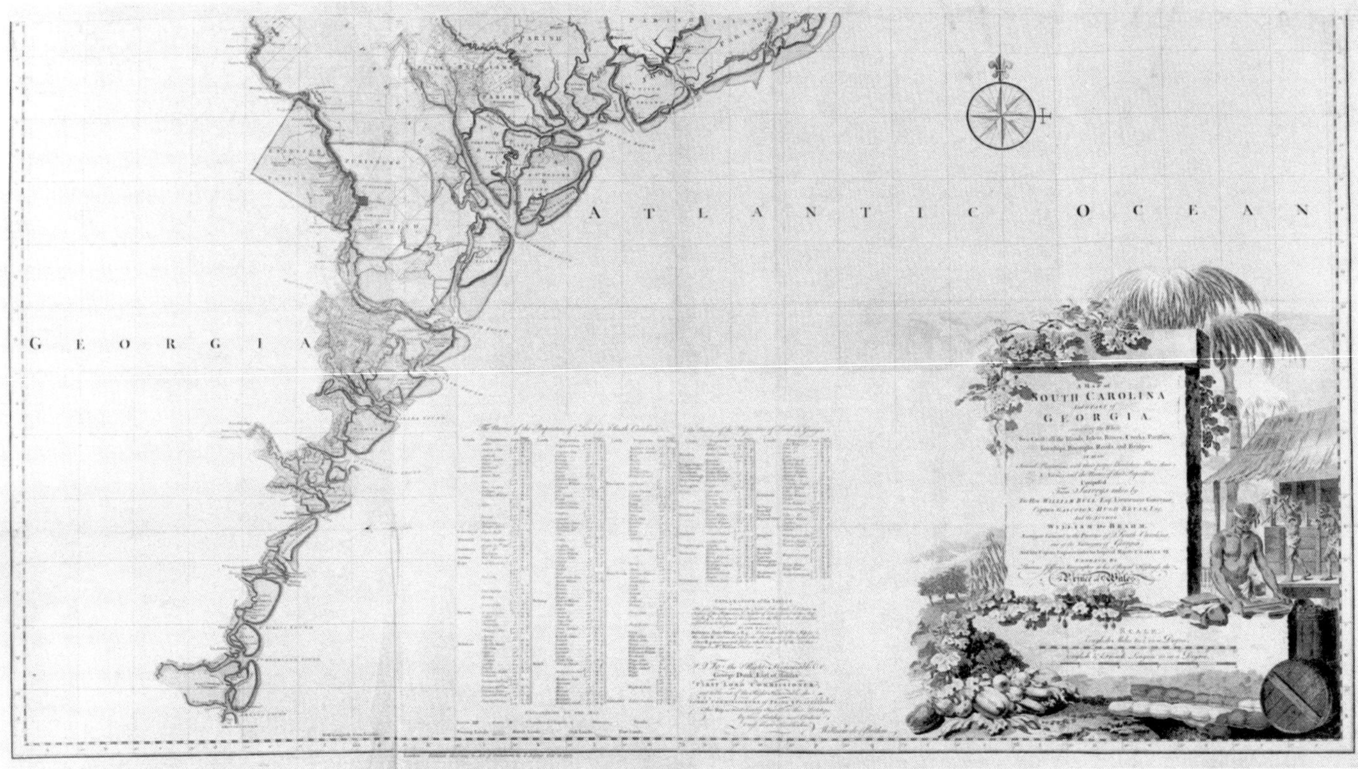

Figure 7. John Gerar William DeBrahm, engraved by Thomas Jeffrys, *Map of South Carolina and a Part of Georgia*, 1757. London: Thomas Jeffrys. H. 53″, W. 48″. Special Collections, The University of Georgia Libraries.

from 1733 and had possibly aided Peter Gordon in his "View of Savanah."[7] However, the first surveyor who made great impact on the colony was a Dutch Protestant, John Gerar William DeBrahm (later William Gerard DeBrahm). Arriving in Georgia in 1751 with a group of Salzburgers, DeBrahm was by 1754 a king's appointed surveyor. By 1757, he had completed his extensive survey of the Georgia and Carolina coastal areas. His "Map of South Carolina and a Part of Georgia" (figure 7/not in exhibition) was vastly superior to any work done before in the region. Its influence would continue well into the next century. It accurately determined, at least for the inhabited areas, the direction of rivers, the shapes of islands and tributaries, and parish and settlement boundaries. DeBrahm was a professional who relied on firsthand observation and measurement rather than depending on the prior work of others, who were a continent and ocean away.

The impact of DeBrahm's scholarly effort, however, was not immediately felt. The April 1779 publication of J. Hinton's "A New and Accurate Map of the Province of Georgia in North America" (figure 8) in the *Universal Magazine of Knowledge and Pleasure* shows little of the detail of the DeBrahm map, although it does have numerous creeks named that are well inland. The dotted line depicting the border of Georgia runs along the south side of the Savannah River and from there along Little Creek at the north. It does not reflect the 1773 purchase of Cherokee lands, which opened up new expanses of territory on both sides of the Broad River. Trading paths are clearly marked because more and more these former "paths" were becoming arteries of travel as settlement stretched out towards the interior. The Okefenokee appears as "Owaquaphenoga whose pass is a secret."

Figure 8. J. Hinton, *A New and Accurate Map of the Province of Georgia in North America*, 1779. *Universal Magazine*, 44, April 1779. H. 13⅛", W. 11¼". Special Collections, The University of Georgia Libraries.

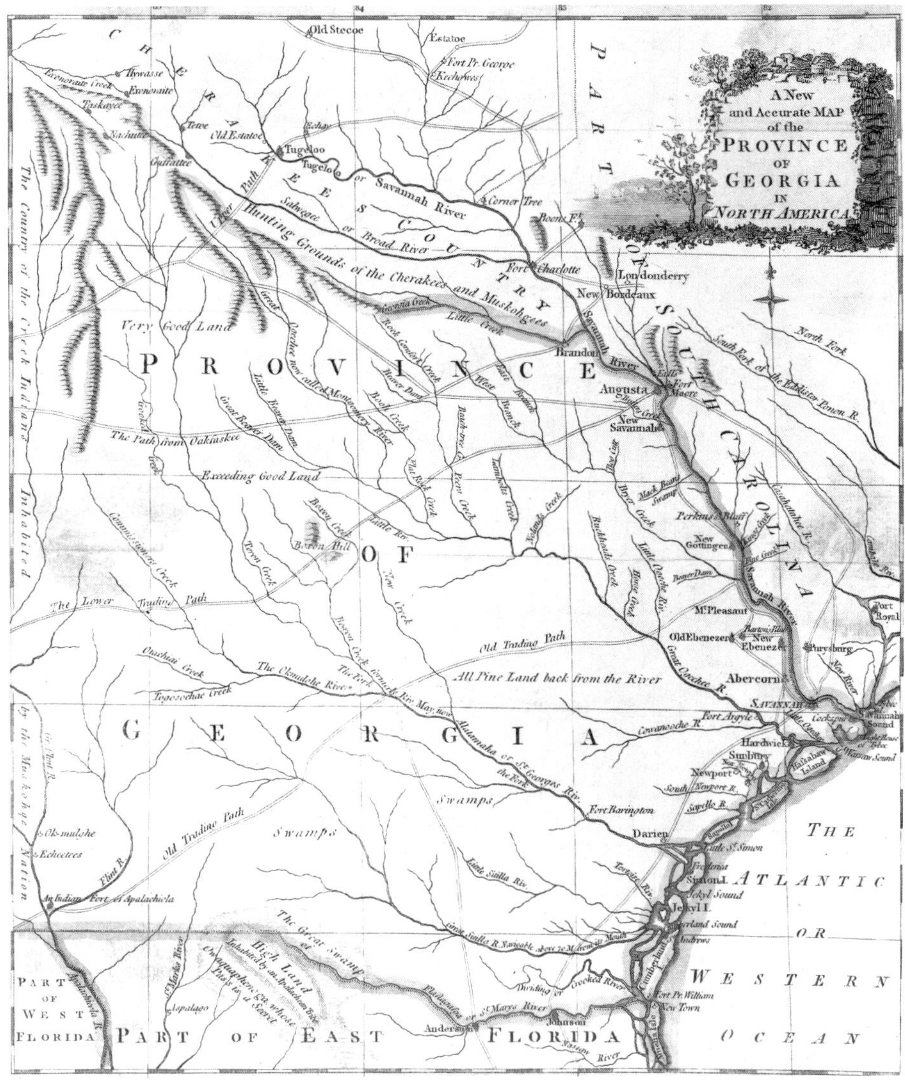

While the swamp is somewhat to the west of its actual position, it is no longer noted as the source for the Alatamaha [sic] River. The Alatamaha [sic] is described with the note "formerly River May," but this notation is an error. The Alatamaha [sic] is given the alternate name "St. Georges Riv." The Oconee River, a prominent feature on the 1748 Bowen map, does not appear at all, though the Great Ogeechee flows well into the Appalachian foothills, listed with its "new" name, the Montgomery River.

For Georgia, the Revolutionary War was more an internecine struggle than a British invasion although certainly both Augusta and Savannah witnessed British seiges. Oddly enough, a map of Georgia provided the detail and definition needed to help the British war efforts in Georgia. The stunning Archibald Campbell "Sketch of the Northern Frontiers of Georgia, extending from the Mouth of the River Savannah to the Town of Augusta" (figure 9) is one of the most beautiful examples of eighteenth-century cartography. The map, developed for military purposes to delineate the route from Savannah along the river to Augusta, presents an accurate rendering of roadways, trails, stream and river crossings, property owners, and terrain.

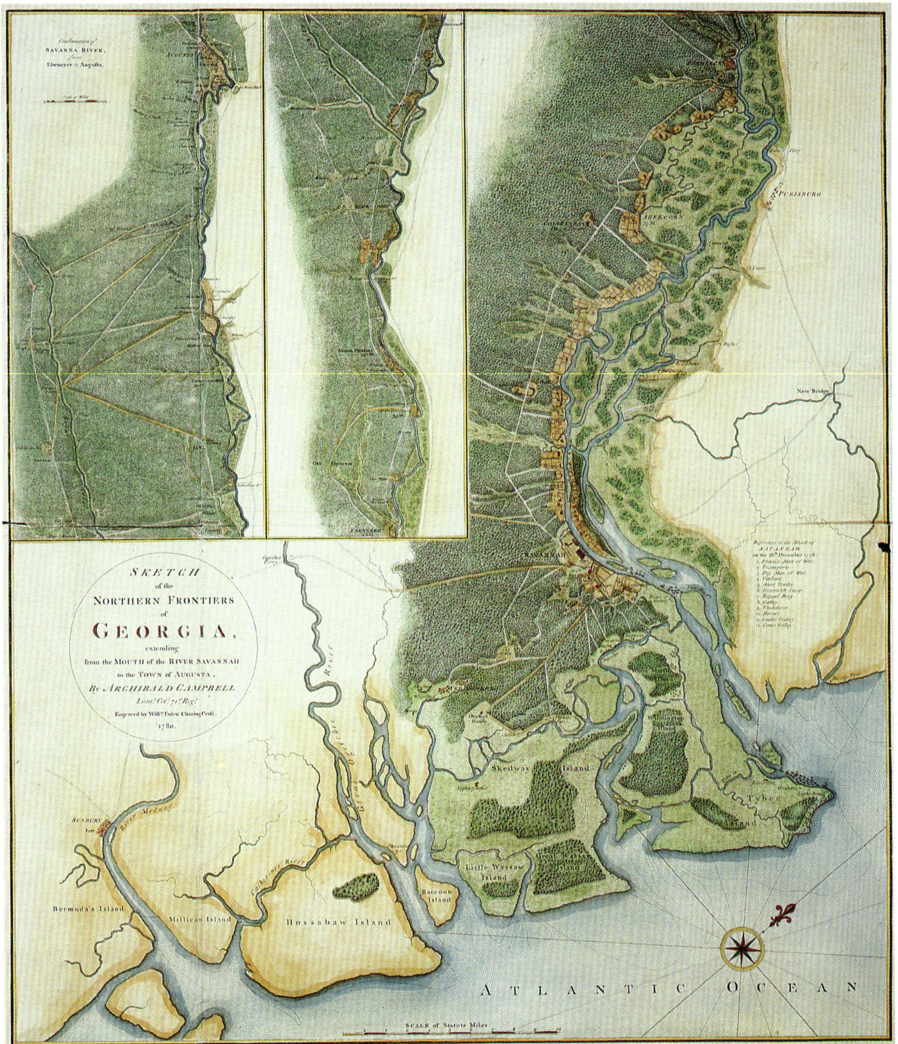

Figure 9. Archibald Campbell, engraved by William Faden, *Sketch of the Northern Frontiers of Georgia, Extending from the Mouth of the River Savannah to the Town of Augusta*, 1780. London: William Faden. H. 28¾", W. 24⅜". Special Collections, The University of Georgia Libraries.

Utilizing DeBrahm to a certain extent, the map is chiefly the product of British engineers working under the auspices of Lieutenant Colonel Campbell. Its engraving testifies to its significance for the British. The engraving was done by William Faden, the successor to Thomas Jeffreys and foremost map publisher in England.

One of the earliest printed maps indicating Georgia's colonial parishes was Bernard Roman's 1776 map of the southern British colonies. The next year, Georgia abolished the parish system in anti-British fervor and established the county system that remains today. Not until 1794 did a map reflect this subdivision of the new state. Philadelphia publisher Mathew Carey had acquired the American rights for an edition of Guthrie's *Geography* and had commissioned a new set of maps. W. Barker engraved the one of Georgia (figure 10).[8] At the time of the engraving, the state had taken on its familiar form, stretching from the Savannah to the Mississippi. Counties were named and their boundaries denoted. The growth of the state in the upcountry is clearly defined with settlements shown at Petersburg, Washington, and Louisville. The Oconee River is well-marked as the western boundary for the ceded areas and the "High Shoal" appears.

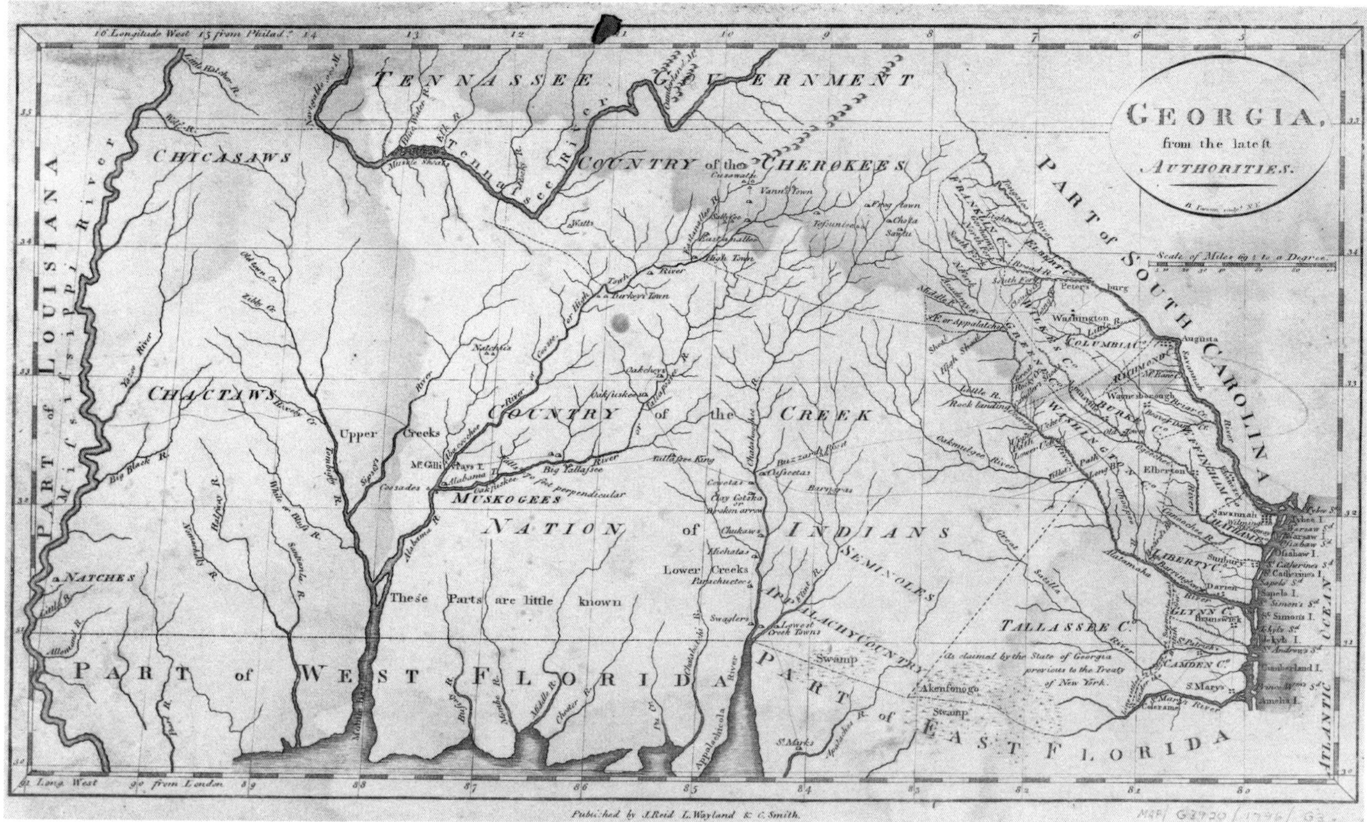

Figure 10. Mathew Carey, engraved by W. Barker, *Georgia from the Latest Authorities*, 1794. Philadelphia: Mathew Carey for Guthrie's *Geography*. H. 9 9/16", W. 16¼". Special Collections, The University of Georgia Libraries.

Most of the state remained Indian land; much of the western territory was simply noted as "These parts are little known."

New Yorker John Reid's *American Atlas* was the first atlas engraved and published in the United States containing only maps of America. As part of this atlas, Reid reissued the Carey map in 1796 reengraved by B. Tanner but with no other changes from the earlier version.

By 1813, both the Mississippi and Alabama territories had been created, thus moving Georgia's boundary eastward from the Mississippi River to the Chattahoochee. The state's boundaries were now substantively fixed, although settlement west of the Ocmulgee River was negligible. Thirty-nine counties were now clustered together—many of their boundaries changed in the ensuing years. A map entitled simply "The State of Georgia" and engraved by Gridley appeared approximately in 1813 (figure 11). Unlike several similar maps of the period, it does not show a sharp westward bend in the upper reaches of the Savannah River, which distorts the Georgia-South Carolina boundary. Instead, it gives a relatively careful rendering. Much of Georgia remains Indian land, and a number of trails are shown into the Creek and Cherokee territories. County seats and courthouses, as well as an expanded road system, are included. In north Georgia the Appalachians, with stylized mountain ridges, are relatively accurately placed among the Cherokee lands.

As early as 1783, the State of Georgia had felt the need for county surveyors and accurate mapping. However, not until the second decade of the nineteenth century was a statewide official survey begun.

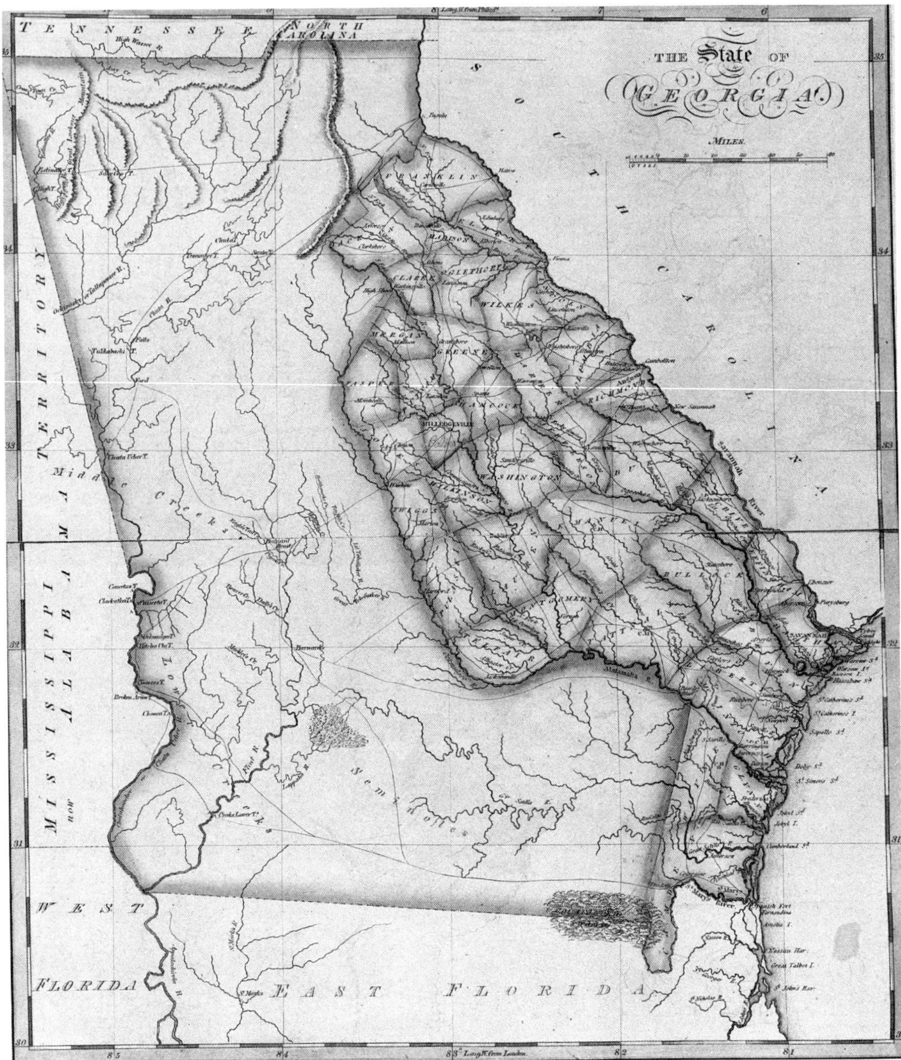

Figure 11. Engraved by Gridley, *The State of Georgia*, ca. 1813. Philadelphia: Gridley. H. 18¼", W. 15½". Special Collections, The University of Georgia Libraries.

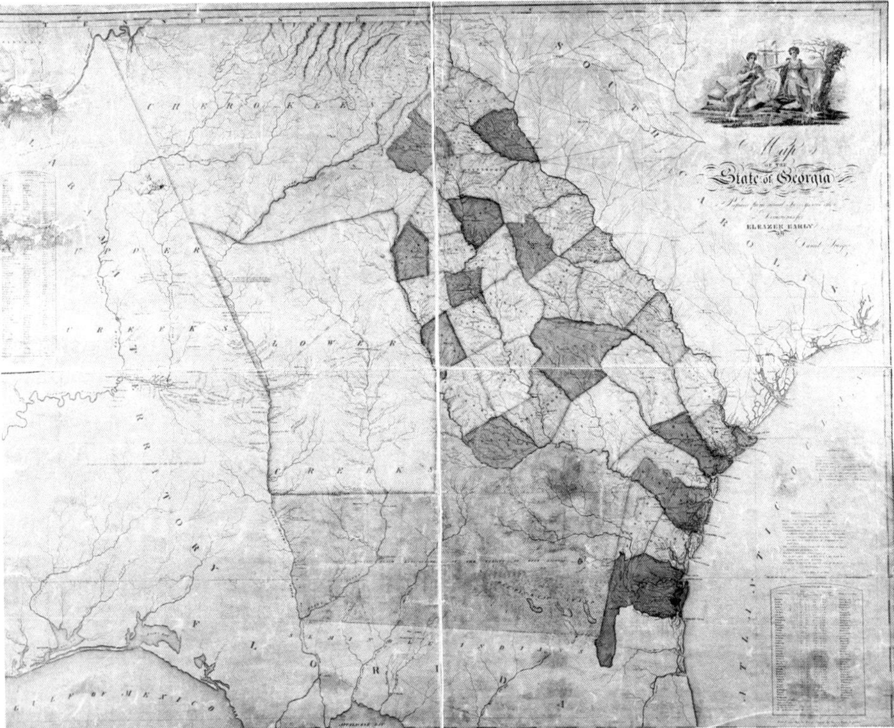

Figure 12. Daniel Sturges, surveyor, engraved by Samuel Harrison, *Map of the State of Georgia*, 1818. Philadelphia: Eleazer Early. H. 44", W. 55". Special Collections, The University of Georgia Libraries.

Figure 13. Engraved by Young and Delleker, *Georgia*, ca. 1830. Philadelphia: Anthony Finley. H. 12″, W. 9⅞″. Special Collections, The University of Georgia Libraries.

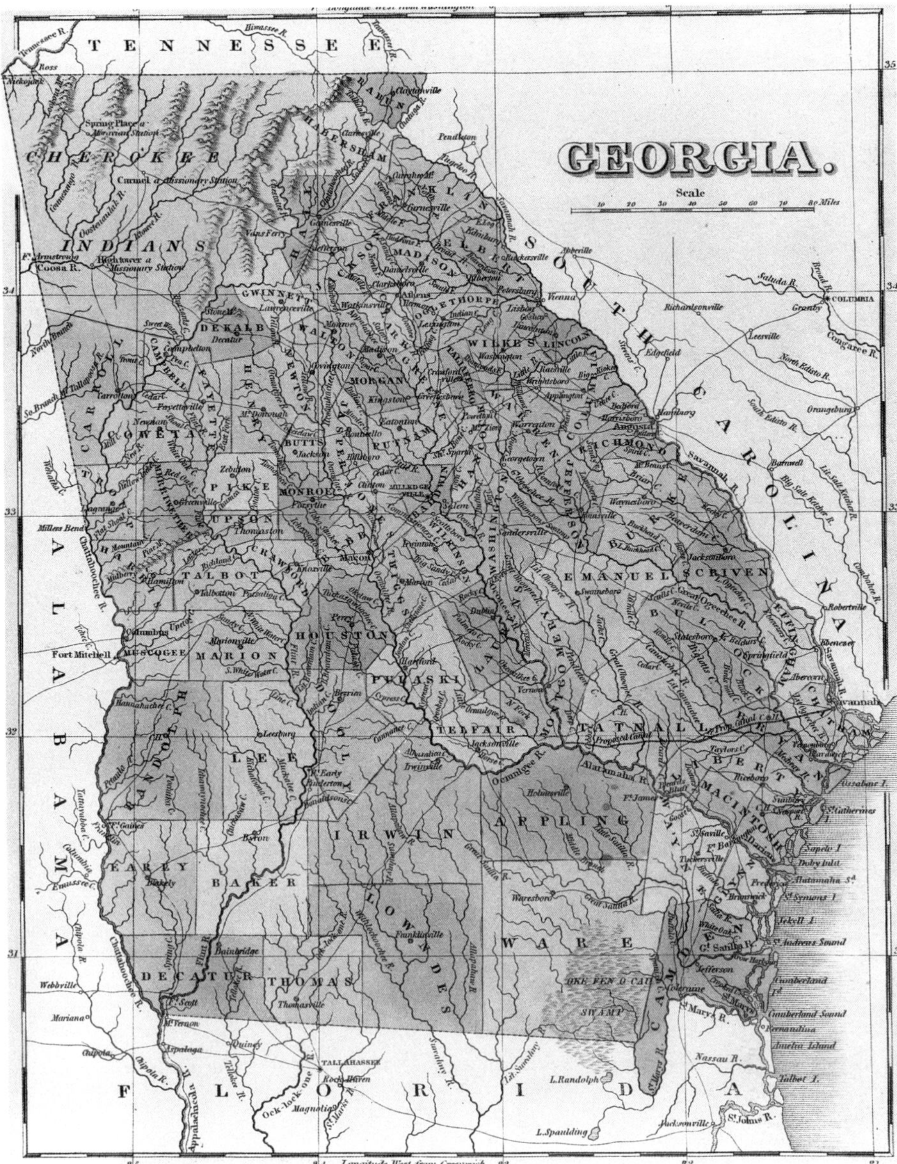

Daniel Sturges, the State Surveyor General, was charged with the project, which proceeded with great care. By December 1818, the map (figure 12/not in exhibition) became available to the public. It was published by Eleazer Early, brother of Governor Peter Early, and engraved by Samuel Harrison in Philadelphia. Scaled eight miles to the inch and sized 44 x 55 inches, it was the first close analysis of the entire state. By comparison, DeBrahm's detailed work encompassed only the coastal and border areas. The project's impact was understandably significant. The map established a standard and provided a "mother map" on which other cartographers could depend.[9]

By about 1815, Philadelphia had become a map publishing center in the United States. What most of these map makers lacked in creativity they made up for in craftsmanship, creating handsomely functional productions. Among the most prominent of these publishers was Anthony Finley, whose large atlas was produced in the mid–1820s and updated and revised continuously for some years afterward. His "Georgia" (figure 13) came out about 1830. It shows the Cherokee

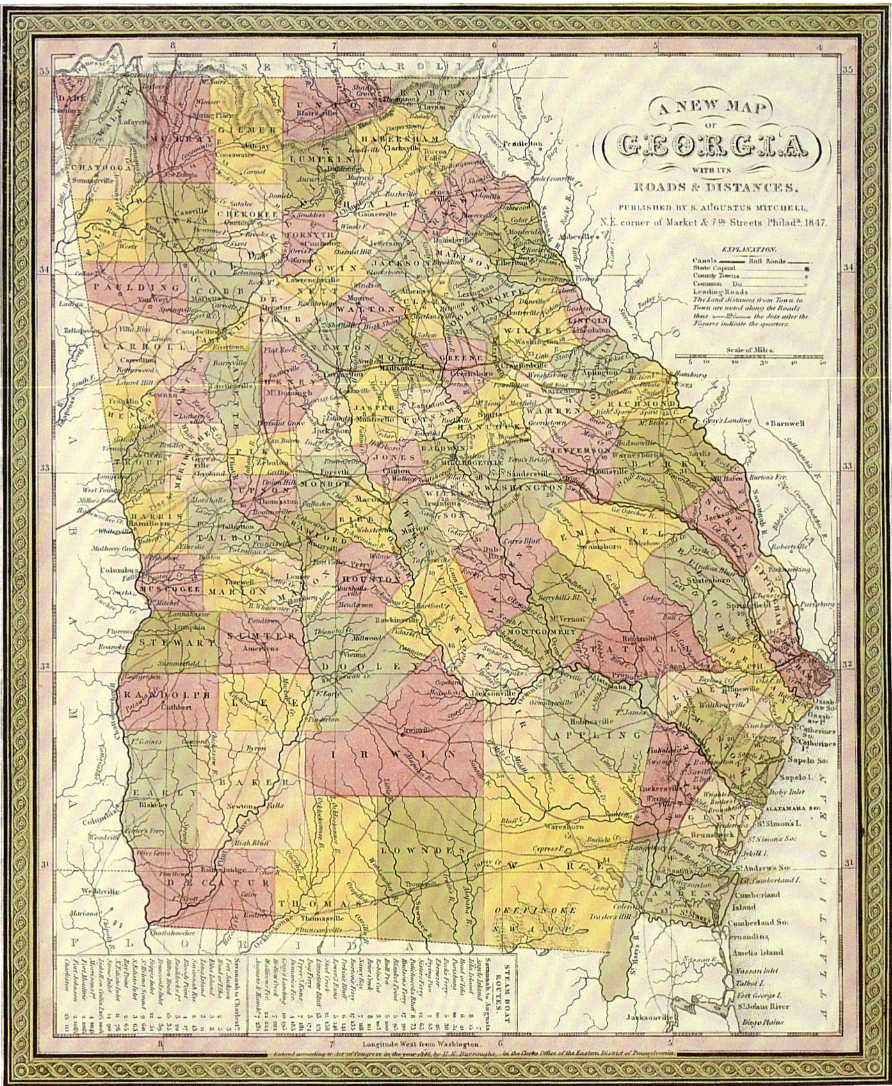

Figure 14. Engraved by H. N. Burroughs, *A New Map of Georgia with Its Roads and Distances*, 1847. Philadelphia: S. Augustus Mitchell. H. 14″, W. 11½″. Special Collections, The University of Georgia Libraries.

territory as still existing, although the Creek cessions were by then completed and counties and their fledgling courthouse sites were dotting the former Indian lands. Stone Mountain appears in DeKalb County, adjacent to the Cherokee frontier, and roads now stretch out to new settled lands in southwest Georgia. Both Macon and Columbus appear and the Milledgeville state capital is noted.

Also a Philadelphian, S. Augustus Mitchell was a prolific producer of maps in the decades before the Civil War. Having taken over Henry S. Tanner's operation, Mitchell employed as many as 250 people in his establishment. Designed for the popular market, his atlases were indeed popular—more than 400,000 copies were sold.[10] His "A New Map of Georgia with its Roads and Distances" was issued in 1847 (figure 14). Gone are all the Indian lands, replaced by numerous counties and towns. Although Atlanta had been settled by 1847, it is not on this map. However, the railroad terminus and extension that gave rise to its development does prominently appear. Mileage between towns is noted and there is an inset table giving steamboat routes.

Over a period of three centuries, Georgia had advanced from unknown land to coastal fringe settlements to thriving and populous antebellum state. From Indian trails and trading paths evolved roadways and railroads. From geographical features constructed only from legend came accurate surveys and cartographic delineations designed not for the curious European observer but for the colonizer and pioneer. Accompanying the desire for development was the necessity for factual information about this area nestled between Appalachian foothills and Atlantic shore, the land we cherish as Georgia.

Robert M. Willingham, Jr.
The University of Georgia Libraries

1. William P. Cumming, et al., *The Exploration of North America 1630–1776* (New York, 1974), 102.

2. William P. Cumming, *The Southeast in Early Maps* (Chapel Hill, 1962), 221.

3. Ibid., 199.

4. Ibid.

5. Louis DeVorsey, Jr., "Historical Maps Before the United States Supreme Court," *The Map Collector*, 19 (June 1982), 27.

6. Cumming, *Southeast*, 210.

7. E. Merton Coulter, *The Journal of Peter Gordon 1732–1735* (Athens, 1963), 6–7.

8. James Clements Wheat and Christian F. Brun, *Maps and Charts Published in America Before 1800, a Bibliography* (New Haven and London, 1969), 132.

9. Walter W. Ristow, "State Maps of the Southeast to 1833," *The Southeastern Geographer* 16 (1966), 39.

10. John Hudson Hollis IV, *Mapping Georgia's Growth 1750–1900* (Atlanta, 1982), 107.

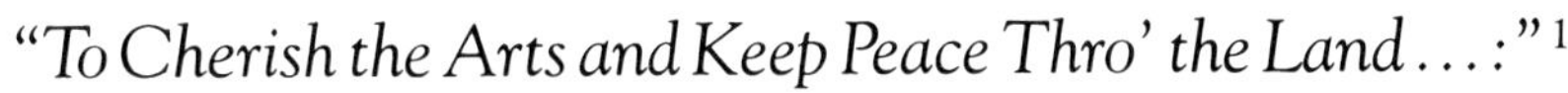

"To Cherish the Arts and Keep Peace Thro' the Land . . . :"[1]

Newspapers Report on Georgia Craftsmen of the Decorative Arts, 1760–1830

Craftsmen have played a major role in Georgia's history from its beginning. This essay emphasizes craftsmen who advertised in Georgia newspapers, but does not include those, for example, who worked anonymously on plantations. The study begins in 1763, when the earliest Georgia newspaper, the *Georgia Gazette*, was established in Savannah. The advertisements indicate that Savannah, Augusta, and other Georgia towns had developed an economy attractive potentially to local artisans. An increasingly affluent society of wealthy planters and professionals, however, developed a definite preference for northern silver, furniture, and architectural styles. By 1830, the trend toward New York fashion was firmly in place. Southern craftsmen continued advertising in newspapers throughout the state, but the merchandise they sold was made primarily in the North and retailed locally. There was little demand for indigenous products.

In attempting to trace the gradual evolution of Georgians from skilled artisans to businessmen, this essay examines the role of craftsmen and their products during Georgia's early colonization; notes the various physical and social developments that helped establish a more sophisticated economic structure; comments on the apprentices and journeymen who worked within that structure; and offers a brief analysis of supply and demand based on price and population. The essay also discusses the role of craftsmen in Georgia's expanding economy and presents various influences on that role.

Craftsmen on the Anne *and the Frontiers of Early Georgia*

Of the 114 passengers who arrived on the *Anne* 12 February 1733, 17 were craftsmen sent on charity by the Trustees of the colony. James Cornock, a plasterer, paid for his own trip (figure 1).[2]

The occupations of all the 2,831 settlers sent to Georgia between 1732–1741 are not known, but the Trustees primarily appealed to laborers, small farmers, and craftsmen, hoping that these diligent people would produce enough silk, wine, and other exportable products

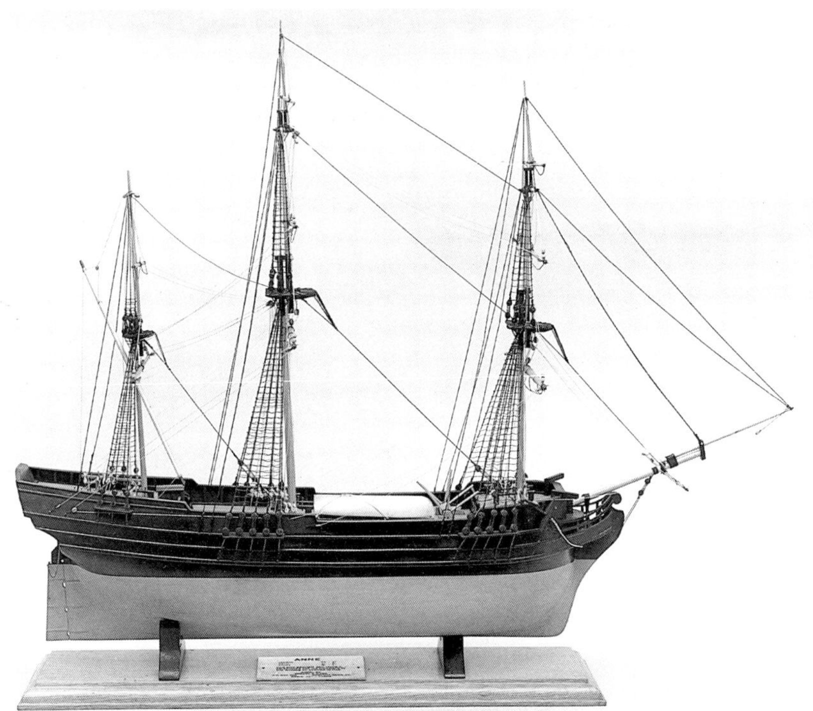

Figure 1. *Anne*, reproduction, 1969. Ships of the Sea Maritime Museum. The *Anne*, helmed by Captain John Thomas, left England on 17 November 1732 with 114 passengers led by General James Oglethorpe. On 13 January 1733, the *Anne* anchored off of Charles Town, South Carolina, and by 12 February, a site on Yamacraw Bluff on the Savannah River had been chosen for the youngest British colony, Georgia.

to make Georgia a successful commercial venture. Carpenters were numerous, as were weavers and silk throwsters, sent in anticipation of a thriving silk industry. Miscellaneous craftsmen represented in colonial Georgia before 1741 include basket makers, blacksmiths, bookbinders, cabinetmakers, calico printers, goldsmiths, gunsmiths, joiners, masons, potters, turners, upholsterers, and watchmakers.[3]

The environment of early Georgia did not encourage these occupations. It was hot, humid, diseased, and dangerous. Twenty-nine of the original colonists died during the first year.[4] Survival became a priority—there was little time for cultural luxuries in the frontier towns of Savannah or Frederica. However, by August 1733, Savannah had 21 houses built:

> and the other nineteen Lotts having no Houses built on them, Mr. Milledge and Mr. Goddard, the two chief Carpenters, offered in the Name of themselves and seventeen of their Helpers, to take the unbuilt Lotts, and give the built ones, to those who were less able to help themselves . . . [5]

(Thomas Milledge and James Goddard were both original colonists.) A 1736 description of Frederica, designed by Oglethorpe as a buffer against the Spanish in Florida, further illustrates the unsettled atmosphere of Georgia during its first few years:

> There is a Town laid out here, and thirty-seven Palmetto Houses built, in which all the People are sheltered till they can build better . . . but the labouring Men which were to have come to the Northward, being not arrived, Mr. Ogle-

> thorpe hired several of our Freeholders to build a Fort, which is now near finished.[6]

Clearly, then, early Georgia was a land in which basic survival skills such as cultivating crops and building houses were initially more essential than the refined abilities of the trained craftsman. As the colony developed, the need for specialized skills increased and the status of the craftsman changed significantly.

Fraternal Organizations in Georgia and Legalizations Benefitting Craftsmen

Freemasonry, the oldest fraternal organization in the world, is guided by "a system of morals (truths) taught by symbols and veiled by allegory," with the objective of "making good men better than they are."[7]

Freemason lodges in the colonies were officially chartered by the Grand Lodge of England, organized in 1717. A 1771 petition from Solomon's Lodge in Savannah to the Grand Master in England states that the Georgia lodge is "the eldest constituted in America except one in New England."[8] "The circumstances surrounding the establishment of the first lodge in Georgia are not known. Only traditions exist to shed any light upon the beginning of the Craft in Georgia."[9]

One tradition is based partially on the personal diary of Mordecai Sheftall, Senior Grand Warden of the Provincial Grand Lodge of Georgia in 1786 and longtime member of Solomon's Lodge No. 1. Sheftall writes that the first Masonic meeting in Georgia, in January 1734, was organized by General James Oglethorpe and conducted under a tree near what became the town of Sunbury. Although no record exists of his having been a mason in England, Oglethorpe is credited as the founder of the craft in Georgia and the first Worshipful Master of the "Lodge at Savannah in ye province of Georgia," chartered officially in 1735 (figure 2).

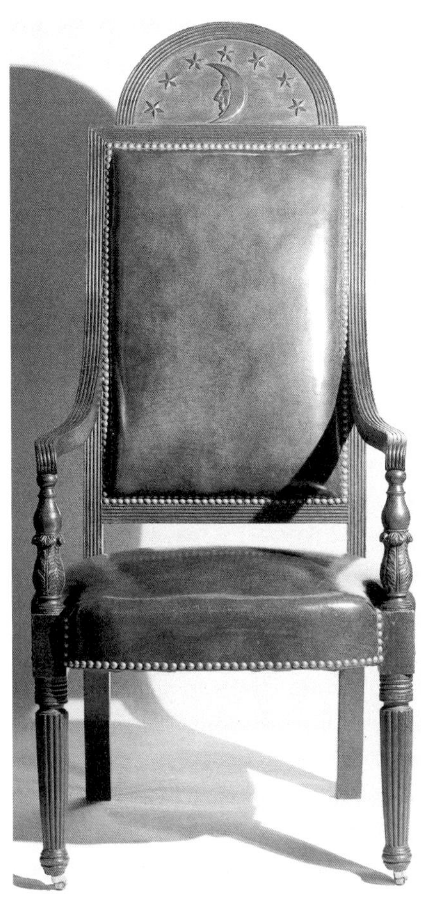

Figure 2. Master Chair, one of a set of nine, including the Senior and Junior Warden chairs, Solomon's Lodge No. 1, Savannah, Georgia, ca. 1810, attributed New York City. Mahogany, H. 57", W. 23⅞". Minutes from the 19 May 1808 meeting indicate the names of a committee appointed to procure "necessary furniture" for the lodge. Serving on this committee was John Scott, a cabinetmaker working in Savannah during 1804–1808. Scott was known to have imported from New York a great deal of the furniture which he sold in his shop. With its reeded frame and turned and reeded legs, this chair is of the New York school. These characteristics are displayed on upholstered furniture, sofas, and easy chairs frequently attributed to the workshop of Duncan Phyfe (1768–1854), who worked in New York City ca. 1800–1840. That the mechanics of the Masonic Lodge preferred New York furniture was indicative of the trend in nineteenth-century Savannah. Owned by Solomon's Lodge No. 1, Savannah.

The Union Society was organized in 1740 for the support of the Bethesda Orphanage, with many of the same members as Solomon's Lodge No. 1. Earliest published accounts of a fraternal meeting in Georgia appeared in the 22 November 1760, *South Carolina Gazette*. The October 28 meeting of the Union Society paid tribute to Royal Governor Henry Ellis:

> We . . . members of the Union Society . . . composed chiefly of mechanics, beg leave to pay our most dutiful acknowledgement . . . for that series of happinesses enjoyed by us . . . . The encouragement given to persons in our station by laws passed . . . to prevent the introduction of negro artificers; the relief afforded us, by the act for the more easily and speedy recovery of small debts; and the benefits resulting from the establishment of public credit; are instances of your excellency's attention to the general good . . . . Be pleased, Sir, to accept . . . a small remembrance of our lasting esteem.

The Society presented the Governor with a "piece of silver plate" inscribed "Georgia / Union Society / Present this token of Public Gratitude / to His Excellency Henry Ellis, Esq. / Their Governor, 28 Oct 1760." Governor Ellis recognized the growing need for protective rules. Creating regulations for Savannah's mechanics was an early progressive step.

In 1750, the charter of the colony was returned to the crown. Before that time, the Trustees dictated regulations that severely hampered the economy and made conditions deplorable for local craftsmen. Editorials in nearby Charleston reflect the negative reactions of that city's mechanics to the commercial policies of Georgia under Trusteeship. James Habersham and Charles Harris's 1759 construction of the first wharf capable of receiving ocean-going vessels opened the door for Savannah's emergence as a thriving port. Along with this development came competition from northern products, a factor that affected the future prosperity of local craftsmen for the next 100 years.

A Digest of the Laws of the State of Georgia, From Its First Establishment as a British Province Down to the Year 1798 Inclusive, published in Philadelphia in 1800, records an act to incorporate the Savannah Association of Mechanics, passed 16 December 1793:[10]

> An Act to incorporate the Savannah association of mechanics. Whereas William Lewden, president; David Moses Vollaton, vice-president; John Peter Lang, secretary; Balthaser Shaffer, Thomas Palmer, John Herb, George Faries, Simon Connor, John Glass, William Henry Spencer, Joseph Roberts, Paul H. Wilkins, John Eppinger, Ezra Plummer, Peter Miller, James Simpson, John Armour, David Gugel, Daniel Gugel, John Trever, James Shaw, Nathaniel Lewis, Michael Asper, Joseph Dunlap, Gabriel Leaver, Elisha Elon, John Cole, John Miller, James Clarke, and Benjamin Bennet, have by their petition represented, that they are mechanics of different trades, residing in the city of Savannah; that they are desirous of placing their various crafts on a more social and respectable footing than heretofore, and of establishing by their united exertions and contributions, a lasting fund for the relief and support of such of their unfortunate brethren, or their families, as are or may become objects of charity; and for those purposes have voluntarily united and formed themselves into a society under the style and name of *The Savannah association of mechanics*. And in order to insure and establish their said institution . . . have prayed the legislature to grant them an act of incorporation.[11]

Also in 1793, the Mechanical Society of Augusta celebrated its third anniversary. "Wine toasts were drank: to Agriculture and the Arts / . . . . May the Indian tribes be employed, (not for) war, but the reverse. / . . . May the principle of barter which . . . hereto prevailed

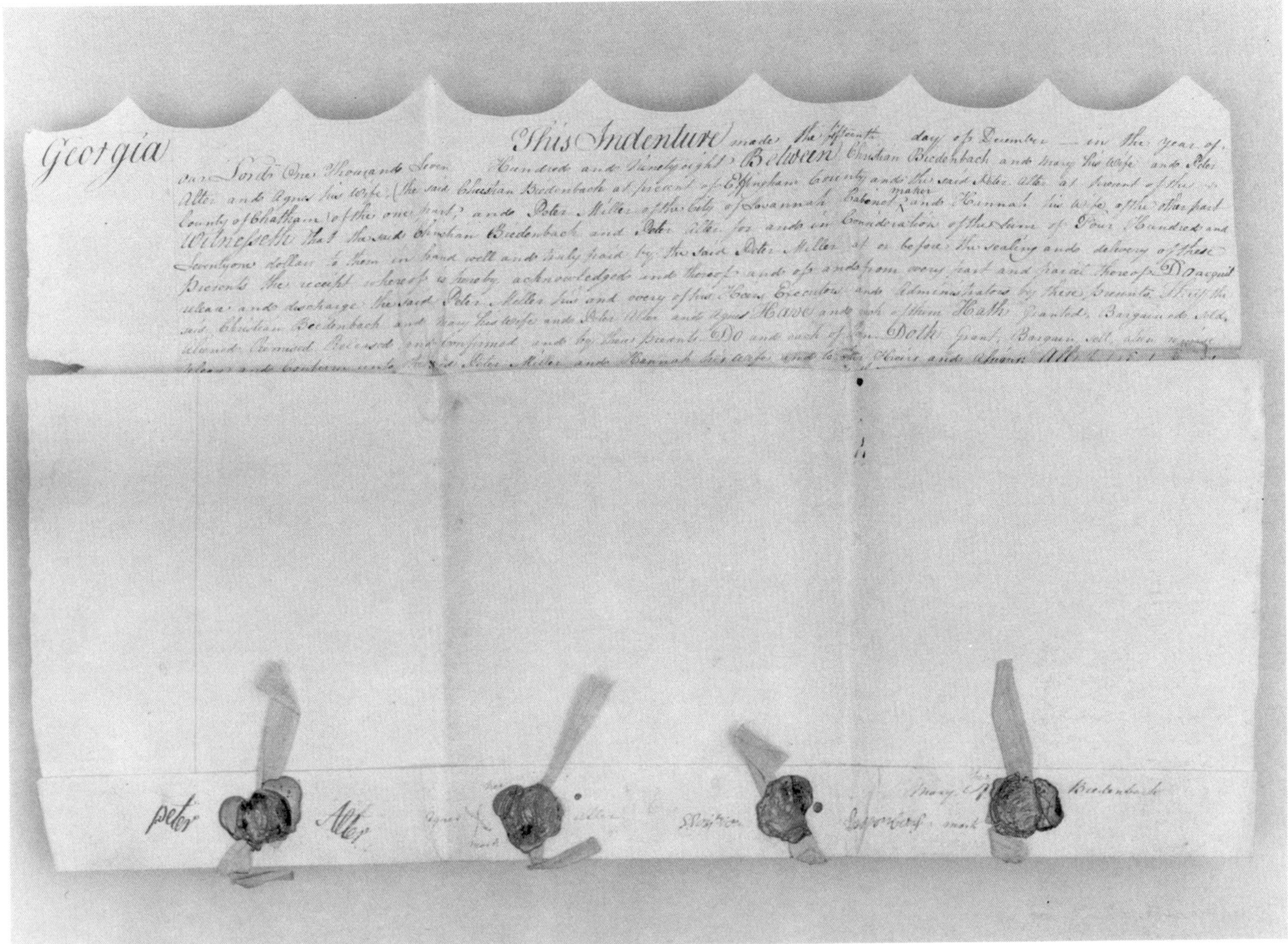

Georgia This Indenture made the fifteenth day of December in the year of our Lord One Thousand Seven Hundred and Ninety eight Between Christian Biedenbach and Mary his Wife and Peter Alter and Agnes his Wife (the said Christian Biedenbach at present of Effingham County and the said Peter Alter at present of the County of Chatham) of the one part, and Peter Miller of the City of Savannah Cabinet maker and Hannah his Wife of the other part Witnesseth that the said Christian Biedenbach and Peter Alter for and in Consideration of the Sum of Four Hundred and Seventy one dollars to them in hand well and truly paid by the said Peter Miller at or before the sealing and delivery of these Presents the receipt whereof is hereby acknowledged and thereof and of and from every part and parcel thereof Do acquit release and discharge the said Peter Miller his and every of his Heirs Executors and Administrators by these Presents ... the said Christian Biedenbach and Mary his Wife and Peter Alter and Agnes Have and each of them Hath Granted, Bargained, Sold, aliened, Remised, Released and Confirmed and by these presents Do and each of them Doth grant, Bargain, sell, alien, remise, release and Confirm unto the said Peter Miller and Hannah his wife and to their Heirs and Assigns All [illegible]

Figure 3. Indenture, Chatham County, Georgia, December 15, 1798. This is a rare surviving example of an indenture, an agreement or contract written in duplicate with the other copy having corresponding notches. The copy given to Benjamin Ansley would have fit the spaces of the notched copy remaining with Peter Miller and his son Jacob, Ansley's new apprentice.

This particular indenture transferred the deed of ownership to town lot number seven in the second Reynolds Ward in the city of Savannah from Peter Alter and Christian Biedenbach to Mr. Peter Miller, cabinetmaker. The original intact seals, with signatures of Alter and his wife Agnes (her mark "X"), Biedenbach and his wife Mary, are rare. It is believed that this was Miller's home, and that his shop was located on what was then South Broad Street, now Oglethorpe. Private Collection.

in most legislative bodies (be) readily abolished, particularly in this state."[12] As these accounts illustrate, by the late 1790s, Georgia craftsmen realized that some type of organization was essential if they were to establish a successful crafts market. Delaying the development of these organizations were Georgia's harsh beginnings as a new colony—beset by hostile intruders and hampered by the Trustee's regulations—and the Revolutionary War, which depleted and disheartened the inhabitants.

Apprentice/Journeyman/Master

The traditional training procedure for apprentices/journeymen, adopted from the English guild system, was practiced in Georgia. The apprentice spent up to seven years with a master learning the "mysteries" of his craft. The responsibilities of both parties were specified in a legal contract, an indenture (figure 3). Following the apprenticeship, the apprentice became an itinerant journeyman, moving from job to job. If successful, the artisan accumulated enough money and experience to become a master and open his own shop, often with a partner. The 24 July 1805 indenture assigning Jacob Miller, son of

Savannah cabinetmaker Peter Miller, as an apprentice to Benjamin Ansley indicates the commitment required of the youngster:

> Georgia
> Chatham County
>
> THIS INDENTURE witnesseth that Jacob Miller, aged about fourteen years with the consent of his father Peter Miller hath put himself, and by these presents, doth voluntarily of his own free will and accord, put himself apprenticed unto Benjamin Ansley of the City of Savannah, Cabinetmaker, to learn his art, trade, and mystery, and after the manner of a Cabinetmaker to serve the said Benjamin Ansley from the date hereof, for and during, and until the full end and term of six years next enduring. During all which term the said apprentice his said Master faithfully shall serve, his secrets keep, his lawful commands every where readily obey; shall do no damage to his Master nor see it done by others, without giving notice thereof to his Master. He shall not waste his Master's goods, nor lend them unlawfully to any; he shall not commit fornication, nor contract matrimony, within said term; at cards, dice, or any other unlawful game, he shall not play, whereby his Master may have damage; . . . he shall not absent himself day or night from his said Master's service with his leave, nor haunt alehouses, taverns, or playhouses, but in all things behave as a faithful Apprentice ought to do, during said term. And the said Master shall use the utmost of his endeavors to teach, or cause to be taught or instructed, the said Apprentice, in the trade or mystery of a Cabinetmaker and procure and provide for him sufficient meat, drink, lodging and washing, fitting for an apprentice during said term of six years. His father Peter Miller to finance said apprentice his Clothing during his apprenticeship . . . [illegible] . . . . And for the due performance of all and singular covenants and agreements aforesaid parties bind themselves, each unto the other, firmly, by these presents.[13]

By the 1790s, it was clear that the struggling journeymen needed protection from inconsistent wage practices. This issue of wage standardization and the question of cash or credit for goods and services caused conflict between masters and journeymen in major American cities in the late eighteenth century. In 1792, cabinetmakers in Hartford, Connecticut, formed a society "for the purposes of regulating the prices of our work; on the principles of dealing in CASH."[14]

Published in 1788, *The Cabinetmakers' London Book of Prices & Designs* established not only a "language of workmanship"[15] but also a basis for employer-employee contracts. A two-year dispute between masters and journeymen resulted in the 1795 publication of the first American volume of cabinetmaking prices, *The Philadelphia Cabinet and Chair-Makers' Book of Prices*. Regional price scales in America tended to be higher than those in London: 50 percent higher in Philadelphia, 75 percent higher in Charleston.[16] This compromise between masters and journeymen in Philadelphia set wage precedents for the whole country as the word spread through the network of mechanical societies. The Baltimore Society, for example, would accept members with a "certificate from any one of our correspondent societies."[17] From 1796 to 1810, journeymen in New York and Philadelphia made $1.00 per 11-hour day. These wages slowly increased to include a cost of living adjustment, so that by 1828 "not less than $1.33⅓ per day was the accepted rate."[18]

The standard pay scale in Georgia is not definitely revealed in newspaper advertisements. A 1788 letter written from a craftsman in Georgia to a friend in Boston states, "They have nominally more than double wages here."[19] In 1795 Savannah silversmith Edward Griffith advertised for workmen in a Charleston newspaper:

> WANTED
>
> One or Two journeymen silversmiths, to go to Savannah to work for one or more months . . . . if steady, may have Twenty Dollars, board and lodging, per month each.
>
> N.B. One who is used to gold and hair work, shall have Twenty-Four Dollars. Apply to the Savannah Packets for passage.[20]

Attaining the status of a master did not assure a craftsman financial security. Only in very rare instances in Georgia could a master craftsman earn an adequate income solely by his practiced skills. Adrian Loyer, a clock and watchmaker and silversmith in Savannah in the 1770s, dabbled in real estate, as did George W. F. de la Huff, a blacksmith in Milledgeville in 1813. Diversified jobs, a prerequisite during the colonial days, became more and more varied by the nineteenth century. J. Thurston, "Grand and Square Piano Forte Maker from London," intended to reside in Augusta "till next Christmas" when he planned "to open a Female Seminary at Edgefield Court-House."[21] Francis Girodon, an "Armorer, Founder, and Mechanist" in Savannah, "repairs umbrellas in the neatest way."[22] Perhaps most enterprising of all was Isaac Anthony, an Augusta silversmith, who invented "super glue":

> SAVE THE PIECES.
>
> The subscriber having found the Patent Cement to answer every purpose, and from the great encouragement he has received in the county of Richmond, has purchased the Patent Right for the State of Georgia.
>
> It may be had . . . in Augusta at my shop, with directions to each stick. This valuable article will cement together Glass, China, and Earthen Ware, as firm as when new, and have a clear sound. Made and sold opposite the New Liberty Pole, at one Dollar per Stick, by / ISAAC ANTHONY[23]

Once the Georgia crafts market was allowed to develop, its procedures differed little from those established elsewhere in America. Georgia's craftsmen were undoubtedly influenced by activities of their counterparts in northern states, not only concerning wages, but also in pricing their products.

Prices

In his book *American Furniture: The Federal Period, 1790–1825,* Charles Montgomery determined a mathematical relationship between labor costs and the retail price of the product.[24] The 1795 Philadelphia price book cited piecework costs for cabinetwork based on how many days were necessary for making a particular item. With a labor cost of $8.00, a clockcase took eight days to make; a pembroke table made in three and one half days had a labor cost of $3.50. The master's retail cost for these goods was $30.00 and $14.00 respectively, or, as Montgomery calculated, an average of three and one half times the labor cost. ". . . If one knows the retail price of a piece of furniture just before or after 1800, he can approximate the time required for making it by converting the retail price into dollars and dividing by 3½."[25]

Unfortunately, Georgia craftsmen seldom advertised the prices of their wares. An early exception appeared in 1763, 25 years before the publication of a pricing book: "Neat Windsor chairs at 10 shillings, or 12 shillings painted, a chair by James Muter."[26] These items were to be sold for cash. The 29 November 1787 issue of Savannah's *Gazette of the State of Georgia* lists William Welscher's "reduced prices" to clean and repair watches:

> A mainspring, 9s. 4d.
> Cleaning and mending the chain, 4s. 8d.
> Best watch crystals, 1s. 4d.
> Hour and minute hand, 2s. 4d.
> And every other article at least 100 percent cheaper than the usual prices.

New York artist Cornelius Schroeder advertised in the *Columbian Museum and Savannah Advertiser* a $15.00 charge for a miniature and warranted "accurate likeness."[27]

The 1820 Census of Manufacturers recorded Georgia craftsmen's inventories, number of employees, payroll expenses, and annual profit. The variations from county to county are evident, with larger communities creating increased demands and larger profits. John McLisky, a Wilkes County cabinetmaker, employed three workers, with $500 capital and $800 annual wages, and he manufactured mahogany "Sideboards, Secretary + Bookcases, Tables, etc. to an annual value of $4,000." McLisky's proximity to the thriving town of Washington made his "establishment a prosperous one, and demands for sale of its manufactures considerable."[28]

On the other hand, Nicholas Nelson, a self-employed cabinetmaker in the southwest frontier county of Early, made "Sideboards, Bureos, Tables, etc." from cheaper woods of walnut, poplar, and pine, whose "Conditions [are] Sorry and has been and the Sale of Manufactures Dull!"[29] The economic center of the Georgia piedmont, Augusta, had a population of 8,608 in 1820,[30] and provided a substantial and sophisticated clientele for Jesse Dimerol, who used

> only mahogany wood to the amount of $1000 annually, employing 4 men and 3 boys, in "Chair Makers work by hand," with capital of $5,000, payroll of $5,000, and other expenses of $300 annually, manufacturing "Chairs and Bedsteads" to the total of $16,000 per year, the "Condition good and in (demand).[31]

In a sense, demographics helped determine the fate of Georgia's craftsmen. The prosperous citizens of the more populated towns created a demand for the goods of the local artisan. In some cases, the craftsman could enjoy an almost flourishing business; however, relatively few indigenous objects from these shops survive.

Natural Disasters and Northern Mechanics

The major obstacle to the understanding of Georgia decorative arts and craftsmen is that few surviving objects can be labeled "Georgian," and even fewer can be firmly dated to the colonial period. The years of the Trusteeship, 1733–1752, were marked by a nonexpanding population, resulting from unpopular laws and constant threats of violence from the French, Spanish, and Indians. This stagnant situation improved somewhat under the royal governors, but the Revolutionary War cut short this progress. Craftsmen did advertise in newspapers immediately after the Revolutionary War, indicating that a potential clientele survived the widespread destruction inflicted upon struggling coastal towns such as Sunbury and Ebenezer. After the 1780s, the piedmont became the focal point of Georgia's post-Revolutionary growth. Savannah would never boast a competitive population to other contemporary port towns. The national reputation of Georgia's coast remained poor for years after the war, as evidenced in this letter written for a Boston paper and reprinted in Richmond in 1788:

> BOSTON, November 19
> Extract of a letter from a gentleman in Georgia, to his friend in this town, September 1788.
> If the fatality of this climate was more generally known, I think it would deter the mechanics of the northern states from venturing hither—more especially if they knew how poorly they were paid for their labor. It is true they have nominally more than double wages here, but they are paid in such truck and trumpery, which, if it could be realized, would not produce one half the real value they receive at home; and three

fourths who spent their summers here, leave their bones, and the fruits of their labour to their employers, who plant them as cheaply as you do potatoes . . . though I believe not so many in hole, as they have got ground enough for that purpose; and it is my opinion, that the grave digger in Savannah, is the most independent planter in the state of Georgia.[32]

In short, Georgia's political and physical climate did not attract large numbers of people, and even fewer skilled craftsmen. Another explanation for the lack of pre–1820 decorative arts could be that natural disasters of floods and fires plagued both Augusta and Savannah, where such household furnishings might have been produced. In 1796, both cities experienced major catastrophes: a flood in Augusta ("On Saturday morning . . . the river rose to an alarming height. . . . in a few hours the [site] of the town was generally under water."[33]) and a fire in Savannah.

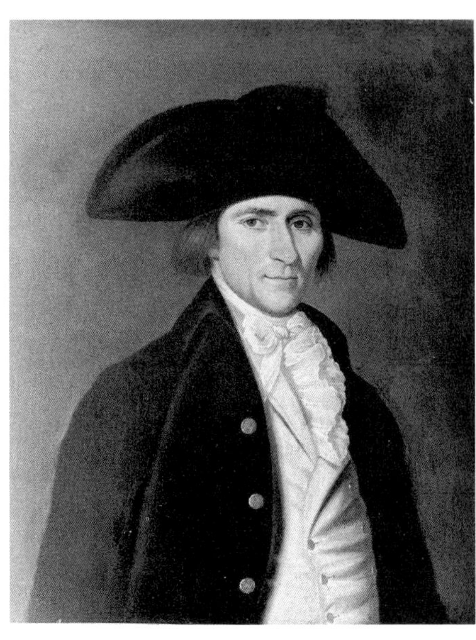

Figure 4. *Robert Bolton*, attributed to Walter Robertson, 1796, oil on canvas, H. 19⅞", W. 23¼". Bolton and his brother John were in the forefront of Savannah's cotton trade in its early years. Bolton's fireproof buildings exemplified the company's leadership position on Factors' Walk. Their venture cargo business was handled by Isaac Hicks, Bolton's agent in New York City. Hicks would consign furniture to the Boltons and also arrange cargoes for Bolton's cotton ships returning from England. Imports from as far away as Rotterdam came through the Boltons' operation (*Georgia Republican and State Intelligencer*, 14 April 1804). Owens-Thomas House, Telfair Academy of Arts and Sciences.

During the conflagration on Saturday night last, in four hours, 229 houses, besides outhouses, &c. were burnt, amounting to One Million of Dollars, exclusive of loose property—375 chimneys are standing bare, and form a dismal appearance—171 houses only of the compact part of the city are standing—upwards of 400 families are destitute of houses. Charities are solicited.[34]

Savannah took many years to recover from the 1796 fire. Most of the destroyed structures were middle-class frame houses, as described by a visitor two years after the disaster: "The houses were frightened about a year ago at a big fire . . . they left the chimnies standing . . . the houses are much the same as they are in Galway, but that the brick part of them is made of wood, and that they are thatched with shingles."[35]

One positive development from the Savannah fire was a new awareness for fire safety. Undoubtedly exploiting this concern was New York City cabinetmaker Joseph Meeks, who in 1798 had "lately arrived," and had for sale "a handsome assortment of elegant mahogany furniture . . . likewise a number of fire buckets."[36] By 1800, fire ordinances were being enforced by firemasters who inspected every three months to insure that there were buckets "equal to the number of fireplaces in the house."[37] "Fire Proof stores to let" were advertised by merchants Robert and John Bolton (figure 4).[38] In 1804, watchmaker Joseph Rice's shop was located in "Bolton's Brick Buildings, nearly opposite the Exchange on the Bay."[39]

Unfortunately, a second major fire devastated Savannah during the winter of 1820. "Savannah has been visited by an awful calamity . . . the whole business part of the town is destroyed."[40] The fire prompted William Jay, architect of many of the Regency-style buildings in Savannah, to recommend "a plan to erect fire-proof stores . . . to use iron instead of timber. . . ."[41] The Hermitage foundry of Henry McAlpin manufactured "castings of all descriptions"[42] for Jay's structures.

Undoubtedly, the most far-reaching consequence of the publicity generated by both the 1796 and 1820 fires reported in northern newspapers was the mass infiltration of northern craftsmen to rebuild the town. They brought with them skills and business acumen and that provided competition for Georgia artisans.

> The passengers in the Good Hope state that a number of the mechanics who went from the northern states to get employment at Savannah, in the building line, after the fire, remain at that place without employment, and in a most destitute situation . . . All kinds of building materials were plenty, and almost without price, owing to the glut from the northward.[43]

These occurrences took place within a 25-year period. The fires took their toll on the future of local artisans by inconveniencing and delaying the productivity of already established businesses and by destroying the locally made wares purchased by a relatively new clientele of middle-class Savannahians. The influx of northern craftsmen came during a time when the Georgia market was already involved with heavy New York trade. By 1830, these factors had joined to dictate the wealthy Georgians' preference for New York styles.

Imports

Imported goods, both foreign and domestic, have bolstered Georgia's craft market since the construction of Savannah's first wharf in 1759. During 1765 and 1767, almost 200 ships entered the port of Savannah from England and the British colonies in Africa and the West Indies, while 114 originated from ports along the American coast, primarily Boston and Salem, Massachusetts.[44] The few surviving port records and advertisements from the colonial period suggest some of the products related to the decorative arts that were imported from England:

> Just imported from Bristol, in the Brig Nelly, Douglas Campbell master, and to be sold by him at Pruniere's Wharff [sic], the following goods . . . looking glasses in walnut frames.[45]

> Adrian Loyer has lately imported from London a complete and fresh assortment of materials suitable for mechanical business, in particular for clock and watch work of all kinds . . . .[46]

> Just imported in the Brigantine Allenton . . . from Liverpool, and to be sold by William Moses, at his store on the Bay . . . mahogany dining and breakfast tables, bureaus, dressing glasses and telescopes, mahogany bedsteads with lawn muskitoe nets . . . . [47]

Before the 1770s, ships entering Georgia ports also originated from Rhode Island and South Carolina, as well as Massachusetts. As early as 1744, consignments of furniture were being shipped from Boston to points along the southern coast.[48]

> The lading for the outward voyages was often the result of previous trading with neighboring colonies and represented various consignments. Piled up in the warehouse, these cargoes awaited the captain's sailing orders . . . The captain was responsible for selling the cargo at vendue and also for investing the proceeds in molasses, sugar, logwood, mahogany, or slaves.[49]

A regular route for packets was established along the coast. Merchants, agents, captains, cabinetmakers, and other craftsmen took advantage of extra space on the ships to gamble on venture cargo shipments. Most major household furniture items entered the Savannah markets from these northern vessels.

By 1789, Congress had passed laws "for the encouragement and protection of manufacturers."[50] A 1788 editorial, "Friends of American Manufacturers," expresses the concern of Philadelphia craftsmen about foreign imports:

> A scheme which thus unites the interest of the . . . merchant, the manufacturer, and the mariner must tend to public good. Let us therefore carefully examine into everything that relates to it, and lay down one rule, never to be deviated from, that whenever we can purchase a home-made article as low as it can be imported, we will decidedly prefer it.[51]

Required were manifests describing all contents of the ships. Duties were imposed on 65 imported items, such as a 7½ percent ad valorem tax on cabinetwares and a 10 percent ad valorem tax on looking glasses. Imports shipped on vessels bought and owned in the United States got a 10 percent discount on these taxes.

During the Federal period, 1790–1820, imports from Philadelphia and New York dominated in both Savannah and Augusta, although products from Providence and Baltimore were also sold.[52] Descriptive lists of available imports included inventories of Philadelphia beef in kegs, New England rum, cast Dutch ovens, Windsor chairs, and "a few boxes coarse Irish Linens assorted."[53] On Waynes Wharf in Savannah, Wilson and Knox had for sale from New York "a large assortment of mahogany furniture, on consignment at cost and charges, also . . . a few sets elegant china."[54] Four hundred Windsor chairs arrived on the schooner *Rolla* from New York in 1808.[55] "Three elegant silver Tea Sets . . . just received from New York," were recorded by the Augusta firm of Huntington & Burrill.[56]

By the 1820s, the import business had boomed. Complex partnerships developed between the agent and the craftsman, who became more businessman than artisan. The activities of Faries and Miller, a firm active during 1817–1819, depict aspects of the New York/Georgia furniture trade and of the gradual transformation of local craftsmen. Both George Faries and Jacob Miller had served apprenticeships under local cabinetmakers and likely had cultivated the skills of the craft—Faries under William Riggs, ca. 1808, Miller under Benjamin Ansley, 1805 (see indenture noted earlier). Both had been in brief partnerships with other men: Adams (John) and Faries advertised on 8 February 1817, on Broughton Street, "opposite Squire Sheftall's, late arrivals from Philadelphia," including "plain and pillar and claw Pembroke tables, lyre card tables, and Grecian couches."[57] The partnership between Jacob Miller and Richard Gorham apparently ended around 22 July 1817, as Miller "continued to carry on the cabinet business . . . . "[58] By August of that year, Faries and Miller had "connected themselves in the cabinet making business . . . they will keep on constant hand an assortment of the most fashionable furniture, from the first manufactories in New York and Philadelphia."[59] By 1818, the firm also had planned a warehouse on the "upper end of Broad Street in Augusta."[60]

One of their suppliers was John Hewitt, a New York cabinetmaker who in 1800 had moved his business to Savannah on Bryan Street, "between the market square and theatre, on Fell's lot."[61] By 1802, however, Hewitt was back in New York. He had established a partnership with Benjamin Ansley offering "elegant warranted furniture."[62] Hewitt had worked with Miller before: "12 cases of furniture, 3 bundles of bedsteads, and 1 chair" had been sent in 1815 to him and two more shipments had gone to Miller & Gorham in March and April 1817.[63] Later that year, Hewitt's agent in Savannah, William Scott, made a contract with Faries & Miller to "accept the bulk of Hewitt's output, paying by notes due in Four months."[64] Four thousand dollars worth of furniture was shipped to Savannah, but by 1818, it had not been paid for.

Dated January 1818, correspondence between Hewitt and his agent William Scott discusses the condition of the market in Savannah: "There is at present no great deal of furniture in Savannah . . . what there is is poor trash." Disappointed by things in Savannah, Hewitt suggested that Scott ship his wares up the Savannah River to Augusta. Scott discovered, however, that doing so was expensive, "from 22 to 24 cents per foot."[65] These circumstances might partially explain Faries & Miller's deliquency in fulfilling their contract with Hewitt. Scott discusses the firm in an 1818 letter to Hewitt:

> They get their furniture from one Clarkson in N Jersey—They talk about establishing a shop in N York next Summer and one of them to remain there, as they think they can then carry on Business to better advantage by supplying their shop here themselves—They have got but very little furniture at hand at present they are complaining of Clarkson's not attending to their orders. I understand the true reason of which this is: that Clarkson wants the money as soon as the furniture arrives here, and that they are not willing to do. They are now indebted to him considerable, and I dont expect he will send them any more until they pay up their arrears.[66]

Their poor credit with northern suppliers undoubtedly prompted this 1819 announcement:

> that they have turned their attention principally to manufacturing, for which purpose they have procured some of the first rate workmen and materials, and will be able to execute orders for any description of Furniture in a style equal to any *Northern City*, and at as low a rate. They hope, by punctual attendance to business, to give satisfaction to those who feel disposed to encourage Savannah manufactories[67] (figure 5).

In 1829, John Hewitt was still trying to collect the 12-year-old debt from "these professing gentlemen . . . whose offers do not comport with religion."[68]

Competition and means of comparison for indigenous goods "executed equal to any in the north or elsewhere . . . "[69] (figure 6a, 6b) were provided not just by the Northern craftsmen and their imports. Charleston's luxurious lifestyle in the mid-eighteenth century contrasted drastically with the lingering frontier-like atmosphere of Augusta and Savannah. South Carolina's economic center was described in 1762 by the *London Magazine*: "Here the rich people have handsome equipages; the merchants are opulent and well bred; the people are thriving and extensive, in dress and life; so that everything conspires to make this town the politest, . . . one of the richest in America."[70]

Many itinerant artists passing through Savannah and Augusta advertised that they came from Charleston. Jeremiah Theus, 1744, Henry Benbridge, 1770s, and Joseph-Pierre Picot de Limoelan de Clorivière, 1803–1806 (figure 7) are examples of portrait painters and miniaturists who worked in Georgia but chose to live in Charleston. Skilled mechanics were also coaxed to Savannah from Charleston. In 1767, silversmith/clockmaker Adrian Loyer boasted that "he has brought up with him from Charleston some compleat [sic] workmen lately from London."[71] Edward Griffith, "watchmaker on the Bay," not only promised prices "as low as can be purchased in Charleston,"[72] but cast aspersions on local craftsmen who advertised falsely about certain portions of their inventories:

> N. B. Mourning rings and hair work excepted, as he does not wish to deceive the public by advertising a business that no goldsmith in Savannah knows anything of; but will always be happy in having it in his power to oblige his customers by procuring such work from Charleston without the least compensation for his trouble.[73]

Merchants and craftsmen in Augusta traded directly with those in Charleston, continuing a tradition of trade that began with the English and Indian fur trade in the late seventeenth century. Oglethorpe had hoped that Augusta as a frontier outpost would challenge Charleston's dominance of this Indian trade, but he was disappointed. Charleston's craftsmen tended to come directly from En-

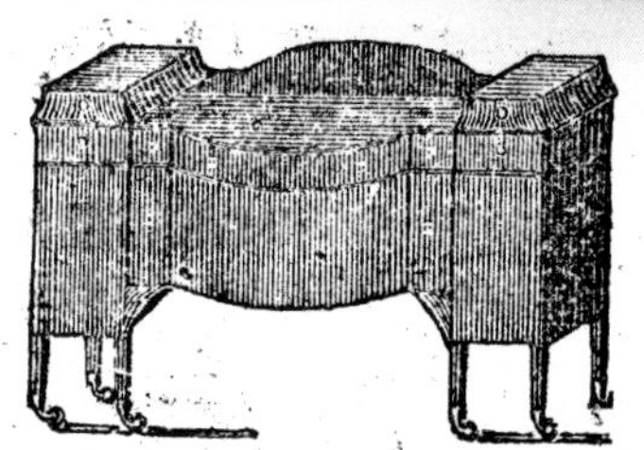

Cabinet Manufactory.

(*Broughton street*)

The subscribers return their thanks to their friends and fellow citizens, for the liberal encouragement afforded them in their business, and respectfully inform them, that they have turned their attention principally to manufacturing, for which purpose they have procured some of the first rate workmen and materials, and will be able to execute orders for any description of Furniture in a style equal to any *Northern City*, and at as low a rate. They hope, by punctual attendance to business, to give satisfaction to those who may feel disposed to encourage Savannah manufactories.

They have now on hand a large stock of Furniture, comprising every article in there line, among which are some of the latest patterns which they will dispose of below the northern prices. Workmanship warranted.

ALSO

A few first quality Hair Matrasses

FARIES & MILLER.

P. S. Merchants and others having orders from the country will find it much to their advantage to give them a call.

dec 7 o 244

Figure 5. Advertisement for the partnership of George Faries and Jacob Miller, active in Savannah 1817–1819; *The Savannah Republican*, 7 December 1819. Special Collections, The University of Georgia Libraries.

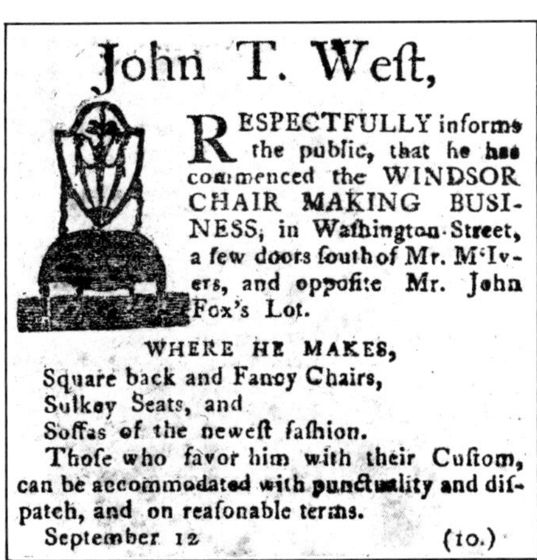

John T. Weſt,

RESPECTFULLY informs the public, that he has commenced the WINDSOR CHAIR MAKING BUSINESS, in Waſhington-Street, a few doors ſouth of Mr. M'Ivers, and oppoſite Mr. John Fox's Lot.

WHERE HE MAKES,

Square back and Fancy Chairs,
Sulkey Seats, and
Soffas of the neweſt faſhion.

Thoſe who favor him with their Cuſtom, can be accommodated with punctuality and diſpatch, and on reaſonable terms.

September 12 (10.)

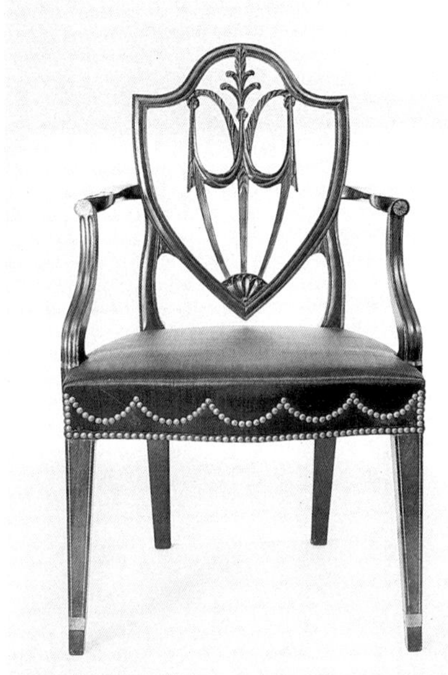

Figure 6a. Advertisement of John T. West, *Augusta Herald*, 12 September 1805; Special Collections, The University of Georgia Libraries.
Figure 6b. Armchair, one of a pair, New York City, 1795–1805, mahogany, ash, cherry, H. 38⅜", W. 21⅛", D. 18". The Henry Francis du Pont Winterthur Museum.
Unmistakable similarities are seen between this New York shield back chair in the Winterthur collection and the chair advertised by John West on Washington Street in Augusta. West professed also to make "square back chairs and soffas of the newest fashion," implying that he also offered upholstering in his shop. Was this chair a copy made by West "equal to any in the north," or did he import it from New York and retail it?

gland. The similarity between Charleston imports and earlier imports from England, such as looking glasses or clock and watchmaking materials, is apparent in this 1808 advertisement by Peter Primrose, an Augusta clock and watchmaker.

> *Peter Primrose*
> Has just received from Charleston
> in addition to his former stock a large assortment of
> Pictures, Glasses, &c. AMONG WHICH ARE,
> Mathematical Instruments, Surveyor's Compasses
> Microscopes and Telescopes,
> Thermometers, Perspective Glasses.
> And a large assortment of JEWELRY.[74]

Imported goods like imported mechanics had both negative and positive effects on the Georgia economy and its emerging craftsmen. The state's rapid growth after the revolution boosted the local market, but also bolstered the already established northern trade. By the 1860s, northern manufactured goods were easily obtained and less expensive. Artisans traded in the skills of their craft in exchange for the business acumen needed by agents and retailers.

Prosperity and Planters in the Piedmont

Georgia piedmont lands ceded by the Creek Indians were opened for settlement in 1773. News of this opening was circulated northward by handbills issued by Royal Governor James Wright, who realized the potential of the upcountry and assured future settlers "that to the end the said settlers may be safe and secure . . . to prevent any interruption to them by disorderly hunters, vagrants and wanderers, or by straggling Indians, a fort will be built . . . . "[75] The Philadelphia Wagon Road stretched westerly from Philadelphia, through the backcountries of Maryland, Virginia, and the Carolinas, and ended near the Broad River Valley close to Augusta. From Virginia and the Yadkin Valley, North Carolina, Scotch-Irish descendants made their way to the new farm lands of Georgia. A Petersburg, Virginia, newspaper reported in 1796 that "upwards of 500 people have lately emigrated from Kentucky to the frontiers of Georgia."[76] Results of the 1800 state census were published in the 4 August 1801 issue of the *Augusta Chronicle* "which the politeness of a friend has enabled us to furnish . . . Indians excepted . . . a grand total of 163,879."

Augusta was the piedmont's center of commerce and banking during early years of the prosperous cotton trade. Georgia's political focus shifted to the upcountry, and the state capital relocated from Augusta (1786–1795) to Louisville, a town created in 1795 specifically for the role. In 1807, it moved from there to Milledgeville where it remained until 1868, when Atlanta became the capital. The rapid growth of Milledgeville, located at the navigational head of the Oconee River, indicated the activity in the Georgia piedmont. Spurred by Eli Whitney's cotton gin, the cotton economy thrived and brought great

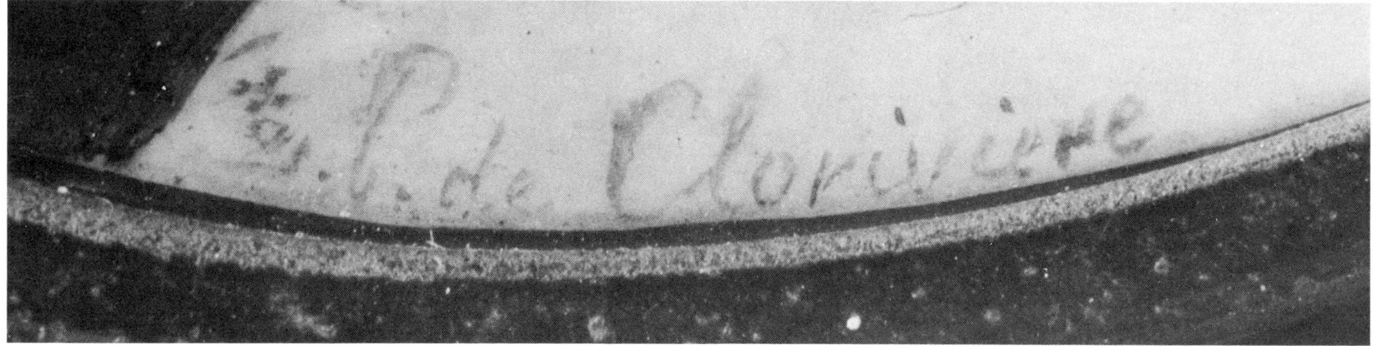

Figure 7. Signature of Joseph Pierre Picot de Limoelan de Clorivière (1768–1826), 180?; on a miniature of Dr. John Alousius Casey of Savannah. De Clorivière lived the transient life typical of many artists passing through Savannah. After arriving in America in 1803, he worked in Savannah during 1803–1806, in Baltimore during 1806–1812, and in Charleston during 1812–1818. In the 24 October 1807 *Augusta Chronicle*, de Clorivière was "in town for a few days . . . and will take likenesses . . . . " He died in 1816 in Washington, D.C.

wealth to many piedmont towns. Excerpts from a lengthy article entitled "Prosperity of Milledgeville," *Georgia Journal*, 28 June 1815, show great pride in the piedmont's progress against great odds:

> The improvement of Milledgeville, in spite of every obstruction, is a source of gratification to all who feel an interest in its welfare. Two years ago, a third of the dwelling houses in it were vacant . . . . With its rapid increase of population, Milledgeville has acquired many worthy inhabitants, among them some industrious mechanics, . . . and no where do those who merit encouragement receive for their labor a better reward. Though an opportunity seldom offers, as a proof that our town has the disposition to patronize the fine arts, we would adduce the extraordinary success of a promising young artist, . . . Nine or ten years ago the spot on which it stands was waste, wild, and uncultivated, the abode of ruthless savages—it is now a flourishing town, contains two thousand souls, presents a pleasing scene of industry and wealth, and is the seat of social refinement, of personal charms, and of polished society.

Craftsmen settled in Milledgeville as well as in other piedmont towns that were exhibiting the same promise described in the editorial. Many settlers who came down the Wagon Road brought with them cabinetmaking traditions that they adapted to local woods and styles appropriate to their new clientele, the merchants and plantation owners. William Robertson sold "To Planters & Purchasers of Cotton," wood screws, "upon an approved plan for Packing Square Bales of Cotton . . . . "[77]

> Huff & Co., from the city of Philadelphia respectfully informs the Planters, Builders, Coach, Chair and Wagon-Makers, with the citizens in and about Milledgeville generally, that by the end of this month, their shop opposite the Eagle Tavern, will be ready to execute with dispatch, orders for any kind of IRON WORK, in the Black & White Smith's Line; Plantation work generally Turning Wrought and Cast-Iron; Screws, for Packing Machine, &c.[78]

Censuses in nineteenth-century Georgia were taken every seven years. The results of the 1817 census were thought to "fall short of the real number, although the tide of emigration has for sometime set strongly to the westward."[79] The post–1820 emergence of new "western" towns such as Macon (1823) and Columbus (1828) attracted craftsmen from Savannah, Augusta, and the piedmont. Their locations on the Ocmulgee and Chattahoochee rivers had made these western towns early centers of Indian trade. In 1830, Macon was described as "a large flourishing town, and has drained all the capital and refinement, not only from Milledgeville, but a great deal from other parts of the state, and is treading fast on the heels of Savannah."[80]

Macon advertisements appearing in pre–1830 newspapers included the "Cabinet and Chair-Making, painting, etc."[81] by the firm of Brown & Wood. William R. Brown continued the business, at least until 1831, and would "manufacture to order any article of furniture . . . has an excellent turner in his service."[82] George Dane, silversmith, clock and watchmaker, from London, was making "large silver spoons for $8 per sett."[83]

The New York trade infiltrated these new western towns after a very short period. Macon had been settled only five years when R. C. Wetmore, No. 4 Fletcher Street, New York City, informed the public of "a superior and general assortment of ware of the newest patterns . . . especially intended for Southern trade."[84]

Georgia Craftsmen and Indians

Indians were a constant threat both on the coast and in the piedmont until the government removed them in 1838. Trade relationships with Indians did not offset the frequent uprisings that deterred new settlers and possible new clientele for local artisans. Craftsmen made few references to Indians in their advertisements; the Indians, of course, were not interested in purchasing New York style furniture or silver and could not afford to have their portraits painted. An exception was Michael Germain, a Savannah silversmith, who advertised in 1790 that "all kinds of Indian Jewellery can be made by the subscriber."[85] In the 20 April 1802 *Columbian Museum and Savannah Advertiser*, Isaac Marquand and Cornelius Paulding offered for sale 400 ounces of silver from the Indians, including arm and wrist bands, gorgets, ear drops, and brooches. These were sold for cash or exchanged for tobacco, cotton, or rice. Josiah Penfield, also a Savannah silversmith, had for sale "one box Beads suitable for the Indian trade."[86]

Few Englishmen seemed to consider the natives as potential trainable apprentices. The Moravians in Salem, North Carolina, however, sent in 1807 craftsmen to two Indian mission sites, one on the Flint River supervised by Colonel Benjamin Hawkins, the other at Springplace, sponsored by James Vann. Correspondence in the Moravian archives in Winston-Salem, North Carolina, relates the experiences of these craftsmen sent to Georgia. Johann Christian Burkhardt, a cooper, and Karsten Petersen, a cabinetmaker, went to the Flint

River; Van N. Zevely, master joiner of the Brothers' House in Salem, went to Springplace.

> They go, not as missionaries but as craftsmen, and will support themselves by their work, under the supervision of Colonel Hawkins, who for many years has sought to promote the culture of this numerous Indian nation, which is estimated at eighty thousand. Br. Petersen is a cabinetmaker, and can also make looms and spinning wheels, which have been introduced among the Creeks and are much sought after. While here Br. Burkhardt has worked with our cooper and with our tinsmith, and has made good progress with both crafts. They will endeavor to learn the Creek language, and will take advantage of such opportunity as they may find in dealing with the nation or with individuals to introduce them to the Gospel.[87]

Even though the number of Cherokees in Georgia was dwindling, New Echota was made the capital of the Cherokee nation in 1825. This nation had a republican government and newspaper, the *Cherokee Phoenix*, first published 21 February 1828, in both English and Cherokee. In the November 1828 issue, J. S. W. White, "housebuilder and cabinetmaker from the city of New York," informed the Cherokee nation that he:

> intends carrying on the business of housebuilding and cabinetmaking in a manner superior to any that has been done . . . N.B. He will take apprentices in the above business. Any native who will come with good recommendation . . . will be taught.
> For further information, apply to Mssrs. David Vann and John Ridge.

By 1833, J. S. W. White had established a business in Columbus on Broad Street, "with an extensive assortment of good lumber and materials . . . to execute furniture of good quality," and "a long experience in the principle cities of the U. S."[88]

Conclusion

The inherent elegance in everyday objects produced by the craftsmen discussed in this essay eluded their contemporaries. Decorative art is an applied art. Pieces we revere today as the work of accomplished artisans were used in the home, not set on museum pedestals.

An early nineteenth-century concept of museums was that they were "depositories of learned curiosities."[89] Neither a silver tea set nor a secretary desk-and-bookcase were considered "curiosities" in the minds of the nineteenth-century intellectuals who were most interested in museums. Josiah Meigs, President of Franklin College in

Athens, wrote in an 1804 *Augusta Chronicle and Gazette of the State* article:

> to excite the attention of the people of Georgia to the establishment in this place, of a *Philosophical Museum*. Even a slight shew of mineral, vegetable, or animal, or the utensils, arms, dress, &c of a Chinese, or an American Indian, or models of useful machines, &c.
>
> Mr. Peale of Philadelphia, and several others have made collections of this kind, which have been sources of wealth to their proprietors.
>
> I, therefore, request, merchants, masters, and owners of ships, and my fellow citizens generally, to preserve for the above purpose, whatever may fall in their way, either abroad or at home.

In 1819, Abner Locke, a schoolmaster in Milledgeville, advertised a museum with "25¢ admittance," which included "a variety of American Antiquities, Portraits, Paintings, Landscapes, &c., &c."[90] At Mr. Mix's museum in Augusta "smoaking (was) strictly forbidden."[91] As for the Georgians who pioneered the traditions of these early museums: "No men ever laboured harder to be taken into notice; none, I presume, were less gratified in their success."[92]

Georgia's progress toward becoming a thriving state that supported local craftsmen was frustrated by many conditions. The early years of the last original colony were violent throughout the period preceding the Revolutionary War; survival took priority. As the port of Savannah prospered and merchants enjoyed economic prominence, goods imported from the North and abroad were preferred by the elite. By the nineteenth century, this trend had spread to Augusta and to the piedmont, where the planters tended to support the imported styles. There is no doubt that homes of working class people were filled with indigenous items, but three major fires, including one in Augusta in 1926, destroyed most of these objects. The signs of regional styles of the Georgia piedmont provide some clues as to what these men advertising in these papers could produce for a receptive clientele. The struggle of the Georgia craftsmen was all but lost by the 1830s, when mass-produced northern goods became convenient, inexpensive, and fashionable.

Jane Webb Smith
Guest Curator

1. From ca. 1790 poem reprinted in 1820 as a "jovial song . . . extracted from a fragment of an old paper . . . probably written about thirty years ago." *American Beacon and Norfolk and Portsmouth Daily Advertiser*, Virginia, 10 March 1820.

2. E. Merton Coulter and Albert B. Saye, eds. *A List of the Early Settlers of Georgia* (Athens: University of Georgia Press, 1949), XII. Museum of Early Southern Decorative Arts computer printout of craftsmen working in Georgia before 1820.

3. The occupations of eighteen craftsmen who were among the original settlers

are as follows: Paul Amatis, weaver; Richard Cannon, calenderer; Thomas Causton, printer of cloth; James Cornock, plasterer; Joseph Fitzwalter, gardener; Walter Fox, turner; Chetwynd Furcerd, apprentice silk throwster; James Goddard, carpenter; Peter Gordon, upholsterer; Samuel Gray, silk throwster; Cornelius Jones, silk throwster; Noble Jones, carpenter; Thomas Milledge, carpenter; Samuel Parker, blacksmith; Samuel Parker, carpenter; Joseph Stanley, weaver; John West, blacksmith; Thomas Young, wheelwright. Coulter and Saye, XI.

4. Ibid., XII.

5. *South Carolina Gazette*, 25 August 1733.

6. Ibid., 1 May 1736.

7. *Freemasonry: What is it?*, Supreme Council, 33° Ancient and Accepted Scottish Rite, Southern Jurisdiction, U.S.A., 1980.

8. First masonic lodge was in Boston, chartered in 1733. William B. Clarke, *Freemasonry in Georgia* (Macon: Masonic Educational and Historical Commission of the Grand Lodge of Georgia, 1933), 25.

9. Ibid., 12.

10. Known occupations of the craftsmen petitioning for the incorporation of the association: William Lewden, carpenter; Thomas Palmer, lumberyard worker; John Herb, gunsmith; George Faries, cabinetmaker; Simon Connor, wheelwright; Peter Miller, cabinetmaker; John Armour, bricklayer; Daniel Gugel, blacksmith; Gabriel Leaver, cabinetmaker; Elisha Elon, bricklayer; John Cole, carpenter. Research files, Museum of Early Southern Decorative Arts, Winston-Salem, North Carolina.

11. Robert & George Watkins, *A Digest of the Laws of the State of Georgia* (Philadelphia: R. Aiken, 1800), 518–19.

12. Elected were William Longstreet, president (inventor of a steam engine patented in 1788); John Catlett, vice-president (silversmith); Robert Creswell, treasurer (carpenter); John Stiles, secretary (silversmith). *Augusta Chronicle and Gazette of the State*, 4 May 1793.

13. Copy owned by descendents of Jacob Miller.

14. Charles F. Montgomery, *American Furniture: The Federal Period* (New York: The Viking Press, 1966), 21.

15. Ibid., 19.

16. Ibid.

17. Ibid., 22.

18. Ibid., 23.

19. *The Virginia Gazette and Weekly Advertiser*, 18 December 1788.

20. *City Gazette and The Daily Advertiser*, Charleston, 15 October 1795.

21. *Augusta Chronicle*, 13 December 1817.

22. *Columbian Museum and Savannah Gazette*, 26 September 1818.

23. *Augusta Chronicle*, 23 July 1813.

24. Charles Montgomery, *American Furniture: The Federal Period*, 23.

25. Ibid., 26.

26. *Georgia Gazette*, Savannah, 8 September 1763.

27. *Columbian Museum and Savannah Advertiser*, 4 December 1807.

28. Records of the 1820 Census of Manufacturers in Georgia, Wilkes County.

29. Ibid., Early County.

30. Edward J. Cashin, *The Story of Augusta* (Augusta: Richmond County Board of Education, 1980), 310.

31. Records of 1820 Census of Manufacturers in Georgia, Richmond County.

32. *The Virginia Gazette and Weekly Advertiser*, Richmond, 18 December 1788.

33. *Augusta Chronicle and Gazette of the State*, 23 January 1796.

34. *Columbian Herald*, Charleston, 2 December 1796.

35. *The Virginia Gazette and General Advertiser*, Richmond, 30 September 1808.

36. *Columbian Museum and Savannah Advertiser*, 9 March 1798.

37. Ibid., 9 March 1798.

38. Ibid., 7 February 1800.

39. Ibid., 21 January 1804.

40. *Louisville Public Advertiser*, Kentucky, 5 February 1820.

41. Frederick Doveton Nichols, *The Early Architecture of Georgia* (Chapel Hill: University of North Carolina Press, 1957), 34; quoted from *The Daily Georgian*, Savannah, 22 January 1820.

42. Ibid., 29; quoted from *The Daily Georgian*, 11 June 1821.

43. *Republican Star and General Advertiser*, Easton, Maryland, 25 April 1820.

44. Katharine Wood Gross, "The Sources of Furniture Sold in Savannah, 1789–1815," Masters' thesis, University of Delaware, 1967, 6.

45. *Georgia Gazette*, 26 January 1764.

46. Ibid., 30 August 1764.

47. Ibid., 13 July 1774.

48. Mable Munson Swan, "Coastwise Cargoes of Venture Furniture," *Antiques*, 55 (April 1949), 278.

49. Ibid.

50. Gross, 58; quoted from *The Augusta Chronicle and Gazette of the State*, 22 August 1789.

51. *Pennsylvania Mercury*, 25 October 1788.

52. Richmond & Allen, cabinetmakers formerly of Providence, Rhode Island, advertised furniture from there. The *Columbian Museum and Savannah Advertiser*, 18 February 1811. Edward Priestley, working in Baltimore, advertised in 1802 "a quantity of excellent mahogany furniture from Baltimore." *Georgia Republican and State Intelligencer*, 15 December 1802.

53. *Gazette of the State of Georgia*, Savannah, 21 October 1784.

54. *Georgia Republican and State Intelligencer*, Savannah, 3 March 1803.

55. *Columbian Museum and Savannah Advertiser*, 9 December 1808.

56. *Augusta Chronicle*, 29 November 1817.

57. *The Savannah Republican*, 8 February 1817.

58. Ibid., 22 July 1817.

59. Ibid., 5 August 1817.

60. *Georgia Journal*, Augusta, 24 November 1818.

61. *Columbian Museum and Savannah Advertiser*, 19 December 1800.

62. Ibid., 17 August 1802.

63. Marilyn A. Johnson, "John Hewitt, Cabinetmaker," *Winterthur Portfolio* 4 (1968), 191.

64. Ibid., 190.

65. Ibid., 191.

66. Ibid.

67. *The Savannah Republican*, 7 December 1819.

68. Johnson, 193.

69. *Augusta Chronicle*, 10 December 1813.

70. "An Account of the City of Charlestown, Metropolis of the Province of South-Carolina, with an Exact and Beautiful Prospect Thereof," *London Magazine* (June 1762), 296.

71. *Georgia Gazette*, Savannah, 1 April 1767.

72. *Columbian Museum and Savannah Advertiser*, 2 March 1798.

73. *Georgia Gazette*, 12 July 1792.

74. *Mirror of the Times*, Augusta, 12 December 1808.

75. Ellis Merton Coulter, *Old Petersburg and the Broad River Valley* (Athens: University of Georgia Press, 1968), 3.

76. *Virginia Gazette and Petersburg Intelligencer*, 29 July 1796.

77. *Georgia Journal*, 29 August 1810.

78. Ibid., 27 February 1811.

79. *The Savannah Republican*, 22 November 1817.

80. Mary Levin Koch, "A History of the Arts in Augusta, Macon, and Columbus, Georgia," Masters' thesis, University of Georgia, 1983, 5; as quoted from Anne Royall, *Mrs. Royall's Southern Tour, or Second Series of the Black Book* (Washington, D.C., 1811), 159.

81. *Georgia Messenger*, Macon, 17 November 1824.

82. *Macon Advertiser*, 2 August 1831.

83. *Georgia Messenger*, 7 December 1825.

84. *Macon Telegraph*, 5 May 1828.

85. *Georgia Gazette*, 11 February 1790.

86. *Columbian Museum and Savannah Daily Gazette*, 5 January 1818.

87. Records of the Helfer Conferenz Furs Ganze, dated 30 March 1807.

88. *Columbus Weekly Enquirer*, 12 April 1833.

89. *Georgia Republican and State Intelligencer*, 10 November 1802.

90. *Augusta Herald*, 18 December 1818.

91. *Milledgeville Georgia Journal*, 19 October 1819.

92. *Georgia Republican and State Intelligencer*, 10 November 1802.

" . . . disarm death of half its terrors":

Commemoration in Mid-Nineteenth Century Georgia

Commemoration in Georgia was essentially the same as in other parts of the country. Although the carving of iconic gravestones had been initiated in the eighteenth century through the dominant activities of New England stonecarvers in communities like Savannah and Midway, the confluence of certain factors, beginning in the 1830s, ensured the widespread acceptance of various motifs in funerary art. Of key importance were the expanding markets for sculpture both nationally and regionally, the increasing availability through mass publication of memorial catalogues and design books, and the flourishing of a unique genre, consolation literature. This literature, written to comfort the bereaved, not only popularized commemorative themes and motifs, but also provides for the contemporary reader invaluable insights into how these motifs were understood from the 1830s until the close of the century.[1]

Equally significant in guaranteeing the universal incorporation of certain motifs into funerary design, and far more dramatic in its immediate impact, was the establishment of Mount Auburn Cemetery in 1831 in Cambridge, Massachusetts, for it served as the paradigm for what has come to be described as the "rural cemetery" movement.[2] Within a decade, cemeteries of vast acreage, sequestered in trees and abounding in floral loveliness, began to appear all along the East coast. The churchyards and municipal burial grounds characterizing the eighteenth century and spilling over into the early nineteenth century had become associated with the spread of disease; and their restricted size meant they could no longer accommodate the dead.

Two of the most impressive of these rural cemeteries are found in Georgia: Rose Hill in Macon and Oakland Cemetery in Atlanta. Founded in 1840, Rose Hill was named after Simri Rose, a newspaper editor and, significantly, an amateur horticulturalist, who was inspired by the "far famed Mount Auburn," as he described that cemetery. Rose selected 50 acres, high above the banks of the Ocmulgee River, a half mile from the burgeoning residential section, and created a garden of botanical splendor to suggest the paradise that awaited the faithful. Both the site and the vegetation of Rose Hill are essential components of the rural cemetery. In his description of the exceptional beauty of Rose Hill's landscape, Rose captures one Georgian's pride in the cemetery's lushness and picturesque tranquility, and offers visitors valuable instruction:

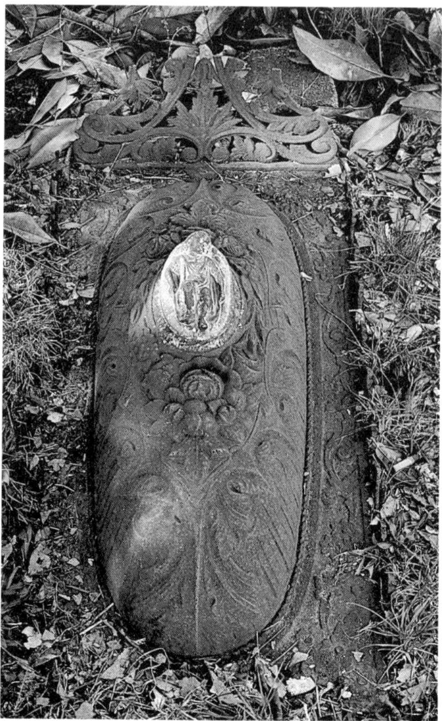

Figure 1. The Myrtis Jentzen marker, 1873, Oakland Cemetery, Atlanta, Georgia. Iron.

> Many who have toured the cemeteries of the North, and even the far famed Mount Auburn, think it far inferior in natural beauty and location to Rose Hill . . . . Around [the pond] are several cypresses and weeping willows, and one rises from a mound in its centre. A variety of *fine roses* are also near it, and *in perpetual bloom.* These are also scattered over the ground, and along the walks and roads, in great profusion . . . . The oriental cypress, from Asia, raises its graceful spire; the balm of Gilead, Norway and silver firs, the hemlock, arbor vitae, cedar, juniper and wild olive, the broom and furze, and even the *humble thorn, from whose branches was plaited the crown worn on* Mount *Calvary* . . . . Most of the Cemetery is thickly wooded by a young and thrifty growth, interspersed with the towering poplar, giant oaks, beech and sycamore: and it is worthy of remark that there is scarcely a tree, shrub, or wild flower, that is known in our country, that may not be found within this area of 50 acres . . . . wild honeysuckle in abundance, woodbine, golden hypericum . . . . The [Ocmulgee] river . . . wheeling around immovable cliffs of granite and flint . . . to mingle in the unfathomed and undefined abyss of eternity, imparts an *instructive lesson,* while the *beauties* of the *scene* disarm death of half its terrors[3] (italics mine).

In 1850, the same year an enthusiastic readership received Cornelia Walter's *Mount Auburn Illustrated,*[4] a work highlighting the history, landscape, and monuments of the cemetery, Oakland Cemetery was established in Atlanta. Originally a six-acre tract, Oakland expanded quickly to its present 88 acres. Like Rose Hill and cemeteries such as Athens's Oconee Hill, which opened its gates in 1856,[5] Oakland stressed the didactic intent of the rural cemetery. This intent was evident in the cemetery's memorials and in its pristine landscape which mollified the inevitability of death through a reassuring recollection of the Heavenly garden. The engravings in Walter's in which comparable halcyon scenes invite the contemplation of one's mortality no doubt fostered the idea of the Heavenly garden.

In proclaiming the Christian's faith in a joyful resurrection, certain funerary motifs predominated throughout much of the nineteenth century. Among the ubiquitous urns, many displaying the flame of immortality (figure 3) and harkening back to the commemorative rituals of the ancient Greeks and Romans, were numerous women and children presented in various guises and gestures. Some are "asleep in Jesus" (figure 1) or are at evening prayer; others, already having become angels, write their brief "histories" on unfurled parch-

Figure 2. (left) The Mary V. Little memorial, 1867, Memory Hill, Milledgeville, Georgia. Marble.

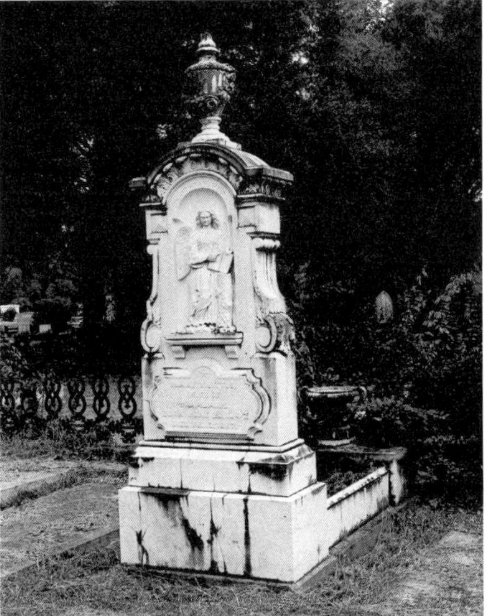

Figure 3. (right) The Robert Freeman memorial, 1856, Rose Hill Cemetery, Macon, Georgia. Marble.

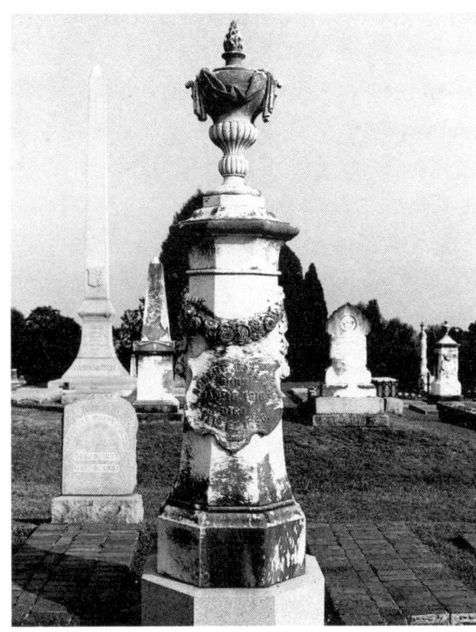

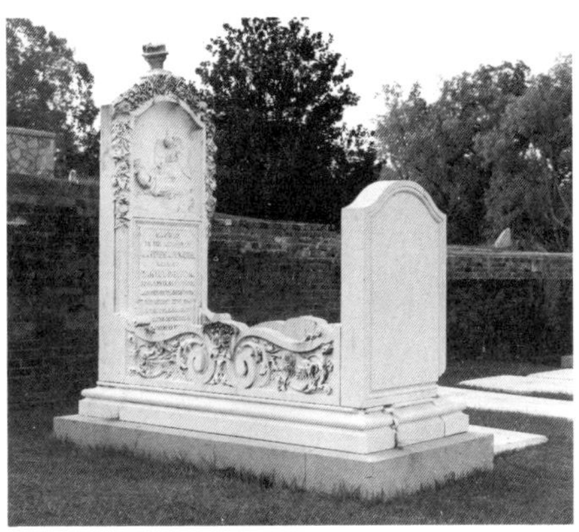

Figure 4. (above) The Narcissa Powers memorial, 1841, Rose Hill Cemetery, Macon, Georgia. Marble.

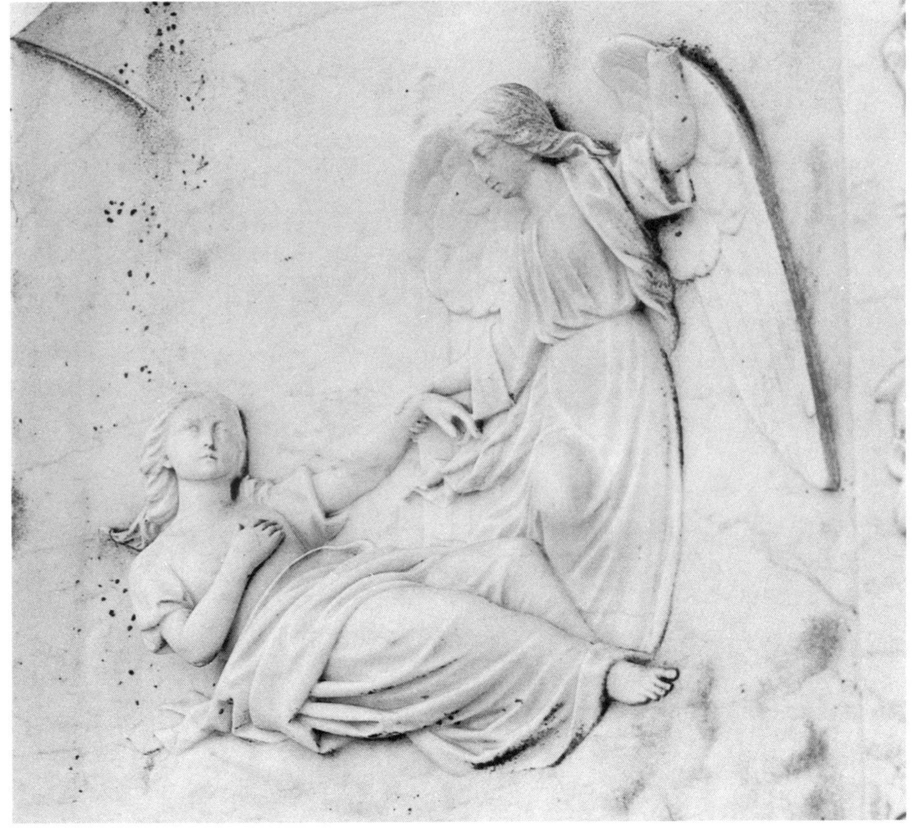

Figure 5. (right) Detail of the Narcissa Powers memorial.

ment (figure 2); while more than a few women are represented as Madonnas and some children are presented in the guise of Christ the Infant Saviour. As an *exemplum virtutis*, the child can also be seen dutifully absorbing Biblical wisdom through the lovingly ministered instruction of his mother, who served as the moral arbiter of the household. Through her teaching of the Scriptures and by her own exemplary conduct, the mother ensured that the goal of the family would be met: they would eventually be reunited in Heaven.

The 1840s and 1850s provide equally powerful manifestations of

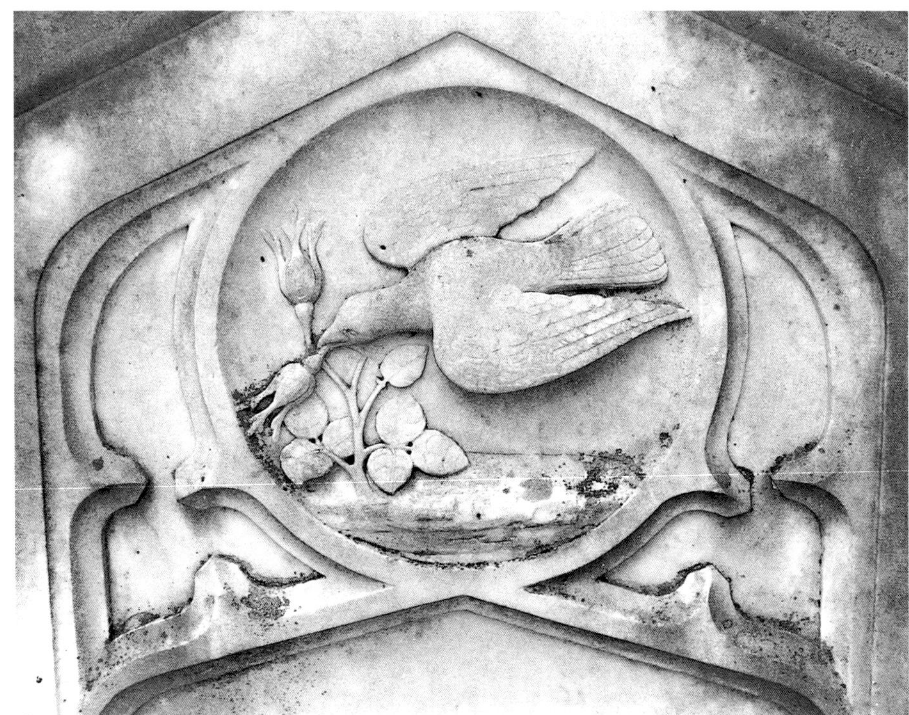

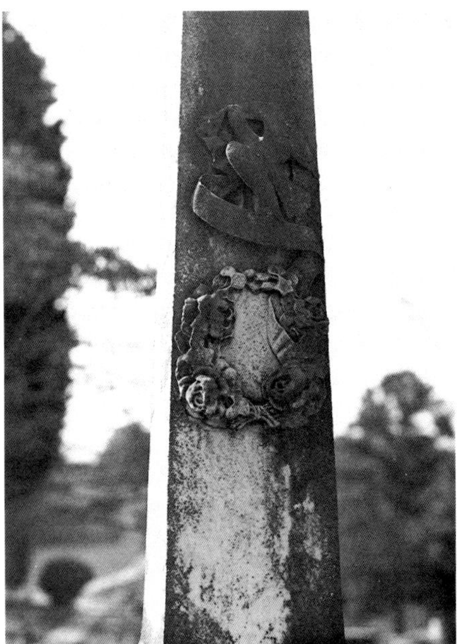

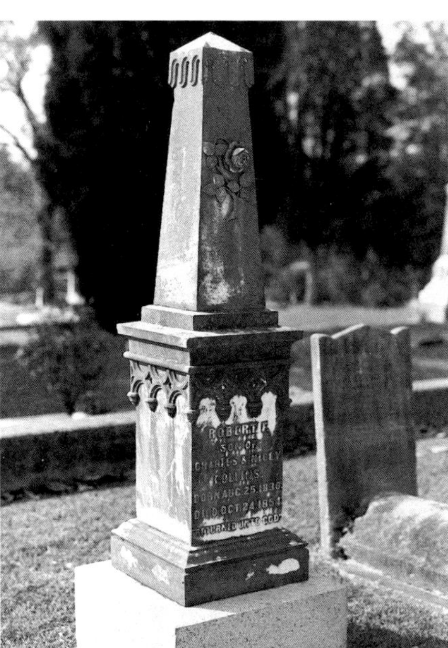

Figure 6. (top) The "Carrie" marker, 1852, Memory Hill Cemetery, Milledgeville, Georgia. Marble. Signed "Dudley and See, N.Y."

Figure 7. (bottom left) The Mary B. Clayton memorial, Rose Hill Cemetery, Macon, Georgia. Marble.

Figure 8. (bottom right) The Robert F. Collins memorial, 1854, Rose Hill Cemetery, Macon, Georgia. Marble. Signed "Ritter's / N.[ew] H.[aven] Ct."

the resurrectional theme. Located at Rose Hill is the earliest memorial on which the female figure appears. The memorial, dated 1841, is for Narcissa Powers who, according to her epitaph, died at age 22 (figure 4). A young woman representative of Narcissa is being lifted from her place of rest by an emissary angel (figure 5). With one hand, the angel grasps Narcissa's limp wrist while with the other she points Heavenward (at some point in time the hand was broken). Having been claimed by God, Narcissa looks beyond the angel in anticipation of her journey to Heaven.

Narcissa's death amidst the jubilation of her assured salvation, although not in her tableau, seems poignant. During this period the language of flowers played an important role in the expression of sen-

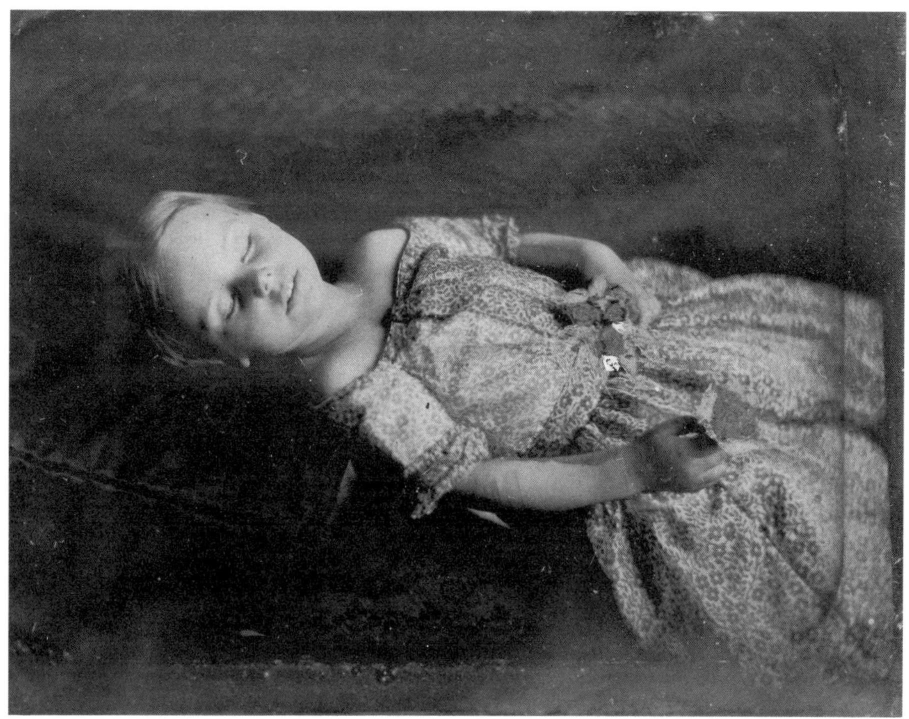

Figure 9. Posthumous daguerreotype of Mary Elizabeth Jones, 1852.

timent. Accordingly, a garland of flowers (see also figures 15, 17, 18, 20) frames the niche; while on the slats of her bed—she is, after all, a slumberer, as the dead were often described in consolatory tracts—appear bouquets of roses, rosebuds, and morning glories. Intertwined with the ivy of undying affection and abiding memory, each of these flowers becomes a declaration of unwavering devotion in the face of death. Numerous symbolic interpretations of flowers appeared in botanical guides and in treatises of sentiment, including such volumes as *The Flower Vase* (1847) and *The Voice of Flowers* (1848),[6] the latter by Mrs. Lydia Sigourney, who was a leading "mourning" poet of the 1840s and 1850s. With its diverse and often exotic plant life the cemetery thus became the locus of another kind of instruction.

In a larger cultural context, the rose or rosebud symbolized the death of the young (figures 6, 7, 8, 9), usually a child or woman, as it no doubt did, appropriately, on Narcissa's marker. Additionally, the rosebud was interpreted as a "confession of love." Of the specific blossoms included in the garland, the columbine meant that "I cannot give thee up," the phlox that "our souls are united," while the zinnias spoke of the ultimate impact of loss: "I mourn your absence."[7]

Milledgeville's Memory Hill Cemetery was established as a municipal burying ground in 1804, the year when Milledgeville became the state capitol, nearly three decades before the initiation of the rural cemetery movement. Nonetheless, Memory Hill was able to accommodate itself to the growth of the community. As a consequence, it became "Victorianized" with time. The landscape was planted according to the standards of the rural cemetery, while the monuments reflect motifs that were widely employed in cemeteries at mid-century and later. The cemetery thus proves unique for study since it bears the imprint of a number of changes in both landscaping and funerary

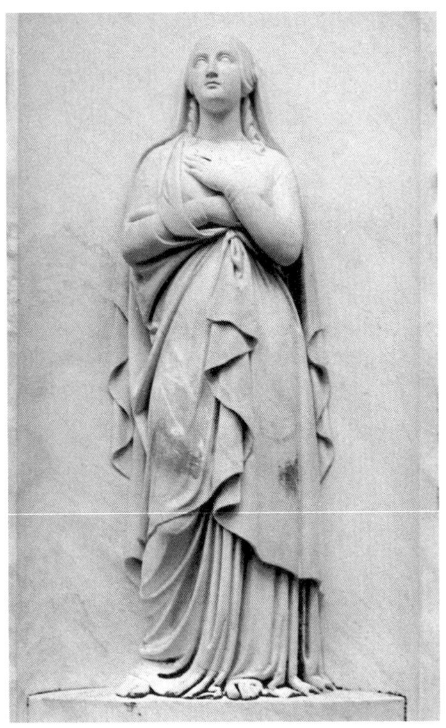

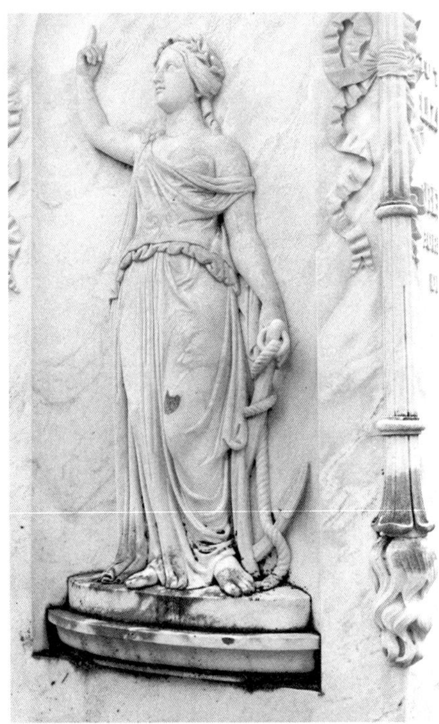

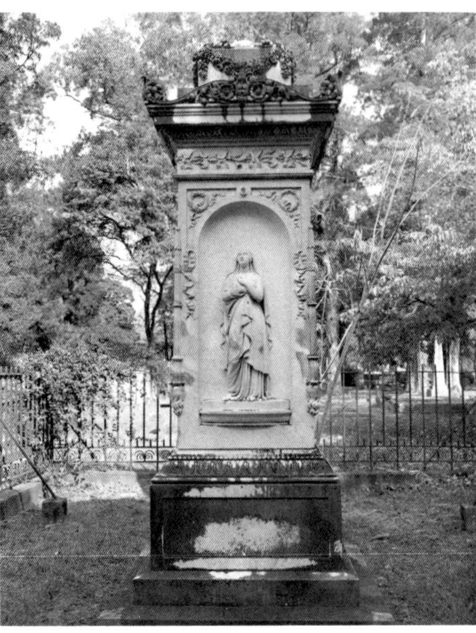

Figure 10. (above) The Elizabeth Taylor memorial, 1858, Memory Hill Cemetery, Milledgeville, Georgia. Marble. Signed "R. E. Launitz, N.Y."

Figure 11. (left) Detail of the Elizabeth Taylor memorial.

Figure 12. (middle) Detail of the Elizabeth Taylor memorial.

art since its inception. A variation on the Powers motif can be found on the Elizabeth Taylor memorial, 1858 (figure 10), in Memory Hill. The Taylor memorial is signed "R. E. Launitz, N.Y.," a stone carver's name that appears on at least a half dozen impressive monuments in this cemetery, including the Lamar and Jordan obelisks. The memorial has two well-executed panels: one featuring a woman looking Heavenward (figure 11), her hands across her chest in a gesture of supplication and piety that can be traced back to the early church; and the other displaying the allegorical figure of Hope, pointing to Heaven, accompanied by her attribute the anchor (figure 12). The extent to which the symbolism of the anchor was understood and embraced during the nineteenth century is revealed in a sentimental verse often memorized by school children and even incorporated into their friendship albums:

> Safely down life's swelling tide;
> May your vessel gently glide,
> And may we anchor side by side
> In heaven.[8]

Together, these figures are a fitting complement to the epitaph, one of the Beatitudes from Christ's Sermon on the Mount:

> Blessed are the pure in Heart
> For they shall see God
> —Matthew Chap. V/Verse 8.

In continually directing our gaze to Heaven with the injunction to "Praise the Lord" (figure 13), the figure announces the optimism borne out of the Christian faith. Such conviction was asseverated not only in consolatory works like *The Christian Home* (1859),[9] but also

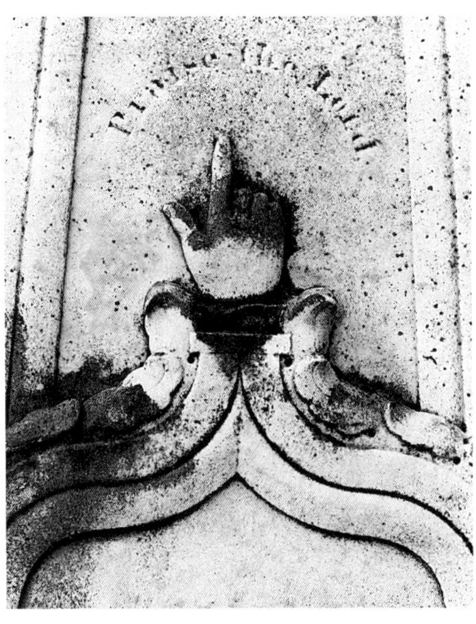

Figure 13. Detail of the Mary A. Blake memorial, 1847, Rose Hill Cemetery, Macon, Georgia. Marble.

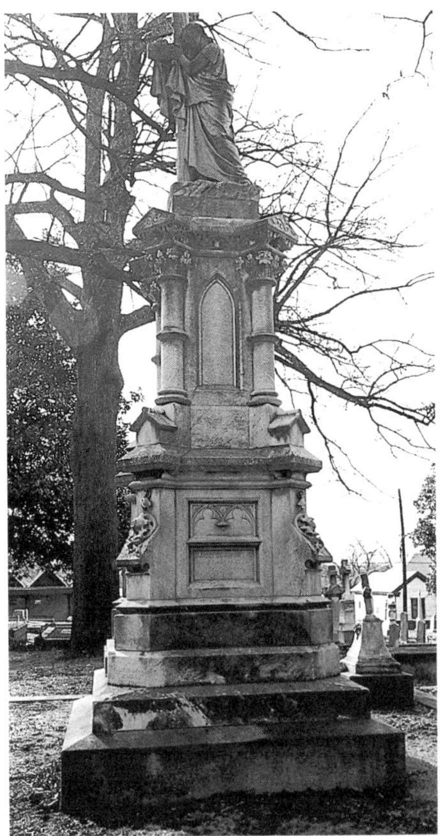

Figure 14. The Dougherty family memorial, 1851–55, Oakland Cemetery, Atlanta, Georgia. Marble. Signed "J. J. Mullan / Builder."

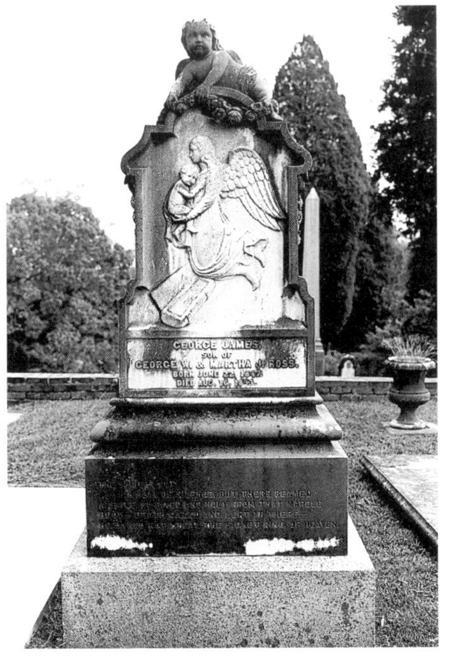

Figure 15. The George Ross marker, 1852, Rose Hill Cemetery, Macon, Georgia. Marble. Signed "R. Barry / Boston, Mass."

in myriad poems like those, for example, of Felicia Hemans, an English poet whose works enjoyed a wide readership in America several decades after her death in 1835. The second and concluding stanza of her "Monumental Inscription" reads:

> But Thou, O Heaven! Keep, Keep what *thou* hast taken,
> And with our treasure keep our hearts on high:
> The spirit meek, and yet by pain unshaken,
> The faith, the love, the lofty constancy—
> Guide us where these are with our sister flown.
> They were of thee, and thou has claimed thine own![10]

Although the female mourner affirms the everlasting life of the spirit, she also indicates the impact of bereavement. On the Dougherty family memorial, signed "J.J. Mullan, Builder" and dated 1851–1855 (figure 14), in Oakland, the classically draped monumental figure seems physically weighted down by her grief. Yet, this is subordinated to the fact that she clings, as the hymn reminds us, to "the Old Rugged Cross," the source of her comfort and spiritual sustenance.

The death of a child, of course, assumes a heightened poignancy, and taps the deepest reservoir of human feeling. Among the mid-century gravestones employing the child motif, the soul's victory over death is once again given precedence. In assuming a rudimentary narrative, the creator of the George Ross marker, 1853 (figure 15), offers a dramatic message of salvation which unfolds with an elevated sense of anticipation and exultation. Having died at age six, George ascends to Heaven in the arms of an angel who has just removed him from his coffin. However, we are privy not only to George's ascent, but also to his placement in Heaven. Sitting atop his monument and holding a festoon of flowers that includes the convolvulus of eternal sleep, George in assuming wings offers visual confirmation of the epitaph "Gone to be an angel" as he assumes his wings. Serenely reflecting this state of grace, George patiently waits to be joined by his family.

The didactic richness of the child motif was such that it was incorporated into the vernacular of daily existence, including Currier and Ives' popular lithograph "The Mother's Dream" (figure 16), published circa 1858–59. The accompanying verse might well serve as an epitaph:

> The great Jehovah full of love
> An angel bright did send,
> Who took my harmless little dove
> To joys that never end.

Similar statements were expressed in *The Christian Home*. The Reverend Samuel Philips spoke of the mother contemplating "that silent nursery" and reminded the reader that the death of a child is part of God's ultimate design for the family's reunion in Heaven:

> . . . death may separate us from them, [but] it does not disunite us. Your departed children . . . are still yours . . . .

> They *represent* your *household* in heaven, and are a *promise* that you will be there also . . . . you are *still one family*, . . . in faith, in hope . . . *in Christ* . . . you can gather those that still remain, and you can tell them they shall meet their departed kindred in a *better home* . . . . With these views of death before you, and with the *moral instruction* they afford, you cannot but feel that your children, though absent from you in body . . . are still living with you in your household, ... (italics mine).[11]

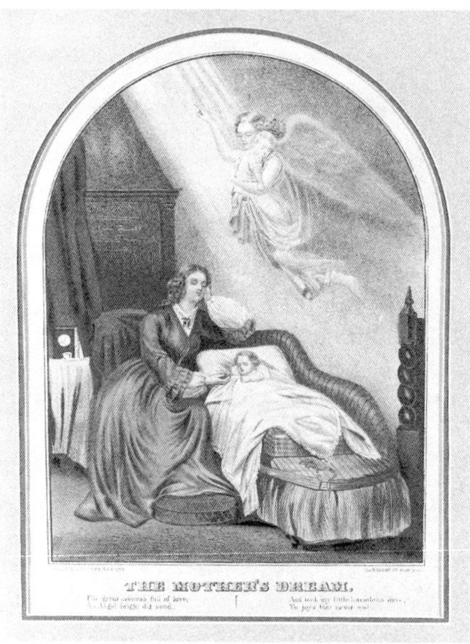

Figure 16. "The Mother's Dream," ca. 1858–59, lithograph, Currier and Ives.

Further, in addressing "the mother who bends in the deep anguish of her soul over the little grave in which the infant slumbers,"[12] Philips characteristically links death with sleep, a concept derived from many Biblical references describing death as a temporary "falling asleep" that is followed by the resurrection of the spirit.[13] For example, in resurrecting Lazarus from the dead, Jesus observes that "Our friend Lazarus sleepeth, but I go, that I may awake him out of sleep."[14]

The motif of the child ascending to Heaven thus played a significant role in mid-century culture and received numerous interpretations in funerary sculpture. A number of such gravestones, in fact, were cut by Macon carver James B. Artope. Originally from South Carolina, Artope apparently established his business in the late 1830s and became Macon's "first marblecutter." It seems his business thrived, eventually becoming a family effort that continued operation after his death in 1883.[15]

Among Artope's signed stones are the Anna Powers and Martha Kirby markers (figures 17, 18). These markers, as well as the one for "Little Robbie" Logan (figure 19), confirm what was a fundamental didactic theme in Victorian consolation and commemoration. More to the point, however, is the eagerness with which the departed Robbie reaches toward Heaven. The literature written especially for children proves illuminating on this matter. For example, in *My Little*

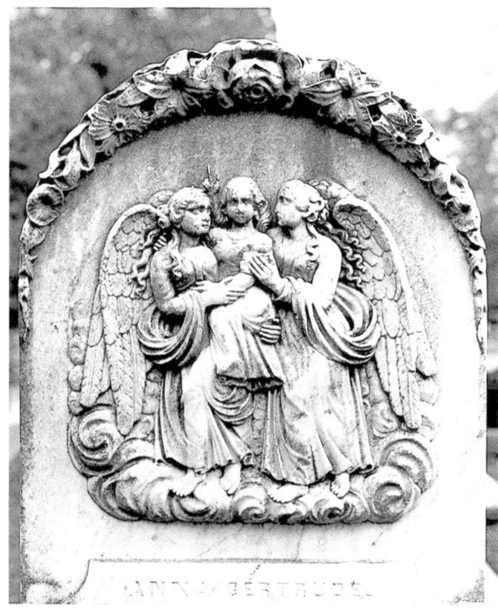

Figure 17. The Anna Gertrude Powers marker, 1859, Rose Hill Cemetery, Macon, Georgia. Marble. Signed "J. Artope & Son."

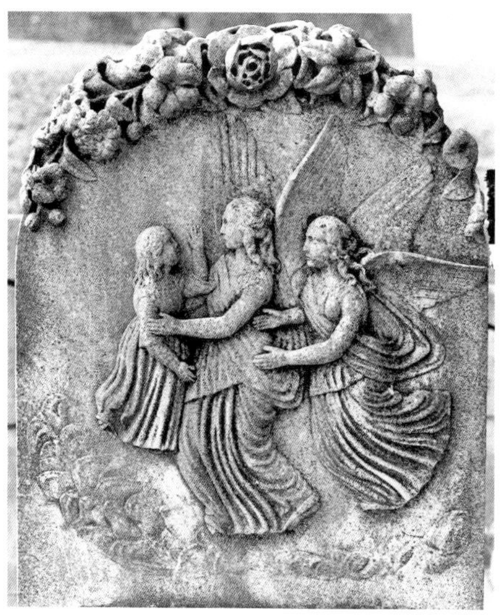

Figure 18. The Martha Kirby marker, 1862, Rose Hill Cemetery, Macon, Georgia. Material unknown. Signed "J. Artope & Son."

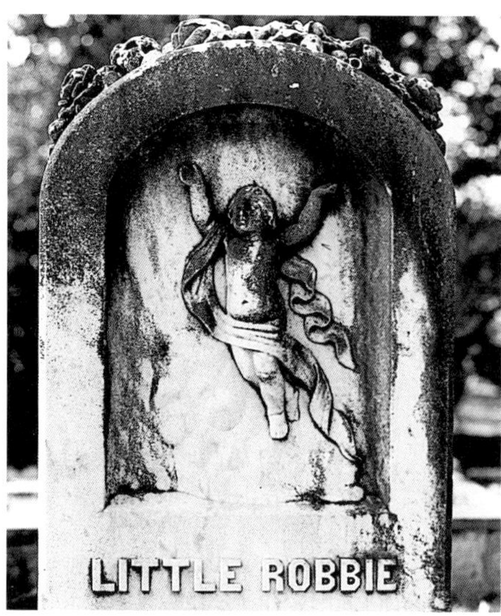

Figure 19. "Little Robbie" Logan, 1859, Rose Hill Cemetery, Macon, Georgia. Marble. Signed "J. Artope & Son, Macon."

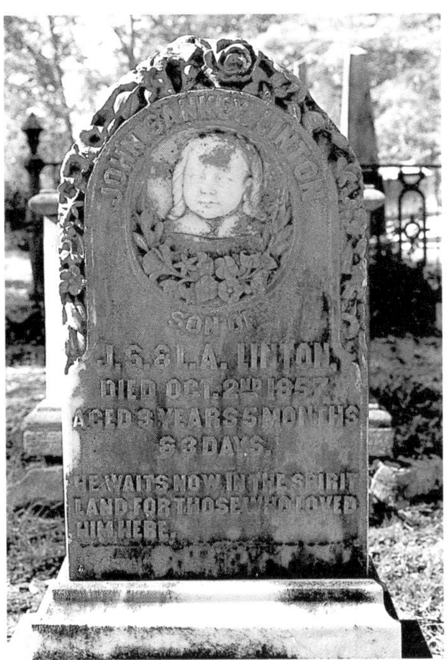

Figure 20. The John Sankey Linton marker, 1857, Oconee Hill Cemetery, Athens, Georgia. Marble.

Hymn Book, an 1836 collection of verses which instilled piety and social virtues, a child concludes his prayer with the following:

> Teach me to live that I may dread
> The grave as little as my bed;
> Teach me to die, that so I may
> *Rise joyful* at the judgement day.[16] (italics mine.)

The passage of time, diminished custom, and the secularization of our culture have dimmed our understanding of and appreciation for these and other commemorative representations (see figure 20) and their accompanying epitaphs. Yet, as long as these monuments remain, their lessons can be rediscovered. If we could indeed learn again to dread the grave as little as we dread our beds, death would be robbed of half its terrors.

Diana Williams Combs
Historic Oakland Cemetery Inc., Atlanta

1. The reader is referred to Ann Douglas, "Heaven Our Home: Consolation Literature in the Northern United States, 1830–1880," *American Quarterly* 30(December 1978), 496–515.

2. See Stanley French, "The Cemetery as Cultural Institution: The Establishment of Mt. Auburn and the 'Rural Cemetery' Movement," *American Quarterly* 26(March 1974), 37–59.

3. George White, *Historical Collections of Georgia* (New York: Pudney and Russell, 1855), 109–111. I wish to thank Barbara Story, the Administrator of Rose Hill Cemetery, for making this information available.

4. Cornelia W. Walter, *Mount Auburn Illustrated* (New York: R. Martin, 1850).

5. My thanks to James Reap and Patricia Cooper for information on Oconee Hill.

6. Miss E. C. Edgarton, *The Flower Vase Containing the Language of Flowers* (Lowell, Mass.: Merrill & Heywood, 1847). Mrs. Lydia H. Sigourney, *The Voice of Flowers* (Hartford, Conn.: H. S. Parsons and Co., 1848).

7. Edgarton, *The Flower Vase*, p. 10.

8. This verse appears in a friendship album I purchased several years ago. The album dates from the 1880s and belonged to Miss Jennie Merritt from Johnstonville, Monroe County, Georgia.

9. The Reverend Samuel Philips, *The Christian Home* (Springfield, Mass.: G. & F. Bell, 1859).

10. Felicia Hemans, *The Poetical Works of Felicia Hemans* (1852), 421.

11. Philips, *The Christian Home*, 327–28.

12. Ibid., p. 336.

13. Of the numerous consolation volumes in which this idea is explored, see The Reverend John Thornton, *Bereaved Parents Consoled* (Nashville, Tenn.: Stevenson and Owen, 1855).

14. John 11:11.

15. *Macon Telegraph and Messenger*, 15, December 1883, 4. My appreciation to Peer Edwin Ravnan of the Middle Georgia Archives for providing me with information concerning James Artope. The reader is also referred to *The Macon Directory for 1860*, apparently the earliest such directory in Macon.

16. *My Little Hymn Book* (Boston, Mass.: Perkins and Marvin, 1836), 57.

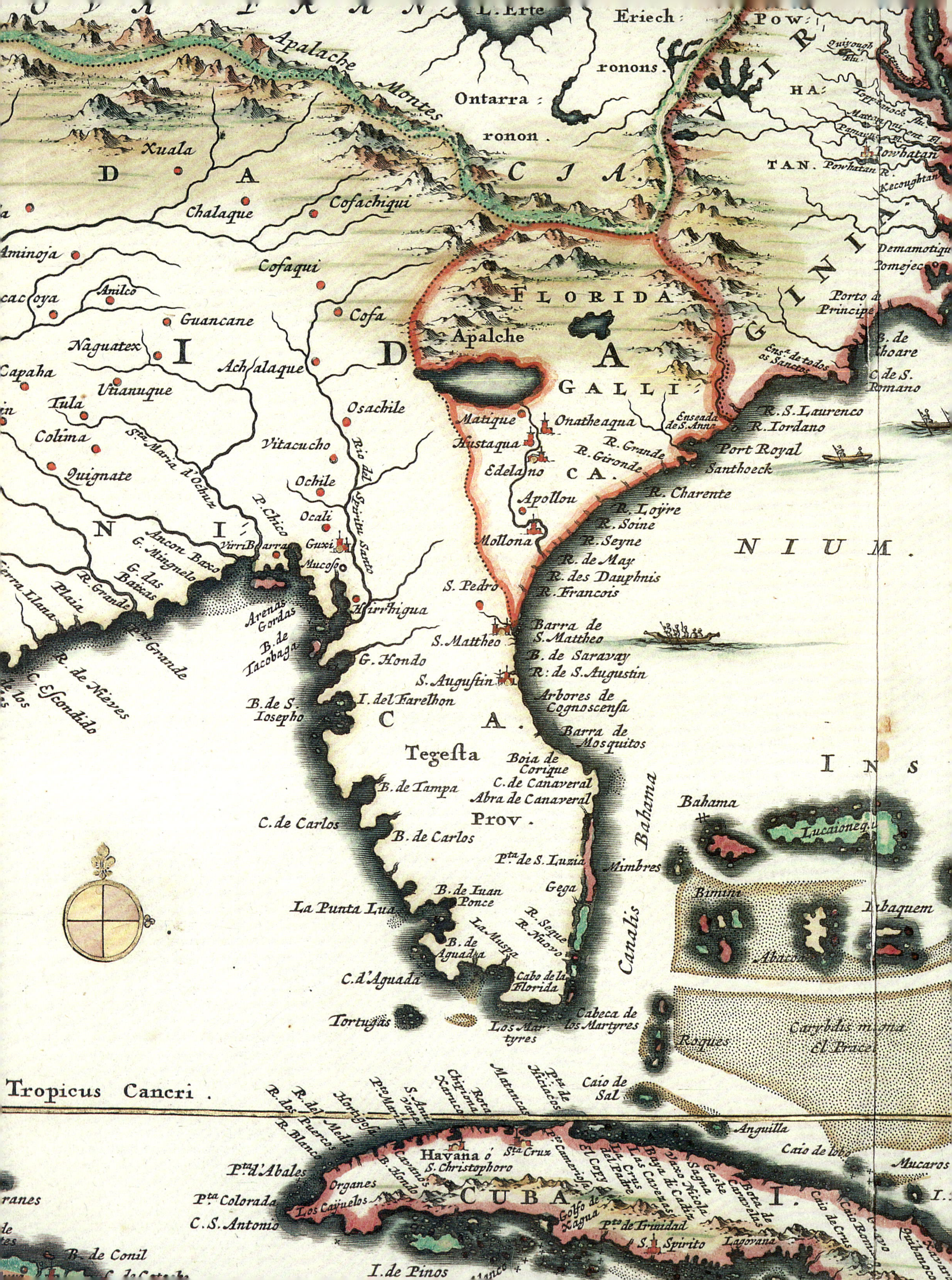

Apalache Montes
Ontarra
ronon
Eriech
ronons
Xuala
Chalaque
Cofachiqui
Cofaqui
Cofa
Aminoja
Anilco
Guancane
Naguatex
Capaha
Vtianque
Tula
Colima
Quignate
Achalaque
Osachile
Vitacucho
Ochile
Ocali
Rio del Spiritu Santo
Sta Maria d'Ochuz
P. Chico
Ancon Baxo
G. Minguelo
G. das Baixas
R. Grande
Plaia
Tierra Llana
Arenas Gordas
B. de Tacobaga
R. de Nieves
C. Escondido
G. Hondo
B. de S. Iosepho
I. del Farelhon
Tegesta
B. de Tampa
C. de Carlos
B. de Carlos
Prov.
La Punta Lua
B. de Aguada
C.d'Aguada
Tortugas
Los Martyres
FLORIDA
Apalche
GALLI
Matique
Onatheaqua
Hustaqua
Edelano
Apollou
Mollona
R. Grande
R. Gironde
R. Charente
R. Loyre
R. Soine
R. Seyne
R. de May
R. des Dauphnis
R. Francois
S. Pedro
S. Mattheo
Barra de S. Mattheo
B. de Saravay
S. Augustin
R: de S. Augustin
Arbores de Cognoscensa
Barra de Mosquitos
Boia de Corique
C. de Canaveral
Abra de Canaveral
Pta de S. Luzia
Gega
B. de Iuan Ponce
La Muspa
R. Seque
R. Nuovo
Cabo de la Florida
Cabeca de los Martyres
R. S. Laurenco
R. Iordano
Port Royal
Santhoeck
Enseada de S. Anna
NIUM.
Powhatan
Kecoughtan
Demamotigu
Pomejec
Porto de Principe
B. de Choare
C. de S. Romano
Bahama
Canalis
Mimbres
Bimini
Lucaioneque
Ibaquem
Abaco
Roques
Carybdis magna el Pracel
INS
Tropicus Cancri
Caio de Sal
Anguilla
Caio de Lobo
Mucaros
Havana ó S. Christophoro
Sta Cruz
Organes
Los Cajuelos
CUBA
Pta d'Abales
Pta Colorada
C. S. Antonio
B. de Conil
I. de Pinos
Golfo de Xagua
Pta de Trinidad
S. Spirito
Lagovana
Matancas
Caio Romano

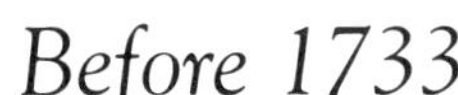

Before 1733

Indians inhabited the Southeast by 10,000 B.C., although little archaeological evidence of their nomadic existence remains. They made their living by hunting large animals, many of which are now extinct, such as the mastadon or the mammoth. A few sites surviving from the Archaic Period (8000–1000 B.C.) reflect a new way of life as the Indians began to collect a greater variety of animals, including fish and shellfish, and to place more emphasis on gathering seeds and nuts. These people laid the foundations for the complex indigenous cultures that were to develop in Georgia over succeeding centuries.

The earliest items included in this exhibition date from the Woodland Period (1000 B.C.–A.D. 800), a time when virtually all aspects of Indian society grew more sophisticated, particularly agricultural practices. Religious rituals and ceremonies became an important component of village life, and the village priest probably served as the communicant with spirits associated with the success or failure of plants and animals. When this priest died, he was buried in a small mound and surrounded by ceramics, stone pipes, weapons, and other artifacts that may have held special significance.

Artifacts, such as those chosen for this exhibition, provide anthropological clues about Indian life during various periods of Georgia's history. The cougar pipe, for example, provides evidence of a keen interest in animal imagery and demonstrates the craftsman's advanced carving skill. Objects in this section of the exhibition trace the development of Indian cultures as they evolved during the Mississippian era and follows them to what is thought to be their peak of sophistication during the Etowah Period (A.D. 1000–1300).

DeSoto's travels in 1540 through the region now known as Georgia brought natives in contact with Europeans for the first time. This contact essentially led to the demise of Mississippian cultures. Through involvement with Jesuit and Franciscan missions as well as trade with Europeans in Charleston, the surviving coastal Indians were exposed to and adopted aspects of European culture. By 1733, when the English colonized the region, little remained of the creative and industrious Indian craftsmen of past chiefdoms.

Nicolaus Visscher, *Insulae Americanae in Oceano Septentrionali ac Regiones Adiacentes*, 1680. Amsterdam: Nicolaus Visscher. H. 18½", W. 22½". Special Collections, The University of Georgia Libraries.

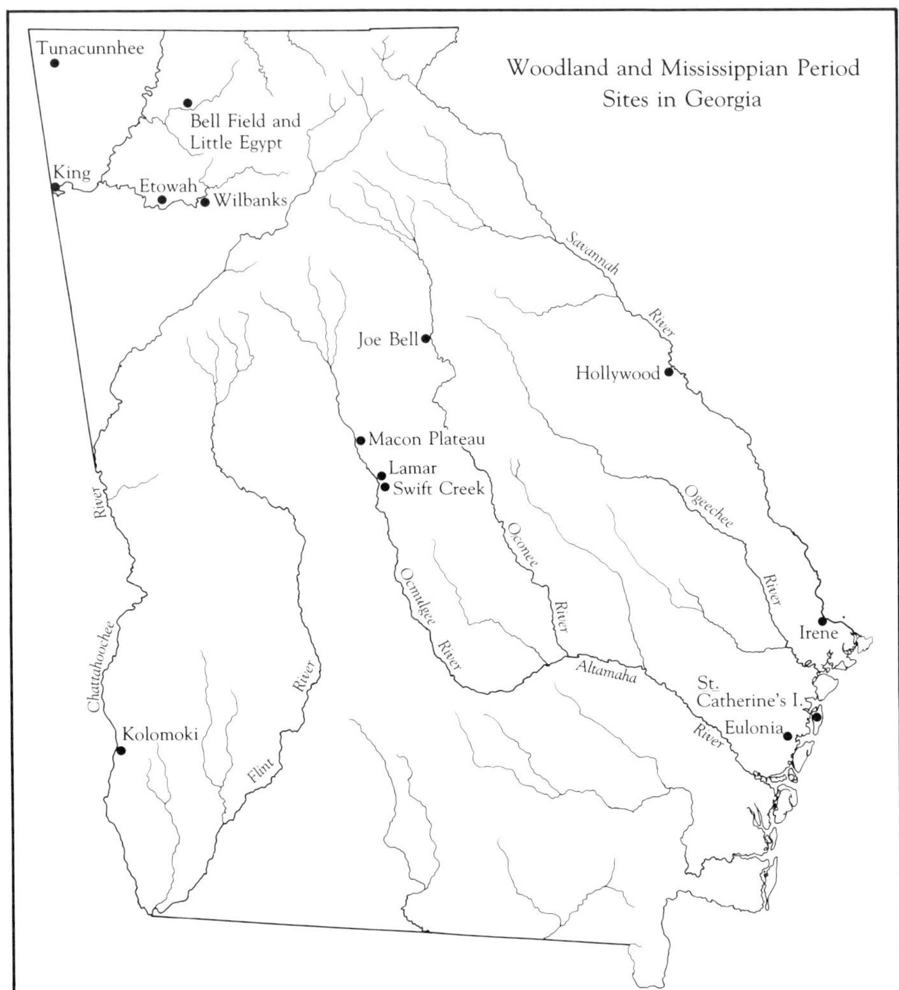

Woodland Period: 1000 B.C.–A.D. 800

North American pottery making begins near the end of the Archaic Period in Georgia. During the Woodland Period, pottery technical advancements took place. Elaborate burial ceremonies as well as the need for utilitarian objects brought new opportunities for artistic expression in this medium. The malleability of unfired clay lent itself to decoration often applied with a paddle [1]. Stylized designs were carved into the paddle, which was then pressed onto the wet surface of the clay vessel. These surface decorations, known as complicated stamps, included fabric-like check and curvilinear and rectangular motifs; each type of design changed over time and varied regionally.

The Weeden Island culture in southwest Georgia produced sophisticated ceramic forms, such as the Kolomoki bird/owl effigy vessel [2]. The holes eliminate the possibility of a practical use; presumably the piece had a ceremonial purpose. However, everyday items, such as pipes and other secular ceramics, are often found in grave sites. The relative quality of these objects may indicate the original owner's status in the tribe. Although both the cougar and platform [3, 4] pipes show the maker's skill in carving stone, the sophistication of the cougar suggests that its owner may have had a higher social ranking than did the owner of the simpler platform pipe.

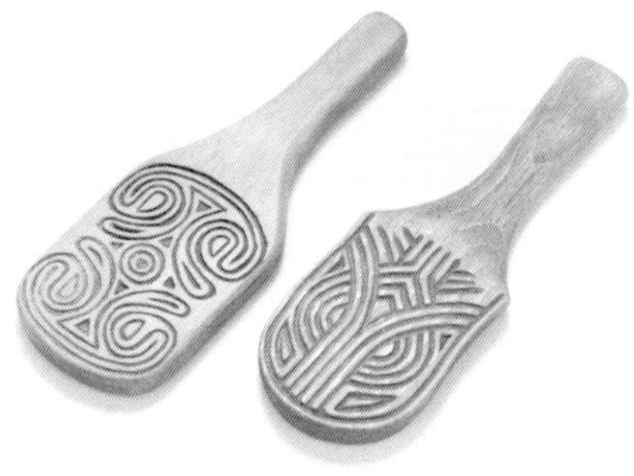

1

1 *Paddle* (Reproduction)

Original stamp from Swift Creek area, Bibb County

Wood

L. 9″

National Park Service, Ocmulgee National Monument

This design, the Swift Creek Complicated Stamp, was originally produced by Woodland Indians on the Ocmulgee River around A.D. 200.

2 *Bird/Owl Effigy Vessel,* A.D. 200–500

Kolomoki Site, Kolomoki Creek, Early County

Ceramic

H. 9″, W. 6″

References: Sears, *Excavations at Kolomoki, Final Report*, 1956, 112; Dickens, et al., *Of Sky and Earth, Art of the Southeastern Indians*, Fig. 106.

Kolomoki Mounds Museum, Georgia Department of Natural Resources, Parks and Historic Sites

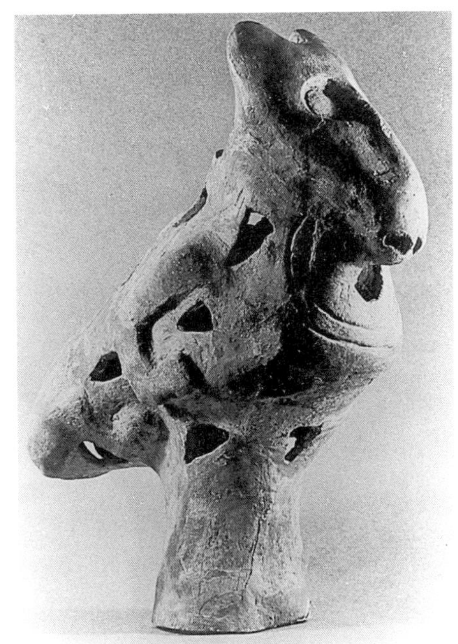

2

3 *Cougar Effigy Pipe*, A.D. 300

North Georgia

Stone

H. 4¼″, W. 8″, D. 1½″

Description: Pipe carved in the form of a cougar with tail carved behind body; head has broken off

Department of Anthropology, The University of Georgia

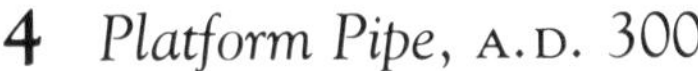

4 *Platform Pipe*, A.D. 300

Tunacunnhee Site, Dade County

Ground stone

H. 2″, W. 4½″, D. 1½″

References: Jefferies, *The Tunacunnhee Site: Evidence of Hopewell Interaction in Northwest Georgia*, 1976, 60.

Department of Anthropology, The University of Georgia

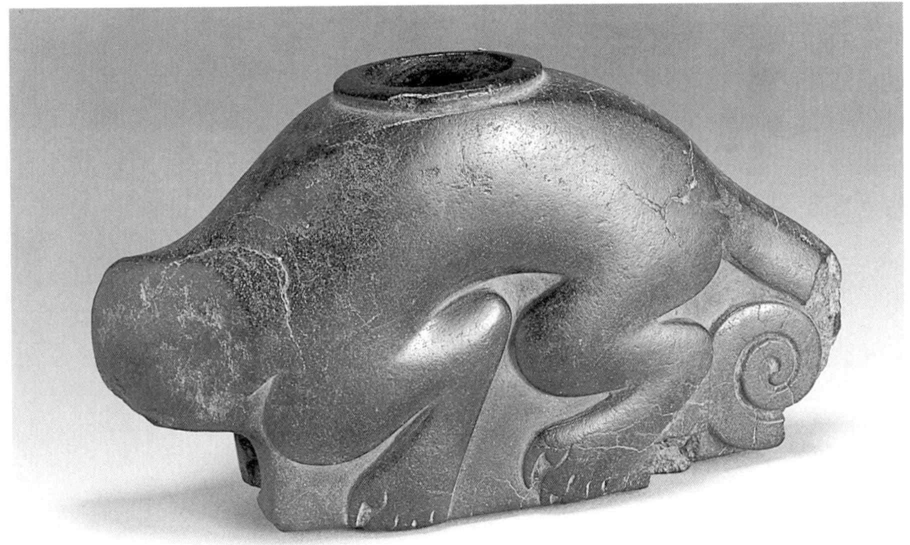

3

Early Mississippian Period, A.D. 800–1300

By A.D. 800, a profound economic and social change, based on the cultivation of corn and beans, occurred in Indian lifestyle. This new type of Southeastern Indian culture was known as Mississippian. Intrinsic to this new culture were large permanent villages built around ceremonial mounds. These villages were stable and therefore provided the organized labor needed to successfully cultivate corn, squash, bean, and pumpkin crops.

As the Indians became more settled and their towns grew, their society became organized into complex chiefdoms whose leaders inherited their positions of power. Mississippian villages and towns were built along

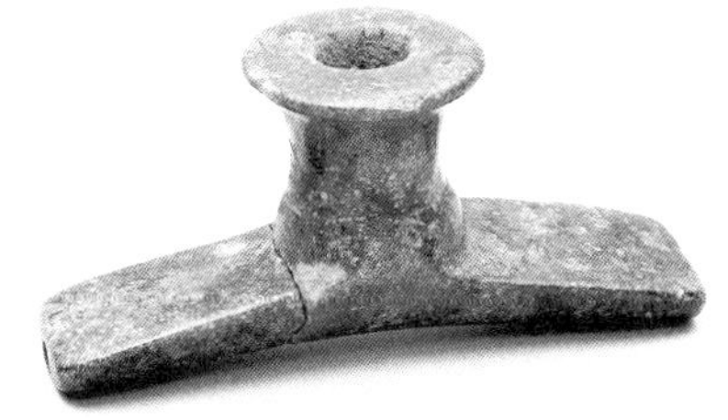

4

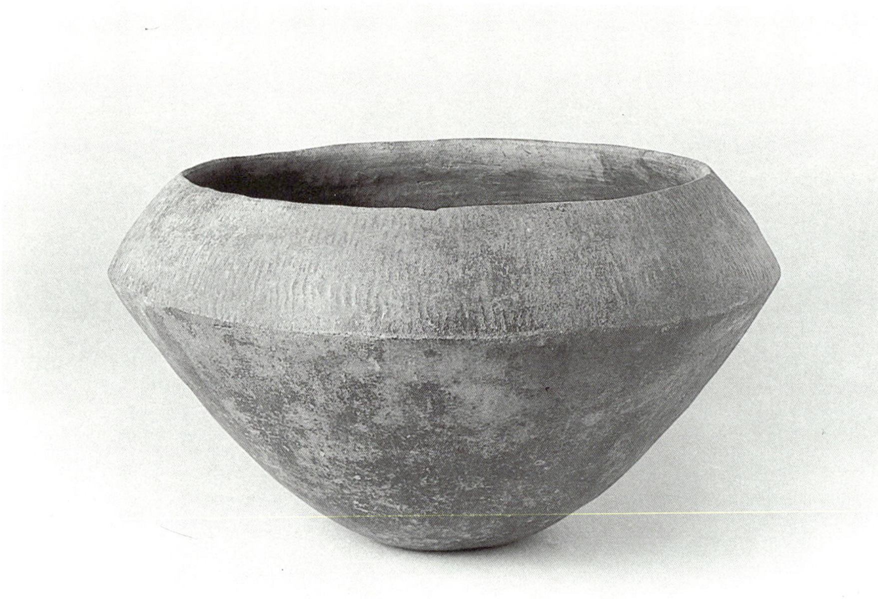

5

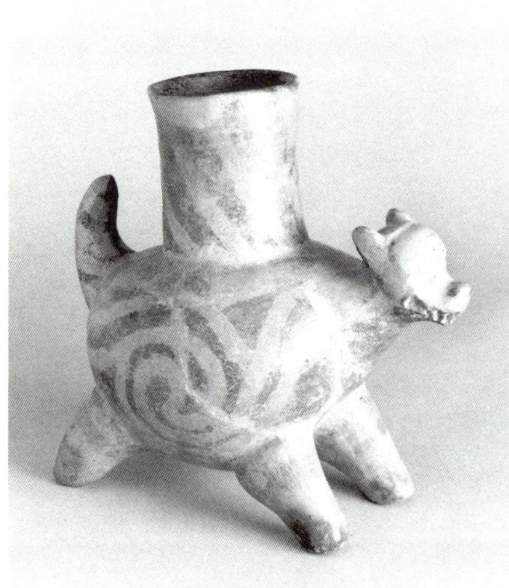

6

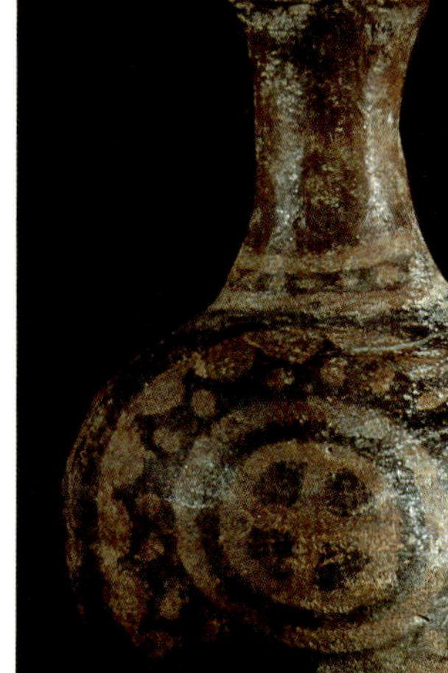

7

rivers and creeks where alluvial soil could be easily worked with primitive tools. Several archaeological sites from the early Mississippian period exist in Georgia, such as Ocmulgee and Etowah.

Accomplished potters, the Mississippian Indians added many new ceramic forms to those of the Woodland era, including plates, cazuela bowls [5], bottles [7], and jars with handles. They also introduced new techniques of decoration such as incising, modeling [8], and painting. One of these, the process of negative painting [6, 7], involved applying a resist or melted wax onto a ceramic form. A motif was incised through the wax layer so that paint could pass through it to the underlying surface; after the "negative" or waxed area was scratched away, a painted image remained.

Burial objects found in northwest Georgia sites, such as Etowah and Wilbanks, reflect the complexities of Mississippian culture. Society at the Etowah mound and village site was at its peak around 1300, when repoussé copper plates [9–10] were worn by officials in the chiefdom. Graphic depictions of priests, warriors, and civic leaders were impressed into the copper with wooden or bone tools. The earspool [12], worn by one of these leaders, as well as the monolithic axe [13], were emblems of civic or religious rank during the Mississippian culture.

5 *Cazuela Bowl*, A.D. 1300

Eulonia Site, McIntosh County

Ceramic

H. 6¼", Diam. 11½"

Department of Anthropology, The University of Georgia

6 *Dog Effigy Vessel*, A.D. 1300

Lower Chattahoochee River area, near Columbus, Muscogee County

Ceramic, painted

H. 10¼", W. 7½", D. 11½"

References: Exhibited in the 1940s, National Museum of Natural History, Smithsonian Institution

The Columbus Museum of Arts and Science

7 *Earthen Bottle*, A.D. 1300

Hollywood Mound, Savannah River, Richmond County

Ceramic, painted

H. 10″, Diam. 7″

References: Thomas, "Report on the Mound Exploration, BAE," 323.

National Museum of Natural History, Smithsonian Institution

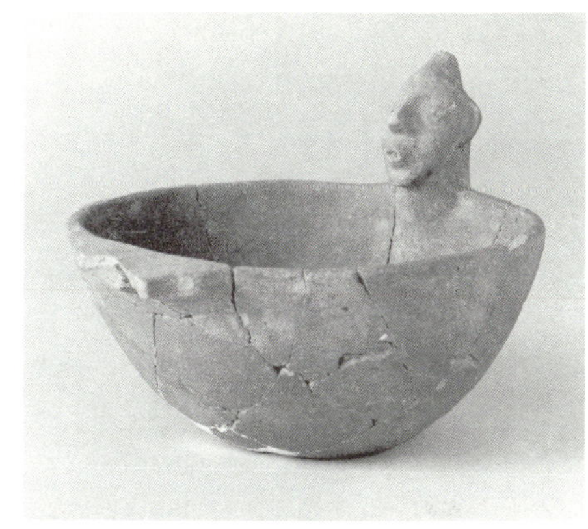

8

8 *Effigy Rim Bowl*, A.D. 1300–1400

Bell Field Site, Coosawattee River, Murray County

Shell-tempered ceramic

H. 5½″, W. 7″, D. 7¼″

References: Kelly, *Explorations at Bell Field, Mound and Village*, Season 1965, 1966, 1967, 1968, 75.

Department of Anthropology, The University of Georgia

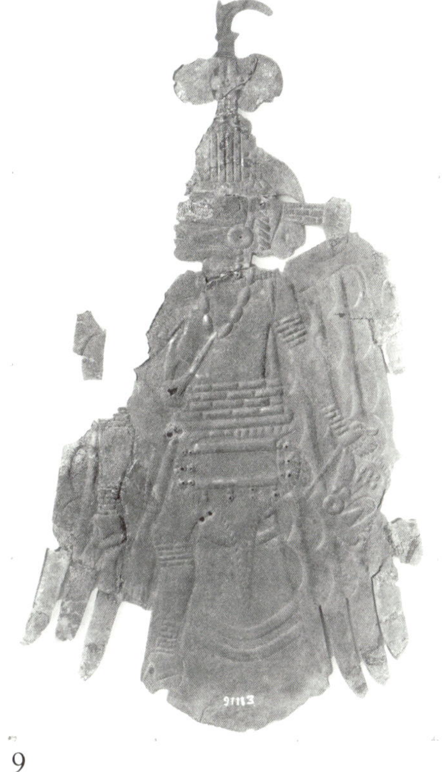

9

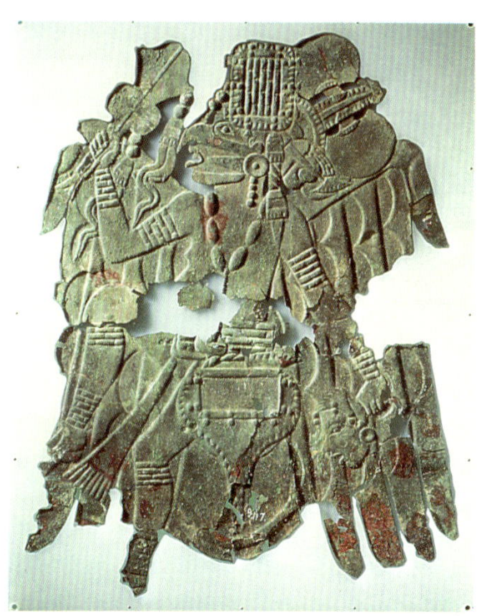

10

9 *Repoussé Copper Plate*, A.D. 1000–1300

Etowah Mounds, Bartow County

Copper

H. 15⅜″, W. 8¼″

References: U.S.N.M. Report, 1896, 501, Fig. 150.

National Museum of Natural History, Smithsonian Institution

10 *Repoussé Copper Plate*, A.D. 1000–1300

Etowah Mounds, Bartow County

Copper

H. 13″, W. 10 1/16″

References: U.S.N.M. Report, 1896, 500, Pl. 59; BAE, Twelfth Annual Report, (1890–1891), Pl. XVI.

National Museum of Natural History, Smithsonian Institution

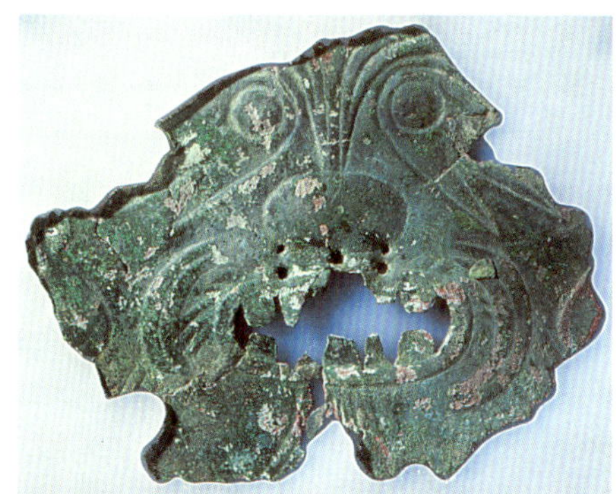

11

11 *Repoussé Copper Plate*, A.D. 1300

Hollywood Mound, Savannah River, Richmond County

Copper

H. 3 9/16", W. 4½"

National Museum of Natural History, Smithsonian Institution

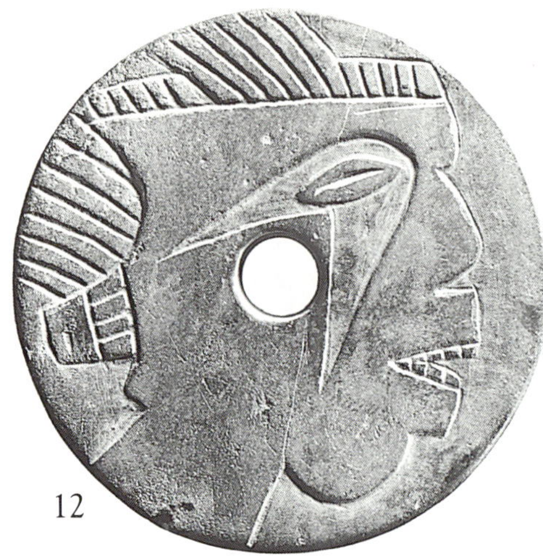

12

12 *Earspool*, A.D. 1300–1400

Wilbanks Site, Cherokee County

Tan claystone

Diam. 2 3/16"

National Museum of Natural History, Smithsonian Institution

13 *Monolithic Axe Head*, A.D. 1300–1400

Ball Ground, Cherokee County

Stone

H. ½", W. 7", L. 11½"

References: *The Waring Papers*, ed. Stephen Williams, 1968, 78–86.

National Museum of Natural History, Smithsonian Institution

13

Late Mississippian Period, A.D. 1300–1600

Ceramics of this later period reflect the influence of the Lamar culture, which flourished in the northern half of the region now known as Georgia, during 1400–1700. Two ceramic forms are characteristic of the Lamar culture: large jars with complicated stamped decoration [14] and cazuela bowls with incised decoration restricted to the rim [16].

Badges indicating civil rank and decorative items of costume were buried with Indians of high status. Pictorial representations were now carved on marine shell rather than repoussé copper plates. Conch shell gorgets incised with stylized serpents, animals, or human faces were believed to have been worn around the neck and were most frequently buried with women and children.

14 *Jar*, 1300–1400

Irene Site, Savannah River, Chatham County

Ceramic

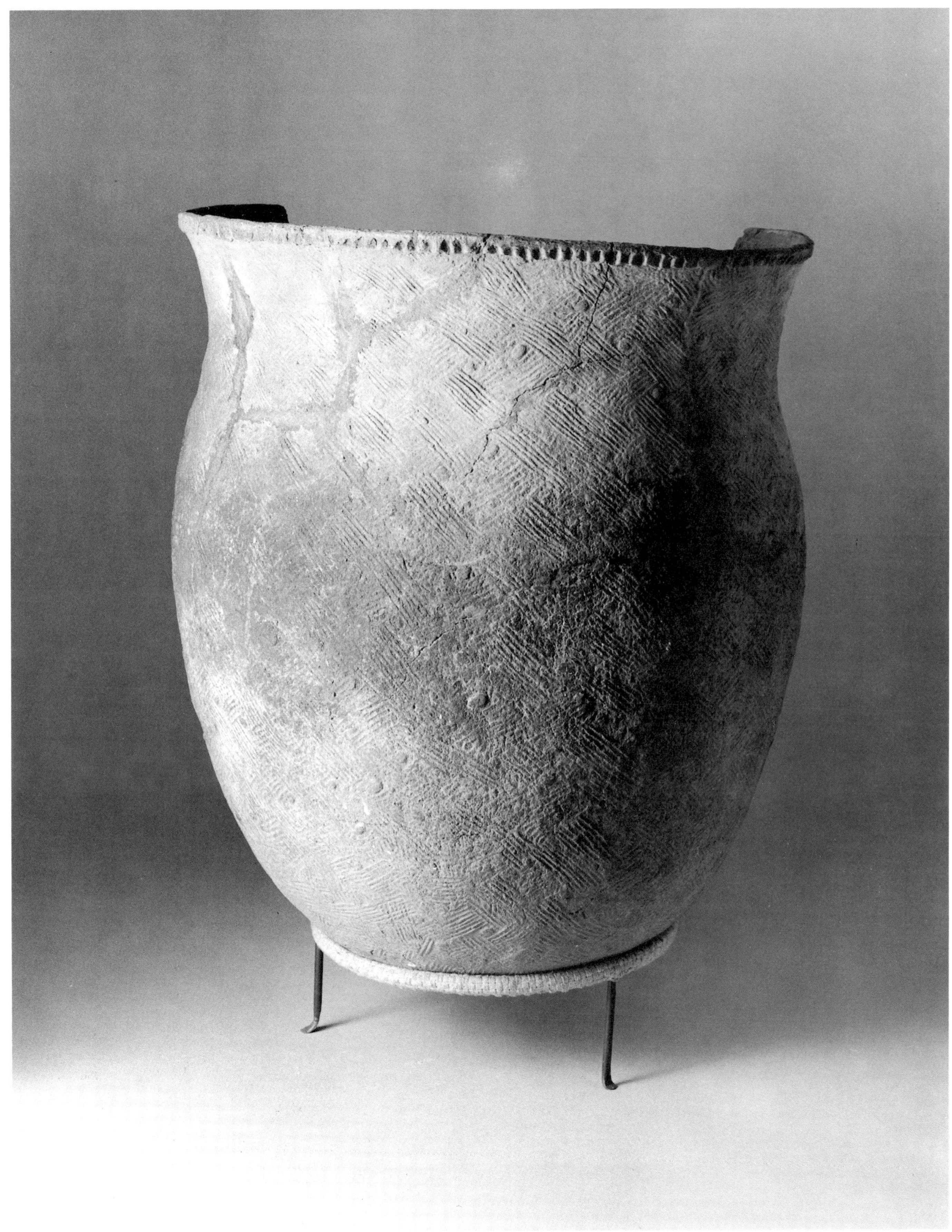

14

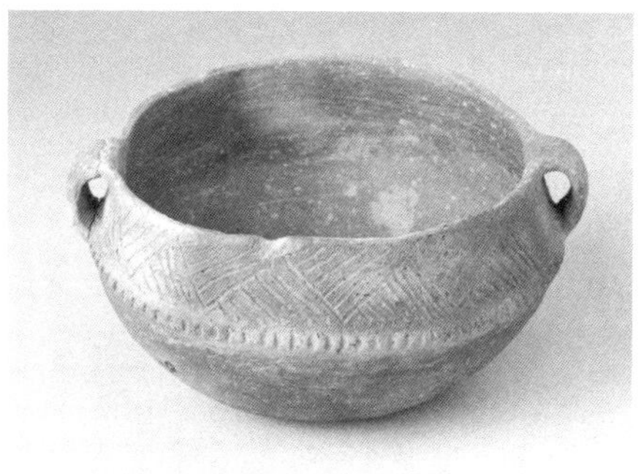

15

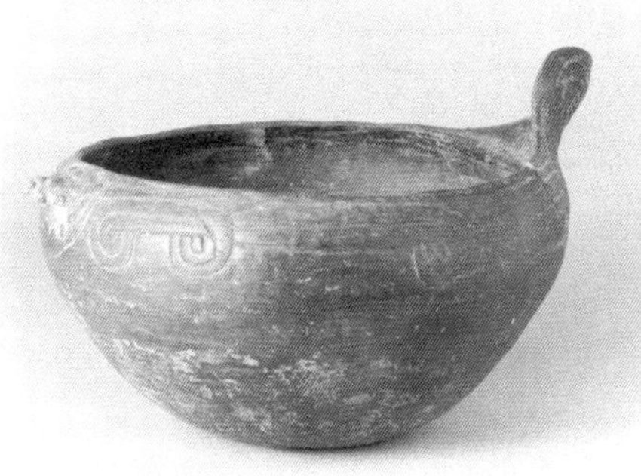

16

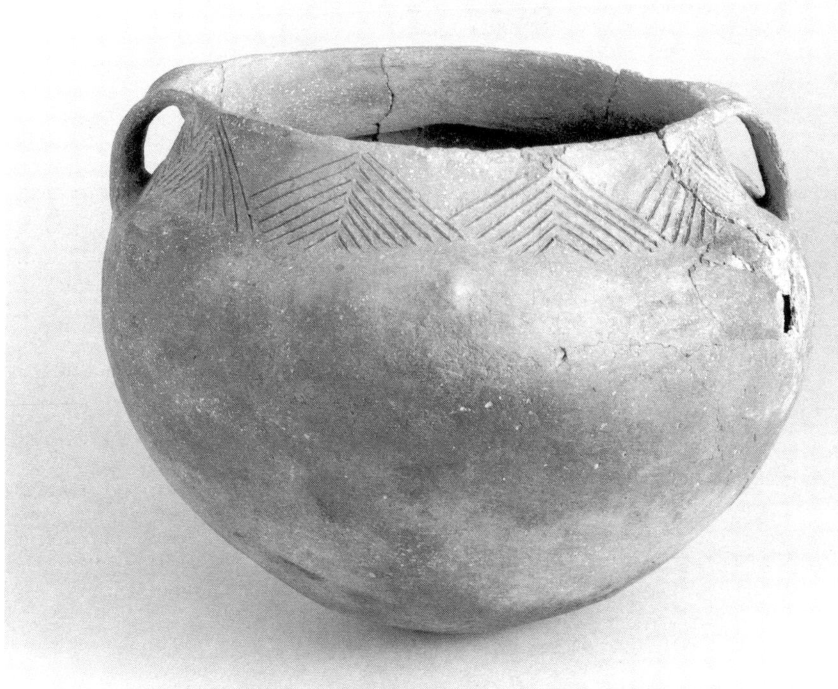

17

H. 17″, Diam. 14″

Description: Vessel with characteristics of the early Lamar phase, pinched folded rim, and Irene complicated stamp

References: Caldwell and McCann, *Irene Mound Site, Chatham County, Georgia.*

Department of Anthropology, The University of Georgia

15 *Bowl*, 1500–1600

King Site, Floyd County

Ceramic

H. 3⅛″, Diam. 6½″

Description: Vessel decorated with incising and punctation; strap handles.

Collection of Mr. Harold King

16 *Cazuela Bowl*, 1500–1600

Little Egypt Site, Coosawattee River, Murray County

Ceramic

H. 7¼″, Diam. 11½″

Description: Effigy bowl in the form of a conch shell with Lamar bold incising around the rim

References: Hally, *Archaeological Investigation of the Little Egypt Site*, 1979.

Department of Anthropology, The University of Georgia

17 *Frog Effigy Jar*, 1500–1600

Little Egypt Site, Coosawattee River, Murray County

Shell-tempered ceramic

H. 6½″, Diam. 9″

Description: Incised rim, legs and nose of a frog modeled on the shoulder

References: Hally, *Archaeological Investigation of the Little Egypt Site*, 1979.

Department of Anthropology, The University of Georgia

18 *Human Effigy Bottle*, 1500–1600

Little Egypt Site, Coosawattee River, Murray County

Shell-tempered ceramic

H. 5¾″, Diam. 4″

Description: Bottle with four-lobed body and effigy human head

References: Hally, *Archaeological Investigation of the Little Egypt Site*, 1979.

Department of Anthropology, The University of Georgia

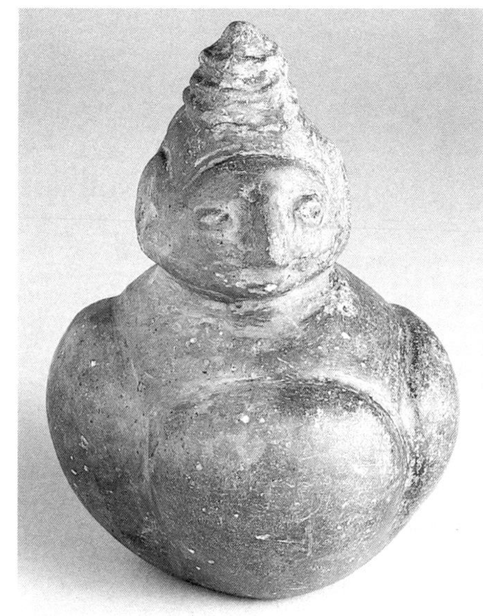

18

19 *Gorget*, 1500–1600

Little Egypt Site, Coosawattee River, Murray County

Conch shell

H. 4½", W. 5"

Description: Incised design of rattlesnake on interior of shell

References: Hally, *Archaeological Investigation of the Little Egypt Site*, 1979.

Department of Anthropology, The University of Georgia

20 *Gorget*, 1500–1600

King Site, Floyd County

Conch shell

Diam. 3 13/16"

Description: Incised design of rattlesnake on interior of shell

Collection of Mr. Harold King

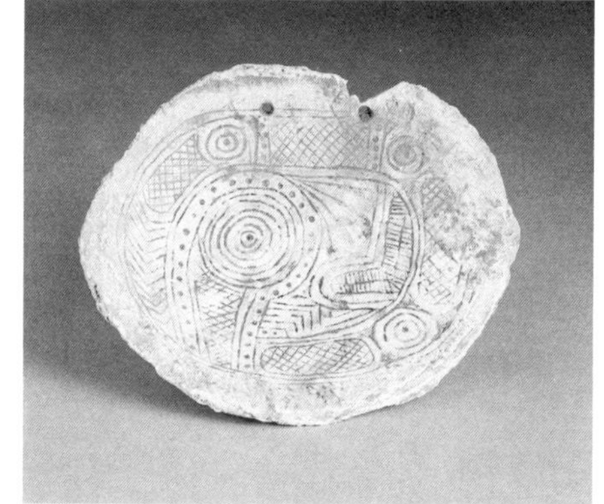

19

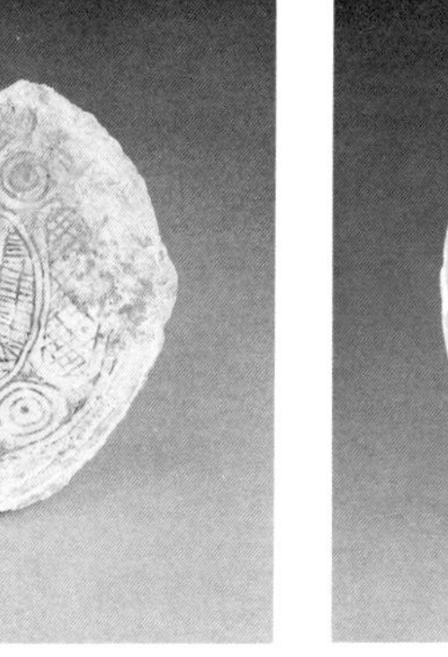

20

21 *Death Mask*, 1500–1600

Little Egypt Site, Coosawattee River, Murray County

Conch shell

H. 7", W. 6", D. 1½"

Description: Pear-shaped gorget; decorated with a stylized face carved in relief.

References: Hally, *Archaeological Investigation of the Little Egypt Site*, 1980.

Department of Anthropology, The University of Georgia

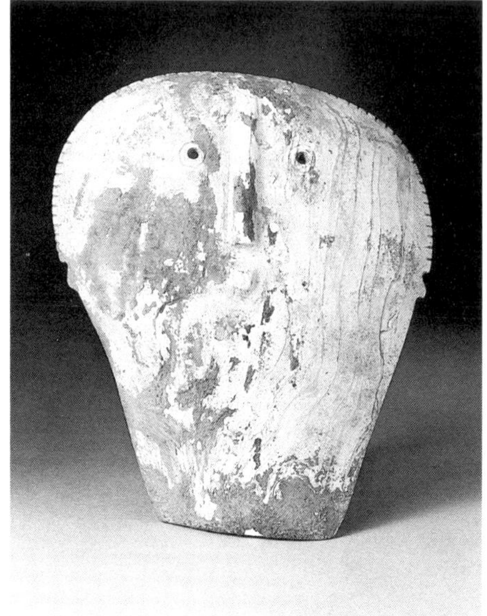

21

Spanish Missions in Georgia, 1565–1683

As early as 1565, the Spanish in Saint Augustine, Florida, began establishing a series of missions along the southeastern coast, from the North Edisto River in South Carolina to the Altamaha River in Georgia. This region became known as the Guale.

The missionaries attempted to convert the Guale Indians to Christianity, but the Indians initially

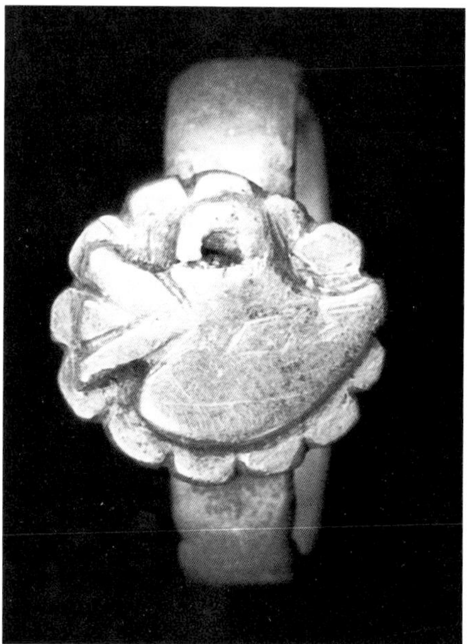

22

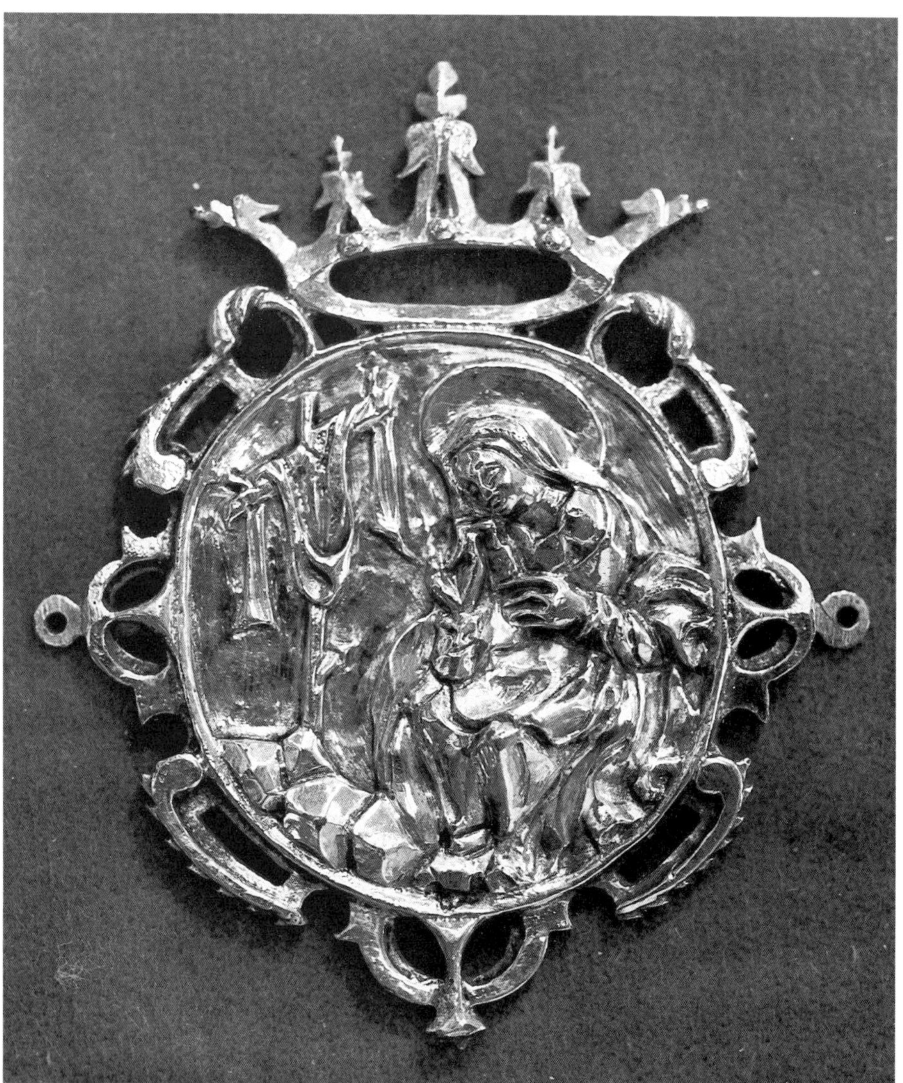

23

resisted. Theirs was an established chiefdom system with centralized leadership and a trade network that stretched into Georgia's interior via the Savannah and Altamaha rivers. Correspondence between the missionaries and civil authorities under Spain's Philip II proves that the Spanish had more than sacred goals in mind (Jones, "The Ethnohistory of the Guale Coast through 1684," 178–210). They needed the Indians to produce food and to provide labor. The Spanish made constant demands upon the Guale, and, as a result, the two cultures were in continual conflict. The Guale Indians rebelled against the Franciscan missionaries from 1575 to the end of Spanish dominion in the 1680s.

During the period of Spanish control, the Guale population declined because of epidemics and fighting with neighboring Indians as well as with the Spanish. By 1675, a large segment of the waning Christian Guale population was located on Saint Catherine's Island. They were concentrated on the southern tip of the island around the mission of Santa Catalina de Guale, which had been established in the 1560s. After the English settled South Carolina in 1670, the British colonists forced the Spanish and Guale to retreat to Saint Augustine. The mission of Santa Catalina de Guale was abandoned after 1683, and by 1689 only 30 Indian families remained on all 14,000 acres of Saint Catherine's Island.

Recently, excavations conducted by the American Museum of Natural History have located several buildings that were part of the mission Santa Catalina de Guale. Archaeological sites have yielded evidence of more than 4000 years of Indian habitation on the island. Imported Spanish artifacts and religious trinkets have been found near the mission church, but these date only from the mid-seventeenth century.

Franciscan churches also served as cemeteries, and hundreds of skeletons of Guale Indians have been found during excavations. Indians were buried so that their arms crossed over their chest and their feet faced the church's altar. Proximity to the altar indicated high social status in the chiefdom. Most of the artifacts exhibited here were excavated from graves; many of the children were found close to the altar. The medallion and ring [22, 23], for example, were presents given by the Franciscans to the Indians, possibly to encourage baptism in the Christian faith (Richard Ahlborn to David H. Thomas, 31 January 1984). The graves of the poor were always placed near the walls of the church; these contained relatively few grave goods, all of which were crude and probably made by the lower-class Indians themselves [24, 25].

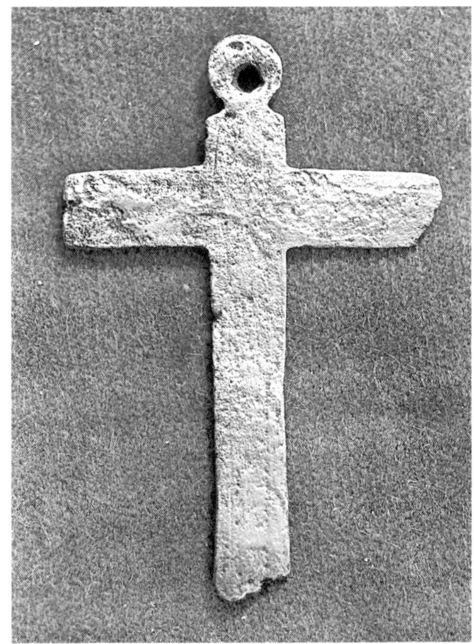

24

22 *Ring*, ca. 1566–1680

European; excavated in Santa Catalina de Guale Mission Site, Saint Catherine's Island, Liberty County

Cast metal

Diam. ½″

Description: "Sacred Heart of Jesus," asymmetrical heart with flame and dagger iconography; based on designs seen in Jesuit trade items of the sixteenth century

Department of Anthropology, American Museum of Natural History

23 *Medallion*, ca. 1566–1680

European; excavated in Santa Catalina de Guale Mission Site, Saint Catherine's Island, Liberty County

Gold-plated silver

H. 2″, W. 2¼″

Description: Loops on the sides possibly indicate clothing ornament; the mourning Virgin beside the rustic cross with Jesus' shroud is taken from sixteenth-century iconography.

Department of Anthropology, American Museum of Natural History

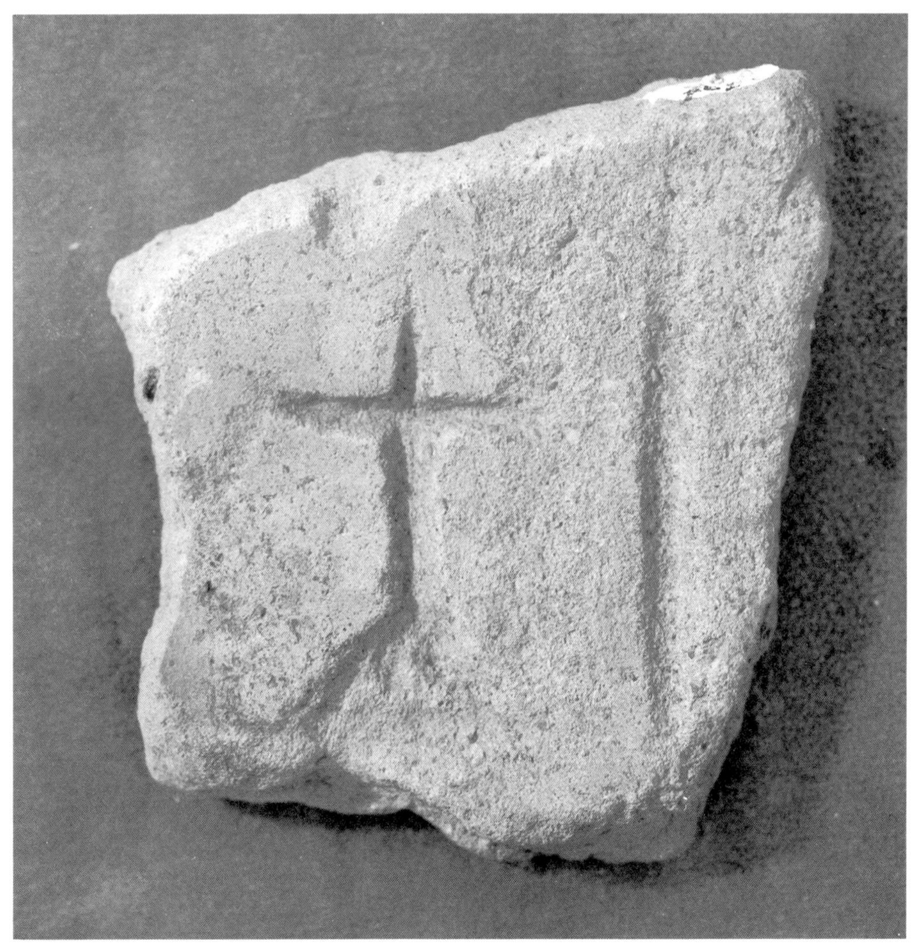

25

24 *Cross*, ca. 1566–1680

European, excavated in Santa Catalina de Guale Mission Site, Saint Catherine's Island, Liberty County

Copper

H. 1¾″, W. 1 3/16″

Department of Anthropology, American Museum of Natural History

25 *Sherd with Cross*, ca. 1566–1680

Guale, excavated in Santa Catalina de

Guale Mission Site, Saint Catherine's Island, Liberty County

Ceramic

H. 2", W. 2 3/16"

Department of Anthropology, American Museum of Natural History

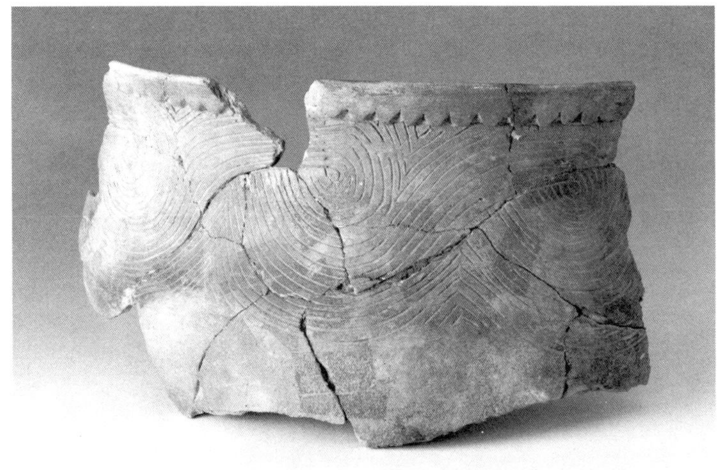

26

Late Lamar/Pre-Colonial Period: 1400–1733

European contact had a devastating effect on aboriginal cultures in Georgia: whole regions of the state were depopulated; mound building ceased; and chiefdoms and other political organizations disappeared. Ceramics production, however, continued to thrive. Two vessels from the Joe Bell site on the Oconee River (ca. 1630)—featuring skillful, evenly spaced incising and meticulously smoothed surfaces—exemplify the fineness of this craft [26, 27].

The growing population of Charleston, South Carolina, settled in 1670, brought traders from that region into Georgia. Soon the Indians became dependent upon guns, woolen cloth, hatchets, knives, and other European-made goods. An interesting product of this cultural exchange was Colono-Indian ware—vessels combining European forms with indigenous decorative patterns [28, 29]. The Indian pitcher [29], found on Colonel's Island, Liberty County, for example, reflects the influence of a common utilitarian form brought by European settlers to the Indians.

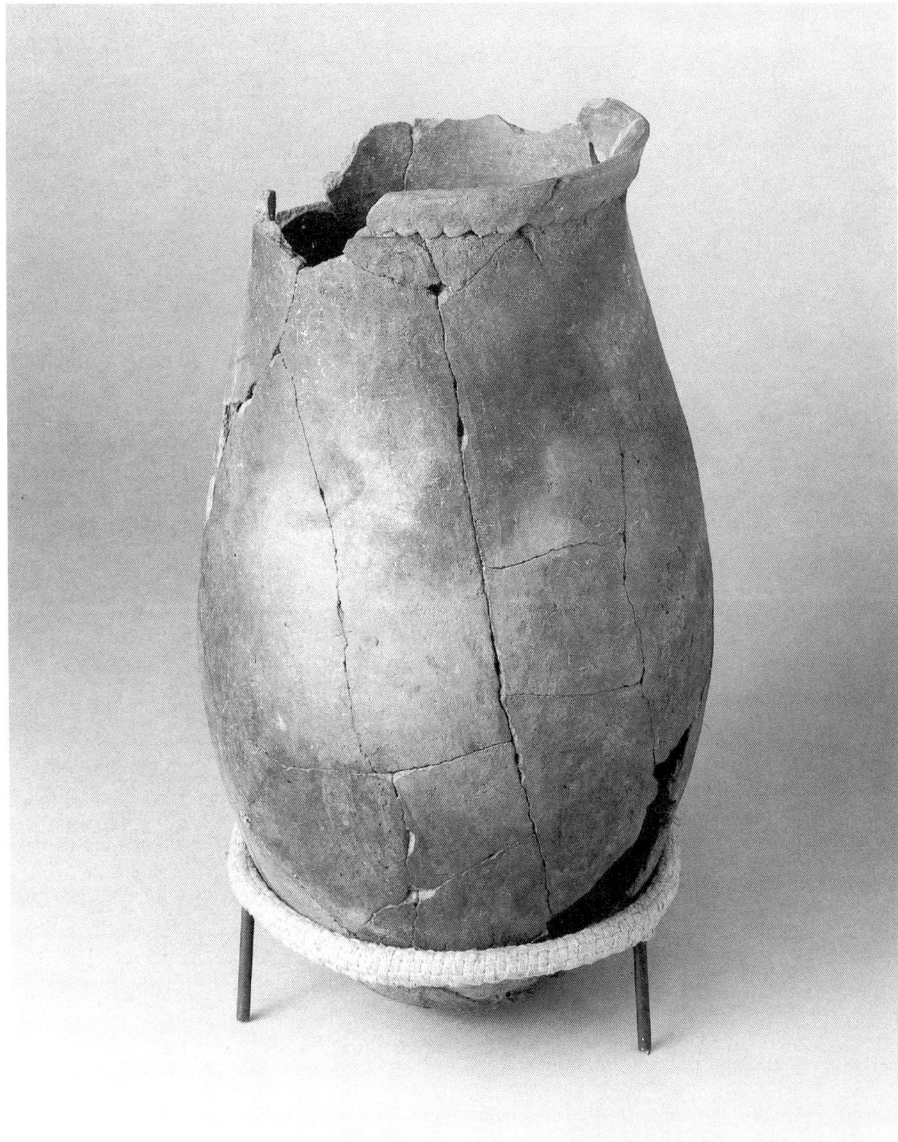

27

26 *Fragment*, ca. 1630–1650

Joe Bell Site, Oconee River, Morgan County

Ceramic

Description: Combination of Lamar bold incising and folded pinched rim characteristics

Department of Anthropology, The University of Georgia

27 *Jar*, ca. 1630–1650

Joe Bell Site, Oconee River, Morgan County

H. 12⅛″, Diam. 7⅛″

Description: Lamar plain jar with folded pinched rim

Department of Anthropology, The University of Georgia

28 *Pitcher/Jug*, late seventeenth century

Colonel's Island, Liberty County

Ceramic

H. 8″, Diam. 7½″

Description: Guale-made vessel with Lamar-like incising and European influenced applied handle

The Columbus Museum of Arts and Science

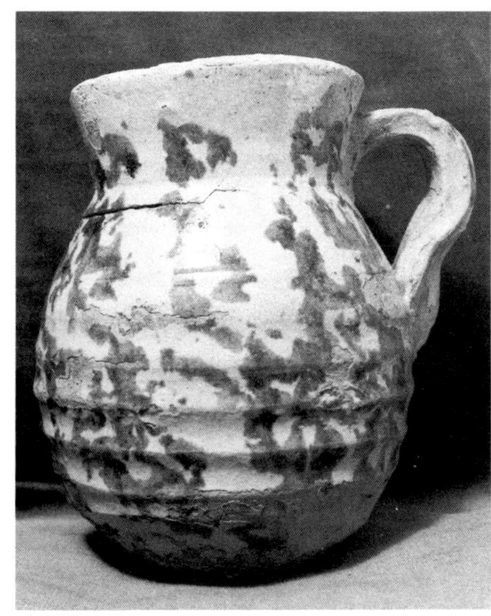

28

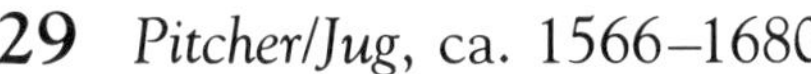

29 *Pitcher/Jug*, ca. 1566–1680

European; excavated in Santa Catalina de Guale Mission Site, Saint Catherine's Island, Liberty County

Tin-enameled earthenware

Diam. 4 9/16″, Diam. 4⅜″

Department of Anthropology, American Museum of Natural History

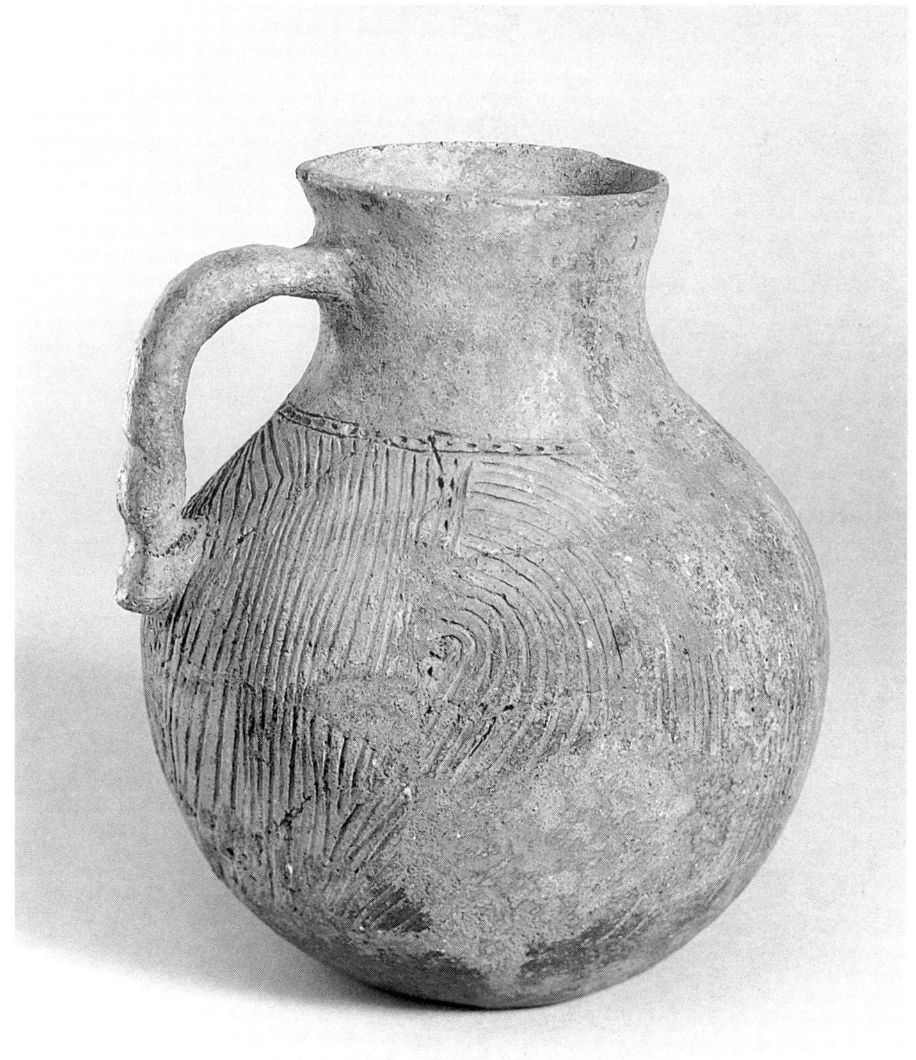

29

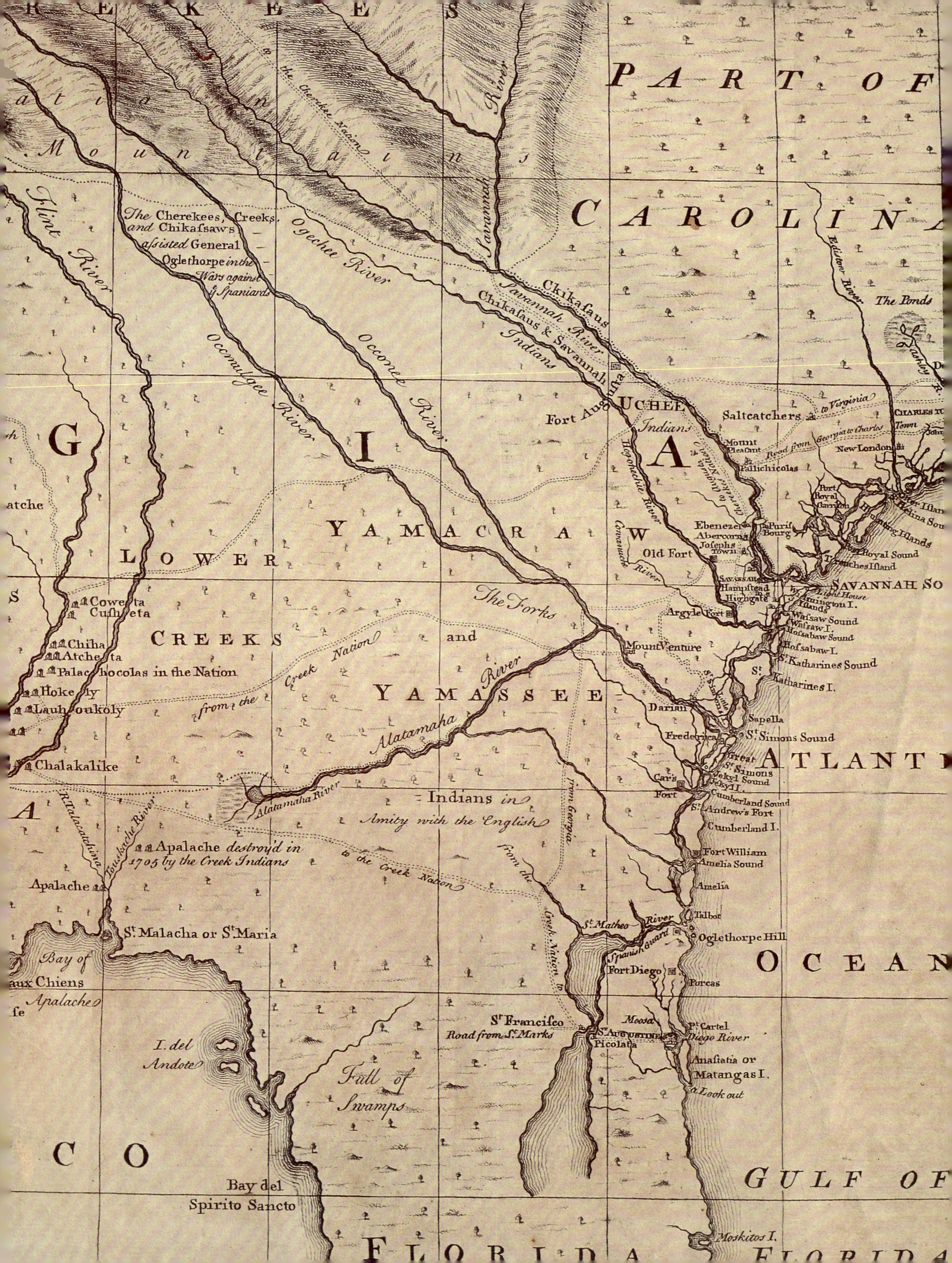

PART OF
CAROLINA
G I A
Mountains
The Cherekees, Creeks, and Chikasaws assisted General Oglethorpe in the Wars against ye Spaniards
Flint River
Ogechee River
Savannah River
Ocmulgee River
Oconee River
Chikasaus
Savannah River
Chikasaus & Savannah Indians
Fort Augusta
UCHEE Indians
Saltcatchers
to Virginia
Road from Georgia to Charles Town
Charles Town
Edisto River
The Ponds
Mount Pleasant
Pallachicolas
New London
Port Royal Garrison
Ebenezer
Abercorn
Josephs Town
Purisbourg
Old Fort
Savannah
Hampstead
Highgate
Argyle Fort
Royal Sound
Trenches Island
SAVANNAH SO
Warsaw Sound
Warsaw I.
Horsabaw Sound
Ossabaw I.
St. Katharines Sound
St. Katharines I.
YAMACRAW
LOWER CREEKS and YAMASSEE
The Forks
Coweta
Cussiteta
Chiha
Atcheta
Palachocolas in the Nation
Hokely
Lauhoukoly
Chalakalike
from the Creek Nation
Alatamaha River
Mount Venture
Darian
Sapella
Frederica
St. Simons Sound
Great St. Simons
Jekyl Sound
Jekyl I.
Car's Fort
Cumberland Sound
St. Andrew's Fort
Cumberland I.
ATLANTI
Indians in Amity with the English
Apalache destroy'd in 1705 by the Creek Indians
Apalache
R. Talacatchina
Tauskeche River
to the Creek Nation
from Georgia
from the Creek Nation
Fort William
Amelia Sound
Amelia
Talbot
St. Matheo River
Spanish Guard
Oglethorpe Hill
Fort Diego
Porcas
OCEAN
St. Malacha or St. Maria
Bay of aux Chiens
Apalache
St. Francisco
Road from St. Marks
Moosa
St. Augustine
Picolata
Pt. Cartel
Diego River
Anastatia or Matangas I.
a Look out
I. del Andote
Full of Swamps
CO
Bay del Spirito Sancto
GULF OF
FLORIDA
Moskitos I.

1733–1790

The second section of the exhibition chronicles Georgia's struggle for stability, from the time of Oglethorpe's arrival in February 1733 through the stagnant period of the English Trusteeship and then through 25 more promising years of royal governorships. The Revolutionary War ended with the Treaty of Paris in 1783. The signing of the United States Constitution in May 1787 officially heralded the birth of the new republic with democratic ideals and new American leaders, most of whom had emerged as a result of military victories during the war.

This section, however, includes activity up to 1790 in order to consider the impact of these historical events upon the stylistic development of Georgia's decorative arts. Scholars generally associate the dawning of the new nation with the end of complete stylistic dependency on London. In the South, though, conservative tastes for British influences in furniture and silver, the Queen Anne and Chippendale styles, continued until about 1790. In the North, locally made furniture boasting neoclassical designs typical of the new Federal period were seen by the 1780s.

The scarcity of Georgia artifacts made prior to 1790 demonstrates the extent to which Georgia lagged behind neighboring colonies. Georgia was the youngest of the southern colonies—100 years younger than Maryland and 50 years younger than South Carolina. Furthermore, the first 20 years of Georgia's history saw little population growth or economic development, primarily because of Oglethorpe's clumsy leadership and the restrictions enforced under the Trusteeship. Georgia's position as a buffer state for prosperous South Carolina to the north, as well as the combined threat of Spanish Florida to the south and French expansionism from the west, earned the colony a reputation as an inhospitable, even violent, territory. Such conditions provided little incentive for new settlers to relocate. The small population, in turn, did not foster a sufficient clientele to attract skilled craftsmen.

The scarcity of artifacts from 1733–1790 may also be due to the Georgia colonists' preoccupation with providing for basic necessities.

Emanuel Bowen, *A New Map of Georgia, with Part of Carolina, Florida and Louisiana*, 1748. London: John Harris. H. 14⅛", W. 19". Special Collections, The University of Georgia Libraries.

The European settlements that date from this period were faced with eking out a basic existence. For most, life never developed beyond a subsistence level. Settlers had little time for pleasures associated with leisure moments, and accessories which accompanied their day-to-day existence were minimal.

When the Trustees returned Georgia's charter to the Crown in 1752, the economic status of the colony was in serious decline. Under the royal governors, conditions did improve, so that by the time of the Revolution, Savannah had become a busy port town. The construction of a wharf in 1759 to accommodate ocean-going vessels made imported domestic goods more accessible to wealthy Savannahians, who preferred furniture from the Continent and the North to that made by local artisans. Locally made goods would have been purchased primarily by the middle class. Savannah remained in British hands throughout most of the Revolutionary War, ensuring the continued availability of European imports. These circumstances certainly discouraged full-scale local furniture production and, further, the war undoubtedly destroyed much of the indigenous furniture that had been produced along the coast. Later, two fires in Savannah (1796, 1820) devastated many frame houses of the middle class that may have contained locally made furnishings.

In light of the rarity of Georgia-made objects surviving from 1733–1790, selection for this section of the exhibition was based on slightly different criteria than that for other time periods: pieces here, though not necessarily made by Georgia artists and craftsmen, relate to some historical event within the first tumultuous years of Georgia's development.

30 *General James Oglethorpe*, 1785

P. Ireland (n.d.)

London, England

Engraving on paper

H. 9 1/16″, W. 6¾″

Inscription: General James Oglethorpe. Died 30th June 1785 Aged 102 said to be the oldest General in Europe—Sketch'd from Life at the sale of / Dr. Johnson's books Feby 18, 1785 where the Genl was reading a book he had purchased without spectacles—In 1706 he had an / ___ions commission in the Guards & remembered to have shot snipes in Conduit mead where Conduit Street now stands.

Collection of Mr. and Mrs. Henry D. Green

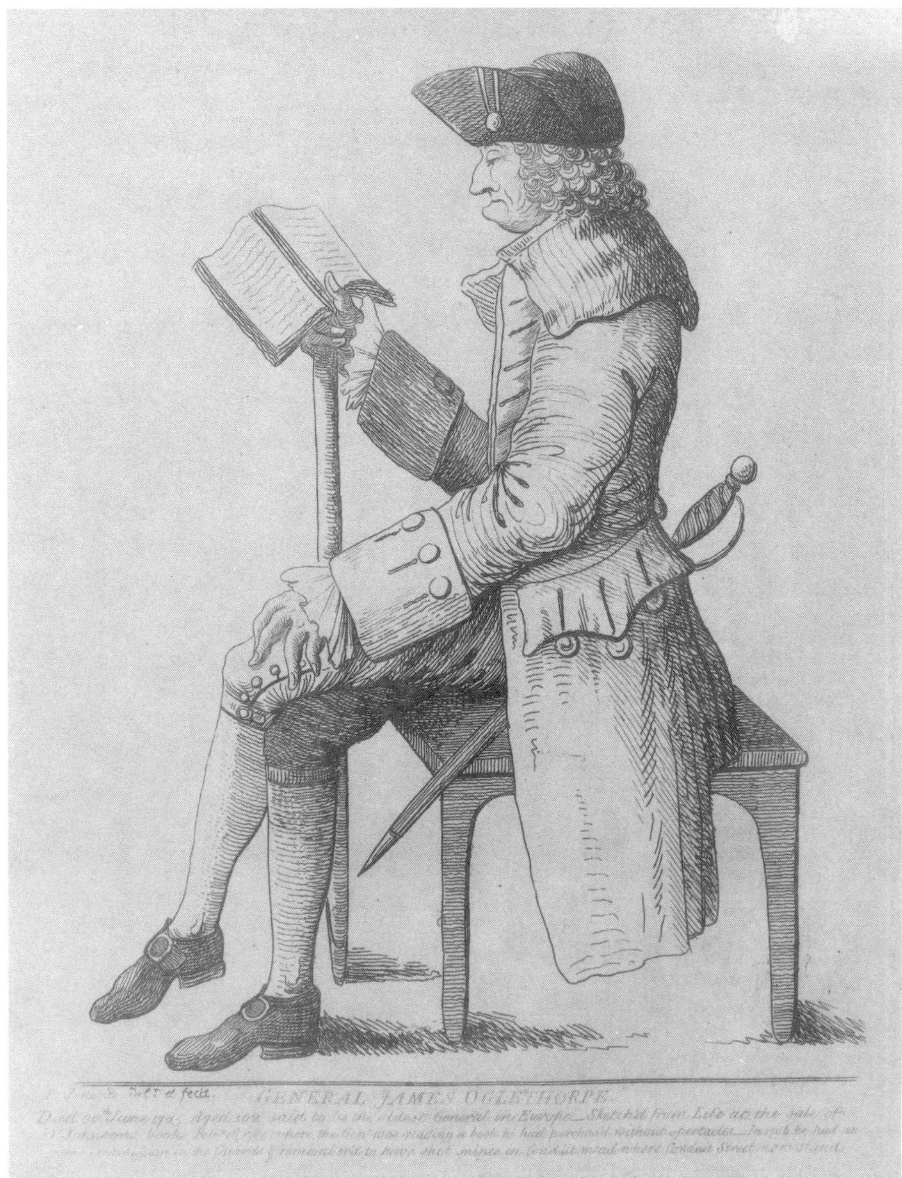

30

James Edward Oglethorpe (1696–1785) had an illustrious military career before his election to Parliament in 1722 as a representative from Surrey. While in Parliament, he investigated the terrible conditions of England's prisons and won the release of thousands of imprisoned debtors. The combination of Oglethorpe's humanitarian fervor and his innate militaristic drive made him the obvious candidate to lead the Trustees' venture to colonial Georgia. Oglethorpe was the only one of the 21 Trustees ever to come to the colony.

Oglethorpe had three major objectives for the new colony: to serve as a military buffer between prosperous South Carolina and the encroaching Spanish, to produce raw materials which England had previously been forced to import, and to open the door to new mission fields among Georgia's native populations. Save for the Battle of Bloody Marsh, his one military victory over the Spanish in 1742, most of his dreams met with discouraging failure. He returned to England in 1743, greatly disheartened. Eight years later, the Trustees decided to give up their charter, returning authority to run the Georgia colony back to the king.

As its inscription indicates, this engraving was executed in London the year of Oglethorpe's death. He continued to cultivate his reputation as a military hero long after his years of active duty. He was a famous character throughout London where it was commonly assumed that he was exceedingly old, in fact 13 years older than his actual age.

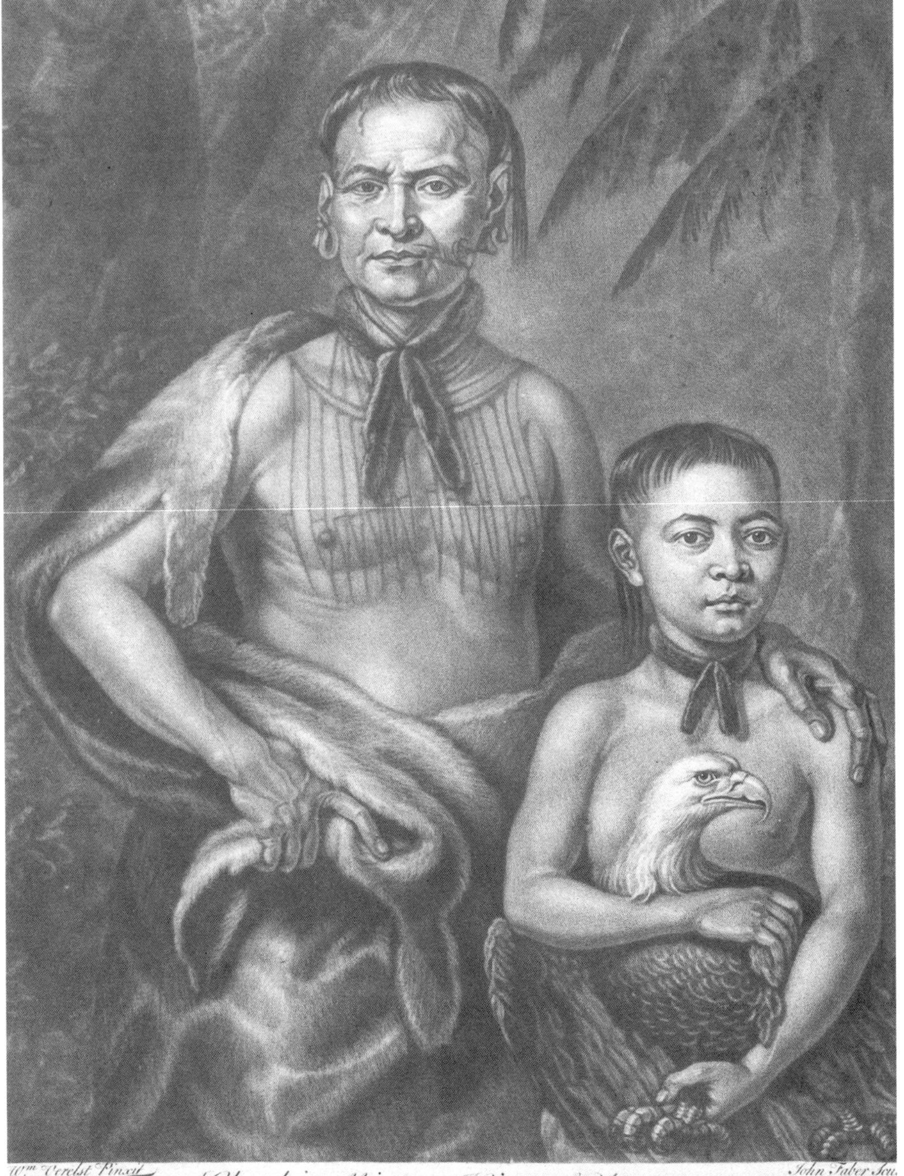

31

31 *Tomo Chachi* [sic], *Mico or King of Yamacraw, and Tooanahoni* [sic] *his Nephew, Son to the Mico of the Etchitas*, 1734–1735

John Faber after William Verelst

London, England

Engraving on paper

H. 14″, W. 10″

References: *Ausführliche Nachrichten*, vol. 1, frontispiece; Jones, *Henry Newman's Salzburger Letterbooks*, 16.

Special Collections, The University of Georgia Libraries

Tomochichi was chief of the Yamacraw Indians, who lived in the Savannah River region and who became an integral part of the early days of the settlement of Georgia. Initial meetings between Oglethorpe and Tomochichi, interpreted by trader John Musgrove, led to a lifetime friendship between the two men. In June 1734, Oglethorpe returned to England and brought Tomochichi, along with his wife, Senauki, and great-nephew, Toonahowi, to meet the Trustees. English artist William Verelst executed this portrait of the chief and his heir. He also painted a well-known scene of Oglethorpe introducing his Indian companions to the Trustees. (The second painting is in the collection of the Henry Francis duPont Winterthur Museum, Wilmington, Delaware.)

Oglethorpe and the Indians returned to Georgia in February 1736. Also on board the ship *Simonds* were groups of Moravians and Salzburgers. Like Oglethorpe, these religious groups considered the chief an admired member of their new communities. A contemporary reported that the Moravians built a house for Tomochichi at his village as well as a house in Savannah, "both in the style of the Moravian house," which means of half-timbered construction (Nichols, *The Early Architecture of Georgia*, 27). One prominent Salzburger, Philip von Reck, mentioned in his journal a visit with Oglethorpe to Tomochichi's house "where he served us pancakes and wine" (Hvidt, *Von Reck's Voyage*, 36). One further example of the Salzburger's regard for the Yamacraw chief was the publication in 1735 of this engraving as a frontispiece in the first volume of

Ausführliche Nachrichten, the published letters of Pastor Bolzius.

Tomochichi died in 1739. Oglethorpe, a pallbearer at the funeral, arranged for the chief to be buried in Savannah according to his wishes.

32 *Artifacts from Fort Frederica*, ca. 1736–1749

Saint Simons Island, Glynn County

a. Scissors
   Iron
   L. 4½″, W. 1″

b. HL Hinge
   Iron
   L. 12″, W. 3½″

c. Table fork with handle
   Iron and ivory
   L. 5″, W. ½″

d. Table fork
   Iron
   L. 6″, W. ½″

National Park Service, Fort Frederica National Monument

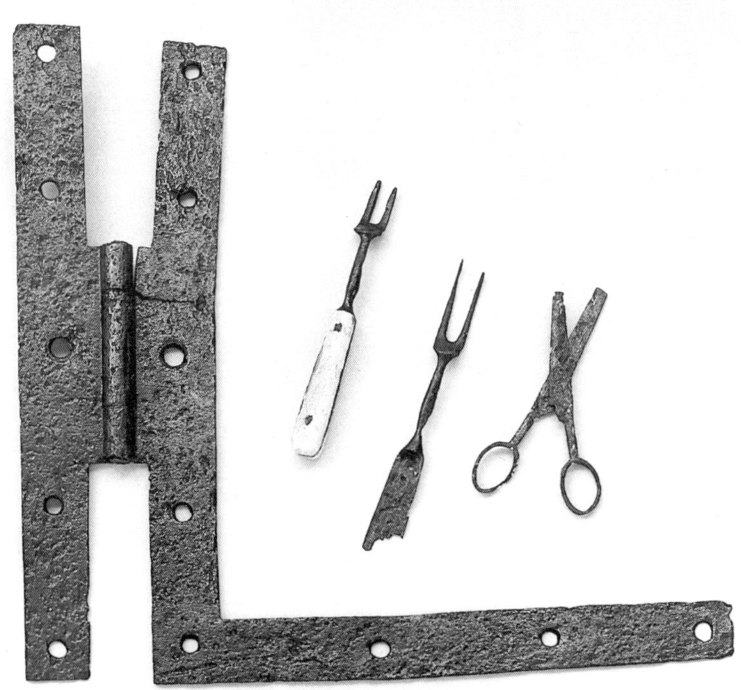

32 a, b, c, d

In 1736, General Oglethorpe laid out the plan for Frederica, named for Frederick, the Prince of Wales and son of George II. The town featured elaborate fortifications against the French and the Spanish. Almost completed in April of that same year, the fort was described in the *South Carolina Gazette* (1 May 1736): "It consists of four Bulwarks, and a Ditch with some Out-Works, frazed round with Cedar Posts, the Works are faced with green Sod, which grows very well . . . ."

Behind the fort grew a thriving town. The first settlers arrived in Frederica in February and March of 1736 and built small huts. According to a contemporary description, "Each Family had a Bower of Palmetto leaves . . . being tight in the hardest Rains, and in regular rows, looked very Pretty" (Nichols, 26). Soon, more substantial, two- and three-story houses of brick, wood, and tabby were constructed, and Frederica began to prosper.

Artifacts such as architectural hardware and European ceramics were found around the sites of several of the known houses in Frederica, such as the John Caldwell House (ca. 1740), the Moore House, (pre–1743), and the Hawkins-Davison House (1736–38).

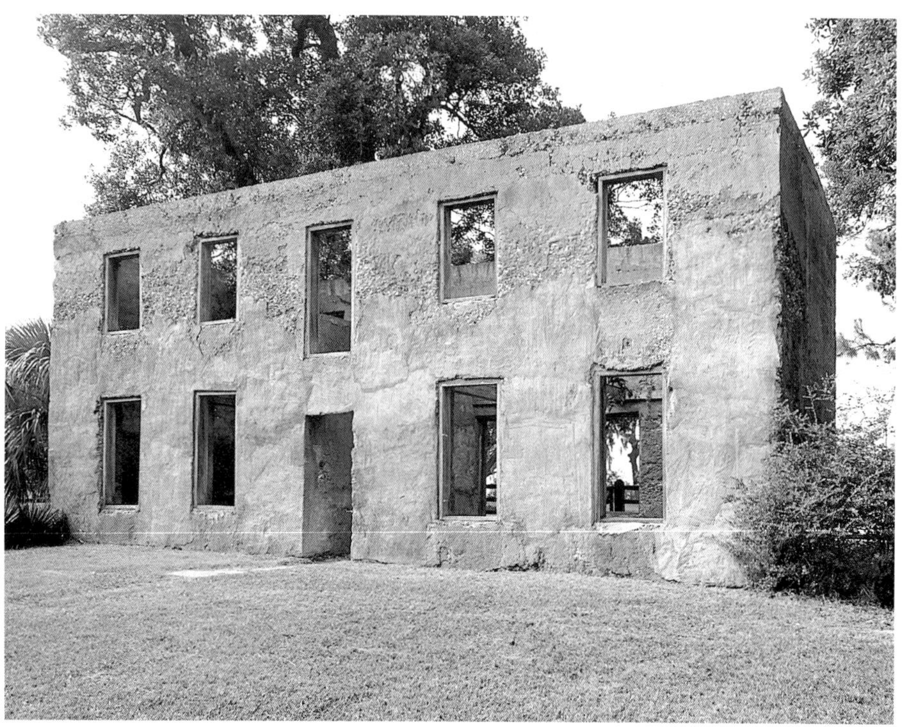

33

While the forks and scissors were imported from England, the HL hinges and shutter hooks were most likely made by the local blacksmiths, possibly by John Harding and his son who were in business in 1740. Thomas Loope, a wheelwright from 1736–43, and Daniel Parnel, a brass founder from 1736–39, prove that furnaces were operating in Frederica and craftsmen were available for producing needed ironwork.

The 1739 War of Jenkin's Ear brought troops to Frederica. General Oglethorpe headquartered his operations against the Spanish here, and the military payroll from the soldiers created new clientele and increased income for local merchants and craftsmen. The defeat of the Spanish at the Battle of Bloody Marsh and the eventual end of the war in 1748 signaled the decline of the town of Frederica, whose economy had begun to rely upon the presence of the regiment. A fire in 1758 destroyed most of the buildings that symbolized the past of the town born of necessity and nurtured by war.

33 *Captain William Horton House*, 1742

Jekyll Island, Glynn County

Tabby, wood, stone

H. 18′, W. 41½′, D. 18′

Description: Two-story tabby ruin; with one standing chimney in east wall, and remains of chimney and hearth on west wall

References: Nichols, *The Architecture of Georgia*, 25, 80; Linley, *The Georgia Catalog*, 23.

Jekyll Island Authority (preservation made possible through the Society of the Colonial Dames of America in the State of Georgia in cooperation with the Jekyll Island State Park Authority)

William Horton was aboard the *Simonds*, along with Oglethorpe, when the ship arrived in Georgia in 1736. A man of some wealth, Horton brought several servants and was granted 500 acres on Jekyll Island by the Trustees. His first house was burned by the Spanish in their retreat from the Battle of Bloody Marsh in 1742. By 1746, Horton either restored the old house or built another.

These ruins reflect several stages of

additions and restoration to the structure. There is evidence that a two-story portico once occupied the south facade. Frame wings were supposedly added after the Revolution, possibly under the ownership of Richard Leake, who bought the entire island in 1784. In 1898, the Jekyl* Island Club, a group of wealthy businessmen who had bought Jekyll to use as a hunting retreat, "restored" the house which was by then in ruins. The house looks much like it did after this effort, described in a letter from the Club Superintendent:

> Tomorrow we finish up the "tabby house" . . . . around the top has been put a layer of concrete . . . . the middle wall has been brought up one and a half story . . . . and lastly a coat of cement over the entire outside . . . . to my mind the picturesqueness has been taken from the ruin, and it looks like a modern house. However, it will last many years now (Ernest G. Grob. Letter to Charles S. Morris, 2 May 1898).

*Jekyll was spelled with one "l" until 1929.

34 *Wall fragment from William Horton House*, 1742

Jekyll Island, Glynn County

Tabby

H. 9¾", W. 17", D. 2¼"

Jekyll Island Museum

This wall fragment shows the tabby construction. It was the first such building material made and used in America. The earliest documented tabby structure dates from about 1670. Tabby was used with varying frequency in coastal South Carolina, Georgia, and Florida until the Civil War.

Tabby's regional popularity was a direct result of the availability of the needed ingredients, as well as its low cost, strength, and fire resistance. It could also be produced on the building site. Because of these characteristics, it was used frequently by Oglethorpe. His Fort Frederica was described in 1743 as a "pretty strong fort of tappy [sic]" (*London Magazine*, 14 August 1745, 395).

Colonial tabby was prepared by mixing equal parts of sand, lime, and oyster shells with equal parts of water. This mixture was then poured into a structure of formwork, or shuttering, of double parallel rows of planks the

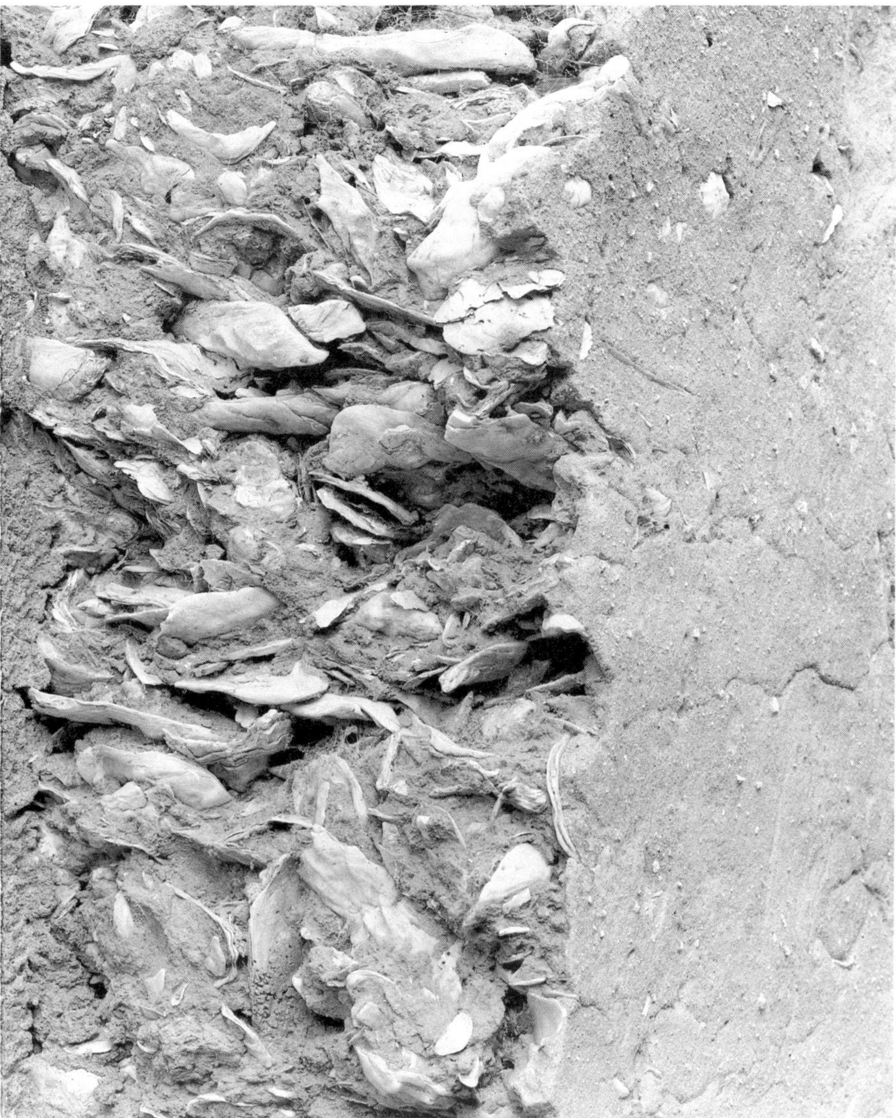

34

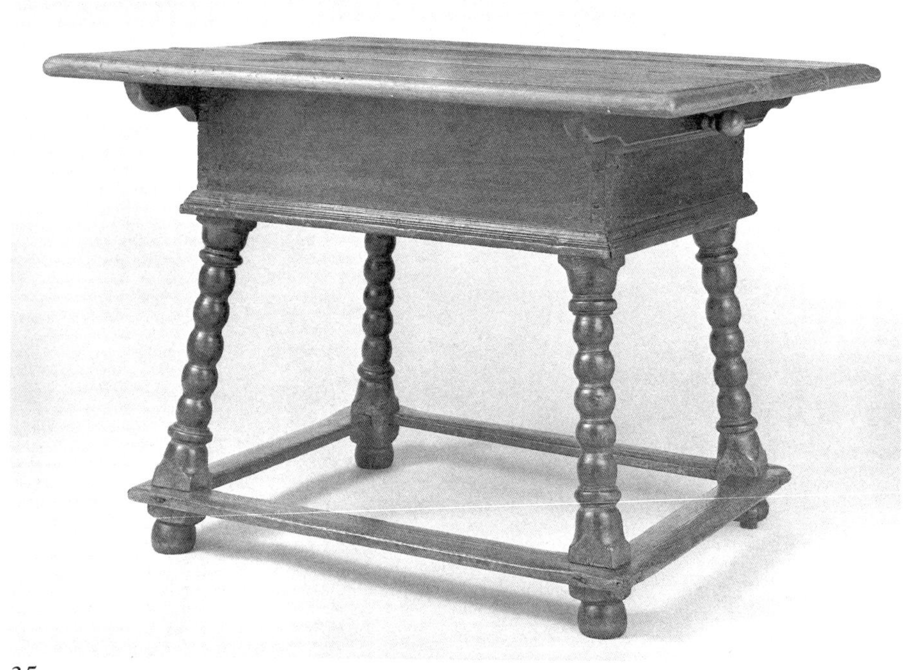

35

length of the wall, allowed to settle, and then left to harden for two or three days. The same forms were reused and the procedure was repeated for subsequent levels. Shorter planks with ample joints allowing for expansion of the hardened mixture would have prevented crumbling over the years. Good tabby needed time to harden. Rushed construction during the colonial period most likely accounts for the scarcity of intact tabby structures.

35 *Stretcher Table*, ca. 1740

Ebenezer area, Effingham County

Primary woods: sweetgum legs; tulip poplar apron; yellow pine stretchers

H. 26", W. 29¼", D. 24½"

Condition: Top restored; feet tipped; originally had a drawer

Exhibitions: *Southern Furniture 1640–1820*, Virginia Museum of Fine Arts, Richmond, 1952

References: Comstock, "Furniture of Virginia, North Carolina, Georgia, and Kentucky," *Antiques* January 1952, 98; Horton, *Museum of Early Southern Decorative Arts Catalogue of Collection*, 25; Morton, *Southern Antiques and Folk Art*, 24; Fairbanks and Bates, *American Furniture, 1620 to the Present*, 327; Poesch, *The Art of the Old South*, 89; MESDA file #S–1162.

Museum of Early Southern Decorative Arts

This stretcher table is believed to have been made by Salzburgers in the New Ebenezer settlement. The first group of Salzburgers landed in Savannah in March 1734, led by Pastor Johann Martin Bolzius. To escape religious persecution, the Salzburgers began leaving Austria in 1731; they immigrated via Holland to a site on the west side of the Savannah River. Laid out for them by Oglethorpe six miles from the river, Ebenezer (meaning "hitherto hath the Lord helped us") proved to be inconvenient, swampy, and sandy. In his journal, Philip Georg Friedrich von Reck relates how he and "Mr. Bolzius had informed Mr. Oglethorpe of the conditions of the Salzburgers, the nature of the soil at Old Ebenezer, and the difficult communications between this place and the other English plantations and had suggested for a real and profitable development of the city of Ebenezer a good and fertile place at the confluence of the Ebenezer and Savannah rivers (Hvidt, *Von Reck's Voyage*, 35). In 1736, Oglethorpe reluctantly allowed the Salzburgers and the third transport, whom he had intended to populate Saint Simons, to relocate at the mouth of Ebenezer Creek, "previously named Red Bluff because of the red clay soil . . . . a good German mile from Old Ebenezer" (Hvidt, *Von Reck's Voyage*, 36). The settlement of New Ebenezer was plotted into city lots with space for a church, school, marketplace, and the first orphanage in Georgia, which was established in 1737.

The style of this table is reminiscent of late seventeenth-century furniture. Since its provenance is of New Ebenezer, however, the piece could not predate 1736.

This Salzburger craftsman created a table reminiscent of a style with which he was familiar—Jacobean transitional William and Mary, characterized by ball feet and heavy stretchers. His possible Germanic training is suggested by the repeated turnings and heavy moldings on this piece. The combination of indigenous woods as well as the retarditaire style illustrates the cultural lag in America's last colony.

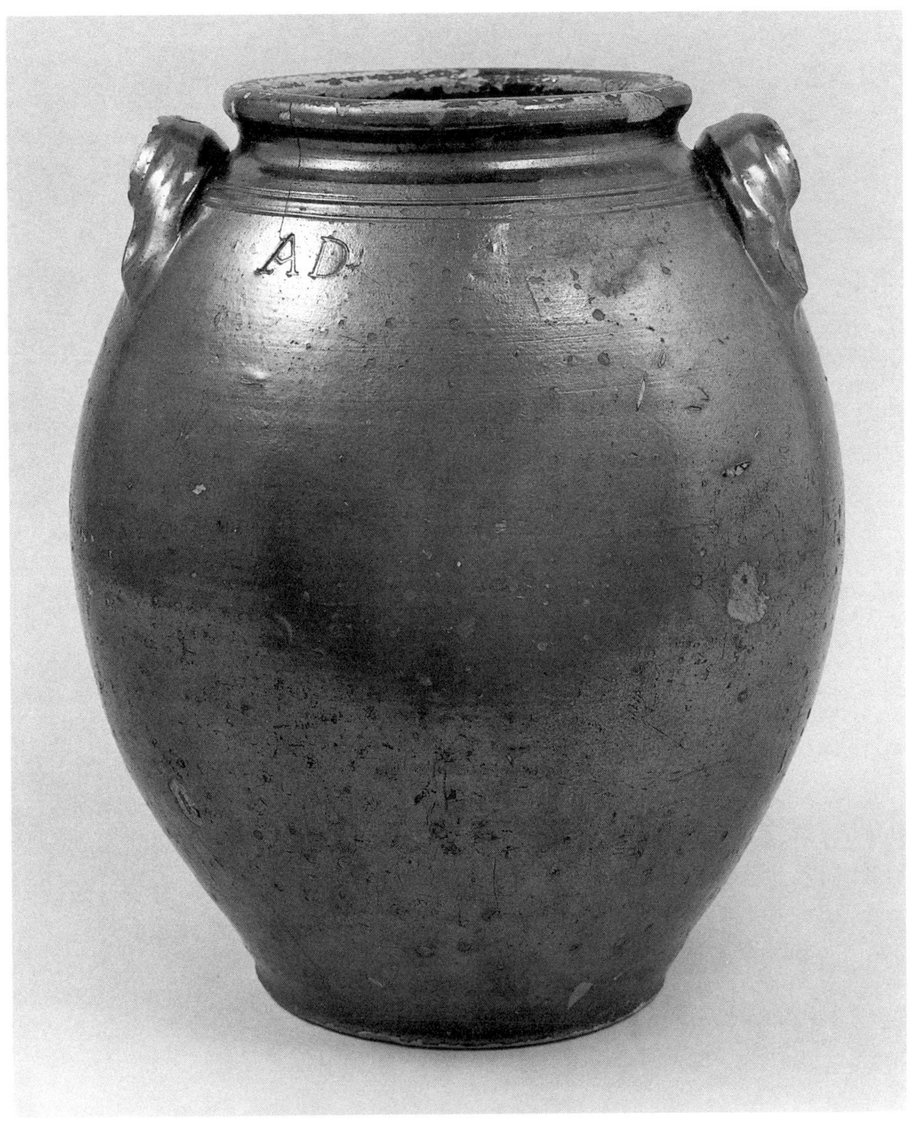

36

36 *Jar* (photoreproduction), ca. 1740

Attributed to Andrew Duché (1710–1778)

New Windsor, South Carolina, or Savannah

Earthenware, lead glazed inside and outside

H. 13″, W. 10½″, Diam. at rim 6⅜″, Diam. at base 6⅛″

Marks: AD

References: Rauschenberg, "The Mysterious Duché," *Luminary*, Winter 1983, 6; Burrison, *Brothers in Clay*, 101–107; Rauschenberg, *Andrew Duché: A Potter . . . a little too much addicted to politics*.

Museum of Early Southern Decorative Arts

Ceramics in colonial Georgia were by and large imported. Few potters came to Georgia from England, although the Trustees were apparently interested in the prospects of exporting fine ceramics along with silk and wine.

Andrew Duché was the third son of

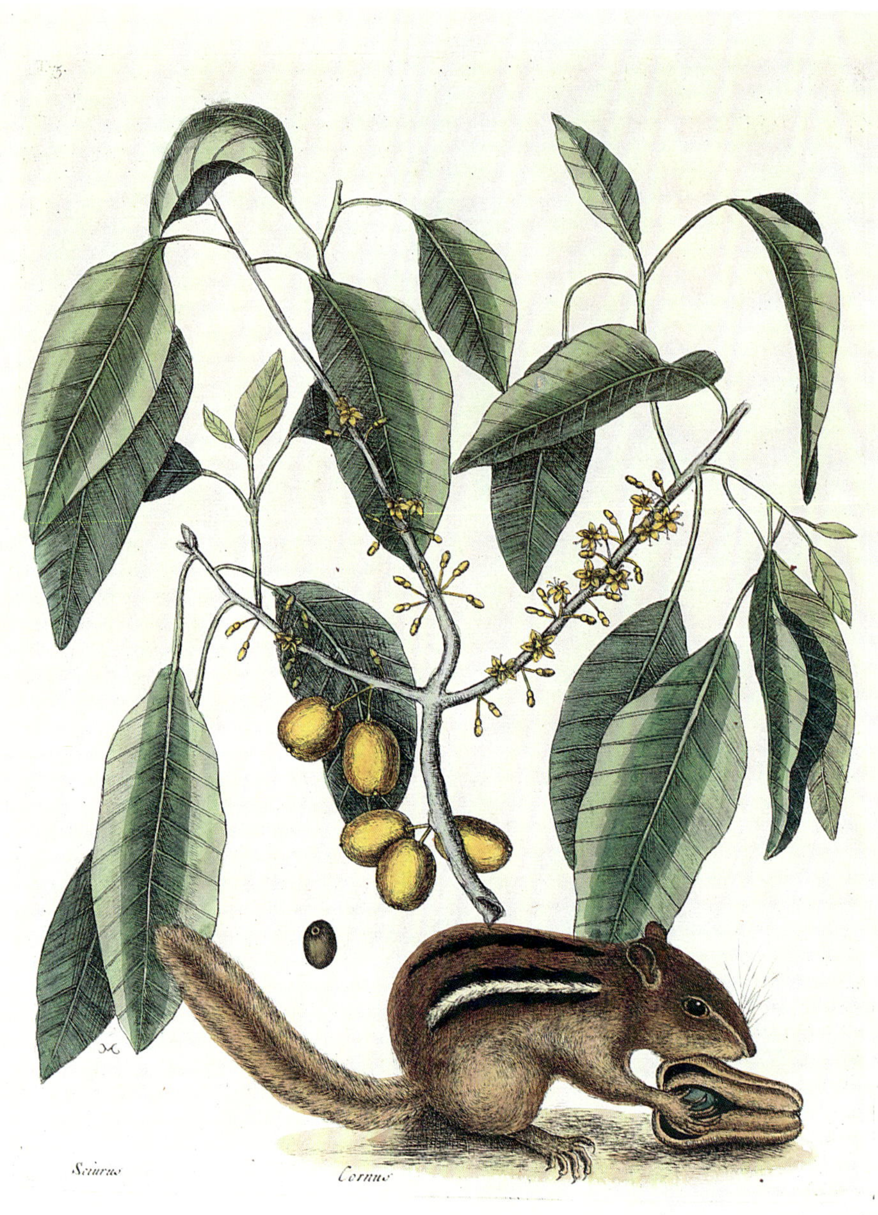

37

Anthony Duché, a Philadelphia potter. Andrew came to Savannah via Charleston and New Windsor, South Carolina, an Indian trading post on the Savannah River across from Augusta. The presence of kaolin in the area spurred Duché's dreams of producing American porcelain, a hard, translucent earthenware previously manufactured in Meissen, Germany. The Trustees backed Duché's endeavor, and a shop and a kiln were built on his lot in Savannah. William Stephens, secretary for the Trustees, informed them of the progress of their investment in a letter dated May 27, 1738 (Burrison, *Brothers in Clay*, 103):

> The encouragement given to a Potter . . . was not ill bestowed . . . . The Master is a sober, diligent, and modest man . . . . his next aim is to do something very curious . . . . He is making some tryal [sic] of other kinds of fine clay . . . which . . . when held against the light was very near transparent . . . . I must conclude it cannot fail of proving a Manufacture that will find good Value abroad.

No examples of porcelain by Duché have been located. Letters of requests for supplies needed from England indicate that he primarily manufactured lead glazed earthenware like this example.

37 *The Ground Squirrel*, ca. 1731–1743

Mark Catesby (1679–1749)

London, England

Etching, colored by hand

H. 13 11/16″, W. 10⅛″

History: Published in *The Natural History of Carolina, Florida and the Bahama Islands*. Vol. II. London: Benjamin White, 1771. Pl. 75 (originally published privately in London, 1731–43).

Special Collections, The University of Georgia Libraries

Ten years before Oglethorpe received the charter to settle the Florida territory into a colony called Georgia, Mark Catesby, an English naturalist, had spent the period from 1722 to 1726 documenting the plant and animal life in the Carolinas and Florida. This visit was his second to America; he had spent 1712 to 1719 in Virginia "viewing as well the Animal as Vegetable productions in their Native

Countries which were strangers to England" (Poesch, *The Art of the Old South*, 32).

Years later, the watercolors Catesby had executed in the field were translated into engravings and published in two volumes from 1741 to 1743. Under the guidance of watercolorist Joseph Goupy, Catesby etched the plates himself. In the text accompanying the illustration, Catesby explains that the nutmeg was indigenous to Georgia:

> The Fruit which the Squirrel is feeding on belongs to a Tree or Shrub which General *Oglethorpe* brought from *Georgia*, by the name of the wild Nutmeg; from its being aromatic, and other circumstances induces me to think it is the fruit of the Plant I have described p. 46 Vol I. which description is imperfect, because the fruit was not then formed.

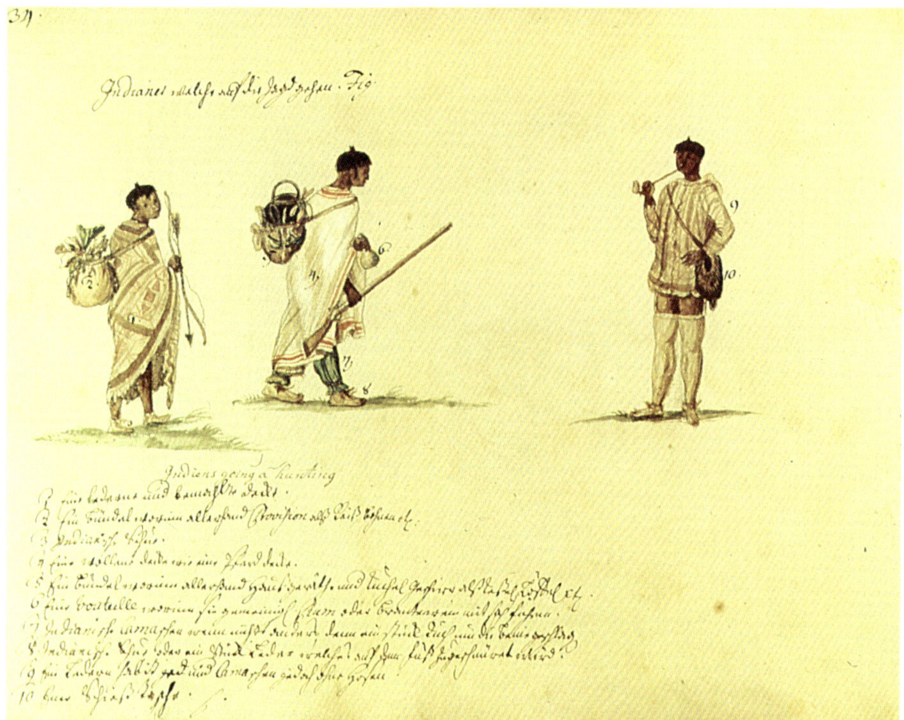
38

38 *Indians Going A-Hunting* (photoreproduction), 1736

Philip Georg Friedrich von Reck (1707–1790s)

Possibly Pallachocolas, a Yuchi town on the Savannah River near New Ebenezer

Watercolor on paper

H. 11⅜", W. 14⅜"

Inscriptions (translated):
1) A painted leather blanket
2) A bag containing all sorts of provisions, like rice, beans, &c.
3) Indian shoes
4) A woolen blanket like a horse cloth
5) A bundle containing all sorts of utensils and kitchenware like a kettle, spoons, &c.
6) A bottle in which they generally carry rum or brandy
7) Indian leggings. If they don't have these, they will at least have a piece of cloth around their legs
8) Indian shoes or a piece of leather which is laced around the foot
9) A leather coat and gaiters, but no trousers
10) A shot pouch

Det Kongelige Bibliotek, Bibliotheque Royale, Copenhagen, Denmark

In February 1736, Philip Georg Friedrich von Reck, who had led the first transport in 1734, returned to Georgia with the third transport of Salzburgers. Before he left Germany, he wrote to the Society for Promoting Christian Knowledge, promising to return with "ocular proof," implying his

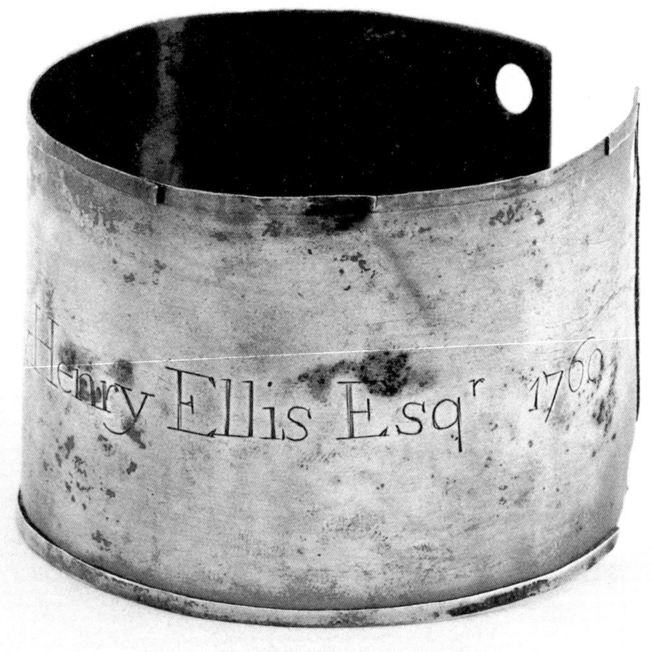

39

intention to produce some form of visual record. This proof was 50 drawings and watercolors by von Reck that, after 200 years of oblivion, have only recently been discovered in the collection of the Royal Library of Copenhagen. He also kept a diary that relates his journey to Georgia on the *London Merchant*, the deteriorating economy of Old Ebenezer, and Mr. Oglethorpe's reluctance to move the Salzburgers up the Creek, as well as the increasing concern and preparation for war against the Spanish.

Dissention with other Salzburger leaders made von Reck restless and dissatisfied. He turned his attention to the comprehension and documentation of the life of New Ebenezer's neighboring Indian tribes, the Creeks and the Yuchis. Many of his drawings are labeled in Yuchi and Creek as well as in German and English—apparently the tireless von Reck was trying to learn the Indian languages.

Trade between the Indians and Europeans had become a way of life for both by the mid-eighteenth century. The Yuchi tribe near Ebenezer made frequent visits to trade deer skins, meat, and corn for money, weapons, and rum. On July 19, von Reck traveled to the Yuchi town of Pallachocolas, 25 miles from Ebenezer: "I have met some thirty men of the Chicasaw Indians . . . . Because this tribe has always had an affection for the English nation, which supplies them with better and cheaper wares . . . . " (Hvidt, *Von Reck's Voyage*, 44). The Indians depicted in this watercolor may have been from this Yuchi town. They wear blankets of English manufacture, and the figure at the right wears a jacket that reflects European stylistic influences. Their guns could have been purchased in Charleston for the price of four deerskins.

39 *Indian Arm Bracelet*, 1760

Possibly Savannah, Chatham County

Silver

H. 2″, Diam. 3″

Inscribed: A Gift of His Excellency Henry Ellis Esqr 1760

History: Excavated in the 1960s from a burial ground in what is now Alabama, but part of the Royal province of Georgia in 1760.

References: Poesch, *The Art of the Old South*, 111.

Collection of James A. Williams

Royal Governor Henry Ellis (1757–1760) recognized the importance of good relations with the Indians, for Georgia's reputation of impending Indian violence had kept away potential settlers. Not all Indo-European relationships were as harmonious as that of Tomochichi and the first English settlers [see 31]. In 1736, Philip von Reck of New Ebenezer [see 38] expresses his evaluation of the Indian character:

> They are very courteous, friendly and hospitable towards strangers, with whom they quickly become acquainted . . . but on the other hand . . . If an Indian is wronged by a European, he kills him or, which is all the same to him, another European. From this it may be seen how dangerous it is to offend an Indian and how soon, through the bad behavior of a single person, an Indian war and the ruin of an entire colony can be brought about (Hvidt, *Von Reck's Voyage*, 48).

This arm bracelet, probably secured with a strip of leather, is representative of Ellis's several successful attempts to prevent the Indians from further impeding Georgia's growth, geographically and economically. In 1757, Ellis had expanded the physical size of Georgia by taking the former Indian territories of Ossabaw, St. Catherine's, and Sapelo islands. The Trustees's hopes of diverting all Indian trade from Charleston to Augusta had not been realized, and trade exploitations on the parts of both Indians and Europeans played havoc with hopes of long-term peace.

40 *Tybee Island Lighthouse*, ca. 1755

Attributed to John Gauntlett, ship's artist on the HMS *Norwich* and *Success*

Off coast of Savannah

Watercolor on paper

H. 16", W. 10"

Mariners' Museum

Located at the mouth of the Savannah River, Tybee Island served as the anchoring point for many ships

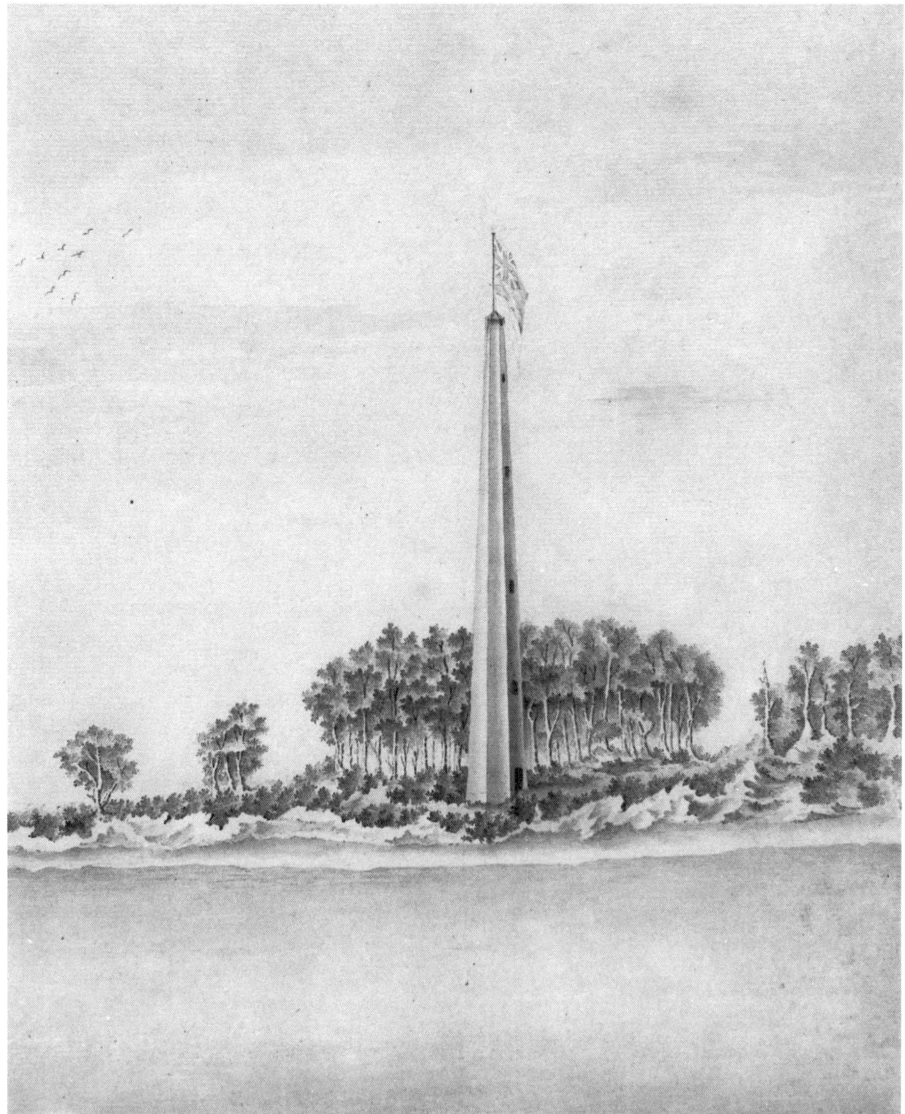

40

THE

SOUTH-CAROLINA and GEORGIA

ALMANACK,

FOR THE YEAR OF OUR LORD
1764.

(Being BISSEXTILE or LEAP-YEAR.)

Fitted to the Meridian of 33 Degrees North Latitude, which renders it ſerviceable to the Provinces of NORTH and SOUTH-CAROLINA, GEORGIA, FLORIDA, and LOUISIANA.

CONTAINING

The GARDENER'S KALENDAR, PROFIT and LOSS in the LATE WAR, and many other uſeful Things.

By JOHN TOBLER, Eſq;

Here, Reader, ſee, in Youth, in Age, or Prime,
The ſtealing Steps of never-ſtanding Time,
With Wiſdom mark the Moment as it flies,
Think what a Moment is—to him that dies.

GEORGIA:
SAVANNAH, Printed by JAMES JOHNSTON.

41

bringing settlers to Savannah. On 16 February 1736, the *London Merchant*, carrying Philip von Reck and 256 others, "went in with the high tide and a favorable wind, passing the high banks into the Savannah River and anchored at Tybee Island" (Hvidt, *Von Reck's Voyage*, 33).

This drawing undoubtedly represents the original lighthouse built by Oglethorpe. It was 25 feet square at the base, 90 feet high, and 10 feet square at the top, and made from "the best pine, strongly timber'd, raised upon Cedar Piles, and Brickwork round the Bottom" (Jones, *History of Georgia*, I, 207).

The lighthouse has been destroyed twice. The 24 January 1793 issue of the *Georgia Gazette* reported to mariners ". . . on Thursday morning the 8th of November, 1792 the lantern of the Light-House on Tybee took fire, and was entirely consumed in consequence of which unfortunate accident no light can appear for sometime." By August of the next year, specifications for "proposals (sealed) will be received by the subscriber (John Habersham, collector for the Customs of Savannah) . . . for furnishing and delivering the necessary materials and executing the following repairs on Tybee Lighthouse." Among these were "a circular hanging staircase from the ground to the lantern floor, height about 90 feet; six floors and twelve window frames with Venetian Blinds." Planks of pine, cypress, and white oak were also required (*Georgia Gazette*, 8 August 1793). Confederate forces partially destroyed the lighthouse in 1862, but it was repaired five years later.

41 *Almanack*, 1764

John Tobler, esq., author; James Johnston, publisher

Savannah

Special Collections, The University of Georgia Libraries

The South Carolina and Georgia Almanack, For the Year of Our Loard 1764 may have been the first book published in Georgia. The *Almanack* was printed in Savannah by James Johnston, who was Georgia's official printer and the editor of the colony's first newspaper, the *Georgia Gazette*, established 1763. At Johnston's shop, Georgians could purchase ink and stationery, books and legal forms, and associated items (Spalding, "Colonial Period," *A History of Georgia*, 55).

42 *James Habersham, Sr.*, before 1772

Jeremiah Theus (1719–1774)

Savannah or Charleston

Oil on canvas

H. 40", W. 36"

Exhibitions: *Tercentenary Exhibition*, The North Carolina Museum of Art, 1963

References: National Society of the Colonial Dames of America, in Georgia, *Early Georgia Portraits, 1715–1870*, 85.

Telfair Academy of Arts and Sciences, Bequest of Miss Emma Wilkins

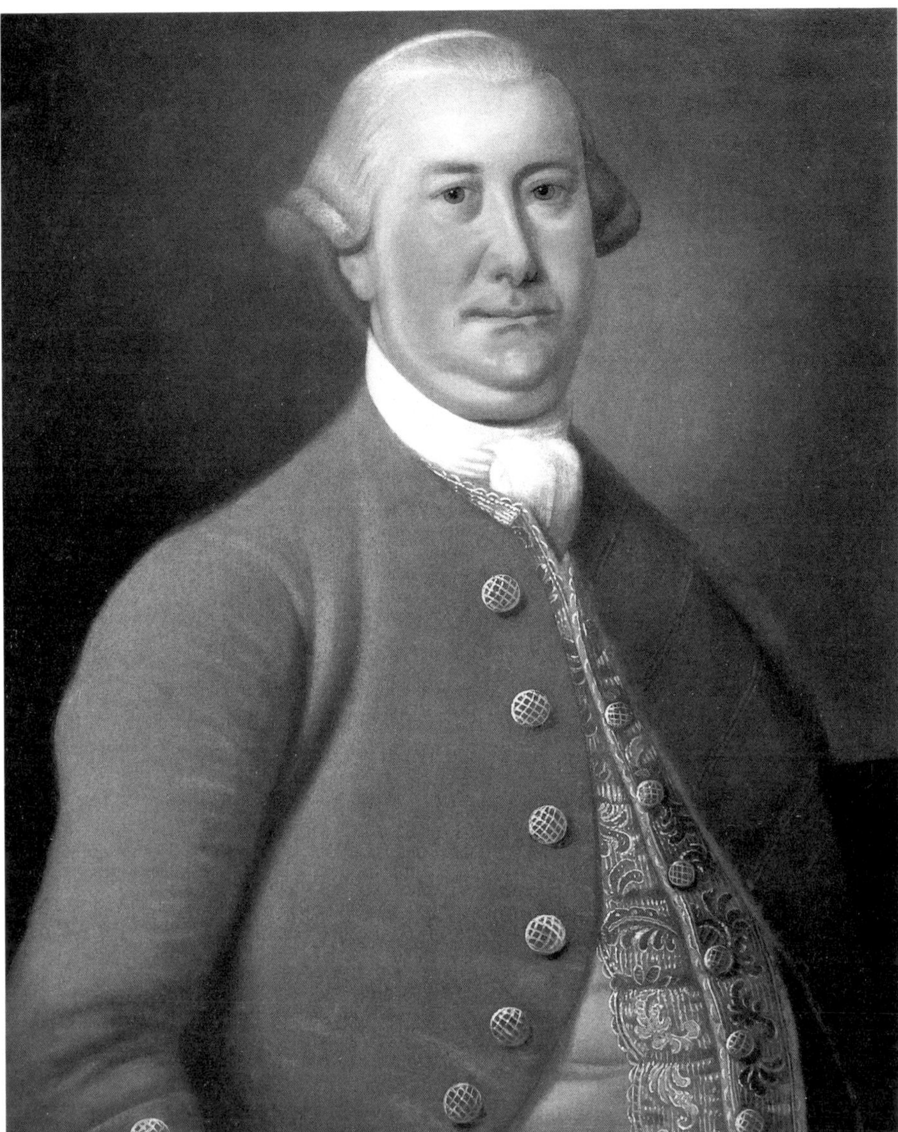

42

Born at Beverly in Yorkshire, England, James Habersham, Sr., (1712–1775) arrived in Georgia in 1738 with his friend, evangelist George Whitefield. Both men became actively involved with the construction and administration of the Orphan House in Bethesda, supported by the New Ebenezer Salzburgers. Habersham was in charge of the educational aspects, and Whitefield the financial. Construction of the grand, Palladian-style house began in 1740. Because of the size and urgency of this project, Habersham, Whitefield, and the Salzburger leader Pastor Bolzius approached the Trustees to allow Negro laborers. Habersham's pressure directly influenced the repeal of anti-slavery laws in 1750, just two years before the Trustees gave up the charter completely.

Habersham established a trading business in 1744, the first in Savannah, and in 1759, the firm had built the first wharf that could accept ocean-going ships. His commercial house sent to England the first shipment of Georgia cotton in 1764, and the firm continued in cotton trade until 1899.

The Revolutionary War period was difficult for Habersham, who had become a political and personal friend of third Royal Governor James Wright. This portrait was probably painted during the period Habersham held public office: he was president of the

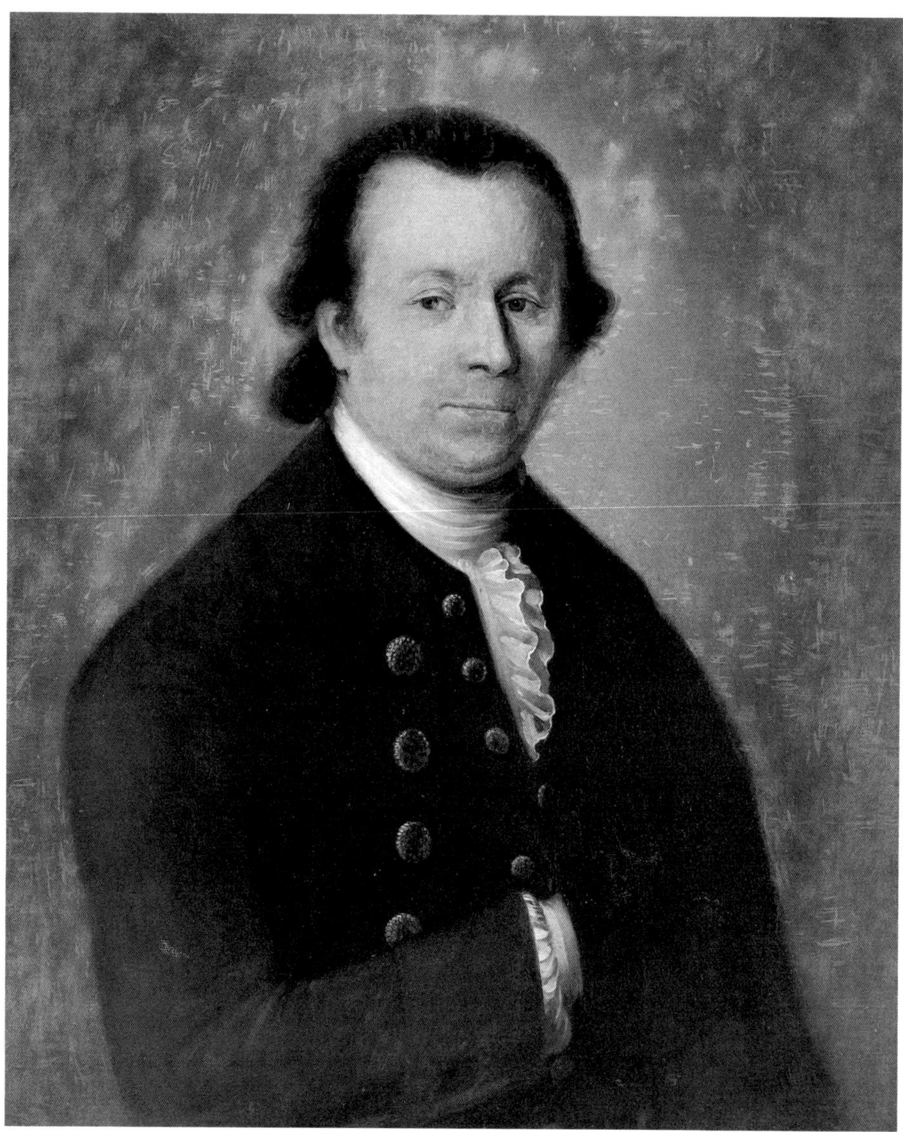

43

Georgia Assembly (1765–1771) and acting governor (1771–1773). Habersham remained loyal to the Crown to the end, while his three sons James, Joseph, and John, emerged as new leaders of the patriots of the American Revolution in Georgia.

This portrait may have been among those to which Habersham referred in a 3 July 1772 letter to prominent Charleston artist, Jeremiah Theus, discussing an "account for my 7 pictures, amounting to 3 hundred and twenty pounds South Carolina currency" (*The Letters of Hon. James Habersham, 1756–1775*, vol. 6, 197).

43 *Button Gwinnett*

Attributed to Jeremiah Theus (1719–1774)

Savannah or Charleston

Oil on canvas

H. 29″, W. 23″

High Museum of Art, on extended loan from Fulton Federal Savings and Loan

Button Gwinnett (1735–1777), born in Gloucestershire, England, arrived in Savannah in 1765 and lived on Saint Catherine's Island. He was in the forefront of shaping Georgia's new government after 1776. One of Georgia's three signers of the Declaration of Independence, he succeeded Archibald Bulloch as president of the Council of Safety.

Internal fighting arose among the Georgia Whigs, pitting factions of the "county party," or radicals, against the Christ Church "city party" conservatives. The feud between Gwinnett, a radical and president of the provincial congress, and Lachlan McIntosh, a conservative Scot from Darien and colonel of the Georgia Continental Battalion, culminated in May 1777, with McIntosh's calling Gwinnett "a Scoundrell and Lying Rascal" before the assembly (Spalding, "Colonial Period," *A History of Georgia*, 76). Gwinnett challenged McIntosh to a duel in which Gwinnett was fatally wounded.

44 *Major General Nathanael Greene*, 1783

Charles Willson Peale (1741–1827)

Philadelphia, Pennsylvania

Oil on canvas

H. 22", W. 19"

References: National Society of the Colonial Dames of America, in Georgia, *Early Georgia Portraits, 1715–1870*, 84.

Montclair Art Museum

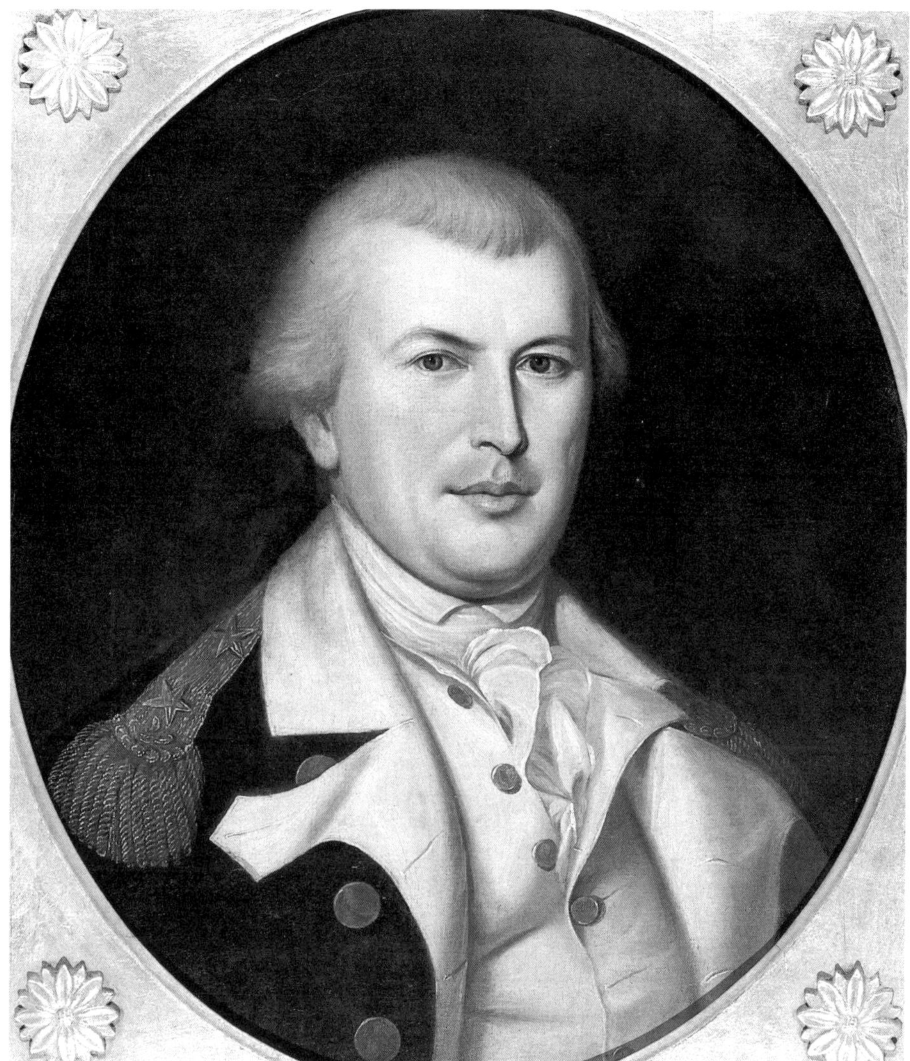

44

Georgia's Continental Army had few successes during the early years of the Revolution. Savannah was captured by the British in December 1778 and remained in enemy hands until July 1782. Sporadic victories in the upcountry were offset when the Tories occupied Augusta, the Revolutionary capital, in May 1780. Only Wilkes County and parts of Richmond County were left in Continental control.

After distinguished performances at Trenton, Princeton, Brandywine, Germantown, and Monmouth, General Nathanael Greene (1742–1788), a Rhode Island Quaker and merchant, had assumed control of the southern army. With few troops available but with savage guerilla warfare techniques, Greene had commanded Georgia and South Carolina militia led by Colonel Elijah Clarke and General Andrew Williamson to a successful siege of Augusta. By June 1781, the upcountry was back in the hands of the Whigs and a new slate of state officials had been elected in Augusta.

As a token of their gratitude, the people of Georgia presented Nathanael Greene with a plantation, Mulberry Grove, where he lived until his death. It was here that Eli Whitney, a tutor on the plantation, designed the first cotton gin in 1793, encouraged by Mrs. Greene.

This portrait was part of Charles Willson Peale's Gallery of Great Men, which he began for his museum in Philadelphia about 1780. Peale wrote in a 1783 letter, "I have painted thirty or forty portraits of Principal Characters. The collection has cost me much time and labor and I mean to keep adding as many of those who are distinguished by their Actions or Office as opportunity will serve" (Richardson et al., *Charles Willson Peale and His World*, 60). Most of these took only one or two sittings with no props or accessories, except to reveal enough of the uniform to show the individual's rank and branch of service.

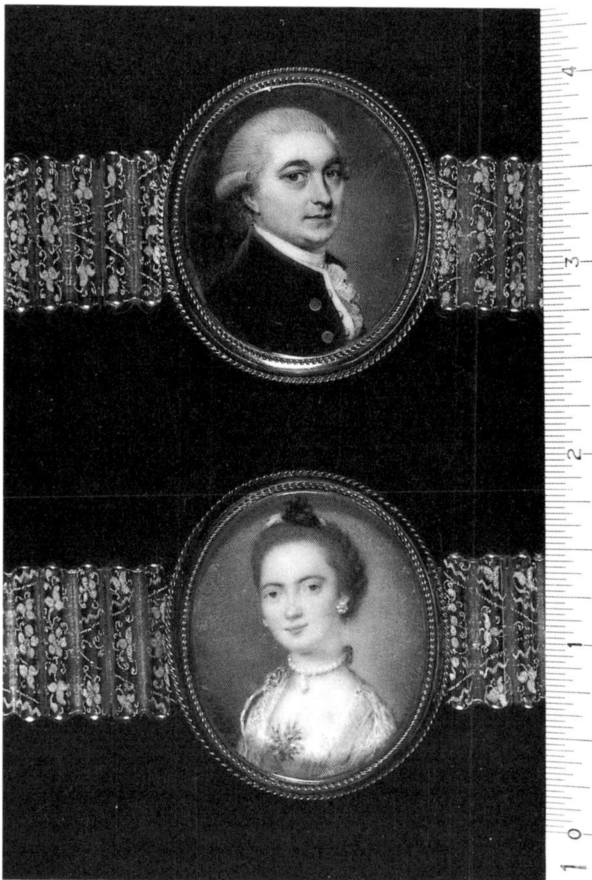

45, 46

45 *Sir George Houstoun*, 1774

Attributed to Henry Benbridge (1749–1812)

Savannah or Charleston

Watercolor on ivory

H. 1½", W. 1¼"

Exhibitions: "Henry Benbridge, American Portrait Painter," National Portrait Gallery, 1971

References: Edith Duncan Johnston, *The Houstouns of Georgia*; Robert Stewart, *Henry Benbridge, American Portrait Painter*, 1971, 70; *Early Georgia Portraits, 1715–1870*, 284–85; MESDA file #S–1313.

Museum of Early Southern Decorative Arts, Gift of Dr. Lucia R. Karnes and Mrs. Jean Rooney Routh

Sir George Houstoun (1744–1795), seventh baronet, was the son of Sir Patrick Houstoun, who sailed to Georgia on the *Anne*. His brother John Houstoun became the second governor of Georgia (1778–1779). A prominent Savannah merchant and plantation owner, Houstoun was a member of the first Council of Safety, organized in June 1775 to oversee the enforcement of the trade boycotts that resulted from the British Intolerable Acts preceding the Revolution. Houstoun was Grand Master of Solomon's Lodge No. 1 in 1785.

The Houstouns were one of several prominent Savannah families painted by Charleston artist Henry Benbridge. Born in Philadelphia, Benbridge was encouraged by his stepfather to study painting in Italy and London. He moved to Charleston after 1771 and remained there until 1800, when he moved to Norfolk, Virginia.

46 *Lady Ann Moodie Houstoun*, 1775

Attributed to Hetty Benbridge (d. 1775)

Charleston

Watercolor on ivory

H. 1 7/16", W. 1¼"

References: See [45]

Museum of Early Southern Decorative Arts, Gift of Dr. Lucia R. Karnes and Mrs. Jean Rooney Routh

In 1774, Sir George Houstoun married Ann Moodie (1749–1821), daughter of Scot Thomas Moodie, deputy secretary under Royal governor James Wright. They had six surviving children. Lady Houstoun died at their Savannah plantation, Retreat, at the age of 72.

47 *George Walton*, ca. 1781

Charles Willson Peale (1741–1827)

Philadelphia, Pennsylvania

Watercolor on ivory

H. 1⅜", W. 1⅛"

Exhibitions: *The Dye is Cast: The Road to American Independence, 1774–1776*, National Portrait Gallery, 1975; *The World of Charles Willson Peale*, National Portrait Gallery, 1982

References: National Society of the Colonial Dames of America, in Georgia, *Early Georgia Portraits, 1715–1870*, 298; Edgar Richardson, et al., *Charles Willson Peale and His World*, 53.

Yale University Art Gallery, Mabel Brady Garvan Collection

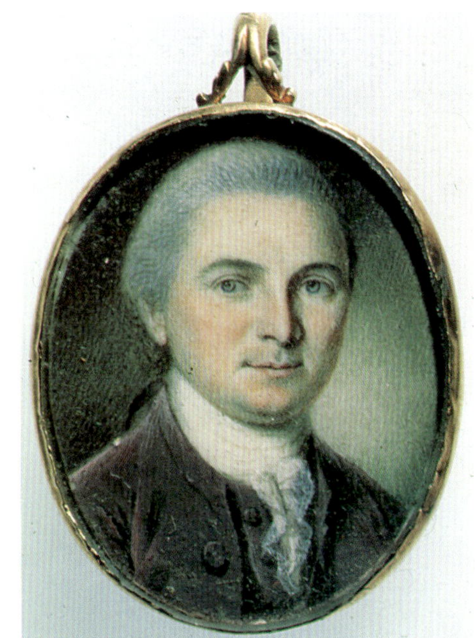

47

In 1769, orphaned George Walton (1741–1804) came to Savannah from Prince Edward County, Virginia. Walton studied law and was admitted to the bar in 1774. His aggressive leadership qualities brought him both military and political prominence during Georgia's restless years during the war. An early patriot leader, Walton was chosen as one of the three delegates to Philadelphia in 1776. He was elected governor in 1779. After the war, his illustrious career continued as he became Chief Justice, United States Senator, and judge of the Superior Court. Walton died in Augusta, where he had been founder and trustee of Richmond Academy.

This miniature was probably executed before Walton left the Continental Congress in 1781. Three years later, Peale had not received the payment of eight guineas for the likeness. He wrote to Walton that his son Raphaelle would be coming to Georgia and could collect at that time: "Having a large family to support at this time it may be doing me a greater favor than if you had paid me much sooner" (Richardson et al., *Charles Willson Peale and His World*, 53).

48 *General Elijah Clarke*

Region unknown

Oil on canvas

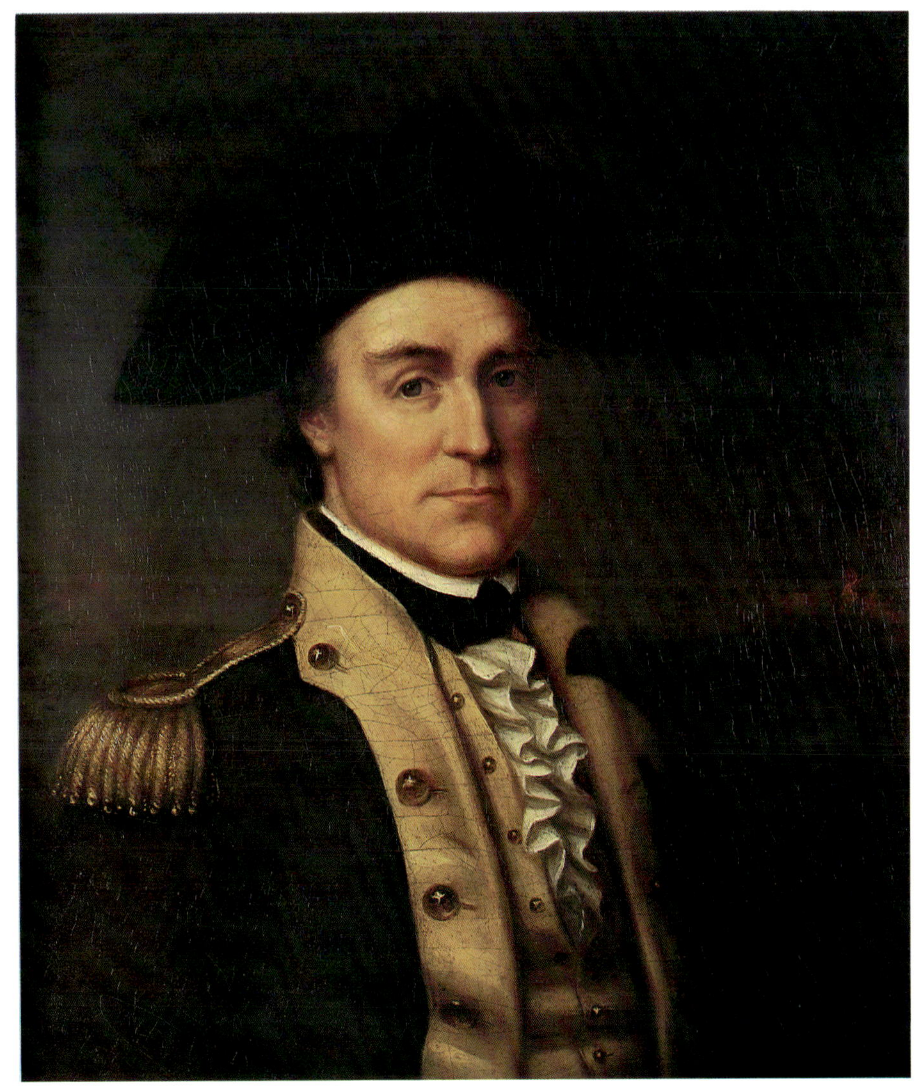

48

H. 30″, W. 25⅛″

High Museum of Art, Bequest of Mrs. Francis Pickens Bacon

Elijah Clarke (1733–1799), an illiterate "cracker," was typical of the military leaders who emerged from frontier Georgia during the Revolution. Born in North Carolina, by 1773 Clarke had settled on Clark's Creek in the newly ceded Indian territory of the piedmont. Like many of these small farmers in northwest Georgia, Clarke joined the patriots' cause and fought in the early unsuccessful struggles to free eastern Florida from British control. After the triumphant Battle of Kettle Creek in 1779, Clarke headed the forts in Wilkes County. Many battles followed, including two attempts to recover Augusta, the second of which was successful. Clarke was wounded four times.

After the war, Clarke was awarded a Wilkes County plantation. He represented Wilkes County in the legislature from 1781 to 1790. Sideline politics, however, were not to Clarke's liking, and he spent the rest of his life trying to organize an ill-fated invasion of eastern Florida. Ironically, the same frontier that had brought Clarke fame also contributed to his demise. As culture blossomed in Wilkes County, his uninhibited lifestyle conflicted with the now thriving and sophisticated piedmont. Clarke died in debt, "disgusted" with the state of Georgia.

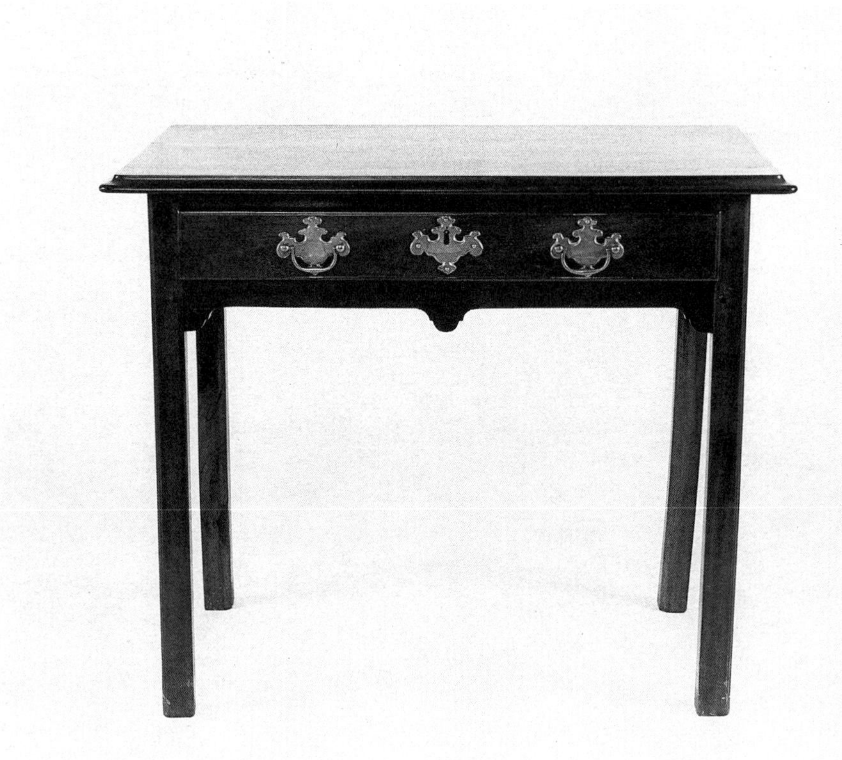

49

49 *Side Table*, 1775–1785

Coastal Georgia

Primary wood: mahogany; secondary woods: yellow pine, walnut back board

H. 28½″, W. 33″, D. 18¼″

Description: Ogee-edged top; chamfered legs; drawer originally had six compartments across the front

History: Descended in the family of Edward Telfair.

References: MESDA file #S–8298.

Telfair Academy of Arts and Sciences

[see following entry]

50 *Blanket Chest*, 1775–1785

Piedmont Georgia

Primary wood: sweet gum; secondary woods: poplar sides and bottom of exterior drawers; yellow pine back; white oak secret interior drawers

H. 33½″, W. 38″, D. 16″

Description: Top hinged at lower ends with original cleats; rosette terminals of imported pulls are inset into drawer fronts; feet are rectangular slides dovetailed into chest sides; heavy dovetailing throughout

Exhibitions: *Furniture of the Georgia Piedmont Before 1830*, High Museum of Art, 1976

References: Henry D. Green, *Furniture of the Georgia Piedmont Before 1830*, 83.

Collection of Mr. and Mrs. Henry D. Green

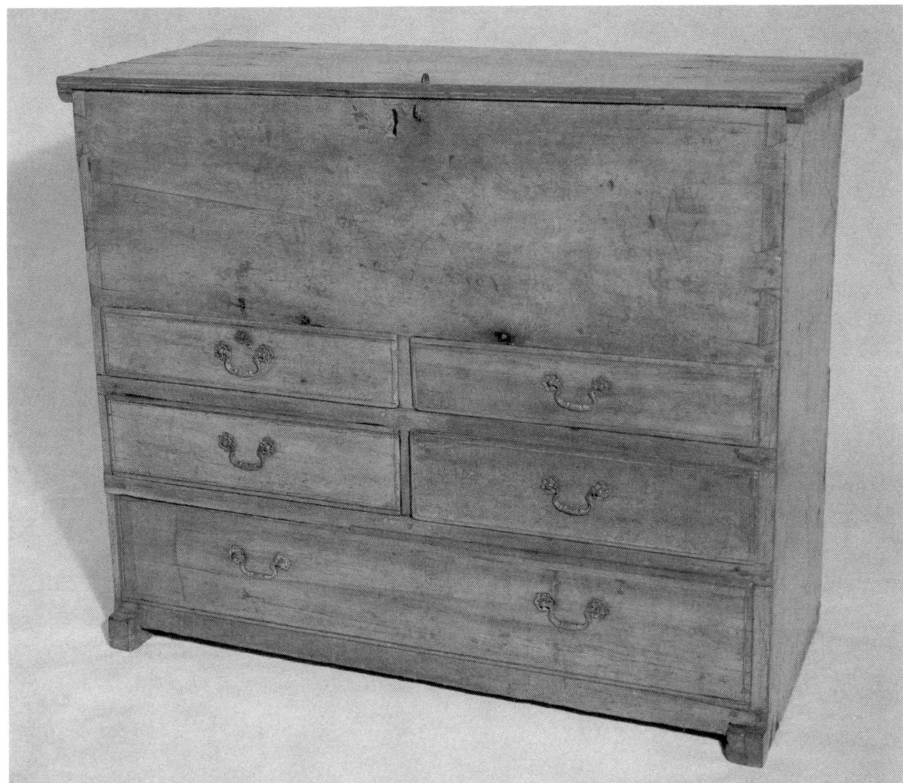

50

This mahogany table from coastal Georgia, possibly Savannah, and the sweet gum chest from the piedmont, illustrate two extremes of cabinetmaking before the Federal period (1790–1820). The table's chamfered-Marlborough legs and molded top are understated references to the Chippendale style still popular in the South. Though few survive, undoubtedly more sophisticated examples of mahogany furniture with elaborately carved details and cabriole legs were available in Savannah. The piedmont, on the other hand, was a newly settled frontier in the 1770s. The need for utilitarian pieces made from locally grown woods, rather than imported mahogany, dictated the types of wares produced by these craftsmen who were recently transplanted from Virginia and North and South Carolina.

Interestingly, during the Revolutionary War, many craftsmen turned to selling real estate as a means of supplementing their income. Some of their advertisements published in newspapers document woods available in coastal regions. In 1774, Adrian Loyer, a Savannah clockmaker, silversmith, and gunsmith, placed an ad in the *Georgia Gazette*: "A valuable plantation 12 miles above Savannah, chief part of it is river swamp . . . . it abounds with plenty of good cypress and other timber" (12 January 1774). And Michael Germain, a silversmith, offered for sale: "a valuable tract of land . . . consisting of red and white oak and hickory" (*Gazette of the State of Georgia*, 1 May 1783).

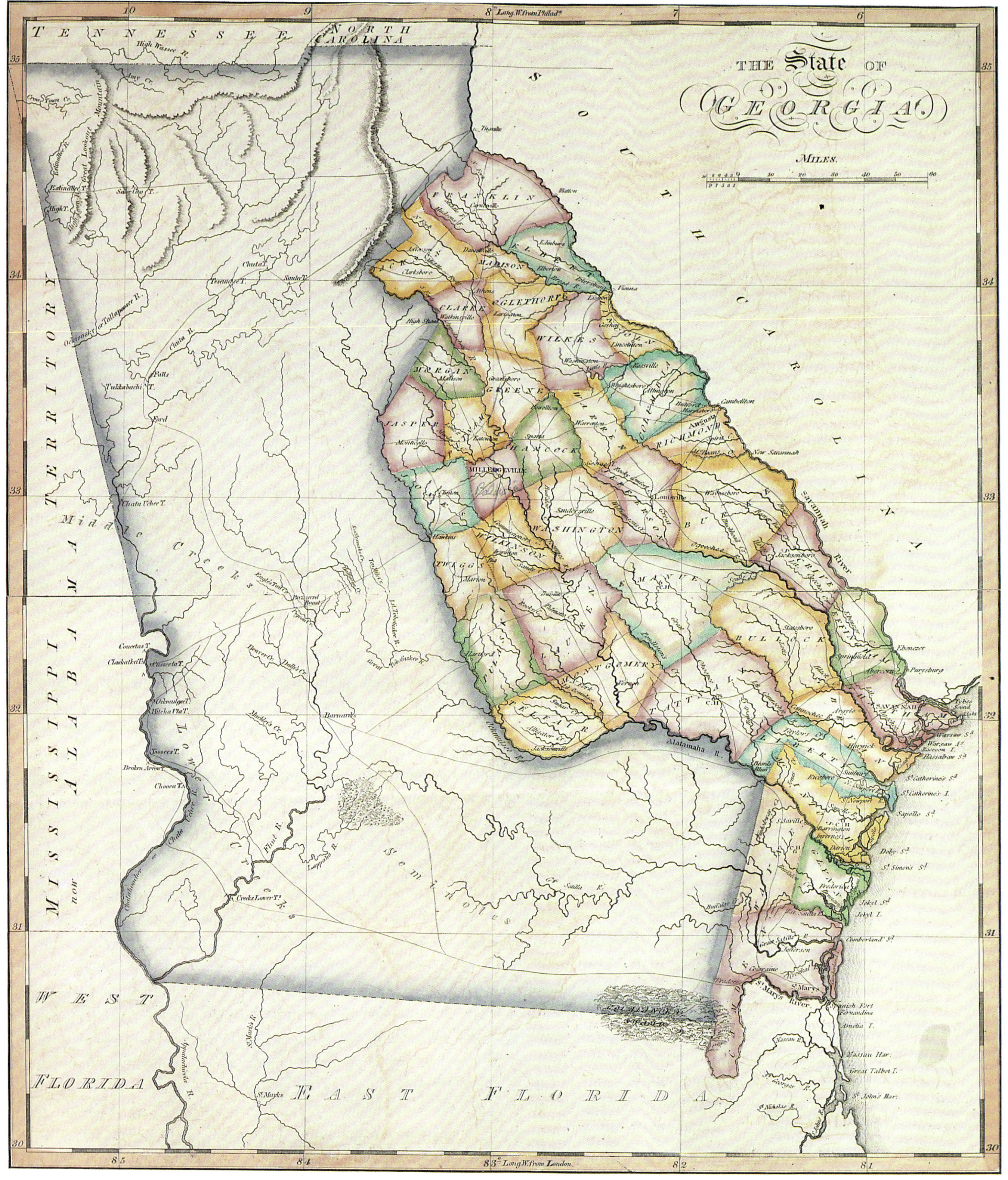

THE State OF GEORGIA.
MILES.
TENNESSEE
NORTH CAROLINA
SOUTH CAROLINA
MISSISSIPPI now ALABAMA TERRITORY
WEST FLORIDA
EAST FLORIDA

1790–1830

This section of the exhibition shows what Georgia cabinetmakers were capable of producing, given peace and a prosperous economic climate. The years after the signing of the Treaty of Paris in 1783 through the early decades of the nineteenth century were encouraging ones for the coastal and piedmont regions: the lowcountry experienced a vigorous recovery after the war, while the upcountry became the center of political power. Further, by 1810, the piedmont was the most populated area of the state. Soon, craftsmen were concentrated in north Georgia communities to supply small farmers, plantation owners, and merchants with furnishings and other goods.

Direct involvement in the War of 1812 temporarily interrupted trade on the coast, but piedmont Georgia enjoyed peace and steady prosperity from 1790 until 1830. Beginning in the 1770s, a constant stream of second and third generation European immigrants from Pennsylvania, Maryland, Virginia, and North and South Carolina traveled south along the Philadelphia Wagon Road, which ended near Augusta in the Broad River Valley, and established a network of farms throughout the fertile Georgia piedmont.

As a result of the New Purchase agreement in 1773, Indian-owned land in the piedmont region was open for settlement. The federal government supported and accelerated Indian removal throughout the state during the years 1790–1830. By the end of this period, only the northwest corner of Georgia remained in the hands of the Cherokees.

To supplement rice cultivation, sea island, or long staple cotton, was introduced to freshwater marshes of the Georgia coast in 1786. The plantation system, which took advantage of slavery, grew up along the marshy coast where earlier small-scale farms had failed.

In contrast, by 1800, the piedmont consisted primarily of small farms that produced tobacco and short staple cotton. Eli Whitney's cotton gin, perfected in 1793, facilitated the separation of the fibers and seeds of this cotton that grew best in the piedmont region. The gin enabled the farmer with even modest acreage to grow cotton in volume. By 1826, Georgia was the world's leading cotton producer.

Engraved by Gridley, *The State of Georgia*, ca. 1813. Philadlephia: Gridley. H. 18¼", W. 15¼". Special Collections, The University of Georgia Libraries.

With hard work a small farmer could become a wealthy planter, and the wealthy planter a shrewd businessman.

During this period, both Savannah and Augusta grew into major commercial centers. Cotton grown in the piedmont and the low-country was traded and shipped from Savannah's waterfront, and many merchants made sizable fortunes operating exchange offices along the wharf, later known as Factor's Walk. By the 1830s, Georgia's socioeconomic structure was flexible and mobile for the white population. The ambitious were generously rewarded.

By the second decade of the nineteenth century, New York and Philadelphia furniture and silver markets were major competition for local cabinetmakers and silversmiths. Complex partnerships, often with one man stationed in the North and the other in Georgia, orchestrated the entrance of large quantities of imported wares into Savannah's port and then up the Savannah River to Augusta. While the upper classes usually preferred these imports, local shops provided facsimile Phyfe-style furniture and possibly pewter ware to the growing working classes.

Regardless of northern influence, 1790–1830 stands as the period from which most examples of Georgia-made furniture and other crafts survive. Nineteenth-century coastal and piedmont newspaper advertisements attest to a lively, competitive market of cabinetmakers, chairmakers, silversmiths, blacksmiths, potters, gunsmiths, and other craftsmen. The 1820 Georgia manufacturers census also provides an impressive listing of successful businesses. However, as is common with most eighteenth- and nineteenth-century southern decorative arts, few Georgia objects can be attributed to specific craftsmen. This exhibition includes two exceptions. Both the Peter Miller pembroke table [61] and the Owen Strange desk-and-bookcase [62] were marked or signed. Additional pieces have been attributed to the coast because of their histories and the woods employed, such as cypress. On the other hand, piedmont pieces evoke a regional style and are distinctive because of their woods, inlaid designs, and construction.

Three highly publicized natural disasters, two fires in Savannah and a flood in Augusta, undoubtedly destroyed a significant quantity of locally made furniture. Fires were a constant threat to Georgians until fire ordinances and the use of iron or brick for building became widespread. Not all explanations for the scarcity of surviving eighteenth- or nineteenth-century crafts can be traced to the period. One can also point to the Augusta fire of 1926 or to the Depression-era antique dealers who carried away and sold off great numbers of piedmont-made sideboards, desk-and-bookcases, and other pieces. It is believed, therefore, that quantities of indigenous furniture are scarce today because of historical events and natural causes. Georgia craft production existed, but surviving pieces are now difficult to unearth.

51 *Dr. Robert Grant*, ca. 1805

Samuel Lovett Waldo (1783–1861)

Saint Simons Island, Glynn County

Oil on canvas

H. 33", W. 26"

Inscriptions on back: Robert Grant / Born July 15, 1762-Leith Scotland / Died Aug. 18. 1843 St. Simons Isl[d]. Ga. / Waldo / pinxt

References: Coulter, *Georgia's Disputed Ruins*, 1937; Lewis and Huie, *Patriarchial Plantations of Saint Simons Island*, 1974; MESDA file #S–3496.

Museum of Early Southern Decorative Arts

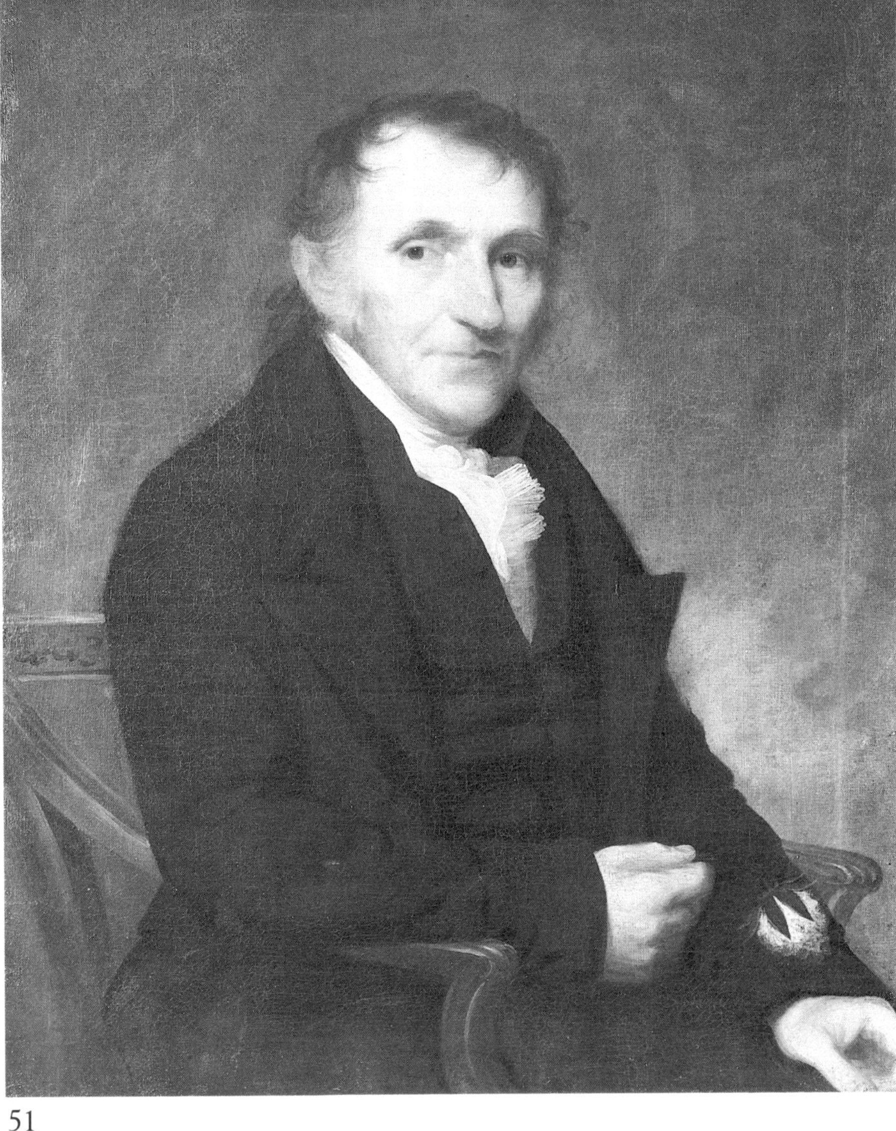

51

Around 1800, Dr. Robert Grant (1762–1843), a physician living in South Carolina, cleared the land for his summer plantation, Oatlands, on Saint Simons Island. Here he successfully raised rice, sugar cane, and sea island cotton, which he holds in this portrait. Grant was an early innovator in the use of canal systems to transport crops to the mills in the early years after cotton replaced indigo as a major coastal crop.

Grant became a warden of Christ Church in 1808, and he and his wife moved to Saint Simons Island permanently in 1834. (See 1860 map of Saint Simons [95] for Oatland's proximity to other prominent plantations such as Hopeton-on-the-Altamaha and Cannon Point [94].)

Samuel Lovett Waldo worked in New York City and was in and out of a partnership with his pupil William Jewett. He was active from 1805 to 1835.

52 *John Milledge*, 1802

Robert Field (1769–1819)

Region unknown

Oil on canvas

H. 7½", W. 5¾"

Inscriptions on back of wooden panel in ink: Hon. John Milledge / Governor Georgia / 1802 / R.F.

Exhibitions: *John Milledge Memorabilia*, Fulton Federal Savings and Loan, 1970

References: Spalding, "John Milledge," *Columns*, 1971; National Society of the Colonial Dames of America, in Georgia, *Early Georgia Portraits, 1715–1870*, 161.

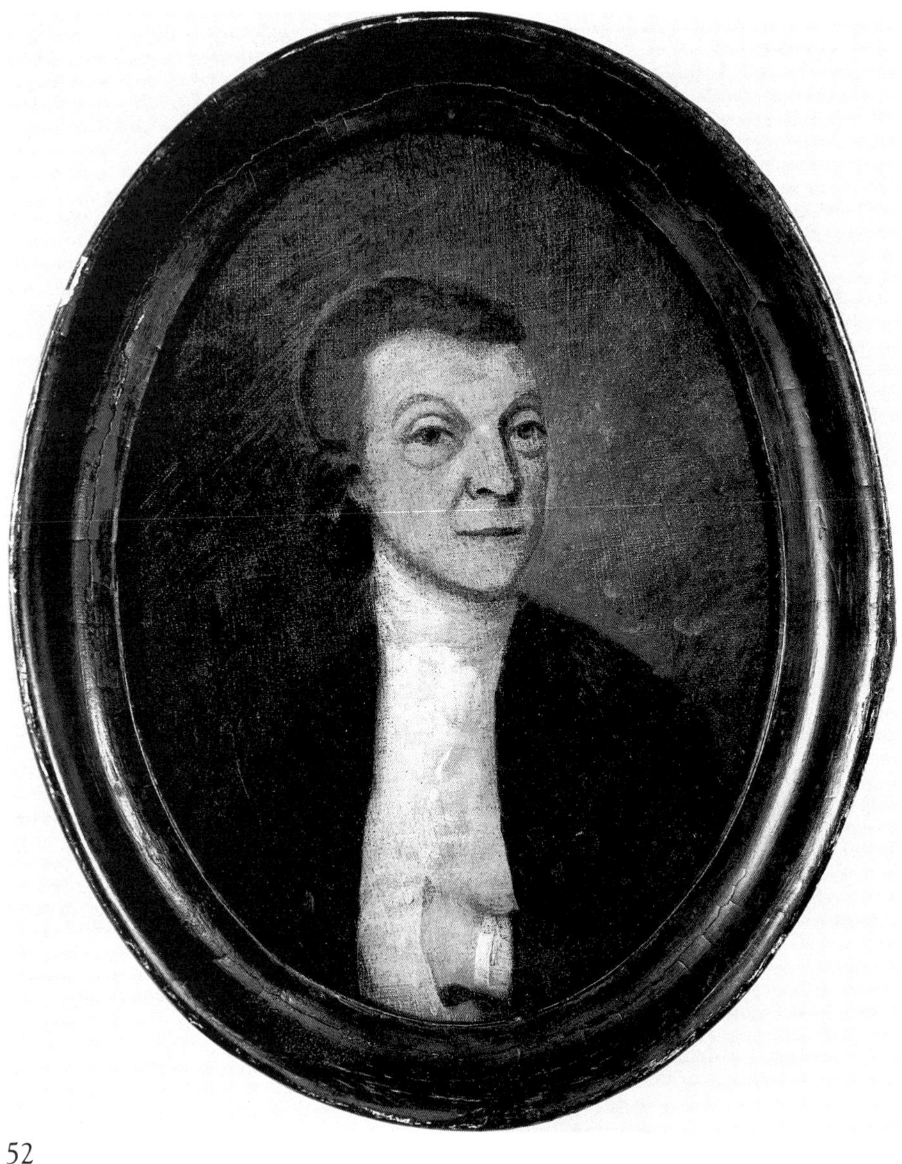

52

Georgia College Foundation, Old Governor's Mansion

John Milledge (1757–1818), whose father had been among the original settlers of the state in 1733, was born in Savannah in 1757. He studied law under Anthony Stokes, chief justice of Georgia, and was appointed attorney general in 1780 during the turmoils of the Revolutionary War. He had fought in the war during 1778–79.

From the Georgia Assembly, Milledge was elected to the U.S. Congress in 1792. From 1795 to 1798, he played a major role in exposing and repealing the Yazoo Land Act. Later he showed great diplomacy in acquiring the Indian land between the Ocmulgee and Oconee rivers. A new capital of Georgia was created in 1803 and named Milledgeville in his honor.

Milledge had been an original member of the Senatus Academicus, the committee that conceived of a public "seminary or college of learning" (Coulter, *College Life in the Old South*, 4). On 27 January 1785, he signed the charter for Franklin College (later The University of Georgia). For years the Senatus Academicus committee disagreed about the location for the institution. During Milledge's term as governor (1802–1806), a hill above Cedar Shoals was chosen, but this land was no longer owned by the State of Georgia. Finally, in 1801, Milledge himself purchased 633 acres on the Oconee River and donated the land to the state for the school.

After serving in the Senate, Milledge retired in 1809 to his plantation, Overton, near Augusta, and died there in 1818.

The artist Robert Field was born in England and studied at the Royal Academy. In 1794, he came to America and painted portraits and miniatures in Boston, Philadelphia, Washington, D.C., and Maryland. He died in Kingston, Jamaica, in 1819.

53 *William Harris Crawford,* 1818

Charles Willson Peale (1741–1827)

Washington, D.C.

Oil on canvas

H. 24", W. 20"

History: This painting was executed when Charles Willson Peale went to Washington to drum up support for his Philadelphia museum. He painted many distinguished men, including President Monroe, Secretary of War John C. Calhoun, as well as Crawford, Secretary of the Treasury, free of charge in exchange for their potential financial support of his museum.

Exhibitions: *Masterpieces in the High Museum of Art*, High Museum of Art, 1966

References: Sellars, *Charles Willson Peale*, 321; *Portraits and Miniatures by Charles Willson Peale*, 58; Lorant, *The Glorious Burden: The American Presidency*, 110; Mooney, *William H. Crawford, 1772–1834*, 211–12; Chambers, *American Paintings in the High Museum of Art: A Bicentennial Catalogue*, 16; National Society of the Colonial Dames of America, in Georgia, *Early Georgia Portraits, 1715–1870*, 49.

High Museum of Art, Gift of Mr. and Mrs. Granger Hansell

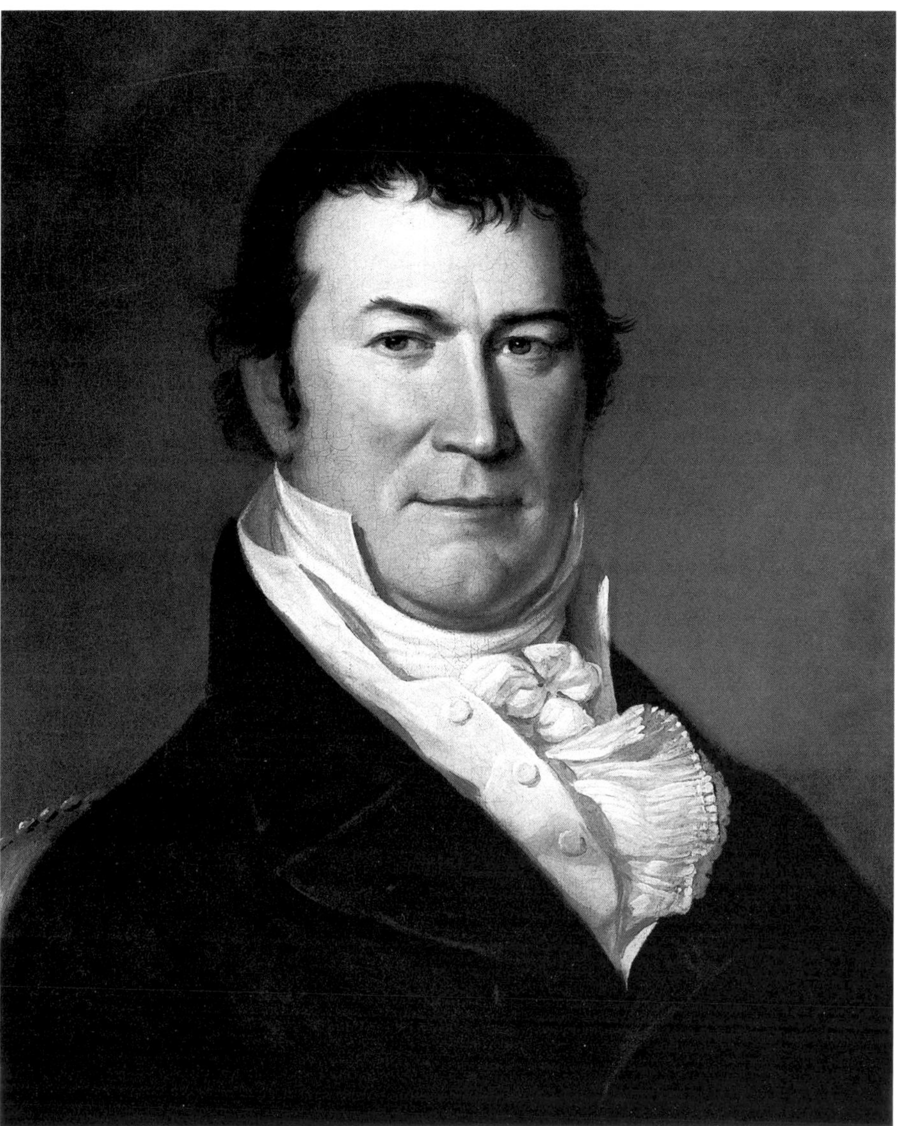

53

William H. Crawford (1772–1834) was born in Virginia but moved to Columbia County, Georgia, in 1783. A former pupil of the Reverend Moses Waddell, president of The University of Georgia from 1819 to 1830, Crawford taught at the Richmond Academy in Augusta before he studied and practiced law in Lexington, Georgia.

Crawford rose to political power in Oglethorpe County during the governorship of James Jackson, a Jeffersonian democrat. At this time, the upcountry was divided into two bitterly opposed parties: the Jacksonians, preferred by the planters, led by Crawford and George Troup, and the rival faction, led by John Clarke, son of General Elijah Clarke [48], and supported by North Carolinians. In 1807, Crawford succeeded Abraham Baldwin in the United States Senate and turned his attention to national politics. George Troup took over the leadership of the planters party in Georgia and led the political struggle against Clarke.

Crawford served as president pro tempore of the Senate, and in 1813 was U. S. ambassador to the Court of Napoleon in France. From 1816 to 1825, he was Secretary of War and Secretary of the Treasury under the administrations of Madison and Monroe.

In 1824, Crawford was a candidate for the presidency, along with Henry

Clay, Andrew Jackson, and John Quincy Adams, but an unfortunate paralyzing stroke caused him to withdraw from the race. Although President John Quincy Adams offered Crawford a cabinet post, the senator had only partially recovered. He returned to his home, Woodlawn, built in 1804 in Oglethorpe County (now Elbert County). He died 15 September 1834.

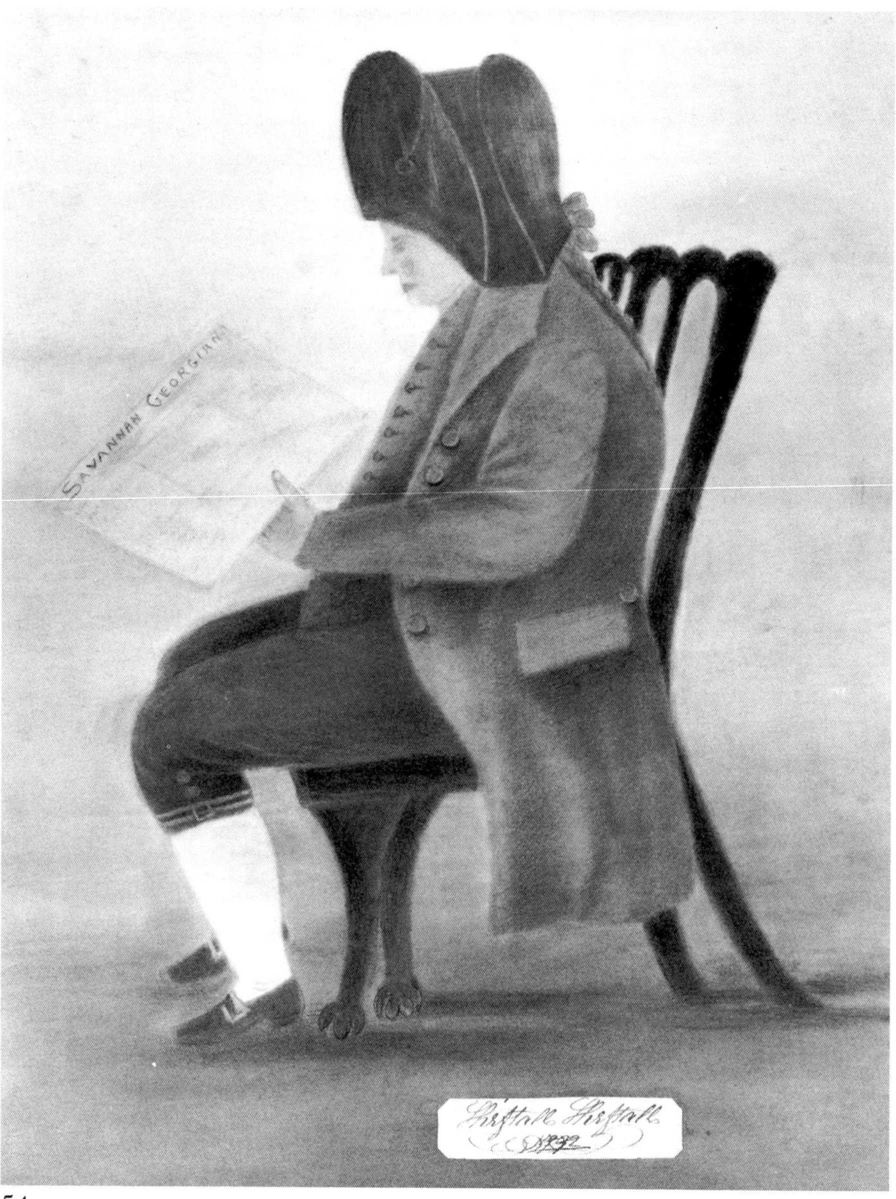

54

54 *Sheftall Sheftall* (photo-reproduction), ca. 1820

Savannah, Chatham County

Charcoal on paper

H. 19½″, W. 15½″

History: The Savannah *Georgian*, which Sheftall holds in this drawing, was established in 1818. This portrait descended in the family of Mordecai Sheftall.

References: Levy, *Savannah's Old Jewish Community Cemeteries*, 60–65; MESDA file #S–8438.

Private Collection

Sheftall Sheftall (1762–1849) was a third generation descendant of one of the original Georgia Jews, Benjamin Sheftall. His father, Mordecai Sheftall, had been a stalwart in the small Jewish community in colonial Savannah, and had financially supported the Georgia and Continental armies during the Revolution. After release from a British prison in Antigua in December 1780, Sheftall Sheftall served as the flag master on the sloop *Caroline Packett* and carried supplies to the Continental army under General William Moultrie in Charleston.

After the war, Sheftall spent a great deal of time in Philadelphia in hopes of recovering from the new government money his father had advanced to support the Continental army. He was elected president of the congregation of Mickva Israel for 1799–1800.

Something of an eccentric, but always the beloved Revolutionary War hero, Sheftall continued to wear the out-of-date clothes of days gone by, including the cocked hat, which earned him the name "Cocked Hat" Sheftall. In 1837, Joseph L. F. Cerveau painted a cityscape of Savannah in which he included a figure standing in front of the Savannah *Georgian* newspaper office, on Bay Street east of Bull; the figure is unmistakably "Cocked Hat" himself, complete with knee-britches. Sheftall died at age 87.

55 *Robert Ransome Billups,* ca. 1827

Attributed to Edwin B. Smith, Jr. (working 1815–1840s)

Possibly Clarke County

Oil on canvas

H. 33½", W. 34¾"

History: Portrait is attributed to Smith because of an inscription on the back of companion portrait of Billups's wife: Painted and presented by Edwin Bt. Smith, Junr. to Mrs. Elizabeth W. Billups, March 1, 1827.

Exhibitions: *Missing Pieces, Georgia Folk Art, 1770–1976*, Atlanta Historical Society, 1977

References: Wadsworth, et al., *Missing Pieces, Georgia Folk Art, 1770–1976*, 4, 34, 35; Bishop, *Folk Painters of America*, 164–65.

Collection of Mr. and Mrs. William W. Griffin

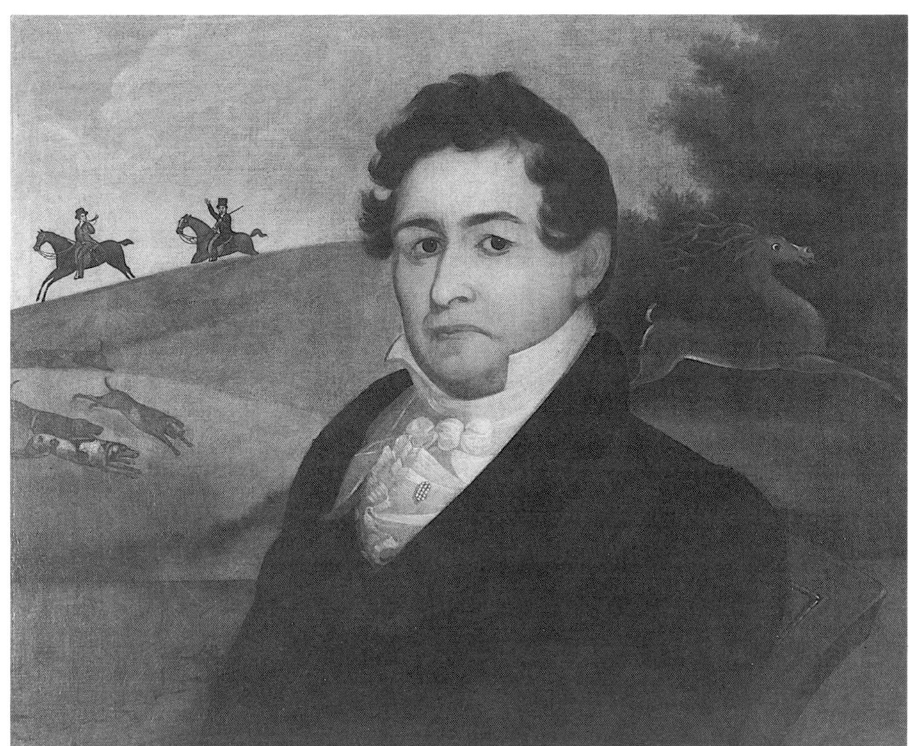

55

Robert Ransome Billups (d. 1836) married Elizabeth Ware Fullwood in Clarke County 11 September 1818. They had three children. Billups was killed 9 June 1836, in the Creek Indian battle at Shepherd's Plantation in Stewart County. His estate inventory (Record book H, page 5, Records of the Ordinary, 23 September 1836) includes an entry for four large frames and pictures valued at $20.00. Two of these framed works must be Billups' own portrait and that of Mrs. Billups. (The companion portrait is signed by Edwin Smith and dated 1827.)

The Billups' son, Edward Swepson Billups, married Mary Richardson, whose father Richard owned the Eagle Tavern (in what is now Watkinsville) from 1836 to 1871. The tavern was built in 1789 as a fort, but had been remodeled to become a stagecoach hotel in 1801. Edward and Mary Billups continued as its proprietors. The portraits of Edward's parents hung in the tavern until 1956, when a descendant gave the building to the State of Georgia.

Edwin B. Smith, portraitist and historical painter, worked in Ohio during 1815–32, and in New Orleans in 1841.

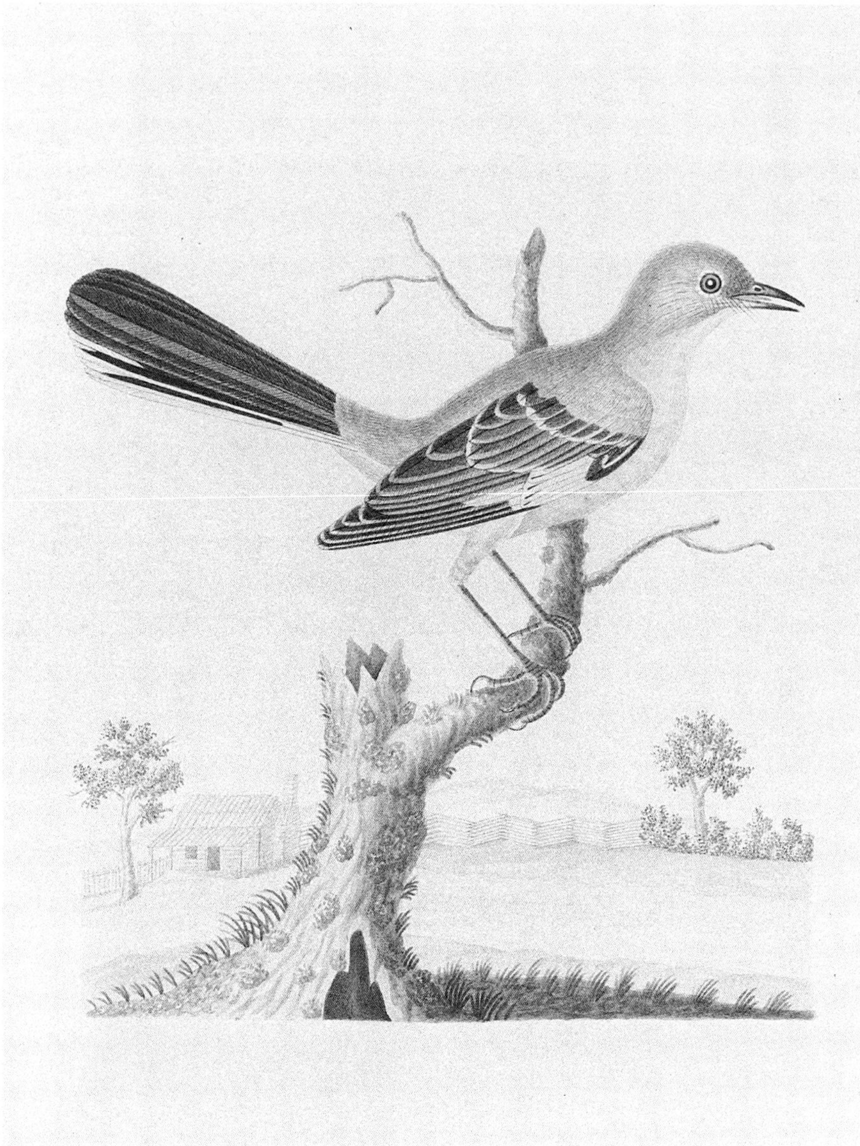

56

56 *Mimic Thrush or Mockingbird (Turdus Polyglottus)*, 1805–1809

John Abbot (1751–ca. 1840)

Burke County

Watercolor and graphite on paper

H. 11¼″, W. 8¼″

Marks: 144

History: One of 55 ornithological watercolors executed during 1805–09 and sold to Chetham's Library, Manchester, England.

Exhibitions: *John Abbot in Georgia: The Vision of a Natural Artist*, Madison-Morgan Cultural Center, 1983

References: Rogers-Price, *John Abbot in Georgia: The Vision of a Natural Artist*, 85 and cover; Rogers-Price and Griffin, "John Abbot: Pioneer Artist-Naturalist of Georgia," *The Magazine Antiques*, October 1983, 768–73.

Amon Carter Museum

Born in London in 1751, by the age of 16 John Abbot had learned drawing and engraving and had developed a "peculiar liking for insects" (Rogers-Price, *John Abbot in Georgia*, 17). He began sketching in graphite butterflies, moths, and the plants they ate; he then applied watercolored details.

In 1773, the Royal Society in London sent Abbot to collect natural history in Virginia. After several disappointments, he moved to Georgia in 1775 and lived 30 miles south of Augusta in Burke County (then Saint George's Parish). After the Revolution, Abbot added birds to his studies in the Savannah River Valley area. By the nineteenth century, Abbot's watercolors had become collectors' items by American and European naturalists, because of not only their precise details but also their beauty. John Francillon, London jeweler and naturalist, had compiled 17 bound volumes containing 2,843 works. In 1791, Francillon served as agent for the sale of 100 bird watercolors to the Chetham Library in Manchester, England. Another set of 55 ornithological drawings, including this one, were sold to the Chetham Library in 1809. Fewer than 200 of the 5,000 watercolors executed by Abbot were ever published, and these by contemporary naturalists in England. Abbot died in Bulloch County, where he had moved in 1818, in the early 1840s.

57 *Spirit Creek; near Augusta, Georgia*, 1820

John Hill (1770–1850) after Joshua Shaw

Richmond County

Engraving on paper

H. 11¾″, W. 15″

Description: Hand-tinted aquatint, from a volume entitled *Picturesque Views of American Scenery, 1820*, published by M. Carey and Sons, Philadelphia

Special Collections, The University of Georgia Libraries

This scene is one of several by John Hill, a prominent engraver from Philadelphia. It is considered the earliest example of a rural landscape recorded in Georgia.

Obviously, a storm was brewing when Shaw made his sketch. Copy accompanying the reproduction guessed as to why the name Spirit Creek was used:

> *Superstition*, which in all countries has peopled the dark and lonely glens with unearthly beings, probably gave its present appellation to this secluded stream. The names of American rivers and creeks, however, are generally far from indicating much poetical imagination. The original Indian names have been too often discarded for others less sonorous, though more intelligible and homely. Sometimes the names of European rivers are borrowed and applied to streams differing in every respect from their foreign prototypes . . . . the wind roared through the forest, and the rumbling of distant thunder might have been mistaken by the "belated cottager" for the hoarse threatening of the spirit of the stream.

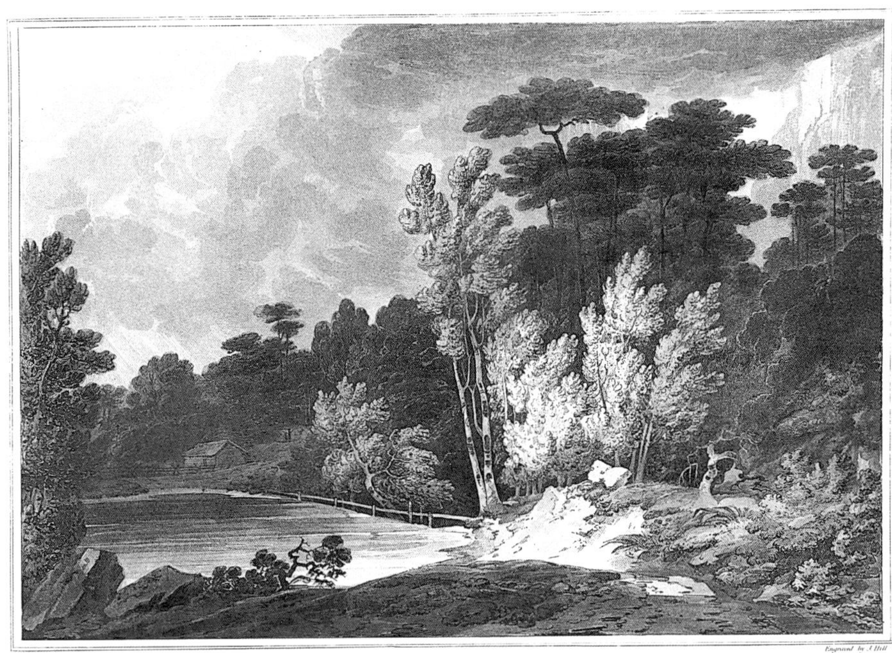

57

58 *Embryo Town of Columbus on the Chatahoochie* [sic], ca. 1830

W. H. Lizars after a drawing by Capt. B. Hall, R. N.

Columbus, Muscogee County

Engraving on paper

H. 9″, W. 11″

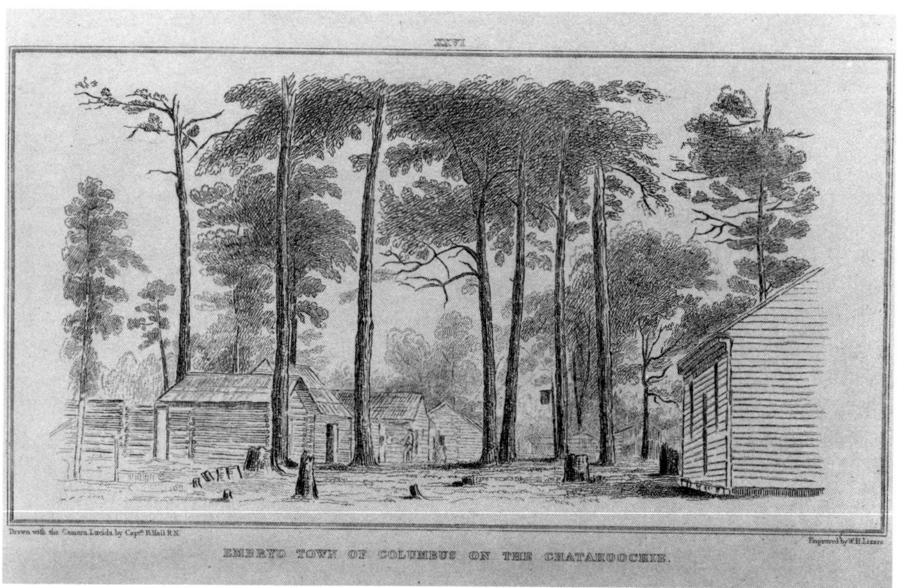

58

History: Captain Basil Hall, R. N., *Forty Etchings from Sketches made with the CAMERA LUCIDA in North America in 1827 and 1828*, published by Simpkin & Marshall, London, 1830, Plate XXVI.

Historic Columbus Foundation

While Captain Basil Hall of the Royal British Navy and his wife traveled through America for 14 months from 1827 to 1828, the Captain recorded scenes with his camera lucida, an apparatus with an arrangement of mirrors that reflects an image on a surface so that its outline can be traced.

The Creek lands between the Flint River and the Chattahoochee were purchased by the United States government during 1825–26. By 1827, a town on the falls of the Chattahoochee was in the planning stages. In early 1828, adventurous settlers, prospectors, surveyors, and artisans looking for jobs were already in the area and living in temporary houses, though the official land sales were not to occur until July 1828.

Apparently, some 900 people were on the scene when Captain and Mrs. Hall arrived in March at the Coweta Reserve (later Columbus, Georgia). The Halls both kept written accounts and described the frontier. Captain Hall commented on the advantages of placing the city on the Chattahoochee River falls: "The new city was to commence at the lower end of a long series of falls, or more properly speaking rapids, over which this great river, dashed in a very picturesque manner. The perpendicular fall being about 200 feet, an immense power for turning mills is placed at the disposal of the inhabitants of the future city" (Worsley, *Columbus on the Chattahoochee*, 74).

In her journal entries, Mrs. Hall noted:

> Basil says he has seen a town without inhabitants, but that he never before saw inhabitants without a town. (74)
>
> All of this is to be . . . for as yet the town is a thick forest, with the exception of some temporary wooden buildings erected to shelter the numerous bidders from all parts of the Union, who are waiting for the sale of lots . . . . (75)
>
> "And now," (their companion) said, as we were on the most rugged beshrubbed part of the path, "You are in the heart of the city." (75)
>
> The little temporary streets . . . presented a very strange appearance, little log and frame

houses, most of them intended to be moved . . . a few months hence. (75)

It was four o'clock when we reached Columbus, . . . and Basil took advantage of the remaining day light to make a sketch. This . . . brought all the idlers to stare, and he soon had a mob around him. (75)

59 *Bedspread*, 1812

Frances Tillman

Savannah, Chatham County

Linen, cotton embroidery

H. 86½", W. 81½"

Description: Embroidered central design of 17 six-pointed stars with an eagle holding three arrows and the olive branch; random embroidered floral design surrounds, but no distinct border; flat woven background; no fringe; fiber is candlewicked; satin, outline, seed, button hole, and couching stitches

Exhibitions: *Missing Pieces, Georgia Folk Art, 1770–1976*, Atlanta Historical Society, 1977

References: Wadsworth, et al., *Missing Pieces, Georgia Folk Art 1770–1976*, 74.

Westville Historic Handicrafts, Inc.

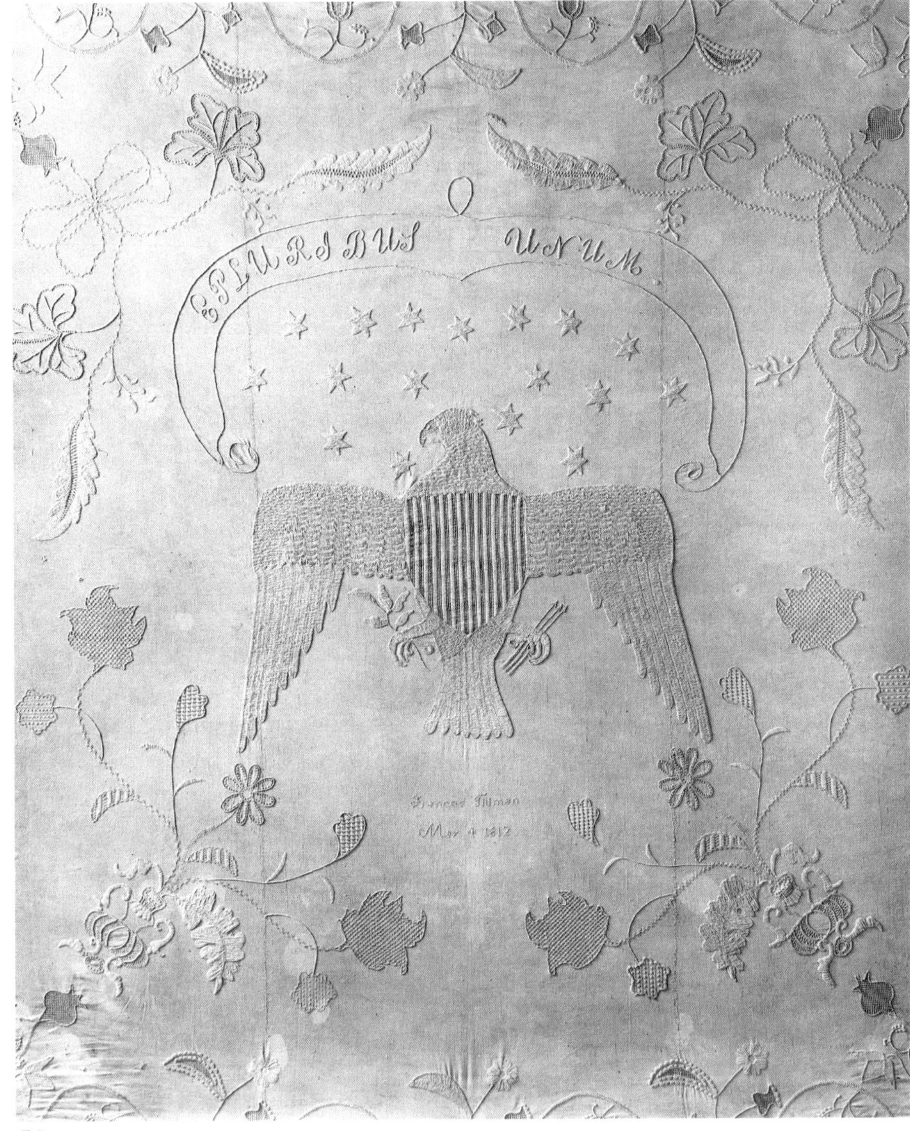

59

Bedspreads and counterpanes were made primarily as decorative covers. Quilts and coverlets, on the other hand, were basically utilitarian—needed for warmth—and secondarily decorative.

Few eighteenth-century textiles exist. Rare indigenous examples were either of homespun linen, Indian cotton, or imported chintzes. These were decorated with a centralized pattern, such as this eagle or the Tree of Life motif [112], surrounded by an undefined border, as a meandering floral design. During the nineteenth century, the border gets progressively more defined and symmetrical. After 1815, cotton cloth from factories was readily available and could be decorated by hand in all white, cotton roving techniques, such as candlewicking (three-ply twisted cotton fiber) and often with the fringe on three sides [60].

Often part of a complete set of canopy, tester, skirt, and curtains, these counterpanes were very large, sometimes 9 x 12 feet, to accommodate the high bedsteads of the nineteenth century. Seams are evident on those made on smaller frames at home, while seamless, professional examples were produced on a larger loomed format.

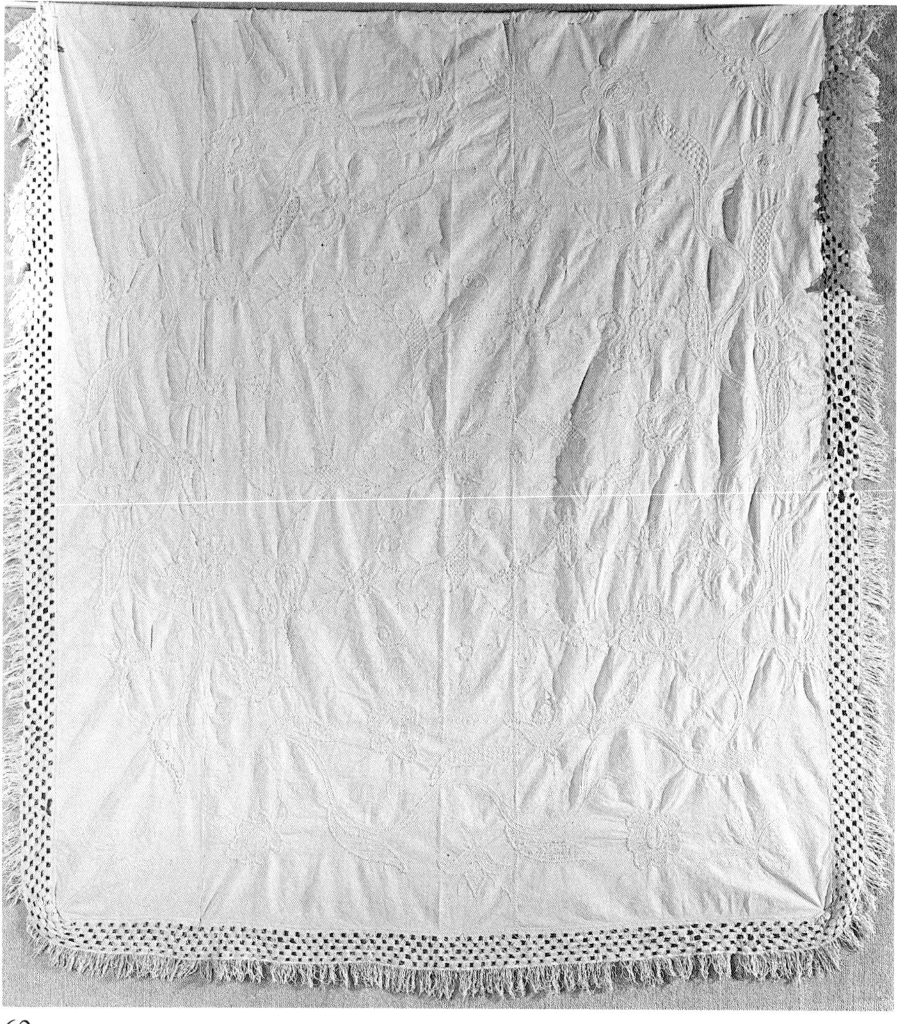

60

60 *Bedspread*, 1815

Sarah Ann Pittman (born 1798)

Madison County

Cotton embroidery on cotton; fringe is linen

H. 86", W. 94"

Description: Flat woven ground with a variety of embroidery stitches: satin, outline, seed, buttonhole, and couching; candlewicking; applied fringe on three sides is loom-made rather than tied; no central design near inscription; leaves and vine designs fill the space.

History: Sarah Ann Pittman was the ninth child of James and Martha Taylor Pittman, who moved to Richmond County, Georgia, from Virginia sometime before the Revolutionary War and died in Madison County in 1850. Sarah married Samson Lay on 11 February 1819, as recorded in the Madison County marriage book. Records of the 1832 lotteries of Cherokee land grants as well as the Gold Lottery of the same year list seven men with the last name Lay; it is possible that Samson and Sarah Ann Pittman Lay moved to northwest Georgia and that their descendants remained there when Cherokee lands became Polk County. The bedspread descended to the donor through her grandmother Annie Hamrick of Polk County, a granddaughter of Sarah Pittman.

Polk County Historical Society

This bedspread made in the piedmont region illustrates some style lag from basic designs of American nineteenth-century counterpanes and spreads. Eighteenth-century embroidered decorations were meandering with a central design that started at a base and spread outward toward imprecise borders. During the nineteenth century, the borders had become formalized around the central design [111]. By 1825, the patterns were more geometric than floral, and by the middle of the nineteenth century, a grid-like structure covered the entire ground [113, 114]. While the overall impression is asymmetrical, the fringe on three sides is typical of the time, 1815, when Miss Pittman embroidered this bedspread. These fringes were manufactured on a loom and sold by local merchants, who imported them from Europe.

Cabinetmaking in Coastal Georgia

From 1790 to 1830, wealthy planters and merchants on the coast were eager to fill their homes with fashionable furniture. Many bought items from New York rather than locally made pieces. Prior to this period, ornate furniture—of heavy mahogany, elaborately carved and styled after Thomas Chippendale's work in England—had been popular in America, even though Chippendale was passé in London by 1788. America soon adopted a new style, called Federal, a direct outgrowth of the new nationalism that was sweeping America.

Federal furniture incorporated neoclassical inlaid motifs, such as urns and swags, which had been revived by Robert Adam in England. Americanized neoclassical motifs symbolized the classical ideals of Greece and Rome which had been the source of the new nation's democratic government. Lighter, more delicate forms were integral to the Federal style, and the use of veneers over cheap woods made furniture more affordable to the growing middle class of merchants and farmers. Cabinet shops in America's important urban centers—Philadelphia, New York, Baltimore, and Charleston—borrowed and adapted designs from English pattern books such as George Hepplewhite's *The Cabinetmaker and Upholsterer's Guide* and Thomas Sheraton's *The Cabinet-Maker and Upholsterer's Drawing Book*, and created their own versions of the style.

Georgia craftsmen also relied on pattern books and produced proficient examples of new Federal forms, such as the pembroke table, card table, and sideboard. Cabinetmakers would have taken note of an 1818 advertisement in *The Savannah Republican* which reported that Seth and James Schenck, bookbinders in Savannah, had just received *The Carpenter's New Guide* by Peter Nicholson, "being a complete book of lines for Carpentry and Joinery with 84 plates . . . $7.50" (15 September 1818).

Exquisite wood was available to the coastal cabinetmaker. Mahogany, used as a primary wood and for veneers, was

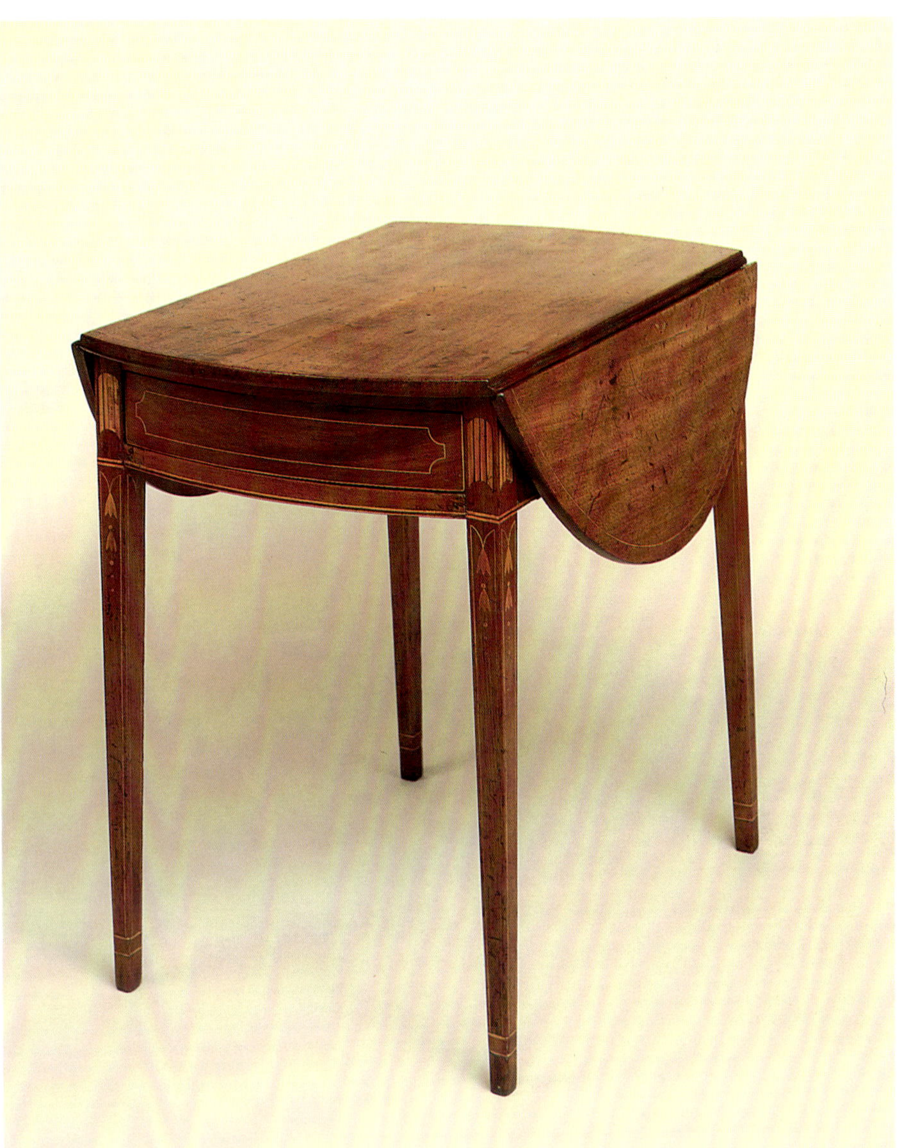

61

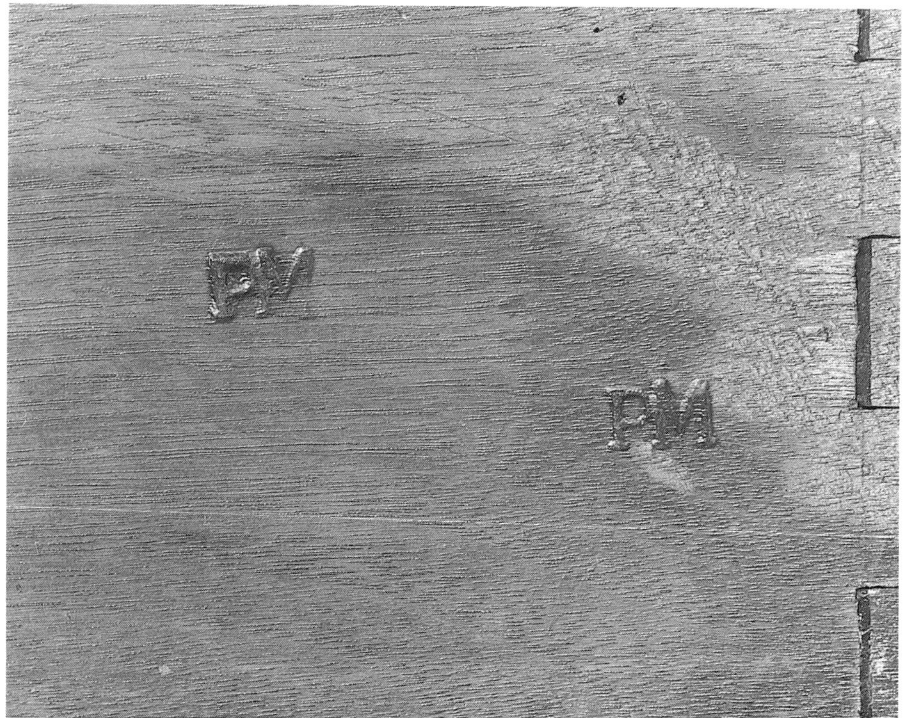

61 detail

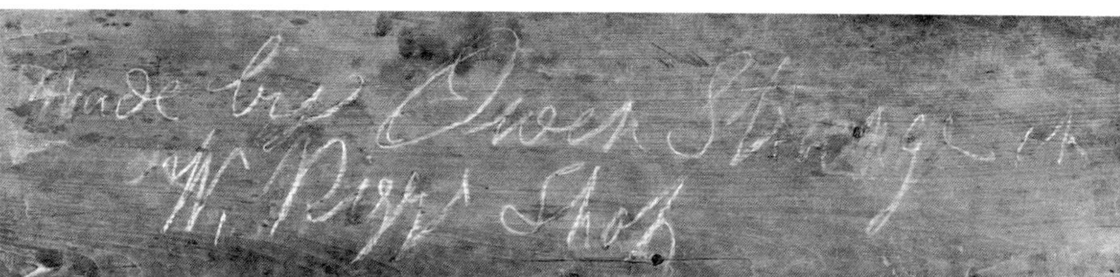

62 detail

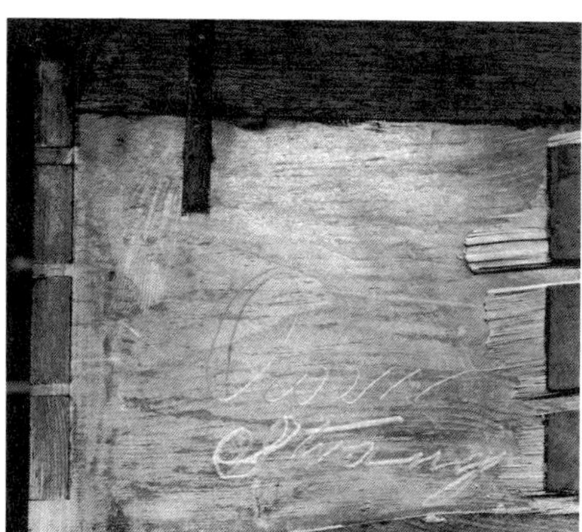

62 detail

collected from West Indian trade routes. Dark mahogany came from Cuba and Santo Domingo, with redder shades from Honduras (Gross, "The Sources of Furniture Sold in Savannah, 48). Before the turn of the nineteenth century, a time of increased trade along the American coast, craftsmen used local woods for the secondary parts of their furniture. These included cypress, yellow pine, tulip poplar, sweet gum, hickory, oak, and red cedar. During the Federal period, however, white pine, earlier associated only with northern-made furniture, became readily available in southern ports. It was employed as a secondary wood, combined with those grown locally.

During this period, chair and cabinetmaking progressed from an individualized craft to a shop format with divided labor. In urban shops, apprentices and journeymen actually completed many pieces, while the master or owner of the shop often received full credit. Owen Strange was one journeyman who apparently desired recognition for his own work. Strange was a journeyman in the shop of William Riggs, who advertised from 1801 to 1810 as a cabinetmaker, upholsterer, and seating chair-maker. The Owen Strange desk and bookcase included in the exhibition was signed in chalk between 1801 and 1809, "Made by Owen Strange in / W. Riggs Shop." Strange announced in 1809 that he had "moved into the house lately occupied by Messrs. Hewitt and Mandeville as a wareroom." Obviously, he had opened his own shop. Whether this happened immediately after he left Riggs is not known, but Riggs no longer advertised after 1810.

The earliest documented evidence of two specialized Georgia craftsmen working under one roof was the partnership between the upholsterer and cabinetmaker. In 1789, Isaac Fell in Savannah was calling himself a "cabinetmaker and upholsterer" (*Georgia Gazette*, 3 December 1789). In 1793, Gabriel Leaver of Savannah had advertised the "upholstery business in all its branches," but by 1795, he needed apprentices for the "cabinetmakers *and* upholsterer business" (*Georgia Gazette*, 22 August 1793, 8 January 1795).

The success of such partnerships was no doubt influenced by the tastes currently in vogue. However, newspaper ads in Savannah, unlike those in the piedmont, tended not to list available upholstered goods nor describe them in detail. Savannah clientele came to prefer Duncan Phyfe's New York style, and inventories of local merchants give evidence of a preference for these late Federal and Empire pieces rather than upholstered ones. There were "dining and pembroke tables" on "pillar and claw feet" [69], "sideboards with carved pillars" [72], "lyre card tables" (*Georgia Journal*, 24 November 1818; Faries & Miller: *The Republican and Savannah Evening Ledger*, 23 November 1815; Langeley & Rindge; *The Savannah Republican*, 8 February 1817, Adam & Miller).

To identify a piece of furniture as coastal, one needs a provenance tracing the piece to a coastal family and/or the use of indigenous woods. Stylistic decoration and construction techniques are not reliable clues to the origin of these pieces. The Peter Miller pembroke table shown here illustrates this dilemma. The inlay on the piece might suggest a South Carolina provenance, since this rendition of a bell flower was used regularly in that state. Yet the table's fully documented history of ownership in the Savannah family of Miller's son Jacob assures its Georgia origin. Because of advertisements, we know that craftsmen were working on the coast, but until more examples are found, a coastal style cannot be defined.

61 *Pembroke Table*, ca. 1800

Peter Miller (working 1788–1810), Savannah

Coastal

Primary woods: mahogany with light wood inlay; secondary woods: yellow pine drawer frame; cypress inner frame and drawer bottom; mahogany gate frame

H. 29½", W. 29⅞", D. 39¼" (open), 20⅞" (closed)

Marks branded twice inside of gate frame: PM

Description: Drawer is without hardware, but has a finger notch set back about six inches under the bottom. Drawer supports are wrought nailed to inner frame; top board has shrunk so that the leaves do not fall straight down. Each leg has string inlay on all four sides with bell flowers on only two sides.

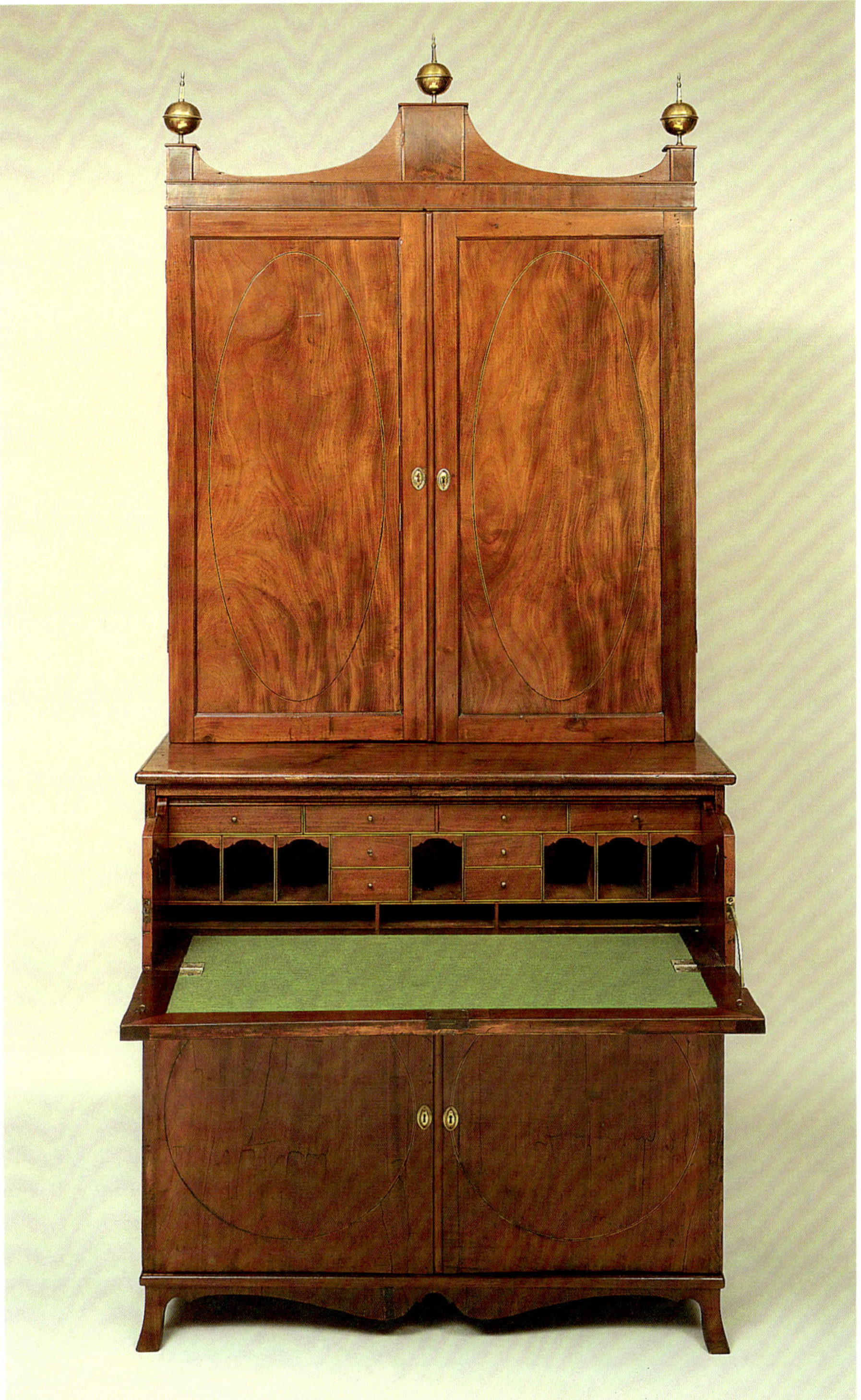

62

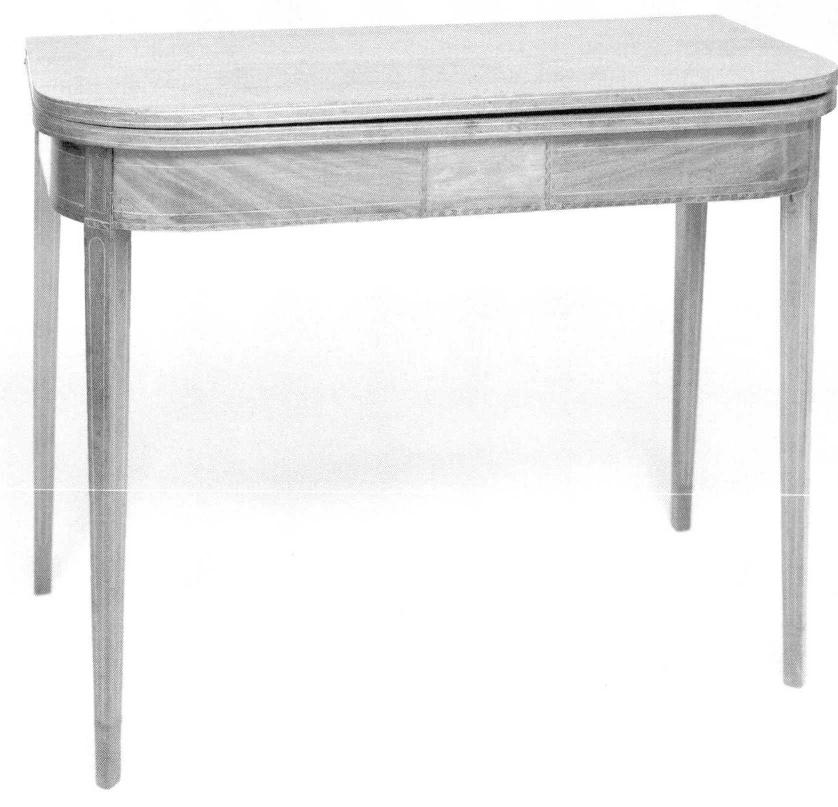

63

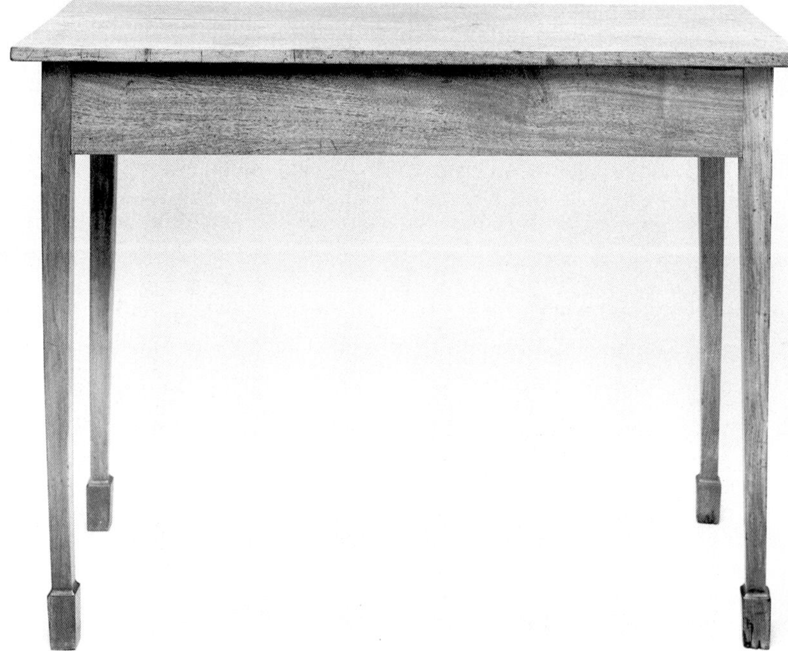

64

History: Descended in the family of Jacob Miller, son of Peter Miller. On 6 August 1807, Peter Miller advertised in the *Republican and Savannah Evening Ledger* that "one double Iron Fore plain, one Jack plain, and a Handsaw, all marked 'PM'" had been stolen.

References: MESDA file #S–8277.

Private Collection

62 *Secretary Desk and Bookcase*, 1801–1809

Owen Strange (working on his own, 1809–1812), Savannah

Coastal

Primary woods: mahogany and mahogany veneer; light and dark wood inlay; secondary woods: yellow pine desk back boards and large drawer sides and bottoms; white pine interior drawer sides, desk drawer back and sides, bookcase back

H. 91⅞", W. 42⅞", D. 33¾"

Inscription in chalk behind secretary drawer: Made by Owen Strange in / W. Riggs Shop.

Inscription carved into side of same drawer: Owen Strang

Description: The desk drawers are linen-type that pull out; all escutcheons replaced. Lack of molding around the bookcase suggests that the upper and lower portions may not have originally been together.

The Columbus Museum of Arts and Sciences

63 *Card Table*, ca. 1800–1810

Coastal, possibly Savannah

Primary woods: mahogany and mahogany veneer; secondary woods: yellow pine inner and front frame; poplar back gate frame; white pine medial brace

H. 29½", W. 38⅝", D. 18¾"

Description: Both legs swing; each back swing leg has a flange which fits over the apron.

History: Descended in the family of Sir Patrick Houstoun, Savannah.

References: MESDA file #S–8480.

Collection of Anne Elizabeth Deméré, in memory of Mr. and Mrs. Raymond McAllister Deméré

64 *Huntboard/Serving Table*, ca. 1800–1810

Coastal

Primary wood: mahogany; secondary wood: yellow pine back

H. 38″, W. 50¼″, D. 22″

Description: Legs taper on all four sides; feet do not.

History: Purchased from a smokehouse in Liberty County, Georgia, before 1930.

References: *Antiques*, October 1930, 336; MESDA file #S–8445.

Collection of Mrs. Sam McCormick

65 *Work Table*, ca. 1810

Coastal, possibly Savannah

Primary woods: mahogany and mahogany veneer with crossbanding; light burl wood veneered on small drawers; light wood inlay; secondary woods: white pine large drawer frame and bottom; white pine small drawer frame; poplar cabinet drawer back and small drawer bottoms

H. 37″, W. 31⅜″, D. 18 7/16″

Description: Cabinet is fastened to base by two screwed batons at each end; the cabinet does not fit properly into the cut-out pattern around top edges of base.

History: Descended in the Charlton and Hartridge families.

References: MESDA file #S–8488.

Private Collection

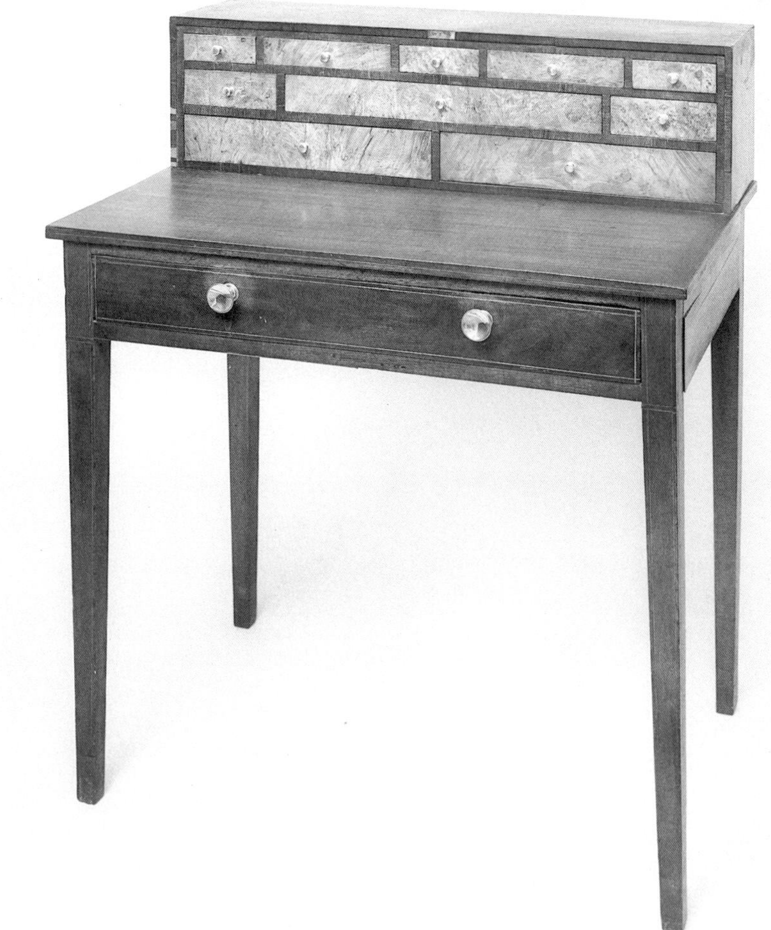

65

66 *Work Table*, ca. 1800–1810

Coastal, possibly Savannah

Primary woods: mahogany with light wood inlay; secondary wood: yellow pine

H. 28¼″, W. 25⅝″, D. 22½″

Description: String inlay on three sides of front legs and on front and sides of back legs; the back board is unfinished and meant to face a wall.

History: Descended in the family of General Henry R. Jackson (1820–1898), Savannah.

Private Collection

67 *Side Chair*, ca. 1810

Coastal

Primary wood: mahogany; secondary wood: white pine slip seat

H. 35¼″, W. 19¾″, D. 16¼″

Marks, second of a set of side chairs marked I-V: II

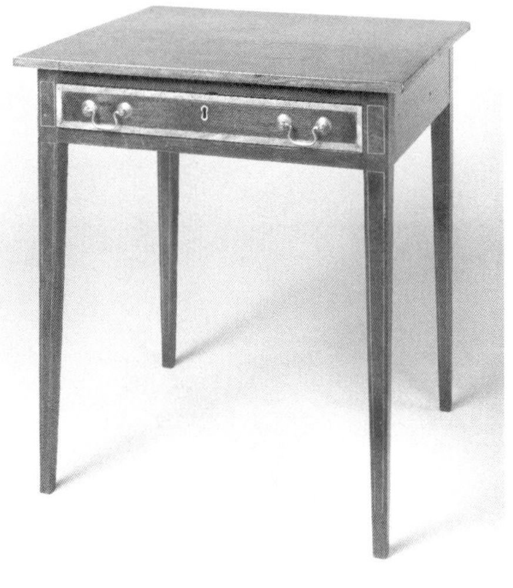

66

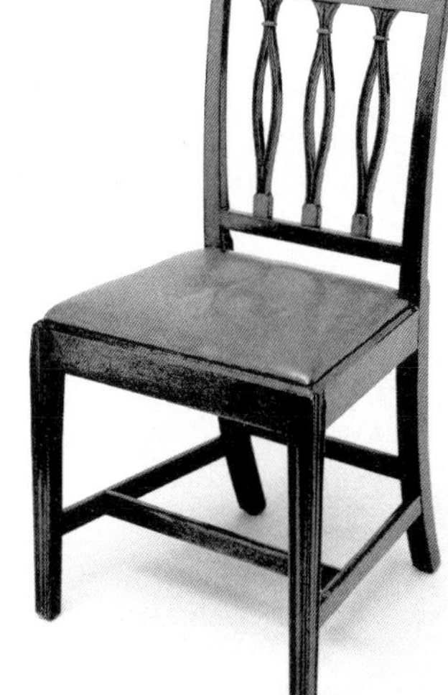

67

Description: Molded front legs taper slightly; mahogany veneer on back chair rail.

History: Purchased from a Savannah family in the 1940s.

References: MESDA file #S–8454.

Collection of Mr. and Mrs. Henry D. Green

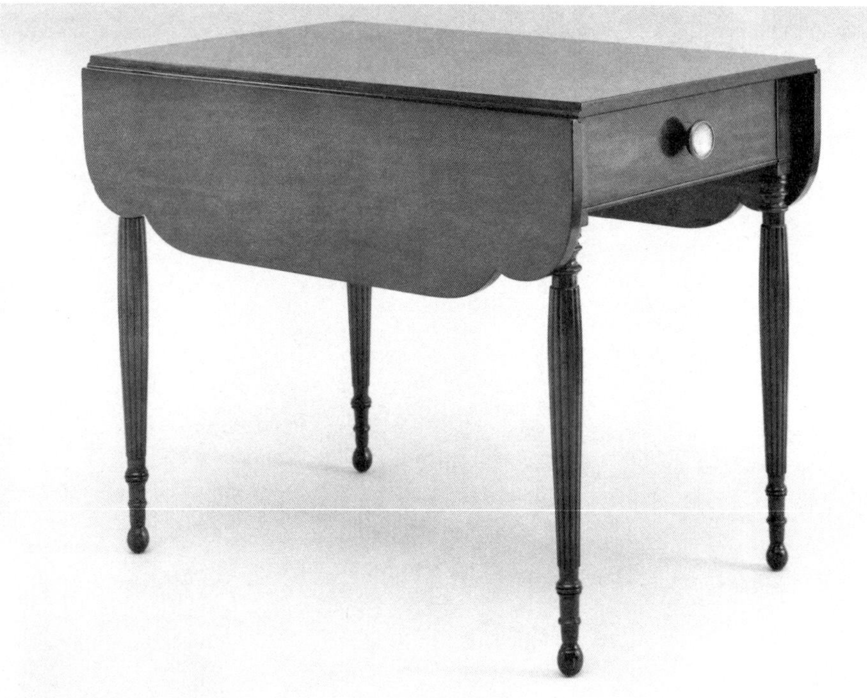

68

68 *Pembroke Table*, ca. 1810

Coastal

Primary wood: mahogany; secondary woods: yellow pine core, cypress drawer sides and bottom

H. 28½″, W. 36″, D. 40¾″

References: Green, "Georgia's Early Governor's Mansion," *Antiques*, December 1968, 867.

Georgia College Foundation, Old Governor's Mansion

69 *Breakfast Table*, ca. 1815–1820

Coastal

Primary wood: mahogany; secondary woods: walnut hinge; cypress core; yellow pine braces

H. 28″, W. 40⅞″, D. 24¾″

Collection of Mr. and Mrs. Dale C. Critz

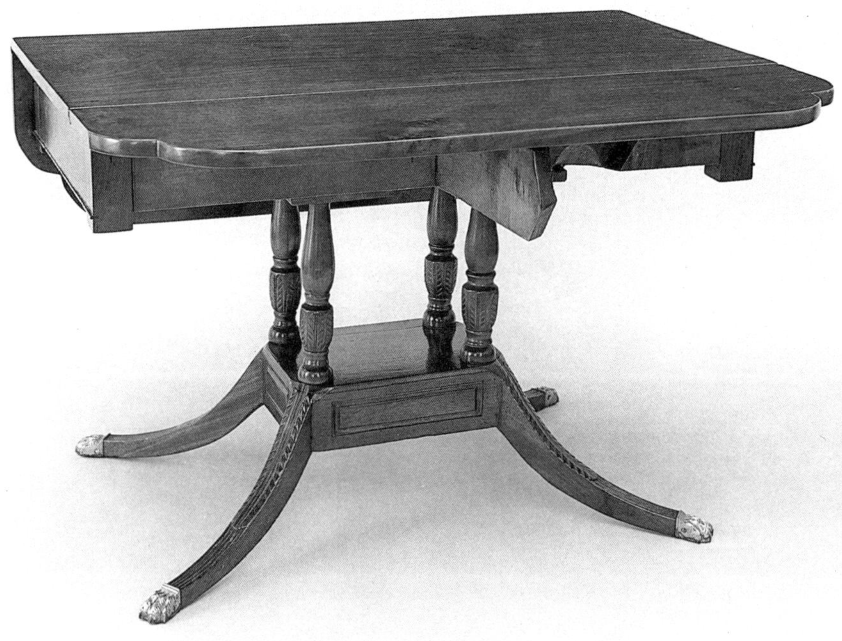

69

70 *Washstand*, ca. 1810

Coastal, possibly New Ebenezer, Effingham County

Primary woods: mahogany and mahogany veneer; secondary woods: yellow pine framing and drawer sides; poplar back and drawer bottoms

H. 37″, W. 25⅛″, D. 17¾″

Description: Front curved frame is laminated and veneered.

History: Descended in the family of Elizabeth Burkhalter Powell (born 1832), whose ancestor, Matthew Burgholder, came to Ebenezer with the third Salzburger immigration on the *London Merchant*.

References: Gnann, *Georgia Salzburger and Allied Families*, 32; MESDA file #S–8470.

Collection of Mrs. A. C. Nichols, Jr.

71 *Huntboard*, ca. 1820

Coastal

Primary wood: yellow pine; secondary wood: white pine drawer back

H. 40", W. 42¾", D. 22"

Description: Drawer front extends beyond applied molding; serves as a drawer stop.

History: Purchased in coastal Georgia in the 1930s.

References: MESDA file #S–8472.

Private Collection

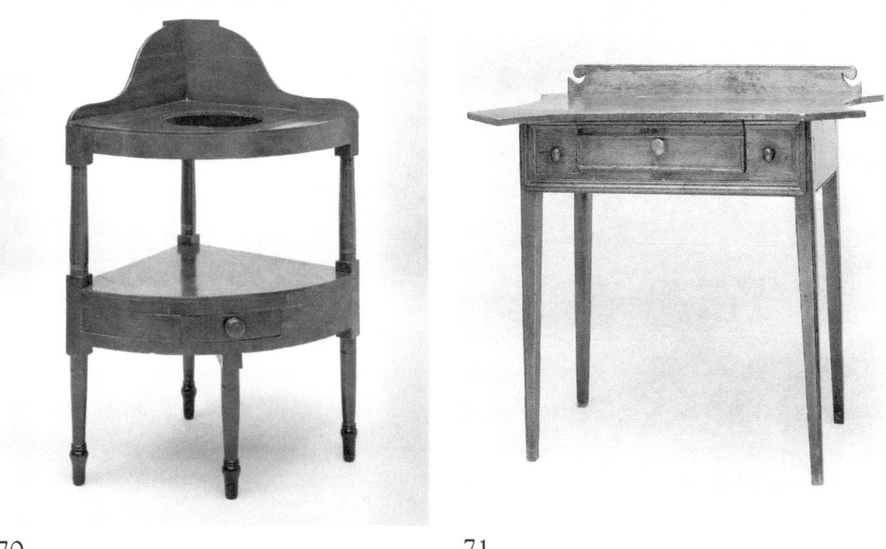

70

71

72 *Sideboard*, ca. 1820–1830

Coastal

Primary woods: mahogany, mahogany veneer; secondary woods: yellow pine, white pine back board

H. 39¾", W. 71½", D. 25" (at center)

Inscription written in pencil inside the backboard: Robert Williamson Harris was born in the year of our Lord 1810-April the 19th day

Description: Drawer front cores are laminated and veneered; recessed panels on case sides; reeded on stiles cut from one piece of wood and applied

History: Purchased in Savannah for the Dickey House Antebellum Plantation, Stone Mountain Park.

Exhibitions: *Furniture of the Georgia Piedmont*, High Museum of Art, 1976

References: Green, *Furniture of the Georgia Piedmont Before 1830*, 47.

Antebellum Plantation, Georgia's Stone Mountain Park

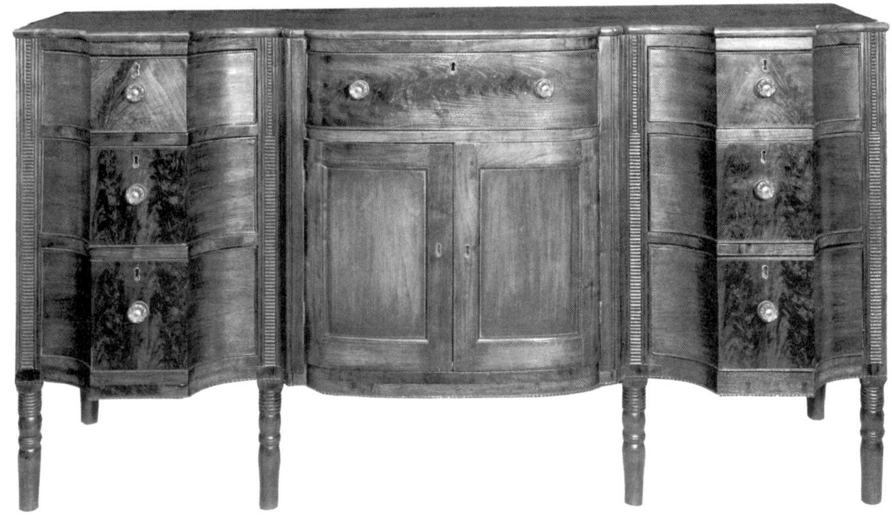

72

Cabinetmaking in the Georgia Piedmont

After the Revolution, the piedmont quickly became the most thriving part of the state. Governor James Wright had arranged for the 1773 acquisition of the area from the Creek and Cherokee Indians. It consisted of two million acres of fertile land in the Appalachian foothills. Recognizing the potential of the piedmont, the governor prompted the government to develop the region—first laying out the town of Washington in what became Wilkes County and then setting up a homestead program that offered 200 acres of land to heads of incoming families. The upcountry soon became a network of small tobacco farmers.

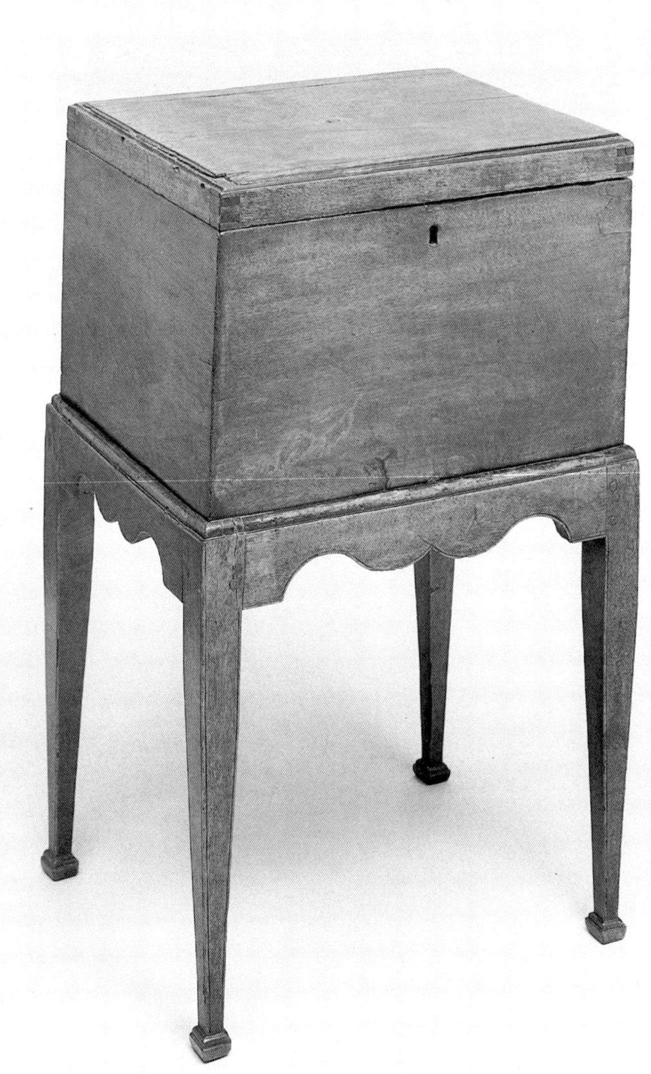

73

Because of the settlement of the piedmont, by 1800, the state's pre-Revolutionary War population of 33,000 had expanded to 162,000.

Although walnut was the preferred primary wood of the piedmont cabinetmaker, sources such as the 1820 Census of Manufacturers of Georgia list a variety of woods in local inventories: maple, burch [sic] (Charles C. Webb and Caswell D. Morris of Jones County), and cherry. Warham Easley of Athens needed "several hundred feet of cherry plank" (*Georgia Express*, 6 August 1808). All grown locally, these woods were used to produce furniture that the small farmer could afford.

Upcountry craftsmen supplied materials and furnishings to prosperous planters as well as to small farmers. Local craftsmen found, however, that it was expensive to transport mahogany, preferred by the wealthy, to Augusta and beyond. Able to accommodate both middle- and upper-class clientele, James Alexander in Washington advertised: "mahogany furniture on moderate terms" and "walnut furniture furnished to those who may require it" (*Monitor*, 3 March 1810). John W. W. Powers, a cabinetmaker on Centre Street in Augusta, sold "plain and ornamental (furniture) . . . . His stock of mahogany is extensive . . . he has been at great trouble in selecting some of the finest shades" (*Augusta Chronicle*, 1 December 1810).

Savannah suppliers rarely advertised furniture hardware in newspapers, possibly because craftsmen there could easily import such items directly from England. Piedmont newspapers, however, announced the availability of "elegant furniture mounting" for the "country cabinetmaker" (*Georgia Journal*, 13 November 1809; *Augusta Chronicle*, 21 May 1814). The estate inventory of Greene County cabinetmaker James Parks lists "1 lot desk mountings, locks and knobs, $14.50." Most likely, Parks' hardware was made in local upcountry foundaries.

Surviving examples of upcountry furniture date primarily from the Federal period. Locally made furniture was often transitional, a combination of Federal details with Chippendale lines and form. For example, the Chippendale ogee bracket foot with inner-crescent curve is associated with piedmont case pieces. The doors of a circa 1810 bookcase made in Franklin County [76] has arched panelled doors characteristic of the Queen Anne period, and the exaggerated overhang and cornice with dentil molding that were typical of the Chippendale era.

Piedmont shops produced mostly standard Federal forms, such as work tables, chests of drawers, three-sectioned dining tables, and sideboards. The types of construction and inlaid decorations used were distinctive; in fact, piedmont furniture evokes the only regional style in Georgia's decorative arts. The number of surviving examples of chests of drawers provide evidence of one school of piedmont craftsmanship, characterized by: graduated drawers, side panels with the apron cut from one piece of wood, serpentine or scallopped apron, applied molding around the top board, and cockbeading around the drawers. Top drawers of chests and work tables have blind locks; lower drawers have metal locks and escutcheons.

The inlays found on this furniture reveal much about the heritage and design sources of the piedmont cabinetmaker. Many pieces have simple string inlay around drawers and aprons and down tapered legs, all commonly found features. Others, such as the desk-and-bookcase made for Margaret or Mary Burns [76], suggest that craftsmen were aware of vine and berry inlays found on furniture of Chester County, Pennsylvania, consisting of string-inlaid half-circles with berries at each intersection or endings or both. The heart found on the fall board of this desk-and-bookcase also resembles motifs on Pennsylvania German frakturs. String inlays ending with a pointed oval and a stylized jonquil, tulip, or bell flower are reminiscent of Kentucky and western Virginia vine designs [77, 78, 81, 82, 83]. Outside the piedmont, "hollow-round," or cut-out, inlays at drawer corners [77] are found on furniture made in Pennsylvania, Kentucky, and the Carolinas, all places of birth for the transplanted Georgia piedmont craftsman.

Two pieces in the exhibition have broad southern significance—the cellaret [73] and the sideboard with patterae or sunburst decoration [85]. Believed to have been produced only in the South, the cellaret, found with tall

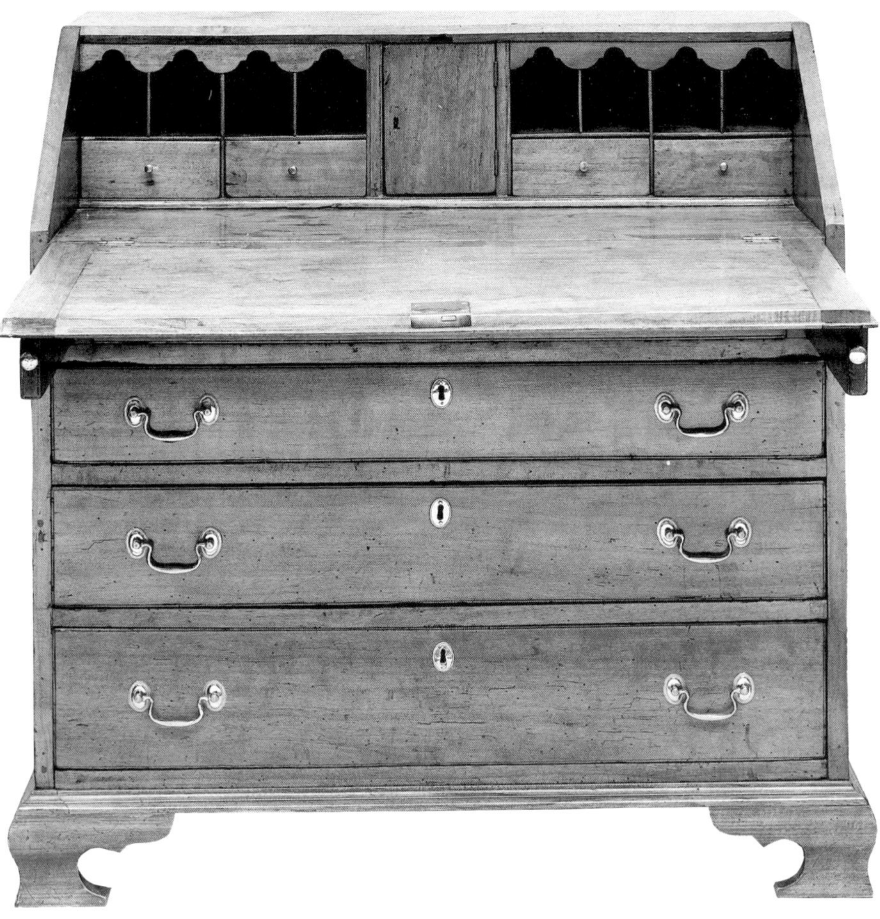

74

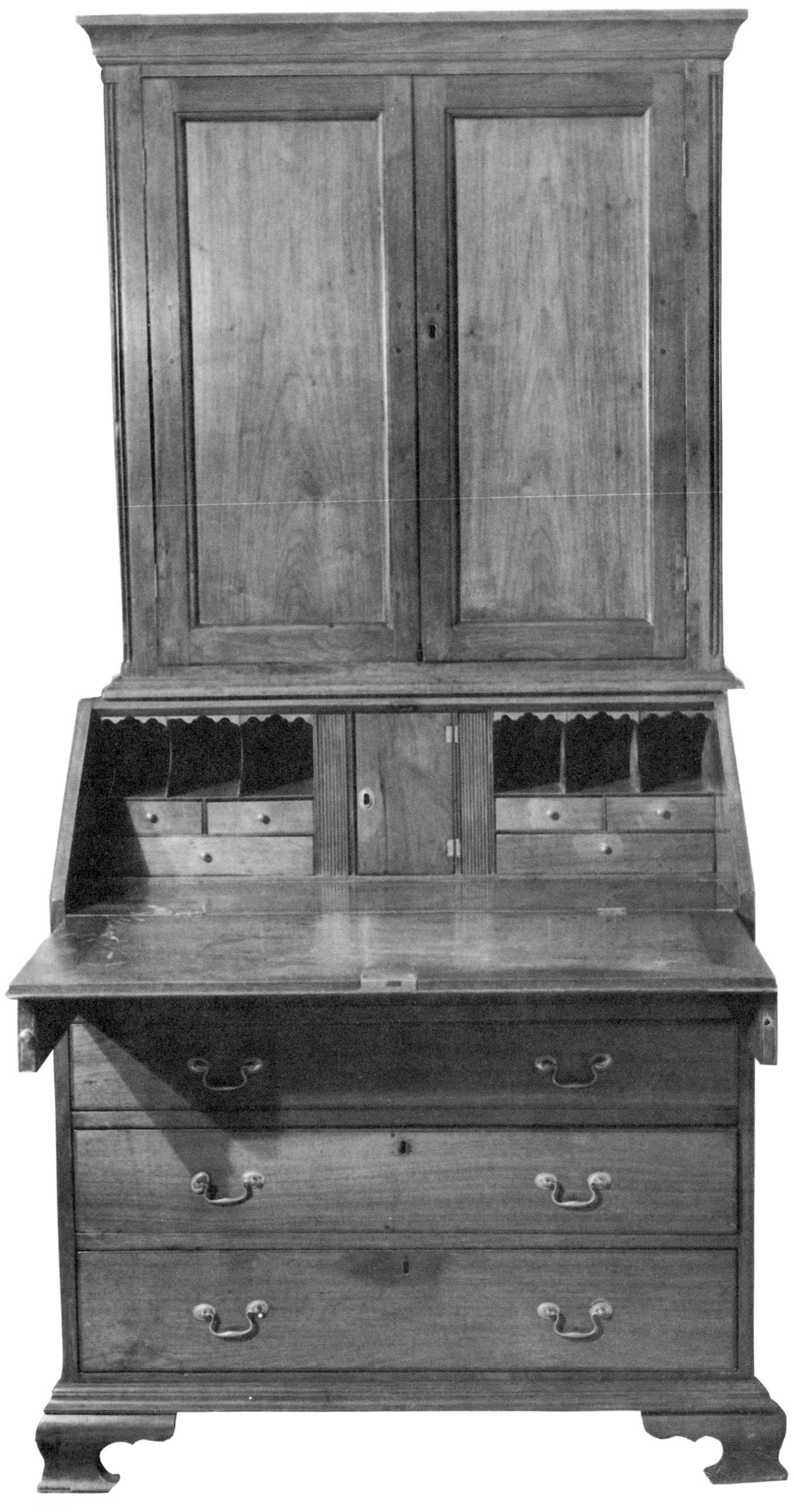

75

legs south of Maryland, was a box with dividers for storing liquor bottles. Though the term "cellaret" has not been found in nineteenth-century Georgia inventories, chests, cases, or stands with or without bottles are frequently listed (Griffin, *Neat Pieces*, 6). The typical Georgia sideboard has three sections with the projecting midsection flanked by quarter-round columns. The sculptural surface seen here was not common in early American Federal furniture; yet the sunburst applied to the drawers of this Madison County sideboard were common architectural features of early nineteenth-century interiors [86]. This neoclassic motif is frequently seen on mantels, door and window jambs, and other woodwork of Federal architecture throughout the South.

The settlers who originally ventured down the Philadelphia wagon road to the Georgia piedmont were second- and third-generation Scotch-Irish—traditionally diligent workers and craftsmen. Unlike the stratified social conditions on the coast, the short staple cotton economy of the piedmont fostered a working class who supported a number of local craftsmen for an extended period of time. These artisans brought their various traditions from Kentucky, Virginia, and the Carolinas, and effectively translated them into an indigenous furniture and a regional style.

73 *Cellaret-on-Frame*, ca. 1800–1810

Piedmont, possibly Athens area

Primary wood: walnut; secondary wood: yellow pine box bottom

H. 29½", W. 17¾", D. 13½"

Description: Box sides have closed dovetail joints and the lid, open dovetail joints; frame has molding on all four sides; serpentine apron has gouged-line carved decoration; legs, cut from solid lengths of wood, taper and end in squared feet; box is divided into twelve sections for storing bottled wines or other liquors.

Exhibitions: *Furniture of the Georgia Piedmont*, High Museum of Art, 1976

References: Green, *Furniture of the Georgia Piedmont Before 1830*, 76; Green, "Furniture of the Georgia Piedmont Before 1820," *Art & Antiques*, January-February 1982, 87; MESDA file #S–6416.

Collection of Mr. and Mrs. Henry D. Green

74 *Desk*, ca. 1800–1810

Piedmont

Primary wood: yellow birch; secondary wood: yellow pine

H. 41½″, W. 40″, D. 20¼″

Description: Ogee bracket foot with crescent curve on inside edge; gouging around large drawer fronts; half-round scalloped interior desk molding

History: Purchased in Nicholson, Georgia, formerly Franklin County, in the 1940s.

Exhibitions: *Furniture of the Georgia Piedmont Before 1830*, High Museum of Art, 1976

References: Green, *Furniture of the Georgia Piedmont Before 1830*, 107; Green, "Furniture of the Georgia Piedmont Before 1820," *Art & Antiques*, January-February 1982, 85.

Collection of Mr. and Mrs. Henry D. Green

75 *Desk-and-Bookcase*, ca. 1800–1810

Piedmont

Primary wood: walnut; secondary woods: yellow pine, oak interior drawer sides

H. 83″, W. 38⅞″, D. 21½″

Description: Ogee bracket feet with crescent curve on inside; gouging around exterior drawer fronts; scalloped interior molding; reeded quarter-round columns on bookcase

History: Purchased in Athens, Georgia, in the 1930s.

Exhibitions: *Furniture of the Georgia Piedmont Before 1830*, High Museum of Art, 1976

References: Green, *Furniture of the Georgia Piedmont Before 1830*, 113.

Collection of Mr. and Mrs. L. Milton Leathers III

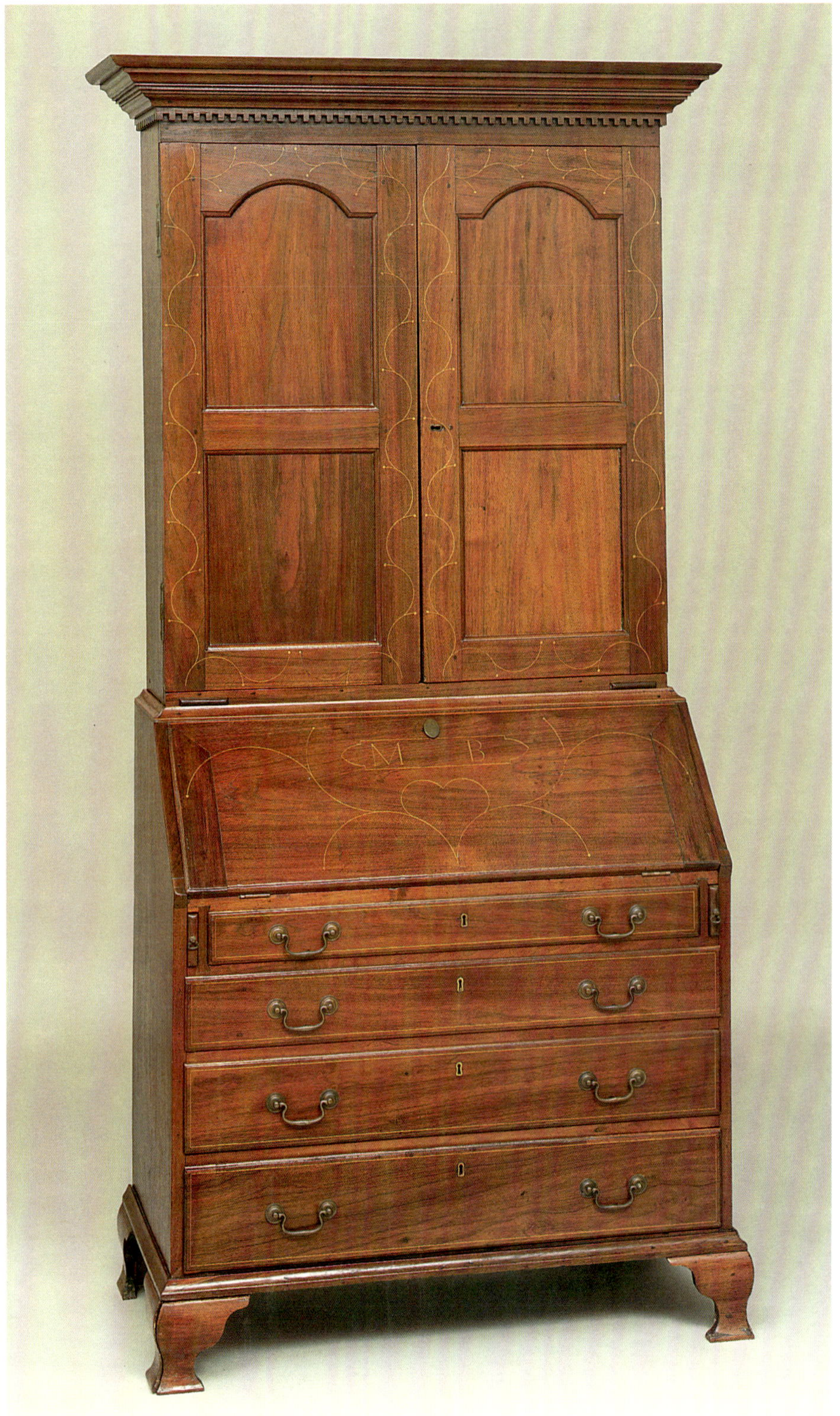

76

76 *Desk-and-Bookcase*, ca. 1800–1810

Piedmont, possibly Franklin County

Primary wood: walnut; secondary woods: light wood inlay, yellow pine

H. 88½″, W. 41¼″, D. 22″

Inlaid on fall board: MB

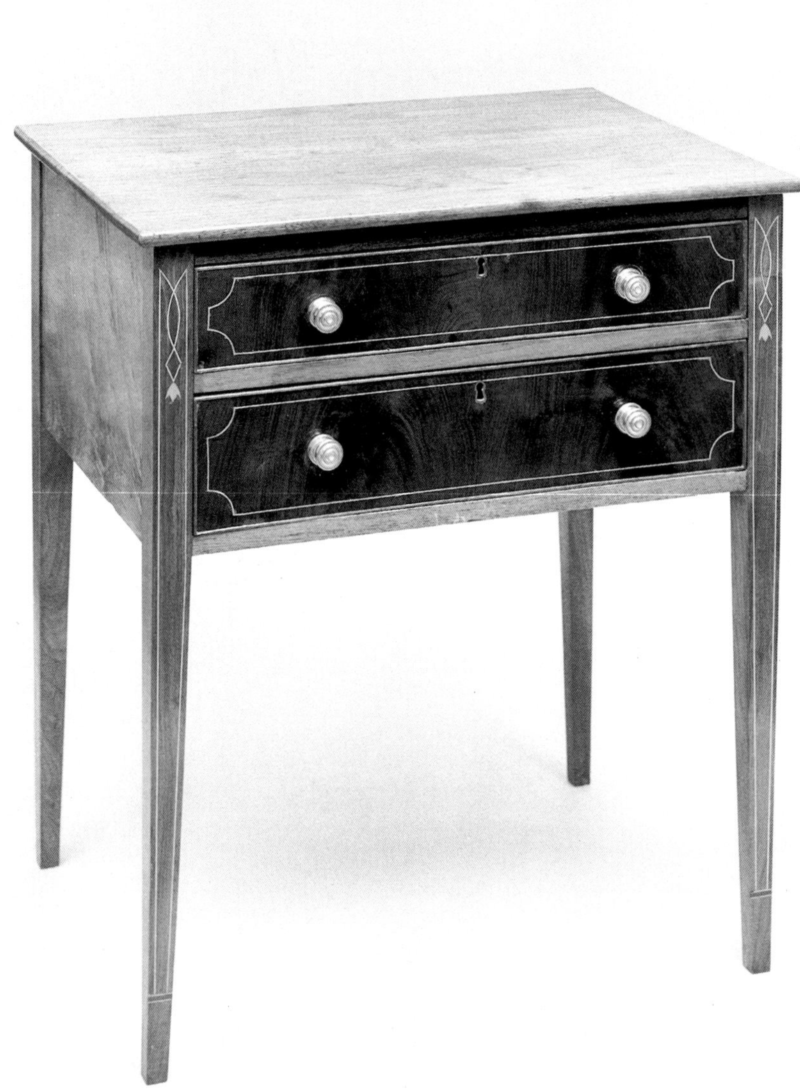

77

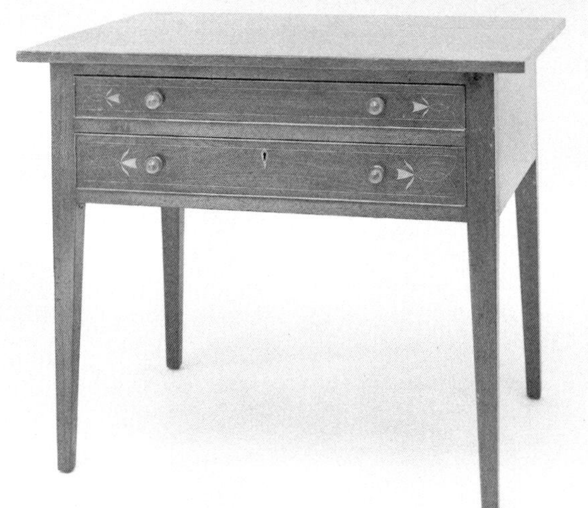

78

Description: Only one original foot; composite crown cornice with molding has exaggerated overhang; thumbnail molding overlaps on exterior drawers; bookcase fits into applied molding desk top; interior drawers marked for assembly with roman numerals in each corner.

History: Purchased from the descendents of Margaret or Martha Burns in Banks County, formerly Franklin County.

Exhibitons: *Southern Furniture, 1640–1820*, Virginia Museum of Fine Arts, 1952; *Furniture of the Georgia Piedmont Before 1830*, High Museum of Art, 1976

References: Comstock, "Furniture of Virginia, North Carolina, Georgia, and Kentucky," *Antiques*, January 1952, 86; Green, *Furniture of the Georgia Piedmont Before 1830*, 116.

High Museum of Art, Purchased with funds donated by the Decorative Arts Acquisition Trust

77 *Work Table*, ca. 1800

Piedmont

Primary woods: walnut top and legs; maple sides; mahogany veneer with light wood inlay; secondary woods: yellow pine drawer sides and back; poplar drawer bottom

H. 28", W. 24½", D. 18⅛"

Description: Leg stiles with inlaid pointed oval and diamond pattern; drawer fronts have string inlay with "hollow-round" corner pattern; applied lip around drawer fronts; original brass keyhole; knobs replaced

History: Purchased in Athens area in the 1930s.

Exhibitions: *Furniture of the Georgia Piedmont Before 1830*, High Museum of Art, 1976

References: Green, *Furniture of the Georgia Piedmont Before 1830*, 57; Green, "Furniture of the Georgia Piedmont Before 1830," *Art & Antiques*, January-February 1982, 86.

Collection of Mr. and Mrs. Henry D. Green

78 *Work Table*, ca. 1810–1815

Piedmont

Primary woods: walnut, light wood inlay; secondary wood: yellow pine

H. 29⅞", W. 35½", D. 25¾"

Description: Cockbeading on drawer edges; blind lock on underside of top drawer; pointed oval with inlaid jonquil-like motif

Exhibitions: *Furniture of the Georgia Piedmont Before 1830*, High Museum of Art, 1976

References: Green, "Georgia's Early Governor's Mansion," *Antiques*, December 1968, 864–67; Green, *Furniture of the Georgia Piedmont Before 1830*, 59; MESDA file #S–6418.

Georgia College Foundation, Old Governor's Mansion

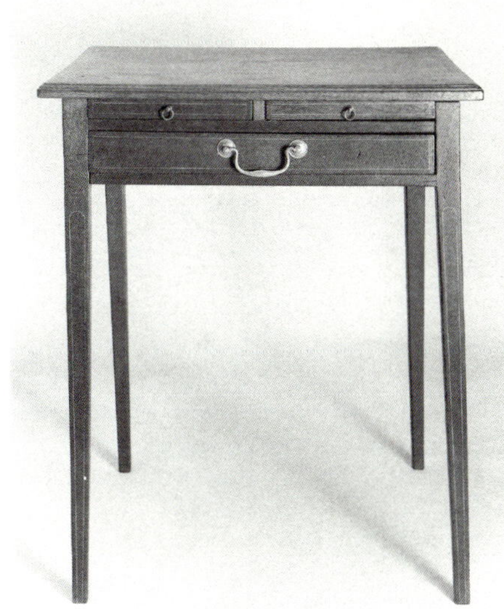

79

79 *Work Table*, ca. 1800–1810

Piedmont, Wilkes County

Primary woods: walnut, light wood inlay; secondary wood: yellow pine

H. 28½", W. 23⅞", D. 18⅞"

Description: Top molded on all four sides; tapering legs have string inlay continuing to floor; blind lock on lower drawer

History: Descended in the Gilbert and Alexander families of Washington, Georgia.

Exhibitions: *Furniture of the Georgia Piedmont Before 1830*, High Museum of Art, 1976

References: Green, *Furniture of the Georgia Piedmont Before 1830*, 53.

Private Collection

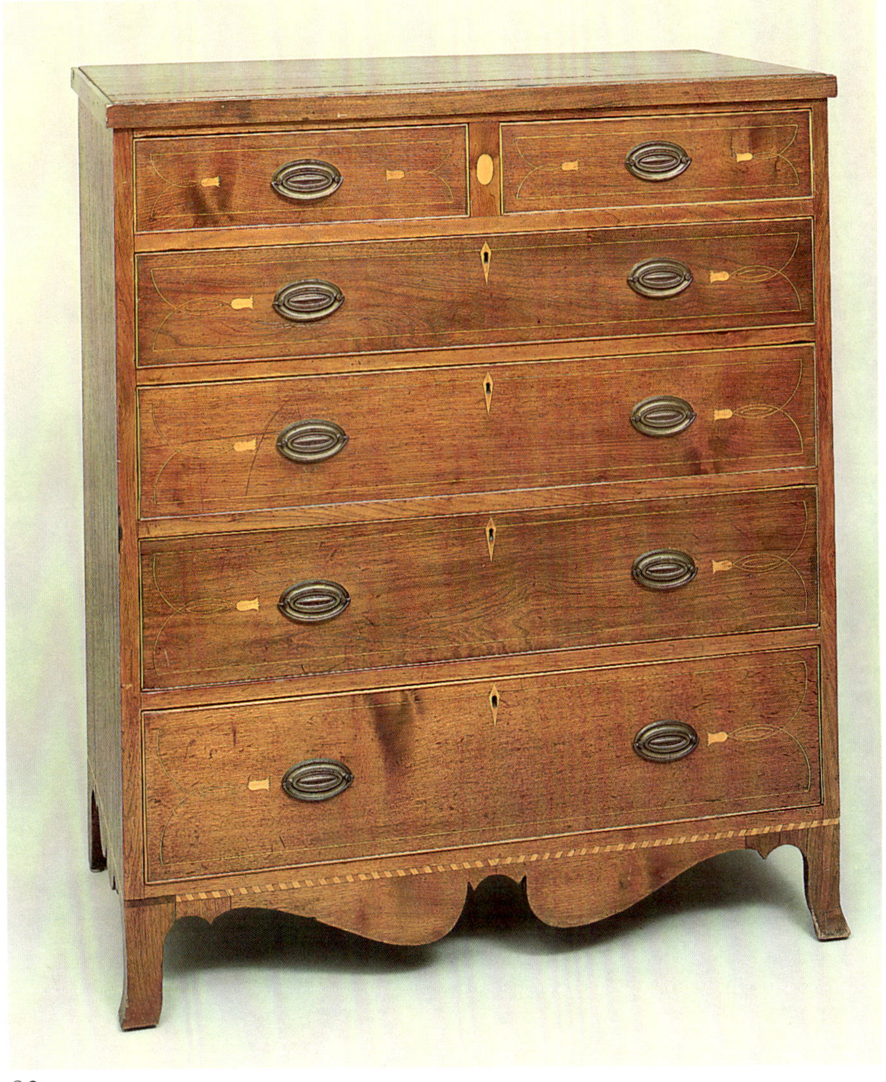

80

80 *Chest of Drawers*, ca. 1810

Piedmont

Primary woods: walnut, light wood inlay; secondary wood: poplar

H. 48¾", W. 41", D. 20¼"

Description: Characteristic of chests made during the Federal period in piedmont Georgia: each side panel is one piece of wood cut to include an apron; graduated drawers; serpentine skirt; French feet; blind locks under top inlaid drawer; surface decoration of pointed ovals, string inlay with hollow-round corners, ending with a flower motif

Exhibitions: *Furniture of the Georgia Piedmont Before 1830*, High Museum of Art, 1976

References: Green, *Furniture of the Georgia Piedmont Before 1830*, 85.

High Museum of Art, Purchase with Decorative Art funds

81 *Chest of Drawers*, ca. 1800–1810

Piedmont

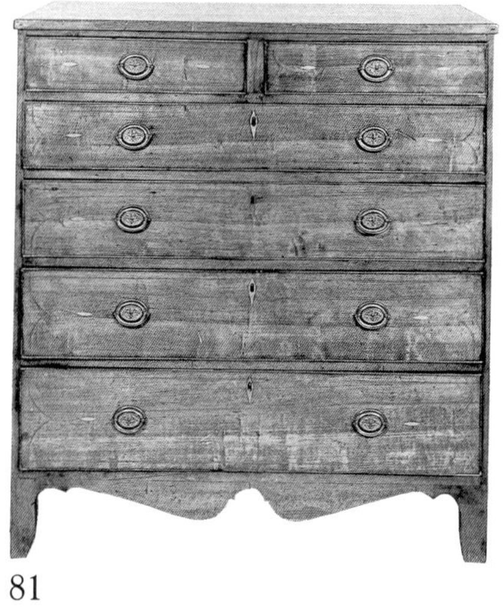
81

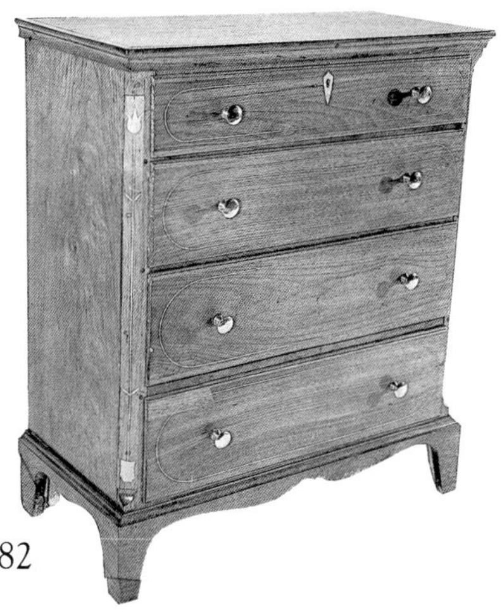
82

Primary woods: yellow birch, light wood inlay; secondary wood: yellow pine

H. 45", W. 40", D. 19½"

Description: This piece is from the same school of craftsmanship as 81; back board slips along routed seams in case sides

Exhibitions: *Furniture of the Georgia Piedmont Before 1830*, High Museum of Art, 1976

References: Green, *Furniture of the Georgia Piedmont Before 1830*, 86.

Tullie Smith House Restoration, Atlanta Historical Society

82 *Miniature Chest of Drawers,* ca. 1810

Piedmont

Primary woods: walnut, light wood inlay; secondary wood: yellow pine

H. 27", W. 22½", D. 11"

Description: Four drawer fronts overlap frame providing a stop; serpentine skirt and squared French feet cut from same board.

History: Purchased in North Georgia in the 1930s.

Exhibitions: *Southern Furniture 1640–1820*, Virginia Museum of Fine Arts, 1952; *Furniture of the Georgia Piedmont Before 1830*, High Museum of Art, 1976

References: Comstock "Furniture of Virginia, North Carolina, Georgia, and Kentucky," *Antiques*, January 1952, 82; Green, *Furniture of the Georgia Piedmont Before 1830*, 80.

Collection of Mr. and Mrs. Albert Dobbs Sams, Sr.

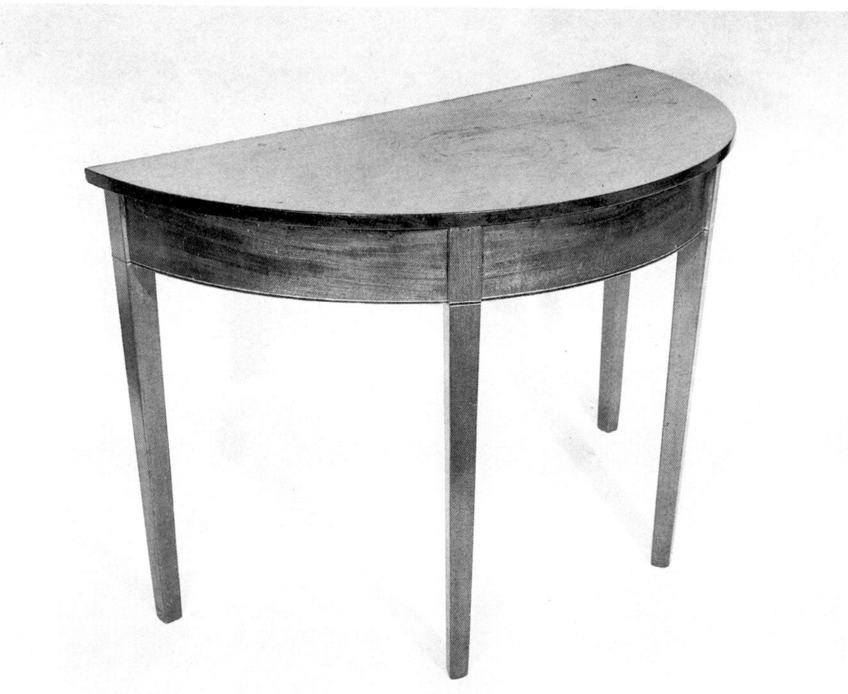
83

83 *Dining Table End,* ca. 1800–1810

Piedmont

Primary woods: mahogany, dark and light wood inlay; secondary wood: yellow pine

H. 29", W. 47⅜", D. 23"

Marks carved underneath on all three parts: SL

Description: End of a three-part dining table; leg stiles extend over the apron; inlay extends from apron edge across legs.

History: Descended in the family of Daniel and Mary Scott Lemle, who married in Louisville, Georgia, on 10 January 1802.

Exhibitions: *Furniture of the Georgia Piedmont Before 1830*, High Museum of Art, 1976

References: Green, *Furniture of the Georgia Piedmont Before 1830*, 70.

Collection of Judge and Mrs. Homer Durden, Jr.

84 *Side Chair*, ca. 1810–1820

Piedmont

Primary woods: mahogany, light wood inlay; secondary wood: yellow birch glue blocks

H. 36¼", W. 19⅝", D. 19⅜"

Description: Single piece shoe and back rail

References: MESDA file #S–11671.

Robert M. Hicklin, Jr., Inc.

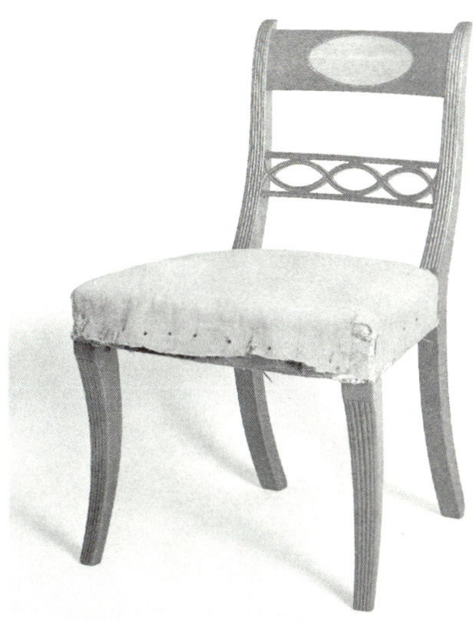

84

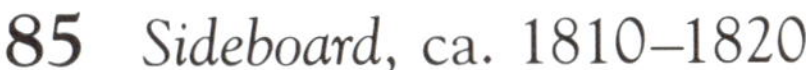

85 *Sideboard*, ca. 1810–1820

Piedmont

Primary wood: cherry; secondary woods: yellow pine, poplar

H. 44½", W. 74½", D. 26⅝"

Description: Top is held by screws set into gouged alcoves in sides and back of case; drawer runners nailed with cut nails; carved patterae or "sunbursts" attached with screws; quarter columns nailed in place; cherry is stained a reddish brown.

History: Descended in the McWhirter family of Fort Lamar, Madison County, Georgia.

References: MESDA file #S–11,700.

Private Collection

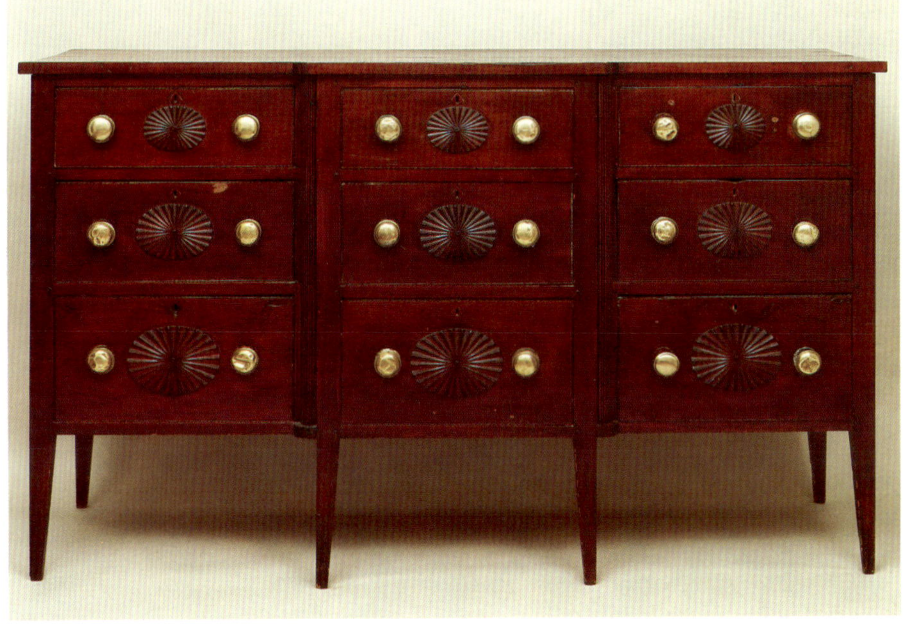

85

86 *Ware-Sibley-Clark House (Ware's Folly)*, ca. 1818

Interior view of double parlors

Augusta, Richmond County

Description: Federal style with late Adamesque details; facade has bow-front tiered portico with delicate columns; flanked with octagonal bays; fanlights above both doors; triglyph and medallionned entablature frieze; the repetition of the oval pattera or "sunburst" motif throughout the interior wood and plaster work is characteristic of other southern Federal architecture.

History: Built by Nicholas Ware, Mayor of Augusta, 1819–1821.

References: Nichols, *The Early Architecture of Georgia*, 124, 128, 133, 135–138, 147; Nichols, *The Architecture of Georgia*, 158–59; Linley, *The Georgia Catalog, Historic Buildings Survey*, 32, 33–35.

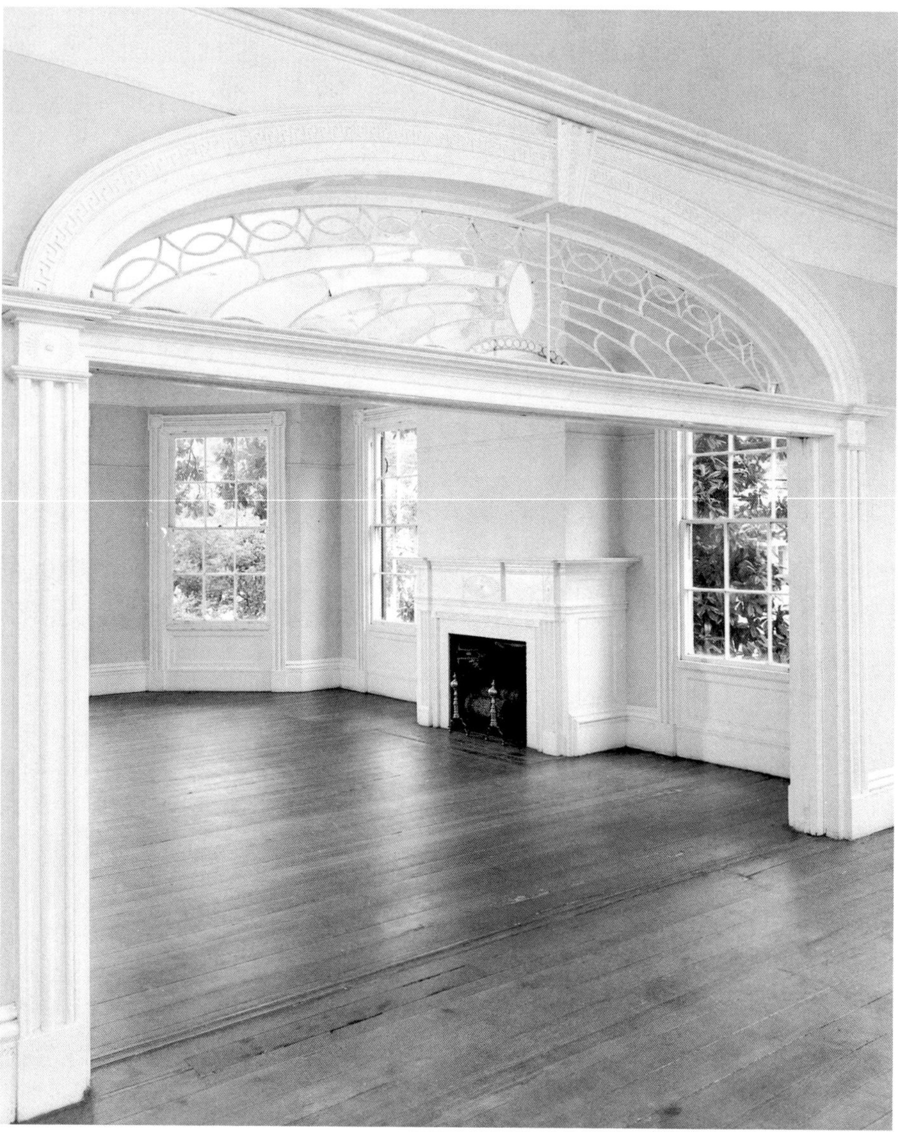

86

Ware's Folly now houses the Gertrude Herbert Memorial Institute of Art

87 *Chief Vann House*, completed 1805

Spring Place, Murray County

Description: Two-story, one-room deep, common bond brick structure has a central hallway which opens out into the double covered porticos. Interior and exterior details have been described variously as Georgian, traditional Federal, post-Colonial, and Cherokee (referring to the hand-carved Cherokee rose design throughout the interior), but the eclectic features evade strict classification.

History: Built by Moravian missionaries for Chief James Clement Vann, sponsor of a mission for the Cherokee Indians. Entry in a Moravian diary for 24 March 1805 notes: "Vann moved into his newly built house today."

References: Nichols, *The Early Architecture of Georgia*, 123, 133, 135, 137, 138, 148; Nichols, *The Architecture of Georgia*, 31, 108–12; Martin and Mitchell, Jr., *Landmark Homes of Georgia*, 42–45; Linley, *The Georgia Catalog, Historic American Building Survey*, 8, 60.

Maintained by Parks and Historic Sites Division, Georgia Department of Natural Resources

After their short-lived settlement in Irene, Georgia, the Moravians relocated in Bethlehem, Pennsylvania, and Salem, North Carolina. Later, they began missionary efforts in Georgia, and in 1801, established a mission, sponsored by James Vann, son of a Scot trader and Cherokee mother, at Spring Place. (Many Cherokees educated at this mission later became leaders in New Echota, Georgia, the future capital of the Cherokee Nation.) Moravian craftsmen completed this one-room deep Federal house for Vann in 1805. Four years later, Vann was murdered in a nearby tavern. One Moravian lamented in his diary entry dated 21 February 1809, "Thus ended the life of one who was feared by many and loved by few in the forty-first year of his life . . . . Vann had been an instrument in the hand of God for establishing our mission in the Nation."

Joseph Vann, James' youngest son, inherited the house and property. By 1834, white settlers had driven Joseph and his family out of the state along with the other Indians. In the 1840s, the Federal government paid Vann, who was then living in Oklahoma, $19,605.00 for Spring Place, including the brick house, 800 acres of farm land, 42 cabins, six barns, five smokehouses, a grist mill, a saw mill, blacksmith ship, eight corn cribs, a shop and foundry, a trading post, a peach kiln, and a still.

The Vann house was constructed of bricks and hardware made on the site. The house interiors have polychrome mantels and moldings; the cantilevered staircase exhibits Germanic training in the skills of the Moravian carpenters.

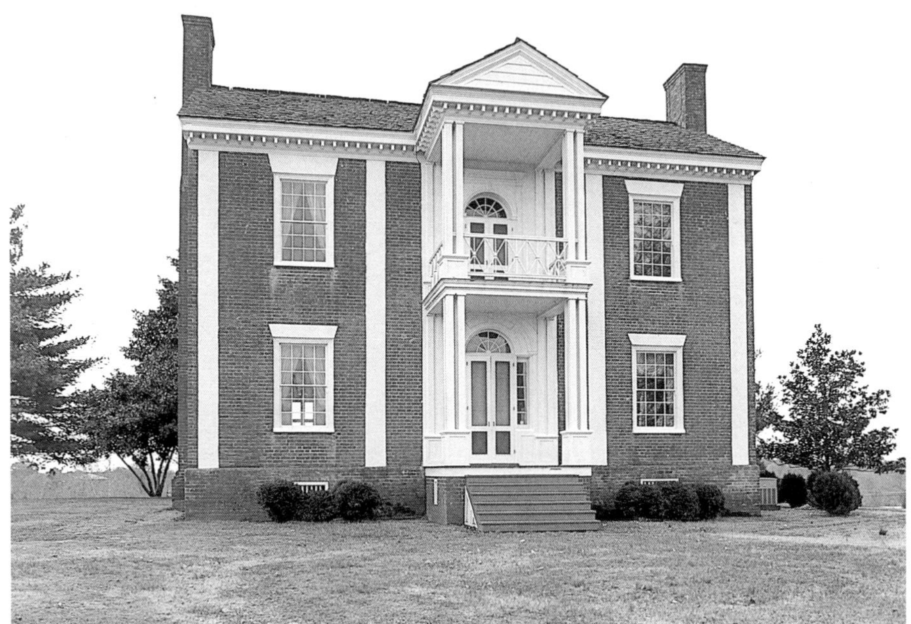

87

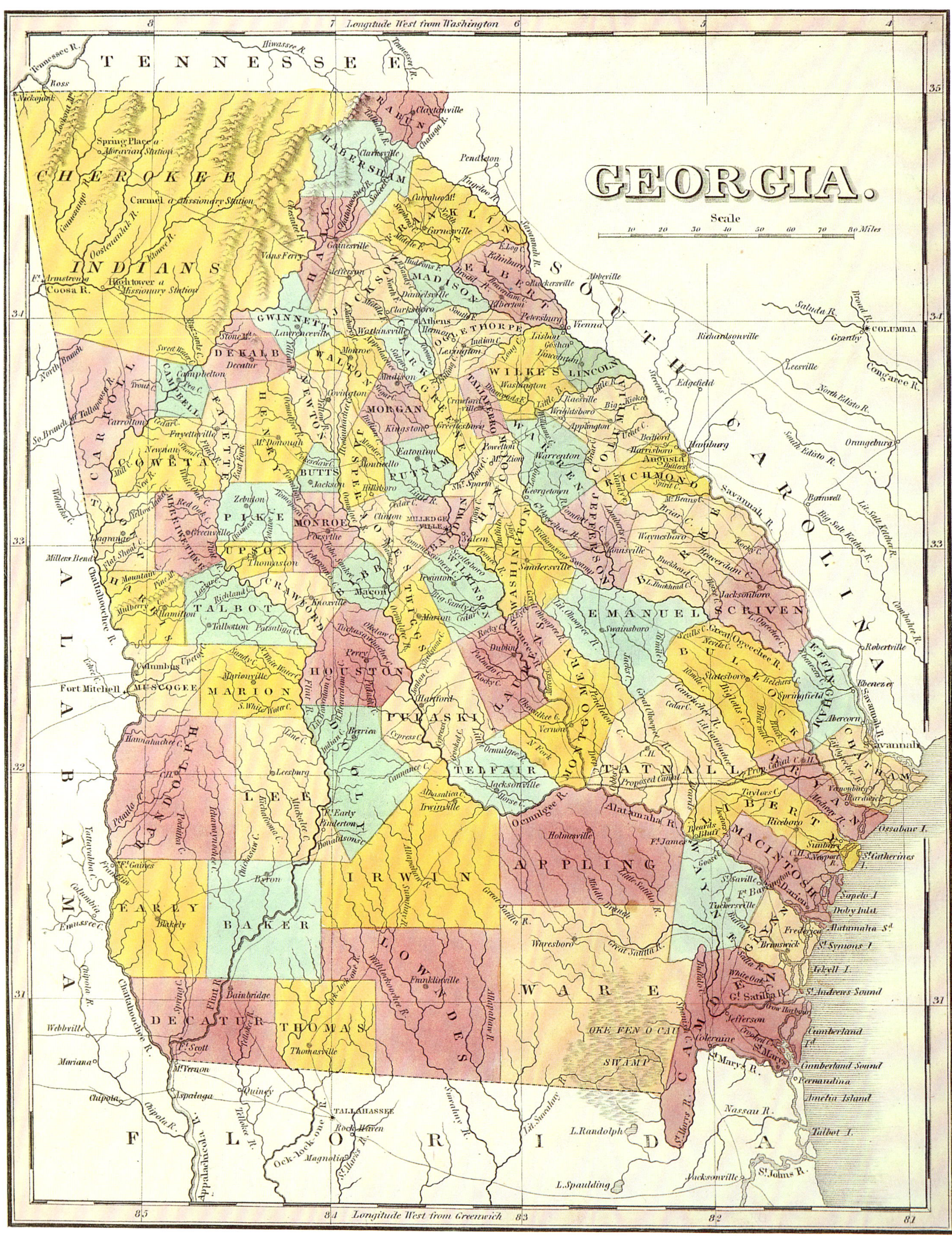
GEORGIA.
Scale
10 20 30 40 50 60 70 80 Miles
Longitude West from Washington
Longitude West from Greenwich
TENNESSEE
SOUTH CAROLINA
ALABAMA
FLORIDA
CHEROKEE
INDIANS
Spring Place a Moravian Station
Carmel a Missionary Station
Hightower a Missionary Station
Coosa R.
HABERSHAM
RABUN
HALL
FRANKLIN
JACKSON
MADISON
ELBERT
GWINNETT
DEKALB
CLARKE
OGLETHORPE
WILKES
LINCOLN
COLUMBIA
WALTON
NEWTON
MORGAN
GREENE
TALIAFERRO
WARREN
RICHMOND
CARROLL
CAMPBELL
FAYETTE
HENRY
JASPER
PUTNAM
HANCOCK
BURKE
COWETA
BUTTS
BALDWIN
JEFFERSON
TROUP
MERIWETHER
PIKE
MONROE
JONES
WASHINGTON
UPSON
BIBB
WILKINSON
EMANUEL
SCRIVEN
HARRIS
TALBOT
CRAWFORD
TWIGGS
LAURENS
BULLOCK
EFFINGHAM
MUSCOGEE
MARION
HOUSTON
PULASKI
MONTGOMERY
CHATHAM
RANDOLPH
LEE
DOOLY
TELFAIR
TATNALL
BRYAN
LIBERTY
MACINTOSH
EARLY
BAKER
IRWIN
APPLING
WAYNE
GLYNN
DECATUR
THOMAS
LOWNDES
WARE
CAMDEN
OKE FEN O CAU SWAMP
Augusta
Savannah
Milledgeville
Macon
Athens
Columbus
Fort Mitchell
COLUMBIA
TALLAHASSEE
Ossabaw I.
S^t. Catherines I.
Sapelo I.
S^t. Symons I.
Jekyll I.
S^t. Andrews Sound
Cumberland I^d.
Cumberland Sound
Amelia Island
Talbot I.
S^t. Johns R.
Jacksonville
L. Randolph
L. Spaulding

1830–1860

By the graces of King Cotton and a 45-year relief from war, between 1830–60 Georgia experienced the most progressive period in its history—agriculturally, industrially, and culturally. The land lotteries in 1832 brought adventurous settlers westward, and the expulsion of the Cherokee Indians to west of the Mississippi in 1838 meant Georgia's boundaries were drawn as they exist today. Georgia's population went from 340,989 in 1820 to 1,057,148 by 1860 (Boney, "The Emerging Empire State," *A History of Georgia*, 163).

Economic and industrial developments in the state were tied to agriculture. A fundamental problem was the cost of shipping cotton, corn, tobacco, and other staples to the market. Other states tried canals as their solution to transportation problems. Except for the successful Augusta Canal completed in 1847, Georgia saw that the best way to close the distance between its growing towns and to transport the products efficiently to surrounding rivers was through a railroad system. The 1837 depression only slightly delayed construction of four major lines: Georgia Railroad Company, Augusta to Athens line, completed 1841; Monroe Railroad Company, Macon to Forsyth, completed 1838; Central of Georgia Railroad Company, Savannah to Macon, completed 1843; Western and Atlantic Railroad, Terminus (Atlanta) to Chattanooga, completed 1851. By 1846, all of the major urban points within the state were connected, and in 1861 Georgia had 18 railroad lines, the largest being the Savannah-based Central of Georgia.

The planters financially supported the railroads and other industrial developments. In 1860, Savannah was the center of Georgia's industrialized efforts, and that year $19 million worth of foreign exports, mostly cotton, left the city's port. Some of these industries across the state included the textile mills in Athens, Macon, Columbus, Thomaston, and Augusta; the lumber industry; turpentine distilleries found in south Georgia; and mining ventures in the Dahlonega area, where a short-lived federal mint was begun in 1838. Established in 1837 as the hub of four railroads, Terminus (later Atlanta) began its rapid growth with industries related to railroad maintenance.

Engraved by William Faden, *The United States of North America with the British Territories and Those of Spain*, 1793. H. 21½", W. 25". Special Collections, The University of Georgia Libraries.

From a socioeconomic viewpoint, new industries and the cotton boom of the 1850s made Georgia's society a flexible one. With hard work and some business acumen, small farmers had equal opportunities to become rich. The most successful of these agribusinessmen became members of what is known as the planters elite, men who owned farms of more than 1,000 acres and 100 slaves. The middle-class farmer, however, was predominant during the 1850s; in 1860, only 3,594 of Georgia's 62,003 farms were "plantations" of more than 500 acres, and most Georgia slave owners had from 30 to 100 slaves (Boney, "The Emerging Empire State," *A History of Georgia*, 163).

The growing proficiency of steam power and mass production made many traditional skills obsolete. Georgia craftsmen realized that making a living through the sale of hand-made goods was impractical. Some increased their profits by selling imported merchandise, much of it produced in large New York or Philadelphia shops. In fact, northern distributors catered to the expanding planters' market throughout the South. Traditional skills survived on the increasingly isolated plantations across the state. By the 1860s, folk wares such as plain-style furniture, functional ceramics, and textiles had become part of the routine of self-sufficient rural communities.

Criss-crossing railroad lines, antebellum Greek Revival mansions, and encouraging cultural developments such as new colleges [100, 102, 103], noted literary authors [101], and even an occasional artist [100] were evidence that Georgia had entered a period of prosperity. During this period, numerous dichotomies emerged: urban versus rural, agricultural versus industrial, black versus white, North versus South. Because almost one half of Georgia's population during this period were black slaves, the most consequential of these conflicts was black against white. By providing cheap labor for plantations as well as industries, the institution of slavery was as crucial to Georgia's economic security as was the cotton seed. By 1861, these disparities had become national issues, leading to a civil war that would destroy much of the progress Georgia had finally achieved after a rocky 130-year history.

88 *Indian Costume*, ca. 1830

Cherokee County area

Black velvet with homespun lining, embroidered designs, cut glass seed, beads, ribbons and tassle

Leggings each: H. 10″ (folded), W. 35″

Pouch: H. 8″, W. 8½″

Broad sash: H. 4″, W. 102″

Breech cloth: H. 13″, W. 47″

Inscribed in ink inside legging and breech cloth: John B. Lamar / Milledgeville, 1832 / To Oliver H. Prince

Description: Five pieces—two leggings, pouch, broad sash, breech cloth; decoration includes seven-pointed star frequently seen in Cherokee Indian designs

History: John B. Lamar (died 1862), son of Zachariah Lamar of Milledgeville, managed Hurricane Plantation, which belonged to Howell Cobb, who married Lamar's sister in the 1830s. Lamar had acquired land in the 1832 Cherokee land lotteries, and obtained the costume there.

Oliver Hillhouse Prince, Sr. (1782–1837), educated at Yale College Law School, settled in Wilkes County in 1819. He moved several times between 1822–35 and spent 1831–35 in Milledgeville. The costume descended in the family of Prince's son, Oliver H. Prince, Jr. It is thought that Lamar presented the teenage Prince with the costume.

National Park Service, Ocmulgee National Monument

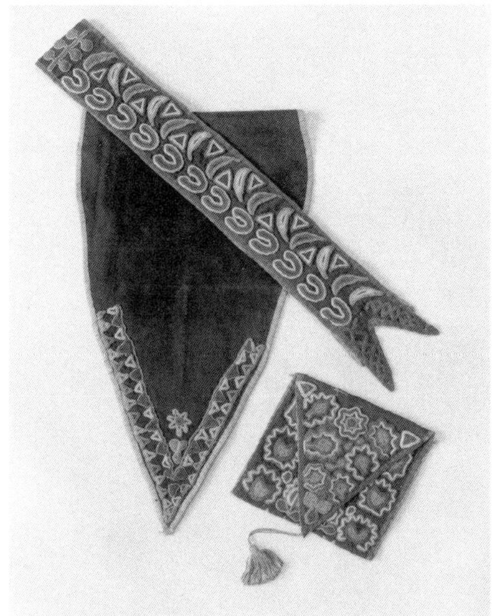

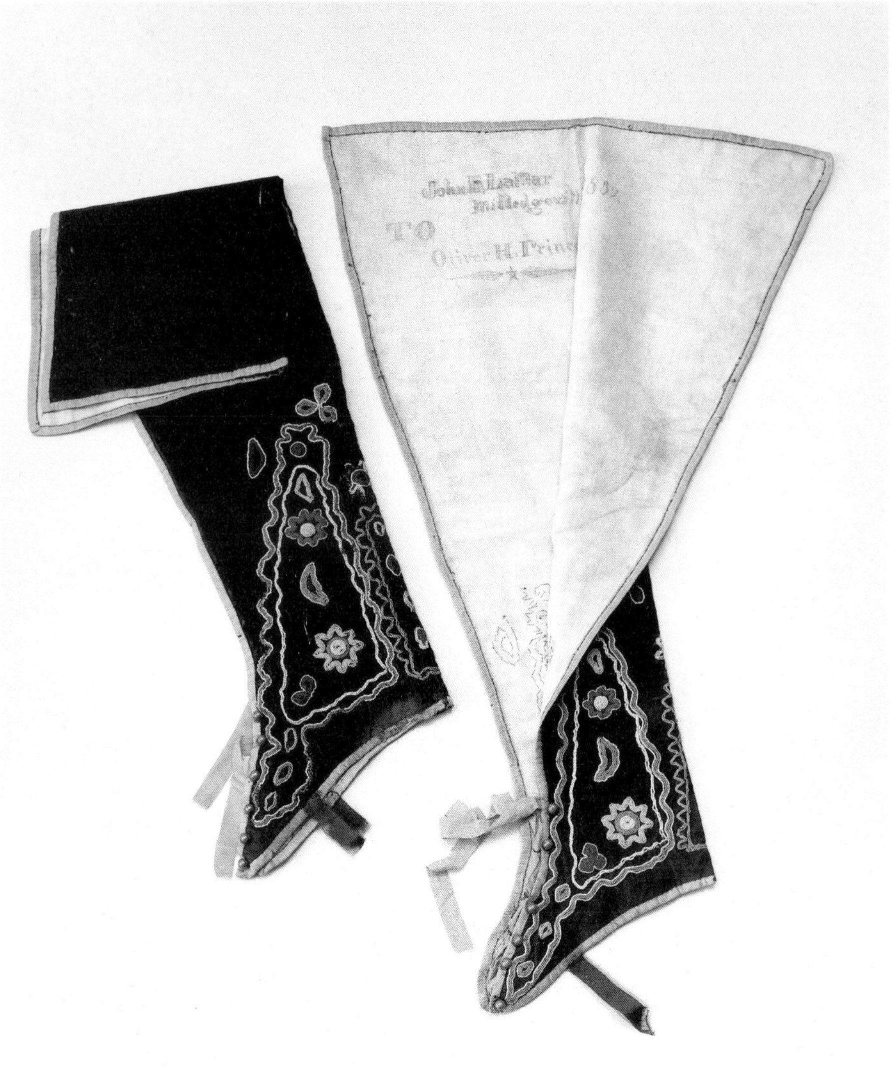

88

One of the consequences of westward expansion was the gradual displacement of the Creek and Cherokee Indians. The 1830 map of Georgia by Finley (figure 13, p. 49) shows that all that remained in Indian hands was land northwest of the Chattahoochee River containing Cherokee missionary stations. Governor George Troup (1823–1827) had been responsible for the final expulsion of the Creeks from the central part of the state by 1827. His successor, Governor John Forsyth, also favored the removal of Indians, as did George Gilmer, who was governor when the federal Indian Removal Act was passed in 1830. The Cherokees persisted by suing the State of Georgia before the U.S. Supreme Court in 1831. The Cherokees won the suit, but President Andrew Jackson refused to enforce the ruling. Heralded for his earlier campaigns against the Indians,

ᏣᎳᎩ 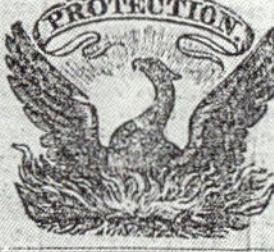 ᏧᎴᎯᏌᏅᎯ.

CHEROKEE PHŒNIX.

VOL. I. NEW ECHOTA, WEDNESDAY AUGUST 13, 1828. NO. 24.

EDITED BY ELIAS BOUDINOTT.
PRINTED WEEKLY BY
ISAAC H. HARRIS,
FOR THE CHEROKEE NATION.

At $2 50 if paid in advance, $3 in six months, or $3 50 if paid at the end of the year.

To subscribers who can read only the Cherokee language the price will be $2,00 in advance, or $2,50 to be paid within the year.

Every subscription will be considered as continued unless subscribers give notice to the contrary before the commencement of a new year.

Any person procuring six subscribers, and becoming responsible for the payment, shall receive a seventh gratis.

Advertisements will be inserted at seventy-five cents per square for the first insertion, and thirty-seven and a half cents for each continuance; longer ones in proportion.

☞All letters addressed to the Editor, post paid, will receive due attention.

AGENTS FOR THE CHEROKEE PHŒNIX.

The following persons are authorized to receive subscriptions and payments for the Cherokee Phœnix.

Henry Hill, Esq. Treasurer of the A. B. C. F. M. Boston, Mass.

George M. Tracy, Agent of the A. B. C. F. M. New York.

Rev. A. D. Eddy, Canandaigua, N. Y.

Thomas Hastings, Utica, N. Y.

met, a decided friend, of similar rank, and his wife *Kapiolani*, who perhaps is second to none in improved manners and Christian character. You would have seen the solid *Hoapiri*, of the same rank, the governor of Maui, recently propounded to the church, the most fearless of all in resisting foreign encroachments, and foremost of all to suppress the vices which derives so much support from abroad. Another of the old phalanx of Tamehamehah would have attracted your notice, *Kaikioeva*, now governor of Tauai, who seems to be desirous to be instructed and to promote our cause; and his wife *Keaweamahi* also, who, as you know, is a respected member of our church, admitted at Tauai. You would have seen, also, the late queen of Tauri, *Deborah Kapule*, and her husband *Simeon Kaiu*, whom we regard as promising Christians. They recently presented their infant son to the Lord in baptism, whom they called *Taumuarii*, out of respect to the characters of those two men.

You would have seen *Kekauluohi*, *Kinau*, and *Kekauonohi*, the three surviving women who were, on our arrival, wives of Rehoriho. The former has, for five years, lived regularly with another husband, gives evidence of piety, and was, last Sabbath, propounded for admission to our church. Kinau, who has recently married *Kekuanaoa*, who accompanied the king to England, now appears friendly, but not pious; her husband whom you would also have seen, is like her in those respects, and is a commander of a small standing force of two or three hundred men, at this place. Kehauonohi has, for about four years, lived single, appears to be a cordial and decided friend of the mission, and is

They have laid aside their vices and excesses, and their love of noise and war. You see every one decently dressed in our own style. Instead of the roaring *hura*, you hear them join us in a song of Zion:

"Kindred in Christ, for his dear sake,
A hearty welcome here receive," &c.

Listen and you will not only hear the expressions of gratitude to us and to God for the privileges they now enjoy, but you will hear these old warriors lamenting that their former kings, their fathers, and their companions in arms had been slain in the battle, or carried off by the hand of time, before the blessed Gospel of Christ had been proclaimed on these benighted shores. Your heart would have glowed with devout gratitude to God for the evidence, that while our simple food was passing round the social circle for their present gratification, the minds of these children of pagans enjoyed a feast of better things; and your thoughts, no doubt, like ours, would have glanced at a happier meeting of the friends of God in the world of glory. When our thanks were returned at the close of our humble repast, though you might not have been familiar with the language, you would have lifted up your heart in thankfulness for what already appeared as the fruits of your efforts here, and for the prospect of still greater things than these.

THE PHILANTHROPIST AND THE HERO IN CONTRAST.

We think the wiser part of the world is growing weary of its great men; or is at least growing more correct in its estimate of greatness.—For thousands of years it has paid its

their labor, and doubting sometimes whether it is not wholly vain. Such living sacrifices, we think, are even more illustrious than the dying self-devotion of martyrs; for it requires more strength to sustain the heart in the weary trial of life, than in the short agony of death. Milton complained with reason, that men were so earnest to celebrate their destroyers, that they had left 'the better fortitude of patience and heroic martyrdom unsung;' but he was too far before his age for even his mighty voice to reach it; we trust that the stern old prophet has found many a heart in our times, to reply to these indignant appeals, which found no answering chord in his own.—*N. A. Review.*

VERSATILITY OF THE FRENCH.

Those who are fond of reconciling apparent contradictions in national character, may find amusement in attempting to account for the singular fact, that the French, who are so remarkable for their constitutional vivacity, and, we had almost said, levity of character, should nevertheless have been unrivalled for nearly a century, in almost every department of scientific research. That they should have taken precedence of other nations in elegant literature, if such were the fact, would not be very surprising; for we should imagine we could discover a decided adaptation to such pursuits, in the prominent features of their character. But when we see them engaged with wonderful ardor and perseverance in those studies, which almost entirely exclude imagination and feeling, and demand for their successful prosecution, the severest efforts of reasoning and abstraction, we witness a phenomenon,

young heads: the flowers on the brink seem to offer themselves to our young hands; we are happy in hope, and we grasp eagerly at the beauties around us: but the stream hurries on, and still our hands are empty.

"Our course in youth and manhood is along a wider and deeper flood, and amid objects more striking and magnificent. We are animated by the moving picture of enjoyment and industry which passes before us; we are excited by some short lived success, or depressed and rendered miserable by equally short-lived disappointment. But our energy and our dependence are both in vain. The stream bears us on, and our joys and our griefs are alike left behind us, we may be shipwrecked but we cannot anchor; our voyage may be hastened but it cannot be delayed; whether rough or smooth, the river hastens towards its home, till the roaring of the ocean is in our ears, and the tossing of his waves is beneath our knell, and the lands lessen from our eyes and the floods are lifted up around us, and the earth loses sight of us, and we take our last leave of earth and its inhabitants, and of our further voyage there is no witness, but the Infinite and Eternal.

"And do we still take so much anxious thought for the future days, when the days which are gone by have so strangely and uniformly deceived us? Can we still so set our hearts on the creatures of God, when we find by sad experience, that the Creator only is permanent? Or shall we not rather lay aside every weight and every sin which does most easily beset us, and think of ourselves henceforth as wayfaring persons only who have no abiding inheritance but in the hope of

89

Jackson joined with Governor Wilson Lumpkin and pressured the Cherokees of New Echota [89] into signing a treaty in which the government gave the Cherokees $5 million to relocate west of the Mississippi. By 1838, the United States Army had forced the last of the 12,000 Cherokee Indians down the "Trail of Tears."

89 *Cherokee Phoenix*, 13 August 1828

Elias Boudinott, editor

New Echota, Gordon County

Special Collections, The University of Georgia Libraries

The Cherokee Nation, whose territories stretched into Alabama, Tennessee, and North Carolina, established its capitol, New Echota, in northwest Georgia in 1825. Life in the new Cherokee capitol increasingly reflected European customs [38]. Excavations have unearthed nineteenth-century European ceramics and clapboards indicating English-style housing. The most important contribution of New Echota was an alphabet developed by Sequoyah (ca. 1775–1843), who was also known as George Guess (Gist) on the frontier [90]. Sequoyah was a silversmith and supposedly marked his works with "George Guess" in script, although no examples of his marked work survive. Sequoyah had been fascinated by the white man's ability to express his thoughts in writing. In 1820, he produced a syllabic alphabet that translated the Cherokee language into writing through symbols or characters. A printing office was built in New Echota in 1828, and the first issue of the *Cherokee Phoenix* was printed on 21 February 1828, in both English and Cherokee. Trained as a missionary at Spring Place, Elias Boudinott was editor of the paper, which cost $2.00 per year for "subscribers who can read only the Cherokee language" (see illustration). The *Phoenix* was defunct by 1834.

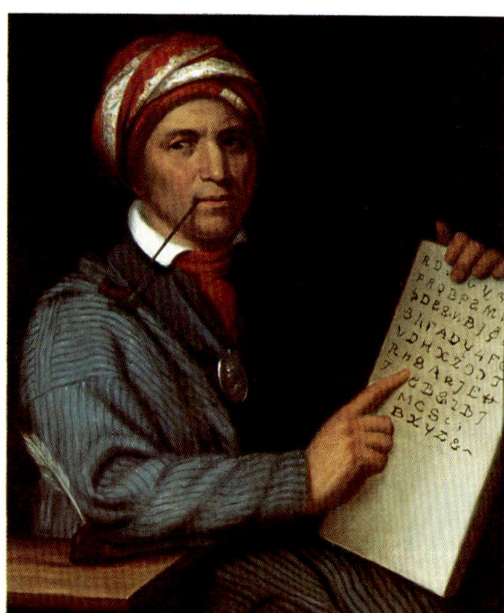

90

90 *Se-Quo-Yah*, 1830–1832

Attributed to Henry Inman (1801–1846)

Philadelphia

Oil on canvas

H. 30⅛″, W. 25″

National Portrait Gallery, Smithsonian Institution

[see following entry]

91 *Se-Quo-Yah*, 1833

Lehman & Duval, lithographers, after Charles B. King (1785–1862)

Philadelphia

Lithograph on paper

H. 19¼″, W. 13⅝″

Inscription: SE-QUO-YAH / painted by C. B. King / Philadelphia Published by E. C. Biddle / from Lehman & Duval Lith Press / Entered according to act of Congress in the year 1833 by E. C. Biddle in the Clerks Office of the District court of the Eastern District of Penn.

References: McKenney & Hall, *History of the Indian Tribes of North America*, vol. 1, 63.

Special Collections, The University of Georgia Libraries

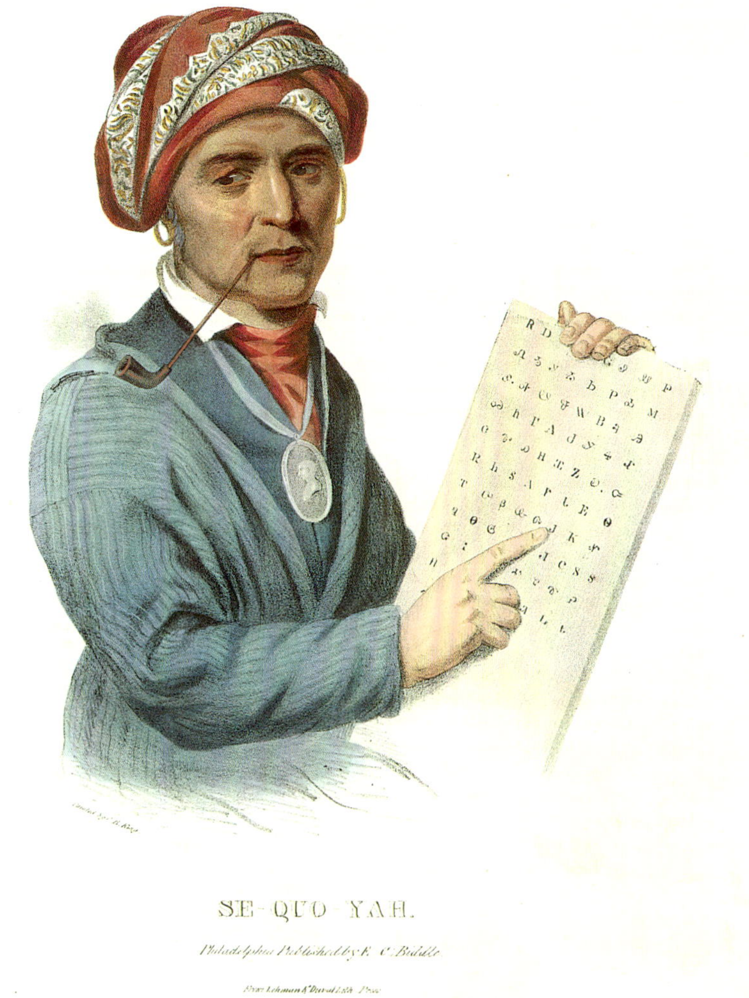

91

By 1824, the problem of removing Indians from the Southeast had become a national issue. Beginning in 1820, delegations of Indians began to come to Washington to plead with the "Great Father," President James Monroe, to spare their lands from the encroaching white settlers. William Lorraine McKenney (1785–1859), Superintendent of Indian Affairs from 1824 to 1830, advocated humanitarian treatment of the Indians, but feared that the Indian culture would soon be extinct. He began a collection "of artifacts relating to the aboriginies preserved there for the inspection of the curious . . . long after the Indians will have been no more" (Horan, *The McKenney-Hall Portrait Gallery of American Indians*, 23). From 1822 to 1842, Washington, D.C., artist Charles Bird King painted portraits of leaders of Indian delegations that came to meet with the President. King charged the federal government $20 for busts and $27 for full-length portraits; by 1842, King had painted 143 portraits and had received about $3,500.

Because he considered these paintings a waste of money, President Andrew Jackson fired McKenney in

1830. But McKenney was still obsessed with preserving Indian culture. He decided to publish the King portraits in a series of elephant portfolios, but the government refused to release the paintings to be copied. Undaunted, McKenney hired New York artist Henry Inman and Cephas G. Childs, the first of several lithographers from Philadelphia, to copy the portraits, which were secretly removed, one by one, for publication. James Hall, author of several books on life on the Western frontier, wrote most of the text for the three-volumed *History of the Indian Tribes of North America*, published from 1837 to 1844. The majority of the original Charles Bird King portraits were donated in 1858 to the Smithsonian Institution, where they were destroyed by fire on 24 January 1865. The Inman collection was given to Harvard's Peabody Museum of Archaeology and Ethnology in 1882.

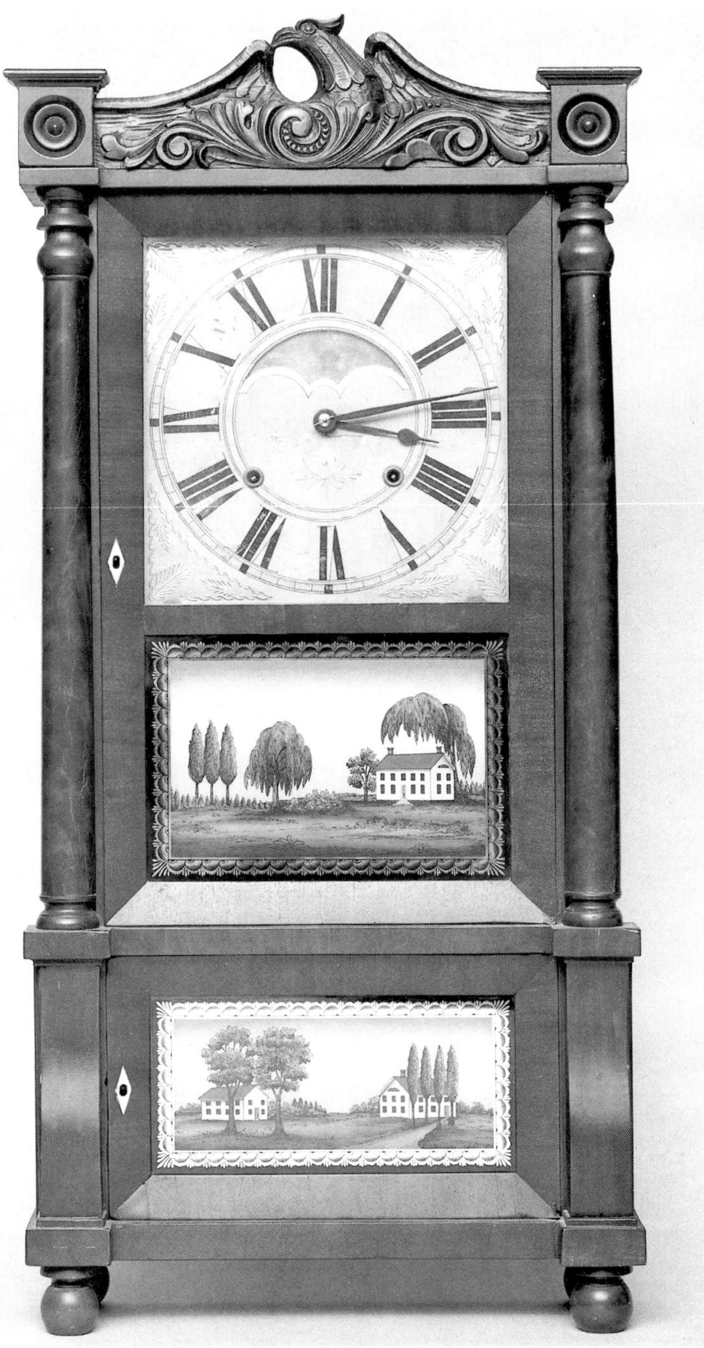

92

92 *Shelf Clock*, ca. 1836–1840

Assembled by Dyer & Wadsworth

Augusta, Richmond County

Mahogany, mahogany veneer, poplar dial with paint, gilding, and mirror, white pine back, ivory escutcheons, glass tablets

H. 37½″, W. 6″, D. 18⅛″

Labeled: Eight Day / CLOCKS / manufactured by / DYER, WADSWORTH & CO / Augusta, Georgia / Directions for regulating the clock / The pendulum ball must be raised to make the Clock go faster, and lowered to produce the contrary effect / WARRENTED IF WELL USED

Description: Empire triple decker shelf or mantel clock, squared pilasters on lower level, round veneered columns above; carved crest with eagle flanked by plinths with "bulls-eye" motif; ball feet; has been restored, tablets replaced; pendulum driven

Collection of Mr. Joe Mack Wilson

Clock and watchmaking in Georgia during this period might more accurately be described as clock and watch repairing or assembling. Contemporary advertisements often listed items for sale such as "watch trimmings . . . chains, seals, keys, glasses, hands, etc, etc" (*Augusta Chronicle*, 21 October 1809) imported from England. Working in Augusta in 1817, Francis Clark revealed the source of his goods: "Superior Gold and Silver patent Lever Watches, from Roskell's Manufactory" (*Augusta Chronicle*, 1 January 1817). The manufactory was located in Liverpool and owned by Robert Roskell between 1800–30, and it produced patent rack lever and cylinder watches. It is assumed that wealthy Savannahians in particular owned tall clocks of English or American make that were popular from the mid-eighteenth century to about 1820; however, none found during field research had Georgia provenances.

By 1816, the focus of American clockmaking had shifted to the Plymouth/Bristol, Connecticut, area, where in 1809 Eli Terry had patented the mass production of interchangeable wooden clock parts. Among the numerous clockmakers in Bristol was Joseph Ives (1782–1862), a clockmaker's son and an innovator in the Connecticut clockmaking industry from 1803 until his death in 1862. Among Ives' inventions was the strap brass, eight-day movement, patented in 1833. Seen on this example, the wrought brass movement could be driven by a pendulum or a fussee spring lever. Like other improvements, this one was expertly marketed by the Bristol clockmaking industry.

By the 1820s, Yankee ingenuity had made its way southward via peddlers employed by Connecticut firms such as Birge, Case & Company, or C. Jerome & Company; these peddlers sold clocks to planters door to door from horse-drawn wagons. Because the clock parts were mass produced in individual shops, the finished product could be achieved simply by acquiring the needed parts and assembling them. Taking advantage of cheap slave labor in the southern states, the Connecticut manufacturers had by the 1830s established factories and supplied brass clock parts and cases to be assembled and distributed. There were assembly shops throughout Georgia—in Augusta, Savannah, Greensboro, Hartwell, and Macon.

Often the Connecticut distributor can be identified by markings on clocks or labels. This shelf clock is labeled by the firm Dyer and Wadsworth, active during approximately 1836–42, whose Connecticut connection was Birge, Case & Company (1834–35) and Case, Willard & Company. The label illustrated in figure A is from another

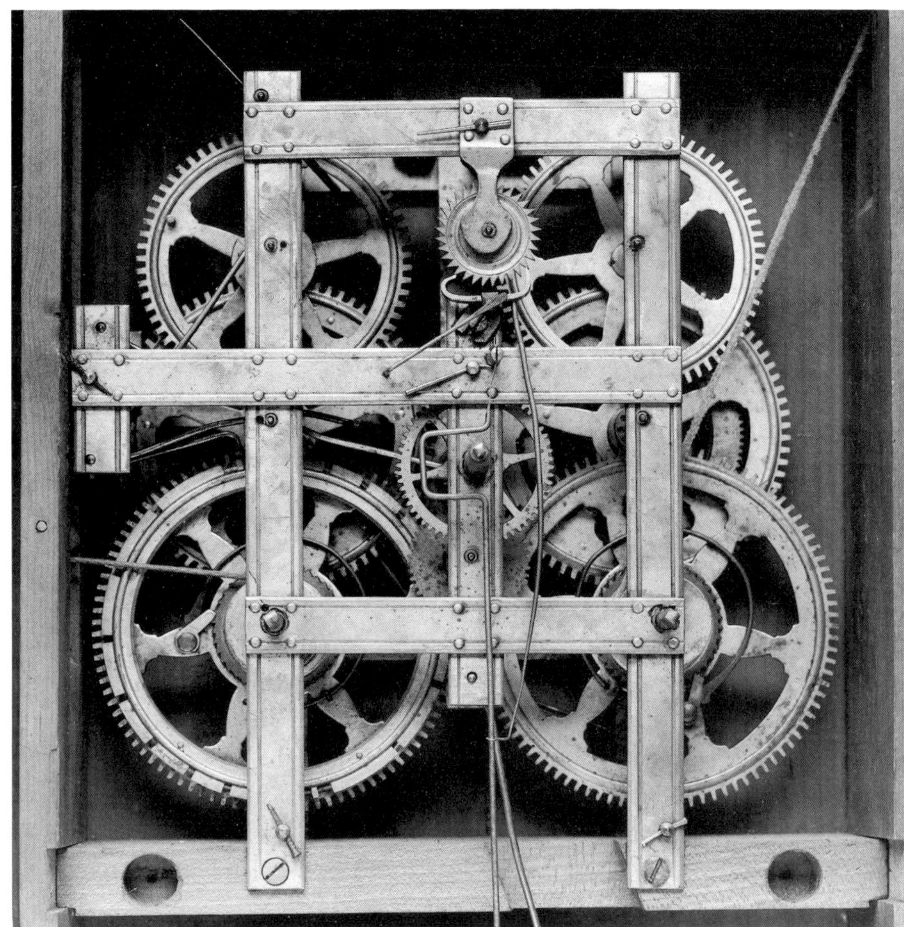

92 detail

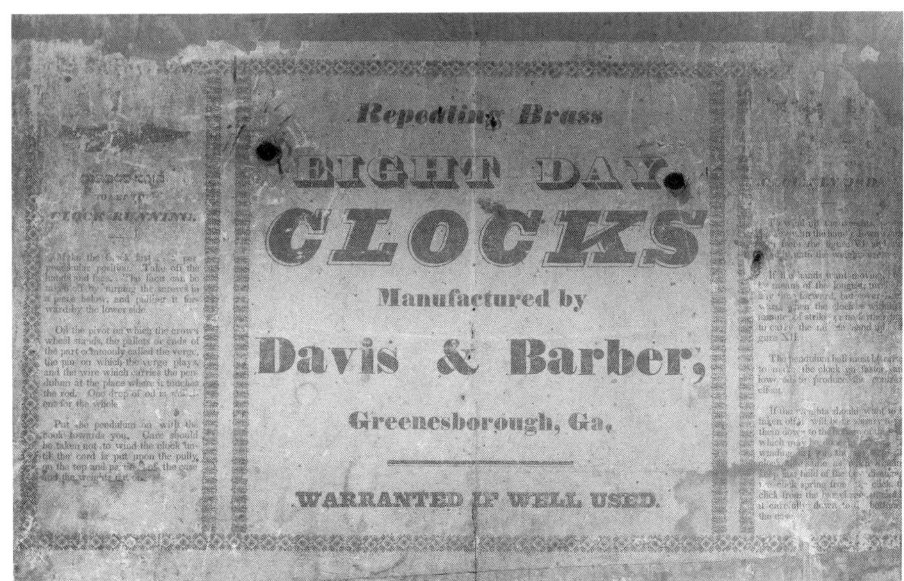

Figure A

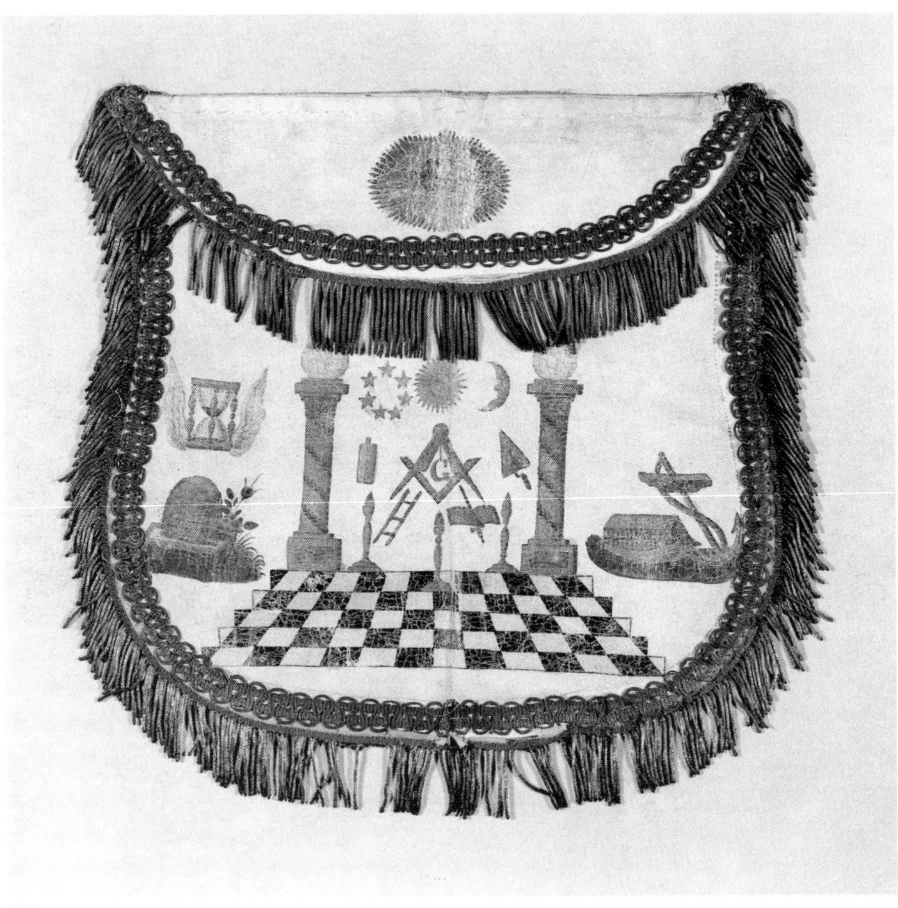

93

firm, that of Davis & Barber, active 1836–50. Parts were supplied by E. C. Brewster & Co., which frequently used the Ives strap movement in their clocks and undoubtedly sent these to be assembled in Georgia.

In his 1816 patent request, Eli Terry describes the advantages of the new shelf clock format over tall clocks: "In being smaller, handsomer, less cumbersome, cheaper including the case, easier moved from one room to another . . . and in having weights in sight so that there is no danger of letting it run down and stop" (Roberts, *Contributions of Joseph Ives to Connecticut Clock Technology*, 41).

By the 1820s, innovations of Bristol developers made clocks available for middle-class farmers and merchants. Clocks such as this one, a version of the "triple decker column case," were priced at approximately $18-$22. Piedmont estate inventories list many clocks ranging from a "mantlepiece clock" worth $20 to a "Paris made clock in bronze case" worth $75.

93 *Masonic Apron*, ca. 1855

Atlanta, Fulton County (then DeKalb)

Lambskin

H. 25", W. 25"

Description: Fringed lambskin apron with Masonic symbols painted and stenciled over standard architectural design, two columns on checkered-grid floor

History: Owned by Dr. Chapmon Powell when he served as treasurer of the Atlanta Lodge No. 59 in 1855.

Atlanta Masonic Library and Museum Association

Begun in England in 1717, the Masonic fraternal organization was established in Georgia in Savannah in 1734. General James Oglethorpe was the first Master of Solomon's Lodge. The earliest reference to the lodge by that name is recorded in a 1771 document: "Solomon's Lodge . . . is the eldest constituted in America except one in New England (Boston)" (*Handbook of Solomon's Lodge No. 1*, 7).

Although not a religion per se, the Free and Accepted Masons follow a system of morals taught by symbols and allegory. The British lodges permitted men to join who were not masons.

These members were "accepted" while those who actually practiced the craft of masonry were called "free."

The tools used in the mason's trade were interpreted as symbols of man's passage through time and life. The masonic pilgrimage was marked by three stages, each represented by one or more of these symbols. Entered Apprentice stage was symbolized by a gauge meaning "time well spent." The square went with the Fellow Craft stage and meant truth and honesty. The trowel of the Master Mason level meant kindness and brotherly love.

Some of these symbols are illustrated on this apron: architectural elements such as the columns and checkered floor represent Solomon's Temple, where Freemasonry was said to have been founded; square and compass together "reminds members to square their actions and to keep them within bounds"; the sun, which symbolizes "intellectual light of which (the member) is in constant search," governs the day, and the moon governs the night; the Worshipful Master is to "rule and govern his lodge with equal regularity and precision"; [see 130] the winged hourglass represents the passage of time or man's pilgrimage through life; and the beehive symbolizes the industry of the masonic trade (Poesch, *The Art of the Old South*, 94–95).

The Atlanta Lodge, chartered in 1847 in what was then DeKalb County, was fifty-ninth in the state. The lodge was located on the second floor of a two-story wooden building on the corner of Lloyd (now Central Avenue) and Alabama Streets; it was above Paul McSheffery's grocery store. Nineteen members were organized under the first Worshipful Master, Leonard Christopher Simpson (1821–1860), a prominent lawyer who was Master of the Lodge in 1847, 1848, 1850, 1851, 1852, and 1855, the year that the owner of this apron served as treasurer.

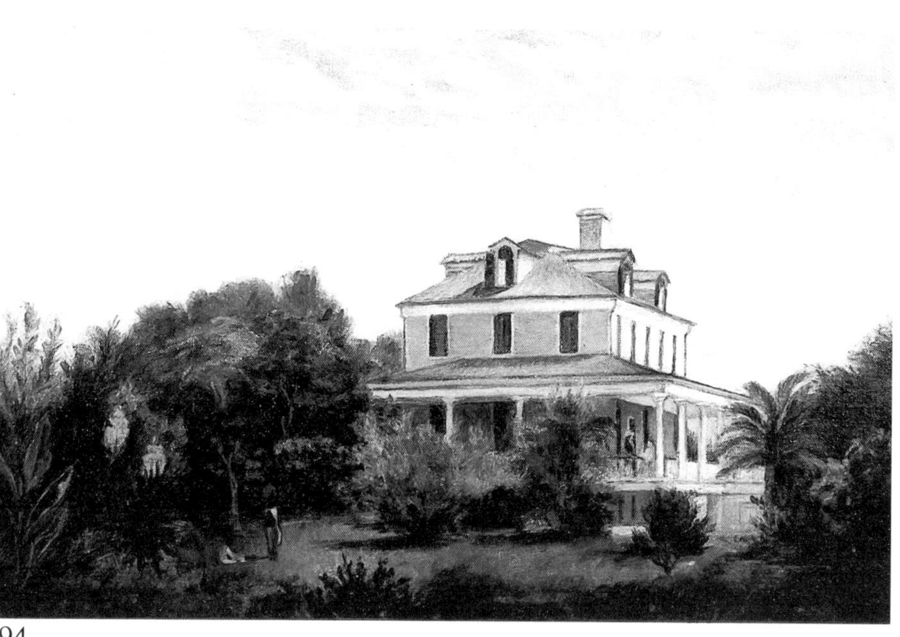

94

94 *Cannon's Point*, ca. 1850

John Lord Couper (1835-ca. 1868)

Saint Simons Island, Glynn County

Oil on prepared artist board

H. 10½", W. 16"

History: John Lord Couper was the

grandson of John Couper, who built Cannon's Point in 1804. This painting was probably executed after the elder Couper's death in 1850. It descended in the Couper family.

Exhibitions: *The Couper Family: Three Generations on Saint Simons Island*, Museum of Coastal History, Saint Simons Island, 1982–84

References: Burnette Vanstory, *Georgia's Land of the Golden Isles*, 160–68; Lewis & Huie, *Patriarchal Plantations of Saint Simons Island*; Nichols, *Early Architecture of Georgia*, 47–48.

Museum of Coastal History

John Couper emigrated to America from Scotland in 1775. Having apprenticed in the import-export business, he moved to Sunbury and opened his own business after the Revolution. In the 1790s, Couper and his partner, James Hamilton, began to purchase land along the Altamaha River. In 1794, Couper purchased a tract on the north end of Saint Simons Island [95] known as Cannon's Point, which had been in the Daniel Cannon family since the late 1730s (Estes, "Daniel Cannon: A Revolutionary 'Mechanick' from Charleston," *Journal of Early Southern Decorative Arts*, May 1983, 12).

In 1804, Couper and his wife Rebecca Maxwell Couper moved to Saint Simons permanently. Couper built and designed Cannon's Point, a Federal style house with pedimented dormers and a one-story piazza supported by delicate columns typical of the period. Cannon's Point had a raised English basement of tabby and clapboarded second and third stories.

This rare nineteenth-century Georgia landscape painting conveys an idea of the plush vegetation that grew around Cannon's Point, a plantation that prospered through the cultivation of sea island cotton; lemon, orange, and peach trees; and date palms imported from Persia. Couper, his son John Hamilton, and Thomas Spalding [105] contributed immensely to agricultural development on the Georgia coast. Through scientific farming techniques, such as water control systems on Hopeton's rice plantation, Couper experimented with growing olive trees, sugar cane, mulberry trees for silk, grape vines for wine, and other exotics. The sugar industry was also a result of these efforts.

After his wife died in 1845, Couper moved to his son's plantation, Hopeton-on-the-Altamaha, where he lived until his death in 1850. Cannon's Point burned at the end of the nineteenth century, leaving only some tabby foundations and a chimney from a cook house.

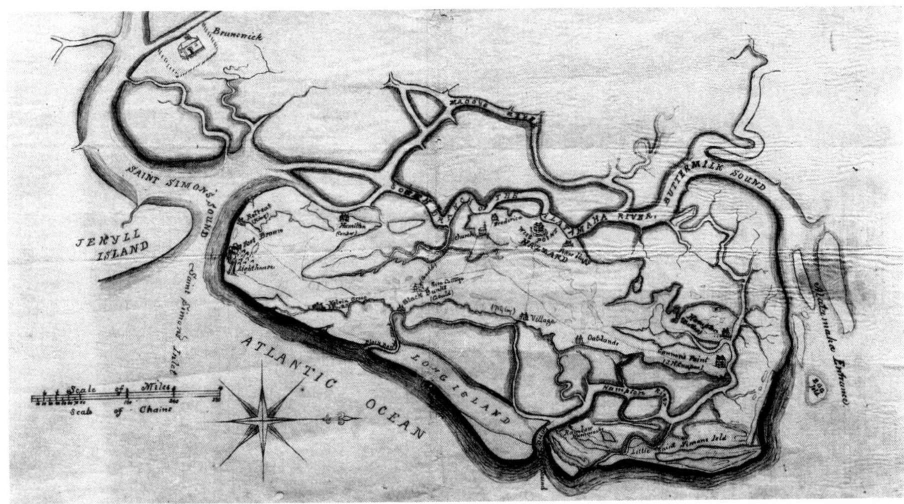

95

95 *Map of Saint Simons Island,* 1861

Saint Simons Island, Glynn County

Pencil and pen on silk

H. 14½", W. 26½"

Museum of Coastal History

During the years 1733–52, the laws of the Trusteeship prohibited rum, large land holdings, and slaves. During the royal governors' period, both the importation of large numbers of West Africans and larger land tracts promoted the plantation system, perfectly suited to the coast's marshy mainland and barrier islands.

Rice and indigo were the staple crops on the coast before the Revolution. Irrigation systems for rice cultivation were destroyed during the war, and indigo exports became obsolete with the British evacuation. In 1786, sea island cotton, a black-seed, long staple cotton, was brought to Georgia from the Bahamas. It changed the economic future of the Georgia coast and sea islands. By the mid-nineteenth century, the cultivation of rice, sea island cotton, sugar, and other crops was the commercial foundation of the plantation system.

In 1830, there were 14 plantations on Saint Simons Island. Their owners were planters who experimented with scientific farming developments. Most of these plantations remained in family hands until the Civil War. Represented on this 1861 map are nine of these plantations; the lighthouse, built in 1810 [104] and destroyed in 1862; and Christ Church, organized in 1808 in Frederica, the fort town settled in 1736 but virtually deserted by 1763 [32]. Listed from the northern end of the island clockwise are the plantations and their owners: Hampton, Pierce Butler; Cannon's Point, James Hamilton Couper; Oatlands, Hugh Fraser Grant; The Village, Alexander

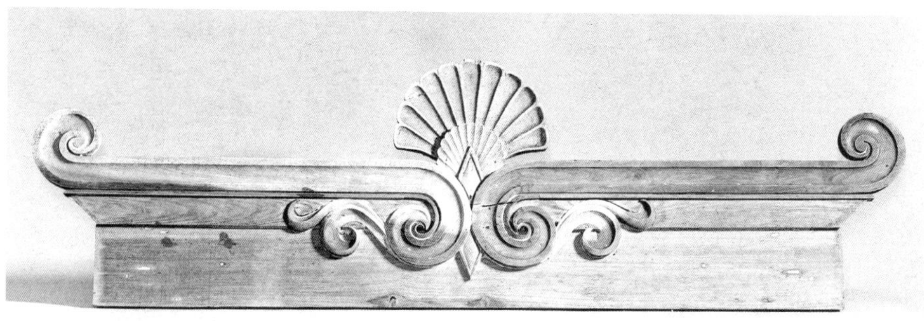

96

Campbell Wylly; Black Banks and Rose Cottage, James Gould [104]; Kelvin Grove, James Postell; Retreat, Thomas Butler King; Hamilton, James Hamilton Couper; West Point and Pikes Bluff, William Whigg Hazzard.

96 *Interior Door Pediment*, 1840–1850

Columbus, Muscogee County

Yellow pine, traces of white paint

H. 21″, W. 71″, D. 1½″

Description: Greek Revival interior door pediment; milled shell at center and applied scroll work on cornice

History: This door pediment comes from the parlor of the Slade House, on the southeast corner of Second Avenue and Fourteenth Street, Columbus. The Slade House was a one-story clapboard house with a simple Doric columned portico.

Collection of Mr. Edward W. Neal

After 1840, Greek Revival was the preferred domestic architecture of the planter elite. Across the state, town after town proudly flaunted these templar emblems of success with their columned porticoes of the Greek classical orders, wide halls with stairways, rooms designated for specific purposes, and interior wood and plaster work that echoed the classical designs symbolizing the republican ideals of Greece and Rome. Other revival styles were popular for civic buildings or for houses built by the new industrialists such as the Italian Renaissance Revival house, known as the Hay House, built by William Butler Johnston (1809–1887) in Macon from 1855 to 1860.

Beginning in the second quarter of the nineteenth century, architects can be associated with structures outside of Savannah. The most prolific of these architects was Charles McCluskey (died ca. 1856), who worked in Savannah in his early years and later designed the Medical College of Augusta in 1835 and the Governor's Mansion in Milledgeville in 1838. Daniel Pratt (born 1799) was the architect of several documented houses in the Milledgeville and Clinton area before he left for Alabama, where he became a wealthy industrialist.

Characteristics of the Greek Revival style were copied from architectural design books and altered to accommodate the climate and other conditions particular to Georgia. Some of these features are: columned porticoes of Doric, Ionic, and Corinthean orders; a one-story back porch; large windows with louvered blinds; a central hall plan; interior wood and plaster work of Greek frets and keys or Roman patterns; and white or off-white paint throughout.

The indigenous plantation plain house was a mid-eighteenth century design dictated by the warm climate and available materials. Details associated with the various revival styles could be applied to the plain-style house with milled woodwork of classical designs that was added to porches, railings, fireplaces, or interior doorways. This Greek Revival door pediment was one such architectural detail from the Slade House, a simple one-story clapboard house with fancy woodwork in the parlor.

97 *Banjo*, ca. 1860

Possibly coastal Georgia

Wide-grained hardwood neck, gourd resonator, hand-forged metal frets

H. 26½", W. 7", D. 2½"

Description: Hardwood of banjo neck has not been tested; four peg holes for strings and another hole by which it could be hung; six frets possibly added later; discoloration from the skin oils on back of gourd suggests three strips of skin had been glued with a rosin-type glue and tied under the body.

History: Purchased from a black family in Savannah

Collection of Howard A. Smith and Robert M. Hicklin, Jr.

The banjo was introduced to colonial American musical history by West African slaves. Late seventeenth-century accounts from the Spanish West Indies describe a stringed instrument with a skin-covered gourd head and with a wooden neck. Also known as banza, banjer, and banshaw, the instrument was first termed banjo in documentation from Maryland and Virginia in 1774. The instrument became associated with southern blacks, who entertained at plantation house parties or who continued African traditions among themselves

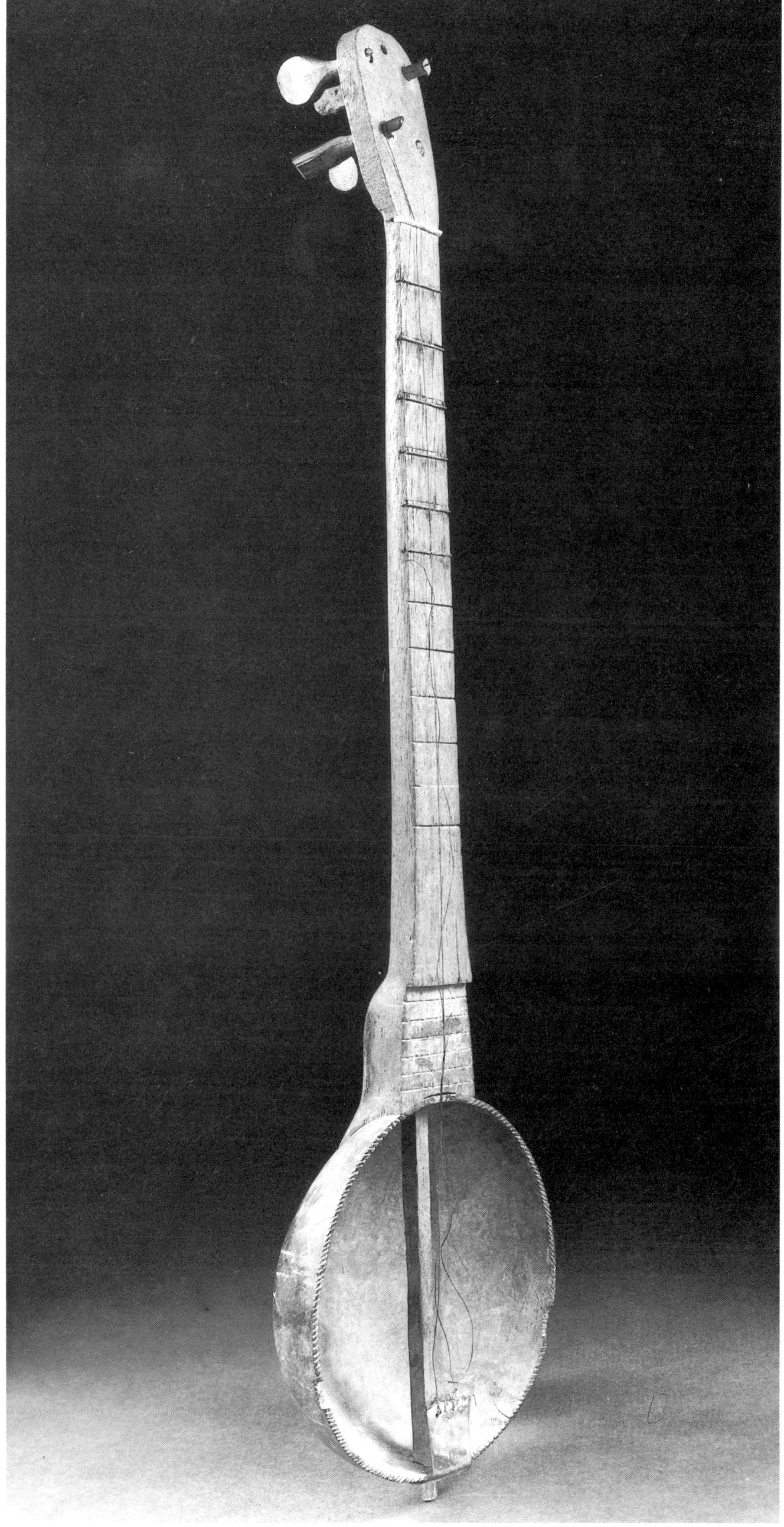

97

during rare instances of leisure time. A watercolor in the collection of the Abby Aldrich Rockefeller Folk Art Collection entitled *The Old Plantation*, painted ca. 1800, records one of these moments on a plantation in South Carolina. In this genre scene, a black man plays a banjo-like instrument while other slaves perform a dance involving swirling scarves.

By the 1840s, the banjo had become popular in traveling minstrel shows and was no longer restricted to the slave culture on southern plantations. Also during this period, a fifth string, known as the chanter, drone, or thumb string, became standard. This five-string banjo is considered the only instrument indigenous to America. Frets were added in the 1850s. The gourd was covered with home-cured hides or skins tacked on or glued and tied around the gourd. Skins of groundhogs, opossums, raccoons, sheep, snakes, or even cats were cut into strips and attached to the banjo head.

Documentation of pre–1860 black crafts is usually lacking—most slaves had no real identity and signing their works had little significance. By the Civil War, plantations had become self-sufficient in production of household items such as plain-style furniture, textiles, white oak basketry, ceramics, and other folk crafts. Undoubtedly, the majority of these items were made by slaves but few of them are signed. It is difficult, therefore, to separate black crafts from white crafts before the 1860s.

Banjoes had become a part of plantation life in Georgia by the 1830s. Frances Ann Kemble, wife of Pierce Butler of Saint Simons Island, in her journal described a ball held on Saint Simons Island in 1838 where "one enthusiastic banjo player seemed to thump his banjo with every part of his body at once" (Kemble, *Journal of a Residence on a Georgia Plantation, 1838–1839*, 131). Although this banjo was owned by a Savannah family, no evidence or documentation has yet been found that proves the instrument was made in the state. However, it is representative of instruments enjoyed by both white and black on the plantation. It offers a small glimpse of one aspect of African traditions continued in the South.

Portraits

Few portrait painters settled in Georgia before the 1840s. They faced the same obstacles that thwarted the successes of other local craftsmen for the first 60 years of Georgia's history. Circumstances were even more prohibitive for the portrait painter, however, since he catered to the elite—the portrait was a status symbol and a luxury, not an object of necessity. Until the 1830s, patrons either commissioned portraits by itinerant artists or traveled to urban centers where they could find established studios. During the cotton boom of the 1830s to 1850s, the piedmont prospered, and wealthy planters in that area who desired likenesses of themselves and their families began to hire the few artists who had settled permanently in the state.

98 *Sarah Jane Abbot Rembert* (Mrs. William Porter Rembert), 1839

Benjamin Bynum (working 1835–1839 in the South)

Athens, Clarke County

Watercolor on ivory

H. 2⅝″, W. 2⅛″

Inscription in ink on paper behind ivory in silver locket setting: B. Bynum Pinx., Athens, Ga. June 6th. 1839.

Description: Miniature is encased in a silver setting with a glass backing behind which a hair sample is displayed. This was painted the same year as Mrs. Rembert's death and was possibly converted to mourning jewelry and placed in this setting.

History: Sarah Jane Abbot (1809–1839) was the daughter of Dr. Joel and Sarah Thomas Abbot of Wilkes County. She married William Porter Rembert of Elbert County on 26 March 1835, and died shortly after this miniature was executed. Rembert is listed in the 1850 census records for Elbert County; the couple had no children. Left to her sister, Ann Abbot Billups (Mrs. John Billups), this miniature has descended through that line of the family to the present owner.

Collection of Mrs. William Tate

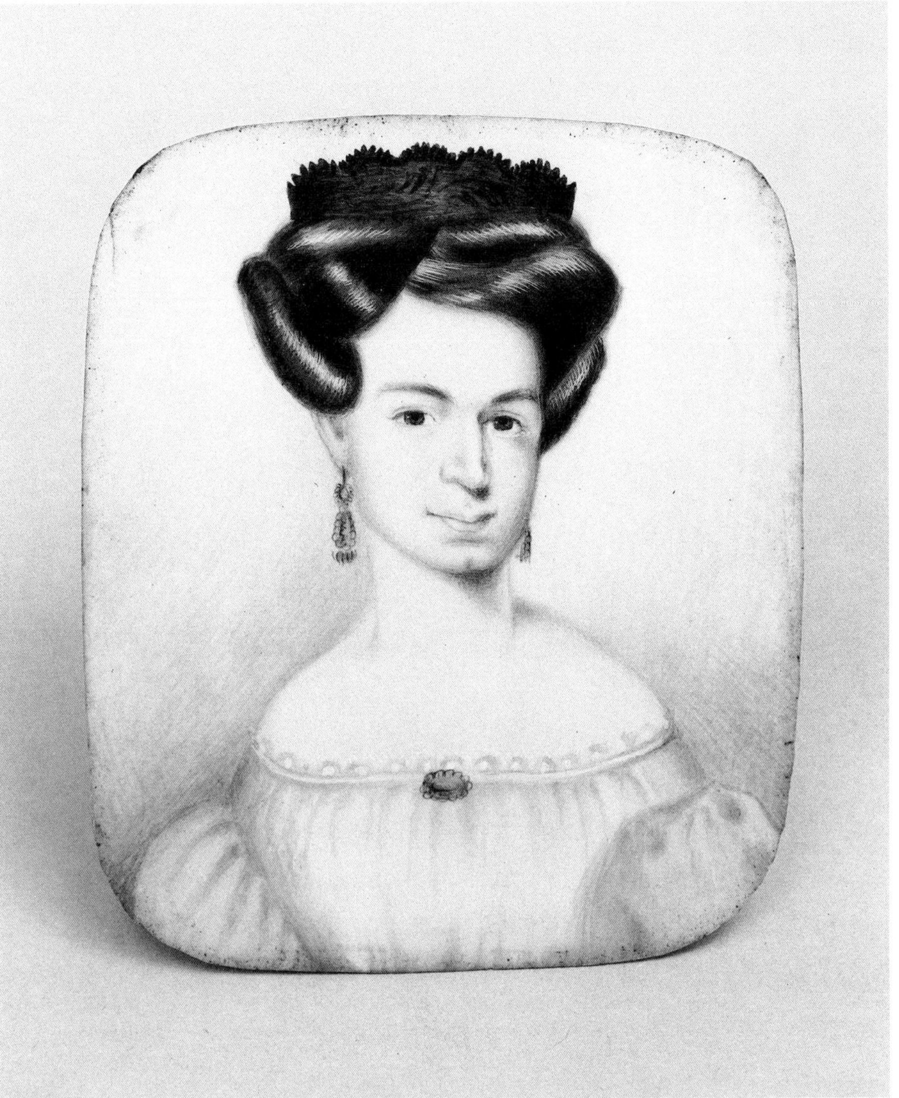

98

Itinerant artists had been passing

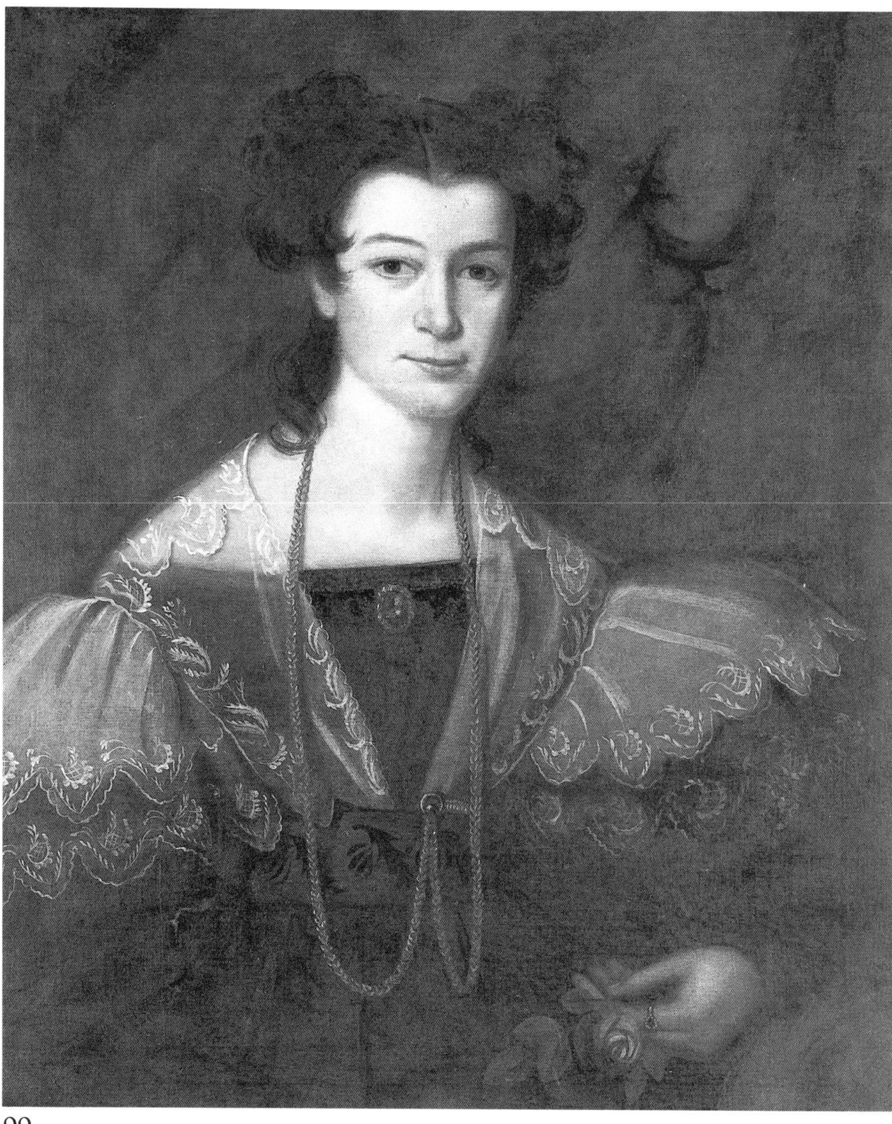

99

through Georgia and advertising in local newspapers since the *Georgia Gazette* had been established in 1763. Benjamin Bynum, boasting illustrious training and eight years experience, spent several years in the Georgia piedmont. His advertisement in the 26 September 1837 issue of the *Georgia Journal* in Milledgeville is typical of those placed by artists seeking patronage from wealthy planters:

> Benjamin Bynum tenders his professional services to the citizens of Milledgevile and its vicinity. Having studied under one of the most celebrated artists of this country, together with 8 years experience, he hopes to share a portion of the patronage extended to Southern artists. B.B. will in all cases give *satisfaction* as regards a *likeness* and a fine picture.
>
> Room at the States Rights Hotel
> Milledgeville, Sept. 26.

The miniature of Mrs. Rembert, then a resident of Elbert County, was painted in Athens on 6 June 1839. Bynum must have moved his studio there from Milledgeville.

99 *Eliza Fannin Walker*, ca. 1840

Madison, Morgan County

Oil on canvas

H. 33½″, W. 26¼″

History: Descended in the Fannin family of Madison, Georgia

Madison-Morgan Cultural Center

Eliza Fannin was the daughter of Isham Saffold Fannin of Madison. In August 1832, Eliza married John Byne Walker (1805–1884) at the home of Adam S. Saffold in Buckhead, Georgia. John was the son of John Walker, who was an owner of an original land lot in Madison, established in 1809, and who built Walkerest outside of town in 1810. John Byne became a wealthy planter, and from 1833 to 1835 he and Eliza built the brick home now known as Bonar Hall in Madison.

100 *Ignatius Alphonso Few*, 1841

George Cooke (1793–1849)

Possibly Oxford, Newton County

Oil on canvas

H. 29¼", W. 24¼"

Signed on column base: G. C. / 1841.

History: This portrait was executed during Few's last year as president of the board of trustees of Emory College in Oxford.

References: *Early Georgia Portraits, 1715–1870*, 70.

Emory University, Office of the President

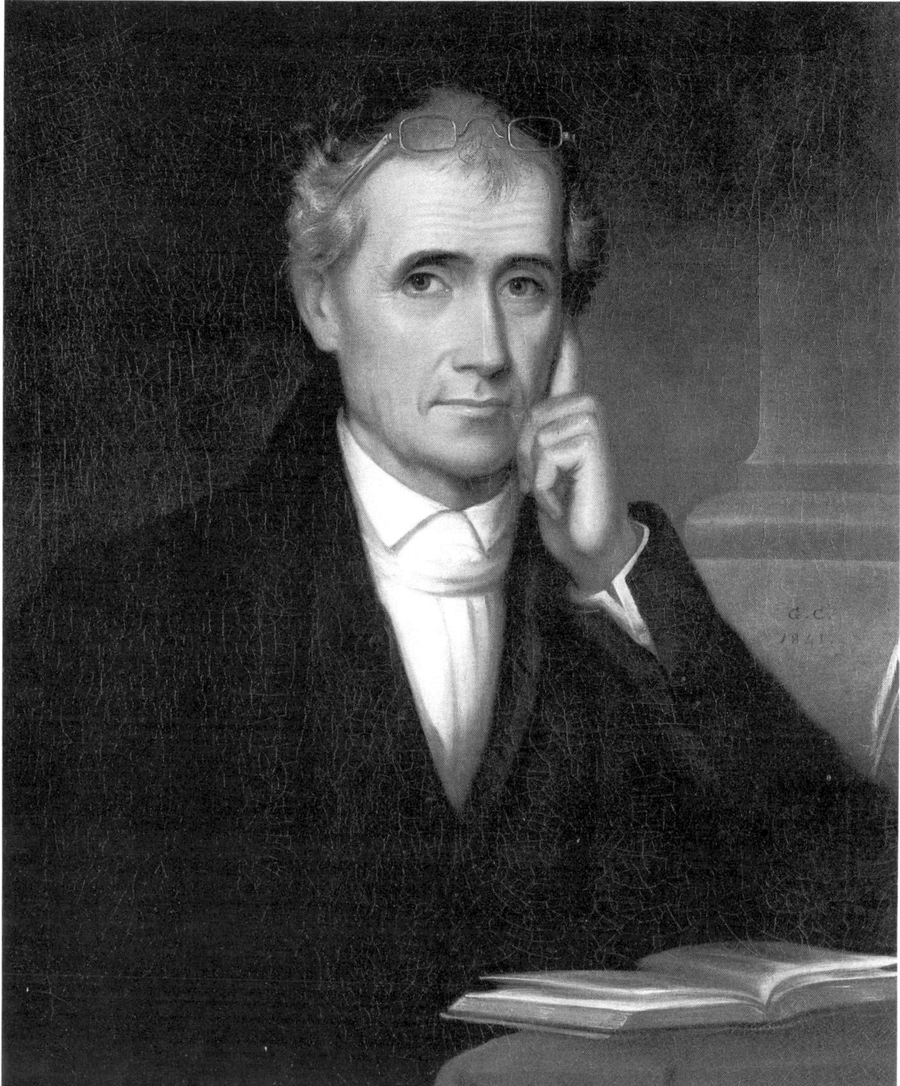

100

Born 11 April 1790 at Mount Pomona Plantation in what is now McDuffie County, Ignatius Few (1790–1845) was the nephew of William Few (1748–1828), one of the two Georgia signers of the United States Constitution. After Ignatius's parents separated, William took the boy to be educated in New York City and Princeton, New Jersey. Few returned to Augusta, Georgia, where he studied law with John Forsyth and Augustus Baldwin Longstreet [101].

Few mismanaged the Columbia County plantation he had inherited from his father in 1810; by 1823, he was practicing law in Augusta. Having developed tuberculosis and fearing for his health, Few became a devout Methodist and was ordained a minister in 1828. John Forsyth, his old colleague from Augusta, was now governor of Georgia and appointed Ignatius chairman and treasurer of the five-man commissioner board [106] to lay out the town of Columbus, where Few was pastor of Saint Luke's Methodist Church until 1833.

As a charter member of the 1831 Georgia Methodist Conference, Few and a committee, which included Major John Park [102], future president of LaGrange Female Institute, established the Georgia Conference Manual Labor School near Covington. The Labor School lasted from only 1834 to 1841, but in 1836, a Methodist college in the new community of Oxford was established and named for the recently deceased Bishop John Emory. By 1856, Emory College was one of three Methodist colleges that were property of the Georgia Conference; the others were Wesleyan Female College and LaGrange Female College [103].

Ignatius A. Few was president of the college and chairman of the board of trustees until 1839, when Augustus Baldwin Longstreet replaced him. He remained chairman of the board until

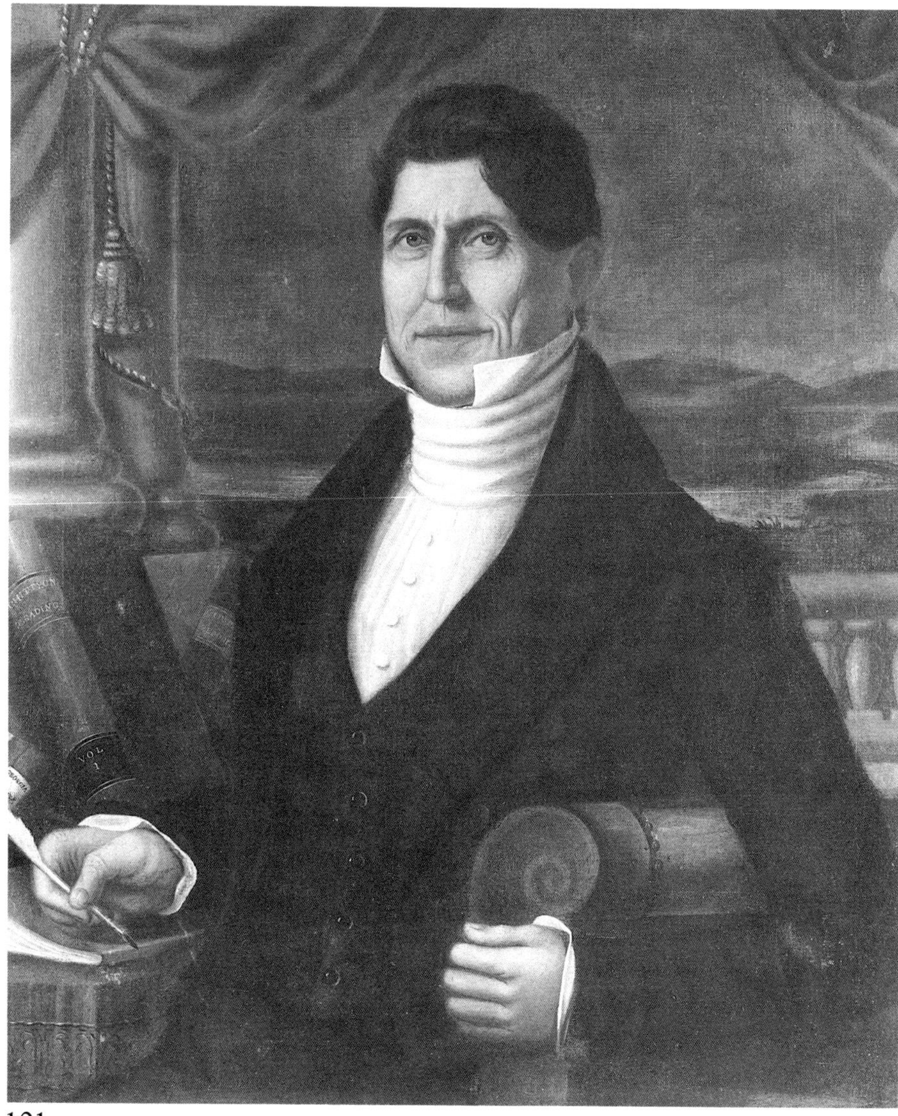
101

1841, the year this portrait was executed. Few died in Athens in 1845.

George Cooke was born in St. Mary's County, Maryland, and was apprenticed to Charles Bird King in Washington, D.C. He painted portraits in Richmond, Virginia, during the years 1816–25. In 1821, Cooke and his wife Maria sailed to Europe, and he trained in Italy and France until their return to New York City in 1831.

Painted for the most part from New York and Washington, D.C., studios, George Cooke's portraits earned him a respectable reputation in the 1830s, but he had hoped to become known for his large historical scenes. This dream was not to be fulfilled, and a disappointed Cooke spent the last decade of his life in the South, particularly Athens, Georgia (1840–44), and New Orleans, Louisiana (1844–49). In New Orleans, Daniel Pratt, Georgia architect turned Alabama millionaire industrialist, became his patron and friend. Cooke died in 1849 in New Orleans.

101 *Judge Augustus Baldwin Longstreet*, ca. 1833–1838

Augusta, Richmond County

Oil on canvas

H. 35 5/16", W. 28½"

History: This portrait was painted sometime between the 1833 publishing of Longstreet's *Georgia Scenes* and his being ordained in the Methodist ministry in 1838.

References: *The Emory University Quarterly*, June 1945, frontispiece; *Early Georgia Portraits, 1715–1870*, 137.

Special Collections, Robert W. Woodruff Library, Emory University

Augustus Baldwin Longstreet (1790–1870), son of William and Hannah Longstreet, was born in Augusta, Georgia, in 1790. He attended Yale College, studied law in Litchfield, Connecticut, and in 1817 began a law practice in Greensboro, Georgia, his wife's hometown. Having represented Greene County in the state legislature and having served as superior court judge during the years 1822–25, Longstreet returned to Augusta in 1827 to practice law.

While in Augusta, Longstreet wrote a series of short stories about life in

Georgia entitled *Georgia Scenes*. In 1833, these began to appear in the *Milledgeville Southern Recorder* as well as the *Augusta State Rights' Sentinel*, which he owned and edited from 1834 to 1836. Edgar Allan Poe praised *Georgia Scenes* as "a sure omen of better days for the literature of the South" (*Dictionary of Georgia Biographies*, vol. 2, 632).

After the death of his eldest son, Augustus gave up the law and became a Methodist minister in 1838. Replacing his Augusta law colleague Ignatius Few, Longstreet was president of Emory College from 1839 to 1848 [100]. From Emory he went to Centenary College in Jackson, Louisiana, in 1849, and then served as president of University of Mississippi from 1849 to 1856.

After a brief period as president of the University of South Carolina, Longstreet began to write articles supporting the southern cause. As the political situation intensified, Longstreet retired to Abbeville, Mississippi, and died in nearby Oxford on 9 July 1870.

102 *Major John Park*, ca. 1860

Charles DeBeruff (working ca. 1860)

Possibly Macon

Oil on canvas

H. 30", W. 24"

Signed above chairback: Chas DeBeruff

History: This portrait and another one like it have descended through two branches of the Park family.

References: *Early Georgia Portraits, 1715–1870*, 180.

LaGrange College

[see following entry]

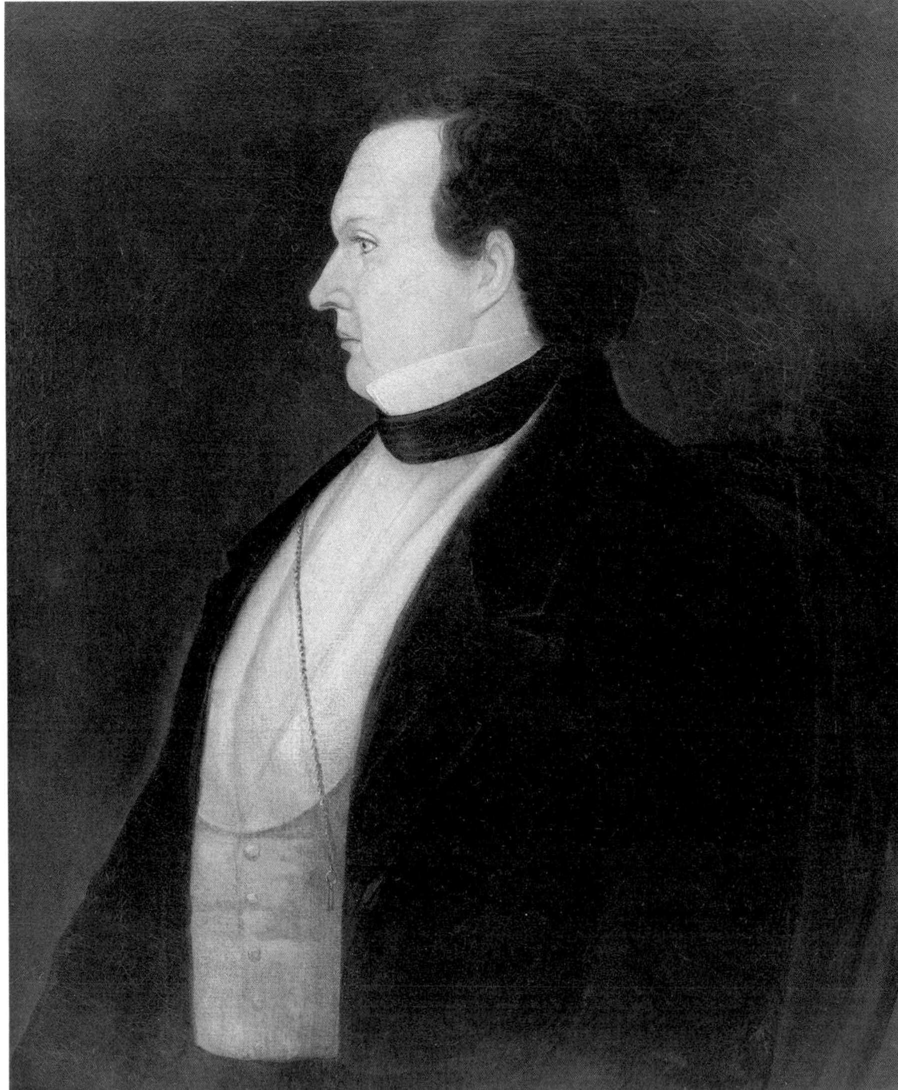

102

103 *LaGrange Female Institute*, 1847–1851

LaGrange, Troup County

Lithograph on paper

H. 3⅞", W. 6¾"

Inscribed in the lower right corner: LEWIS & BROWN LITH. 272 Pearl St. N Y

History: This lithograph of College Home, built 1842, was published from 1848 to 1850 on diplomas and catalogues; the name was changed to LaGrange Female College in 1851.

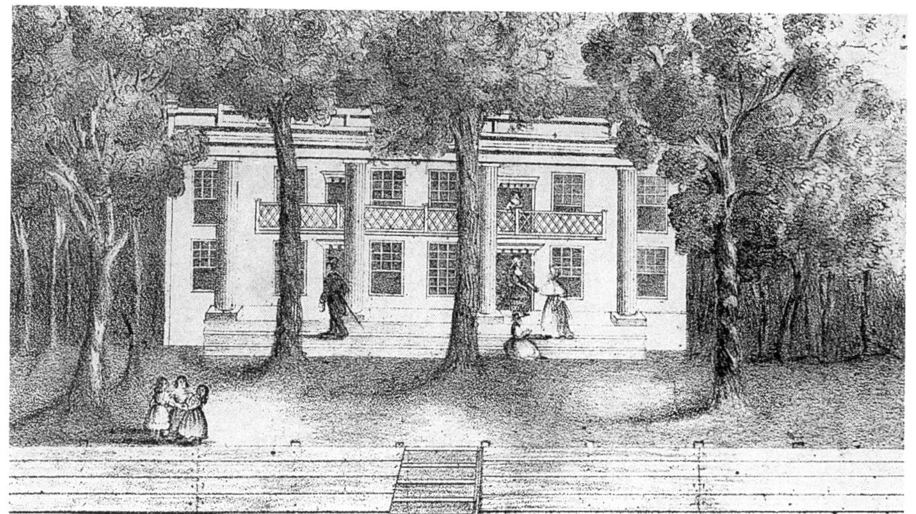
LA GRANGE FEMALE INSTITUTE.

103

References: *Catalogue of the Teachers, Pupils, and Patrons of the LaGrange Female Institute, for the Scholastic Year Commencing Jan 15th, ending Nov 1st 1848*, frontispiece.

LaGrange College

In 1825, the same year that the Creek Indians were removed from the area between the Flint and Chattahoochee rivers, a law was passed to provide higher education for women. When the first Georgia school for women, LaGrange Female Academy was established in 1831, the town of LaGrange was only three years old. The name LaGrange was adopted as a tribute to General LaFayette, whose home was named Chateau LaGrange.

Methodist minister Rev. Thomas Stanley from Athens was the first president of the academy, but he died during his second year there in 1832. The second president was Major John Park (1800–1849), born at Sandy Creek in Jackson County and graduated from Franklin College. Park had established schools in Gainesville and Fort Valley before he became a trustee of Ignatius Few's [100] Manual Labor School in Covington and a charter trustee of Emory College in 1836. He left LaGrange Female Academy in 1842. Park died in Greenville, Georgia, in 1849.

Three Montgomery brothers—Joseph T., as president, Hugh B. T., and Telemachus F.—bought the academy and moved it to its present location on the hill. In 1842, a four-columned Greek Revival building called the College Home had been completed. In 1847, the state granted permission to present baccalaureate degrees, and the school became LaGrange Female Institute, the first college accepting women in Georgia. (Franklin College in Athens did not accept women.) In 1851, the school was accredited as LaGrange Female College and offered graduate Mistress of Arts degrees by 1856. Also in 1856, the Montgomery brothers sold the college to the Georgia Methodist Conference, which also controlled Emory College and Wesleyan Female College in Macon.

The motto of LaGrange Female College in 1858 was "Pour raffinir le monde il faut eduquer les femmes," meaning, "To refine the world, it is necessary to educate women."

104 *James Gould*, ca. 1830

Possibly Saint Simons Island

Oil on canvas

H. 26½", W. 23½"

History: The original portrait of James Gould was painted in New York while Gould was visiting his sons at Yale College. Subsequently, two copies were made, one for his older son James, who lived in Black Banks Plantation, Saint Simons Island, Georgia, and the other for Gould's sister, Mary Gould Gaylor, of Utica, New York. This portrait is the one given to James, which was hung in Black Banks Plantation until 1906. It has remained in the hands of Gould descendents.

Museum of Coastal History, Given in memory of Agnes Campbell Hartridge by Mr. and Mrs. Alfred L. Hartridge

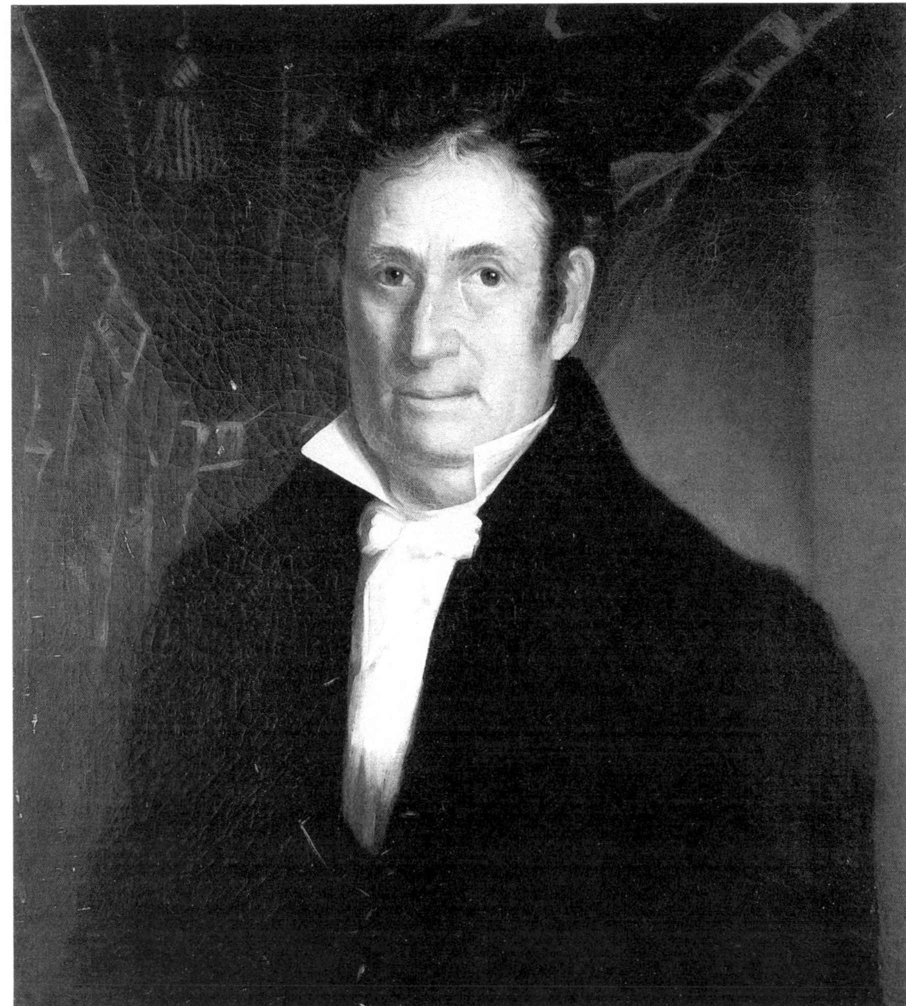

104

In 1807, James Gould (1772–1852), born in Granville, Massachusetts, contracted to build a lighthouse on the southeast side of Saint Simons Island to light the sound and inlet. The project was to cost $13,775. On 21 June 1810, Gould ran the following advertisement in the *Republican and Savannah Evening Ledger*: "A bricklayer to work on the Light-House at Saint Simons Island, to whom good wages and fare will be given if application is made immediately . . . " The structure, a 75-foot octagonal tower with a 25-foot base that tapered to ten feet, was made of tabby. The bricks referred to in the ad were undoubtedly made on the site. This structure was destroyed in 1862 by Confederate troops trying to inconvenience the Union ships.

In 1810, President Madison appointed James Gould keeper of the lighthouse, a position Gould held until 1837. Gould lived on St. Clair Plantation on the island, where the original of this portrait remained until it was stolen or burned during the vast destruction on Saint Simons during the Civil War.

Gould died in 1852 and was buried in Christ Church yard, Saint Simons Island, Georgia.

105 *Thomas Spalding*, ca. 1845

Attributed to John Maier (1819–1870)

Possibly Sapelo Island or Milledgeville

Oil on canvas

H. 29½", W. 24½"

History: Descended in the Spalding family of Savannah, Georgia

References: Coulter, *Thomas Spalding of Sapelo*, frontispiece; *Early Georgia Portraits, 1715–1870*, 214.

Georgia Historical Society

Born in Frederica, Saint Simons Island, in 1774, Thomas Spalding was the only child of James Spalding, who ran a prosperous trading business amidst the ruins of the fort town that had been deserted since 1763 [32]. The family of his mother, Mergery McIntosh, had been original settlers in the Highland Scotch town of Darien. After the Revolution, James Spalding, initially a Loyalist, regained respect from his fellow Georgians; by 1790, he owned 94 slaves and 5,550 acres and was the wealthiest man in Glynn County.

Educated in New England, Thomas Spalding studied law in Savannah and was admitted to the bar in 1795. Spalding had an illustrious political career: serving in the Georgia House of Representatives in 1794; attending the state constitutional convention in 1798; and serving in the Georgia Senate 1803–04, 1808–10, 1812–14, and in the United States Congress in 1806. He soon focused his attention on the agricultural, economic, and cultural welfare of coastal Georgia.

In 1802, he sold his estate, Orange Grove, that had been built on Saint Simons in 1797, and bought 4,000 acres on Sapelo Island in McIntosh County. Along with other planters on the Georgia sea islands—James Couper, his son James Hamilton Couper [94], and William Whig Hazzard—Spalding pursued scientific agricultural developments that made these islands leading commercial producers of rice and sea island cotton. The planters published their findings in agricultural journals such as *The Southern Agriculturist, American Farmer*, and *Southern Farmer*. Despite the success of Spalding's experiments with sugar cane, begun with stalks from the Gould garden at Cannon's Point [94], the sugar industry in Georgia did not progress much farther than Spalding's own mills on Sapelo Island.

Spalding's resourcefulness was not restricted to agriculture; he also revived the use of tabby construction for all of his buildings on Sapelo. Tabby had been popular during the eighteenth century because of its strength and the availability of needed materials [34]. For similar reasons, in 1812, Spalding built his house and surrounding buildings and sugar mills from tabby, which had been out of favor since the 1762 demise of Frederica. Spalding discussed the practicalities of tabby in an article entitled "On the mode of constructing Tabby Buildings, and the propriety of improving our plantations in a permanent manner" in the December 1830 issue of the *Southern Agriculturist*:

> I was born in the old town of Frederica, in one of these tabby houses; while the wooden buildings have been burnt or rotted down . . . these tabby buildings are as . . . imperishable as . . . granite or marble . . . except for the ruin produced . . . by ruthless pilferers who carried away tabby blocks to be used in constructing Saint Simons Lighthouse and other buildings on the island (Coulter, *Thomas Spalding of Sapelo*, 131).

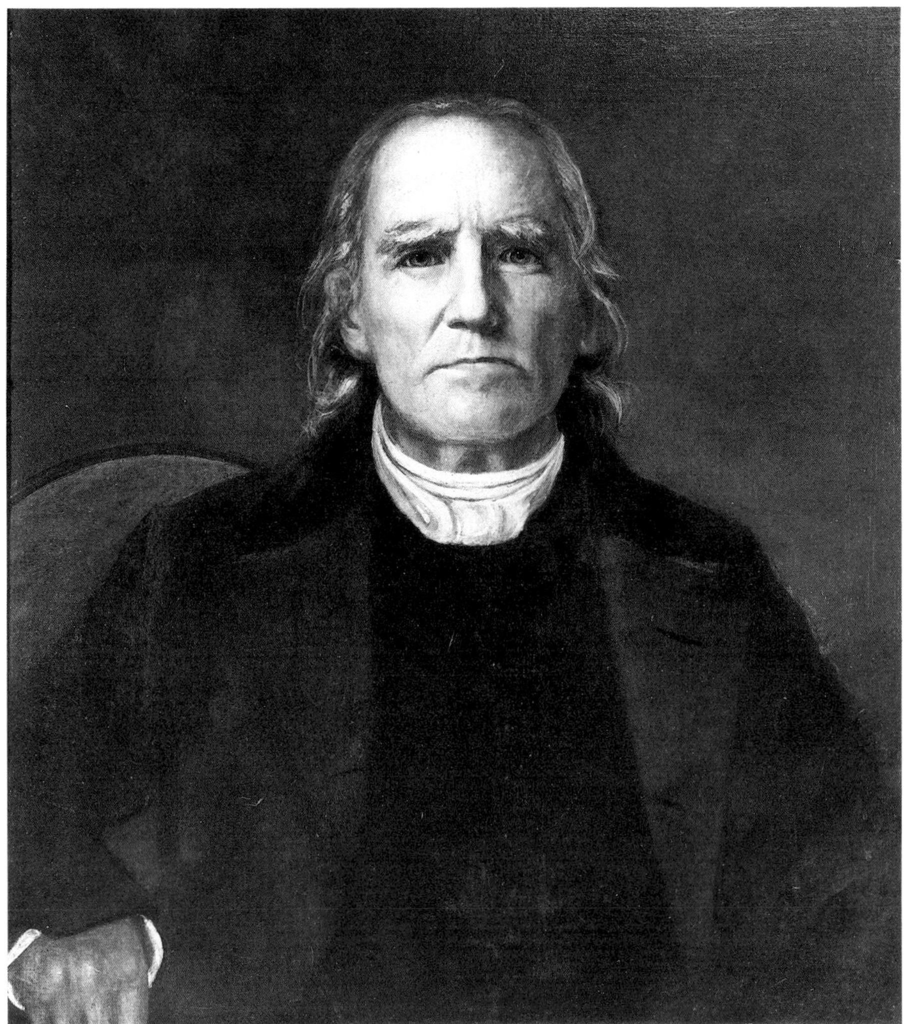

105

Spalding wrote in a letter of 1844 that he "built good tabby from rough gravel taken up from bed of Altamaha near Darien" (Gritzner, "Tabby in the Coastal Southeast"). Spalding's basic formula was the same as Oglethorpe's, but the result was much more refined. Spalding believed that tabby had "a beauty that belongs, as well to the cottage as to the palace, for magnitude is not one of its qualities" (Coulter, *Thomas Spalding of Sapelo*, 129).

Thomas Spalding was noted for extending hospitality to visitors in his Sapelo house. He helped to establish the Bank of Darien and the Georgia Bureau of Public Works. At age 77, he was elected president of the state convention in Milledgeville. On his journey back to Sapelo he died in his son's home in Darien.

Having come to America from Germany in 1840, John Maier had relocated in Atlanta by 1850. Maier was Atlanta's first professional portrait painter, but he traveled to Savannah, Augusta, Columbus, Athens, Washington, Sparta, Fayetteville, and Crawfordville during his 25-year career. His portrait of Howell Cobb, painted in 1870 and now hanging in the State Capitol, was his last portrait. Maier spent the last five years of his life in total blindness.

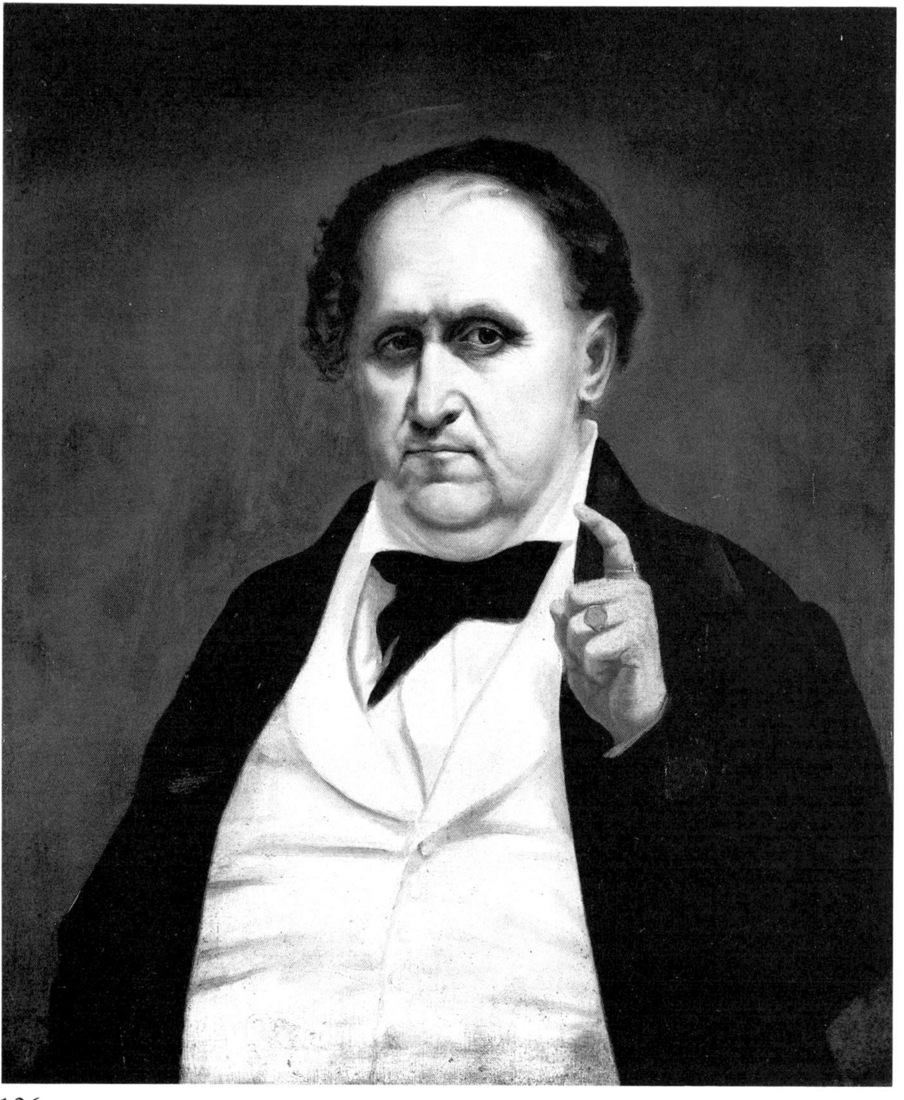

106

106 *Dr. Edwin L. deGraffinried*, ca. 1855

Columbus, Muscogee County

Oil on canvas

H. 29″, W. 24¼″

History: Portrait descended in the family of Dr. deGraffinried

References: Worsley, *Columbus on the Chattahoochee*, 59; *Early Georgia Portraits, 1715–1870*, 60.

Collection of F. Clason Kyle and other descendants

Dr. Edwin L. deGraffinried (1798–1871) was born in Virginia and educated at the University of Pennsylvania. He had been appointed by Governor John Forsyth to a five-man board of commissioners to lay out the new trading town of Columbus on the Coweta Falls on the Chattahoochee River [58]. Others on the board were Ignatius Few [100], Philip H. Alston, Elias Beall, and James Hallam. By 10 June 1828, deGraffinried had moved to Columbus from Greene County when the two-week land lottery began. The signatures of the five commissioners can be found on the receipts for one-fifth of the total price bid at the lottery.

DeGraffinried, who lived on what was then Oglethorpe Street, was one of four doctors in Columbus. He not only attended to the white settlers but also vaccinated the Indians against small pox. In 1834, he helped establish the first Episcopal Church on the west side of what is now First Avenue; he became a Vestry member of this church. DeGraffinried died in Columbus on 7 December 1871.

107 *Children of Archibald Thompson McIntyre*, ca. 1858

Thomasville, Thomas County

Oil on canvas

H. 30″, W. 24″

History: Descended in the family of Archibald Thompson McIntyre, Jr. (1852–1897), far right. On the left is America (1854–1894), and Hugh James (1850–1890) in the middle. An 1834 sampler was signed by Archibald Thompson, Sr.'s sister Hannah, who spelled her name "McIntyre"

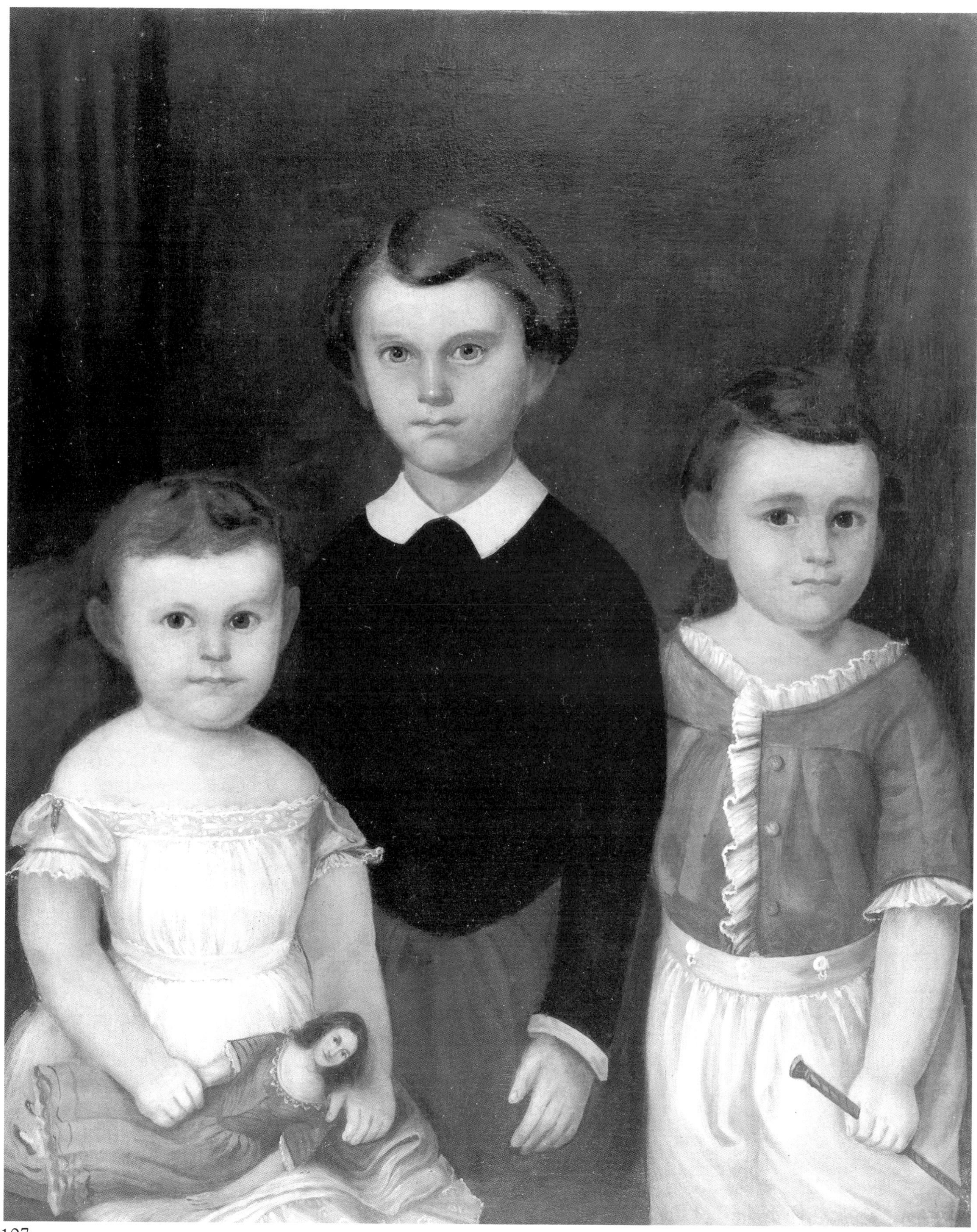

107

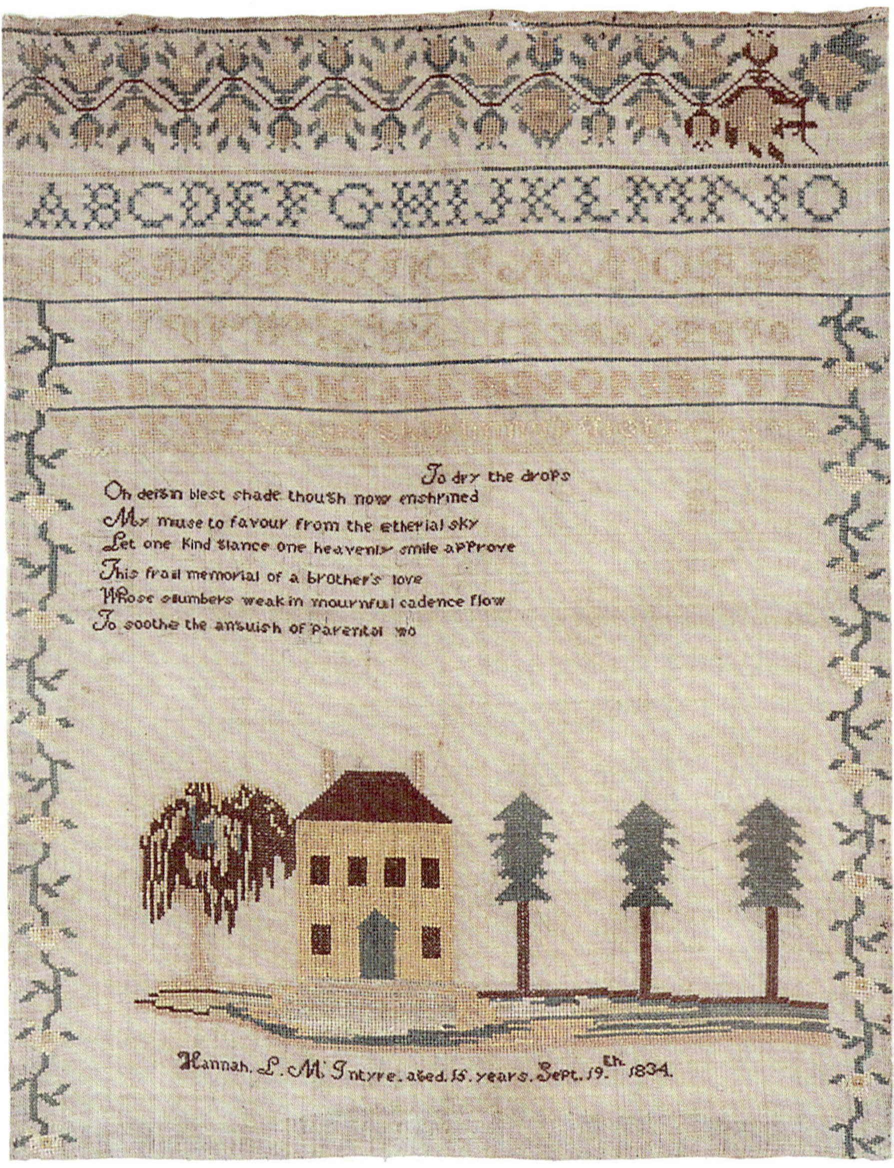

108

[108]; the family currently uses "MacIntyre."

References: *Early Georgia Portraits, 1715–1870*, 152.

Thomas County Historical Society

Archibald Thompson McIntyre, Esquire (1822–1900), was one of 11 children born to Archibald and Hannah Lawson McIntyre, who came to Thomasville from Twiggs County in 1828. McIntyre, one of three brothers to live to adulthood, married America Young, daughter of Michael Young, also of Thomasville. McIntyre practiced law in town with his brother-in-law William Joshua Young (1828–1883).

In 1856, A. T. McIntyre, Sr., purchased 153 acres of land west of town on the Lower Cairo Road and built Box Hall in the Classical Revival style in 1857. Although McIntyre is listed as a reference in an 1860 newspaper advertisement by Thomasville architect John Wind, it is not certain if Wind helped McIntyre build the house. The original Box Hall burned in 1930.

The children of Archibald and America McIntyre lived to produce a third generation of McIntyres who were distinguished citizens of Thomas County: Henry McIntyre Herbener, William Irwin McIntyre, Judge Hugh James McIntyre, Archibald Thompson McIntyre III, Remer Young McIntyre, and William Fraser McIntyre.

Textiles

By the 1850s, mechanization had touched the domestic textile market in the form of machine-made cotton cloth and factory weaving. Particularly common was the Jacquard double loom that mass-produced seamless coverlets with corners left open for embroidering names and dates of owners. Quilters, weavers, and needleworkers on plantations were only indirectly affected by the conveniences of ready-made cloth. They continued to sew hand-decorated, appliquéd [111], friendship [114], and album [113] quilts as well as woven coverlets from home-spun flax [110]. These southern creations have inspired some of the traditional folk designs found in textiles today.

Samplers, or "exemplars," were demonstrations of complex stitches or copied patterns. Young girls produced them with pride, in either northern schools or southern homes, where needlework was one of a young girl's domestic responsibilities [108, 109].

Seventeenth-century American samplers were narrow, vertical strips of linen with patterns filling the ground. By the mid-eighteenth to nineteenth centuries, samplers were square or oblong. Rarely original, the designs were drawn on linen with a pen or pencil. They included alphabets and floral patterns combined with verses, pastoral scenes, and architectural portrayals. Specific biographical data was usually included, such as name, age, date, and location.

Before 1850, woven coverlets were made completely on a loom, with fibers for the warp and weft prepared by the weaver. Preparing flax for spinning the thread was very time-consuming; as a result, few early eighteenth-century settlers wove their own bedclothing. By the late eighteenth and early nineteenth century, undyed linen and cotton were being used for the warp, the threads running the length of the loom; wool for weft, the colored yarns carried by a shuttle across the warp to make the pattern. Home looms produced woven panels approximately 40 inches wide and 90 to 108 inches long. These panels were sewn together to create a coverlet of the desired width.

By the nineteenth century, the warp was usually cotton rather than linen. The overshot technique, the simplest to weave, incorporated a three-thread construction: a cotton warp; a cotton selvage weft; and a colored weft for the pattern, frequently wool dyed with indigo. Generally, overshot coverlets were made before 1850.

Quilts are essentially two layers of cloth between which is cotton padding. Quilts were prominent in America from 1750 through the 1860s. Even though heavy bed clothing was not always necessary in the South, cotton quilts were especially popular in the region after the 1800s.

Decorating the top layer of the quilt began with assembling cut-out swatches of fabric, such as imported chintzes from discarded garments.

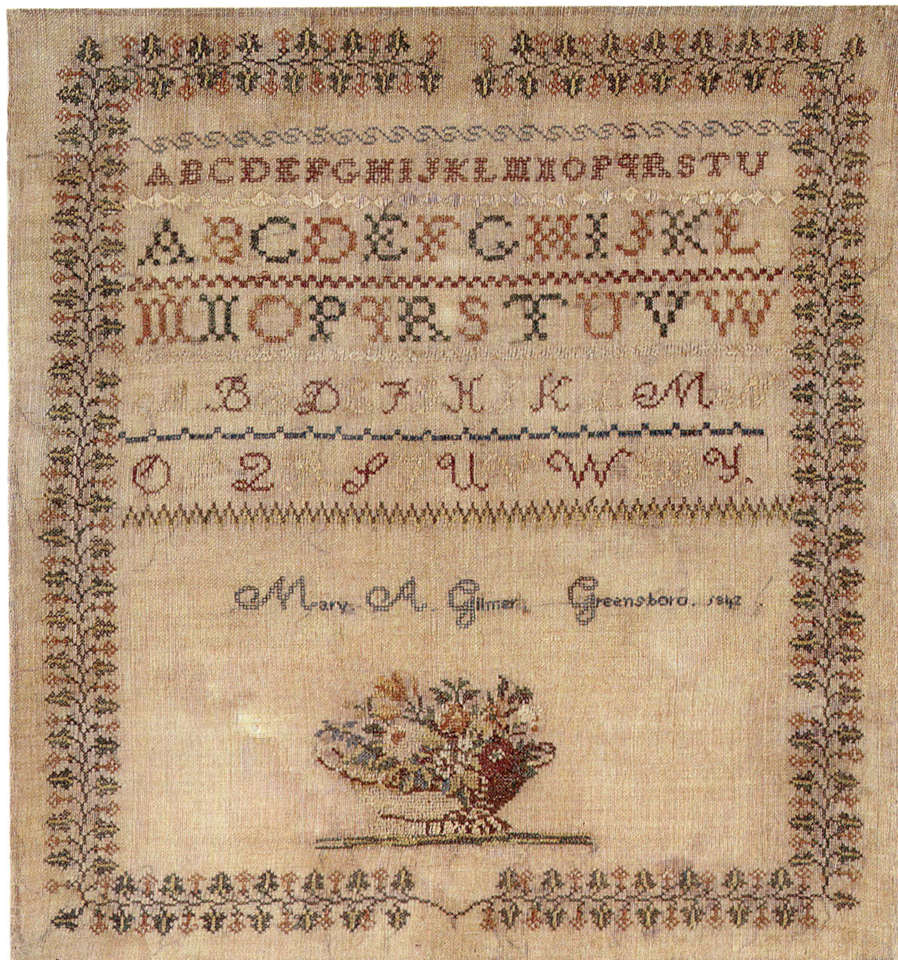

109

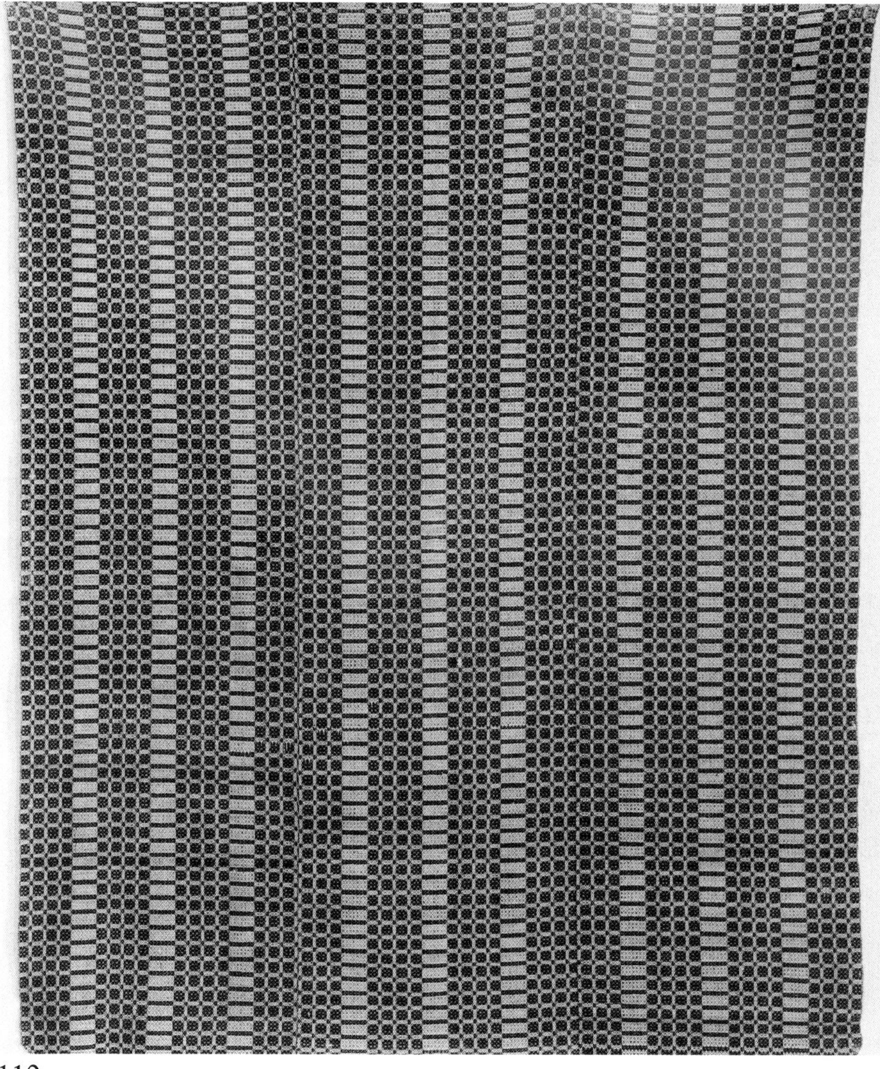

110

Swatches were appliquéd or pieced and stitched to a plain ground. The top layer was joined to the cotton padding and bottom cloth with quilting stitches. These stitches, often outlining appliqués or other designs, created slight relief, and diagonal or latticed lines were tightly stitched over the area free of design [111]. Borders were rare in early examples but by the 1820s had developed into a clearly defined area around a central design. The "Tree of Life" was a popular motif for the center of the quilt [112]. By the 1830s–40s, quilts often had two or more borders, separated by a plain background; the inner borders were geometric and the outside ones were broader with straight or scalloped edges [111, 112]. Symmetry increased by the 1850s and a grid or latticed frame covered the entire area. Album quilts [113] have different appliquéd motifs, often birds and flowers, in each square of the grid.

Friendship quilts [114] are examples of "pieced" work. Individuals would create their own appliquéd squares and sign them in honor of a friend. These squares would be pieced together and put on a quilting frame. A pattern was traced around cardboard all over the pieced work and several women would begin quilting. Quilting, then, was not only a crafting of utilitarian textiles but also a social event in the rural areas and plantations that grew proficiently self-sufficient as the nineteenth century progressed.

108 *Sampler*, 1834

Hannah Lawson McIntyre (1819–1889)

Thomasville, Thomas County

Cotton on linen

H. 23", W. 17½"

Signed in brown stitches, beneath the house scene: Hannah L. McIntyre. aged. 15 years. Sept 19th. 1834.

Description: Flower and vine border; Georgian style house with weeping willow on the left and three pine-like trees to the right. Mourning verse: To dry the drops / Oh deign blest shade though now enshrined / My muse to favour from the etherial [sic] sky / Let one kind glance one heavenly smile approve / This frail memorial of a brother's love / Whose slumbers weak in mournful cadence flow / To smooth the anguish of parental wo.

History: Hannah Lawson McIntyre was the daughter of Hannah Lawson and Archibald McIntyre, who came to Thomasville from Twiggs County in 1828. Hannah was one of 11 children. Her younger brother Hugh is the subject of this eulogy. Hannah married John Scott Wyche of another Thomasville family. Her will was probated in April 1889, and she left her estate to Fraser Livingston McIntyre, wife of her nephew Archibald Thompson McIntyre, Jr. (1852–1897), seen in the portrait [107].

Thomas County Historical Society

109 *Sampler*, 1842

Mary A. Gilmer (n.d.)

Greensboro, Greene County

Cotton on linen

H. 17″, W. 18½″

Signed: Mary A. Gilmer, Greensboro, 1842

Description: Leaf on vine border; black stitches on basket restored

History: This sampler descended in the Gilmer family.

High Museum of Art, Gift of Mr. William Gilmer Perry

110 *Coverlet*, ca. 1840

Nancy Carter Tucker (1820–1903)

Oglethorpe County

Wool on cotton

H. 79″, W. 98½″

Description: Indigo blue and white overshot weave; warp is loose.

Collection of Mr. and Mrs. Jack P. Atkinson

111 *Quilt*, 1832

Mrs. Mary Elizabeth Clayton Miller Taylor

Savannah, Chatham County

Cotton

H. 106″, W. 100″

Signed in ink under middle appliqué: A. G. Taylor / from his / Grandmother / 1832

Description: Quilt with appliquéd fruit baskets, birds, flowers, and cherubs; printed border 7½″ wide, second border in zigzag pattern; ground is small, printed flower pattern

History: Descended in the Miller family.

References: MESDA file # S–9382.

Museum of Early Southern Decorative Arts

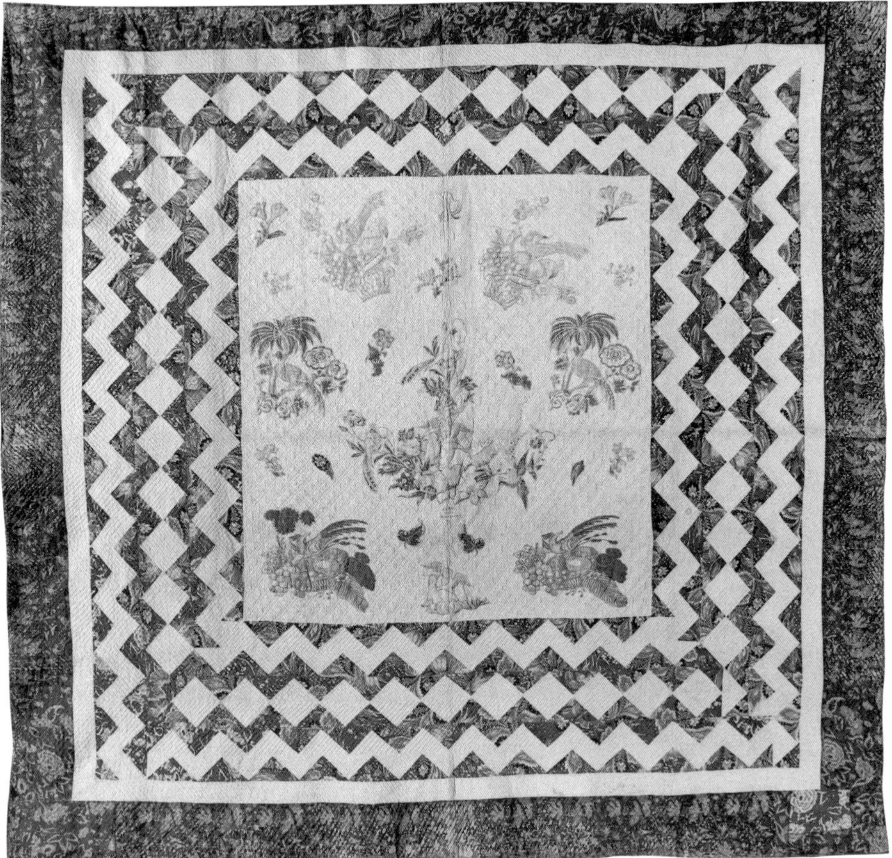

111

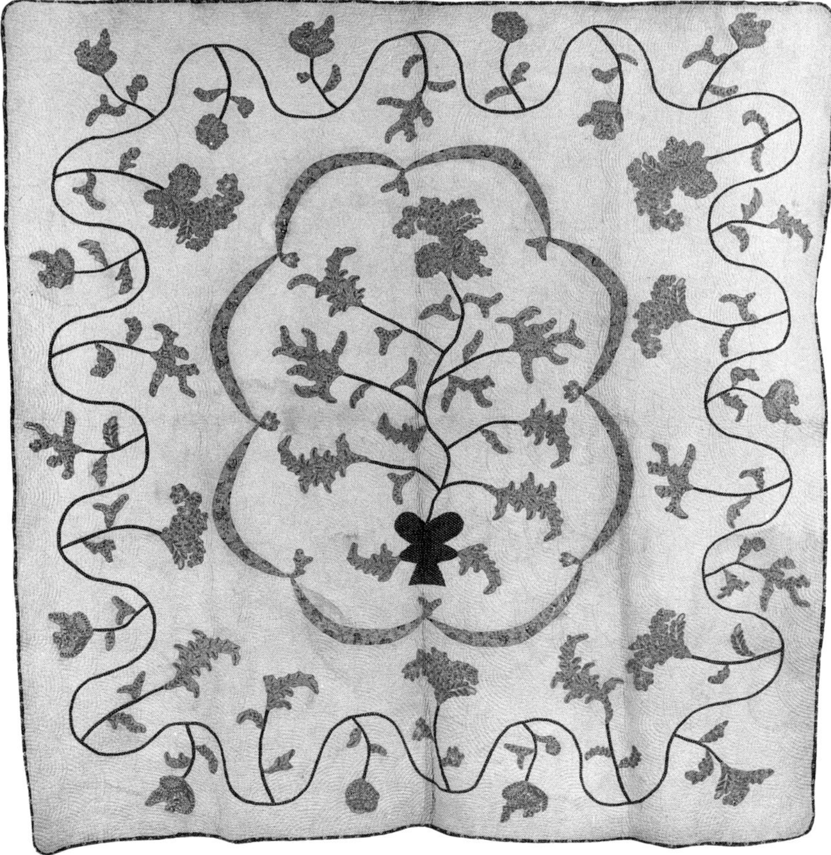

112

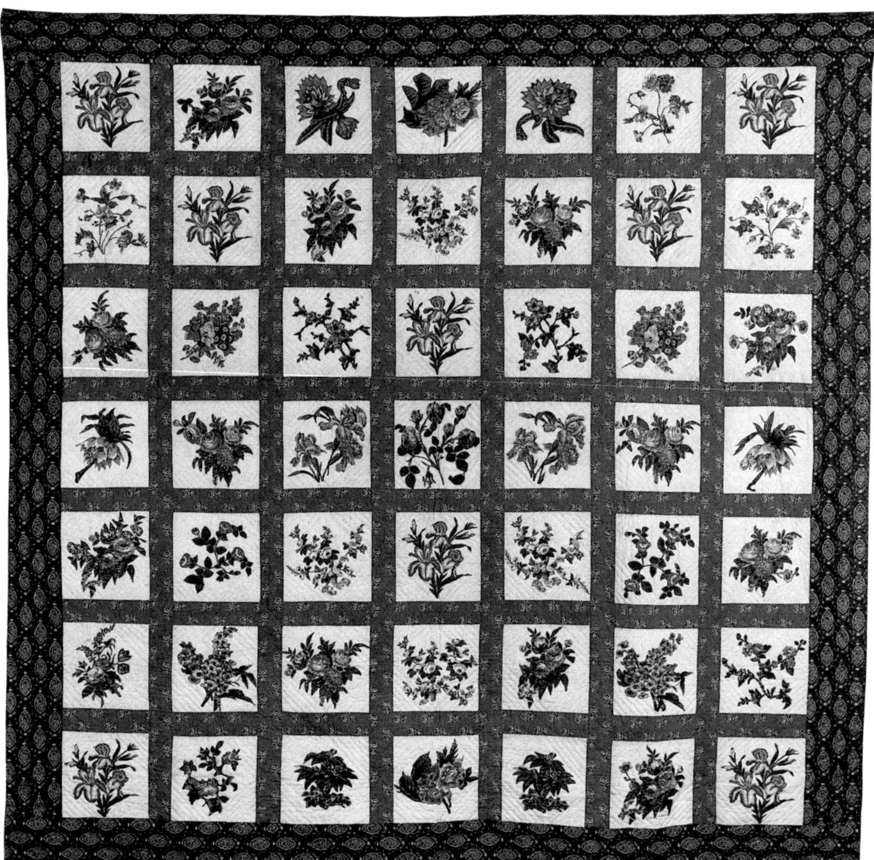

113

112 *Quilt*, ca. 1835–1845

Jane Griffith Eberhardt (1807–1859)

Elbert County

Cotton and wool on cotton

H. 80 1/5", W. 80 1/5"

Description: Plain and twill weave cottons, with appliqués of blue resist-dyed cotton, cotton chinz, wool; now predominantly brown in color; "Tree of Life" central appliqué with trailing vines and leaves and scalloped appliquéd border; appliqués sewn with rose-colored thread; the whole is quilted in a scallop shell or fan pattern

Exhibitions: *Southern Comfort: Quilts from the Atlanta Historical Society Collection*, Atlanta Historical Society, 1978

References: Reynolds, *Southern Comfort*, Atlanta Historical Society, 32.

Atlanta Historical Society

113 *Quilt*, ca. 1850–1860

Montevideo Plantation

Liberty County

Cotton

H. 92½", W. 91¾"

Description: Album quilt, 49 appliquéd English floral chintzes representing 18 different flowers; grid work of flower printed red cotton; border of red cotton in another print; white cotton backing that folds over the edges

History: This quilt was made by a member of the Reverend Charles Colcock Jones family, whose letters were published in *The Children of Pride*. In a letter dated 5 August 1862, Mrs. Jones mentions a "chintz spread," perhaps referring to this particular quilt (Myers, ed., *The Children of Pride*, 945).

Exhibitions: *Four Cheers for Atlanta*, Atlanta Historical Society, 1975; *Southern Comfort: Quilts from the Atlanta Historical Society Collection*, 1978

References: Reynolds, *Southern Comfort*, Atlanta Historical Society, 30; *The Magazine Antiques*, June 1978, 1224.

Atlanta Historical Society

114 *Quilt*, ca. 1860

Wilkes County

Cotton

H. 98¼", W. 95¾"

Signed: 25 signatures in ink, one on each square

Description: Friendship quilt, 25 appliquéd squares pieced together after being made individually by different friends of the owner; quilted overall; each square is approximately 17¼" x 17"; printed cotton forms grid

History: Descended in the family of the recipient of the quilt, formerly Miss Boswell of Wilkes County, Georgia

Exhibitions: *Missing Pieces: Georgia Folk Art, 1770–1976*, Atlanta Historical Society, 1976

References: Wadsworth, *Missing Pieces*, 77.

Collection of Dr. and Mrs. J. Turner Bryson

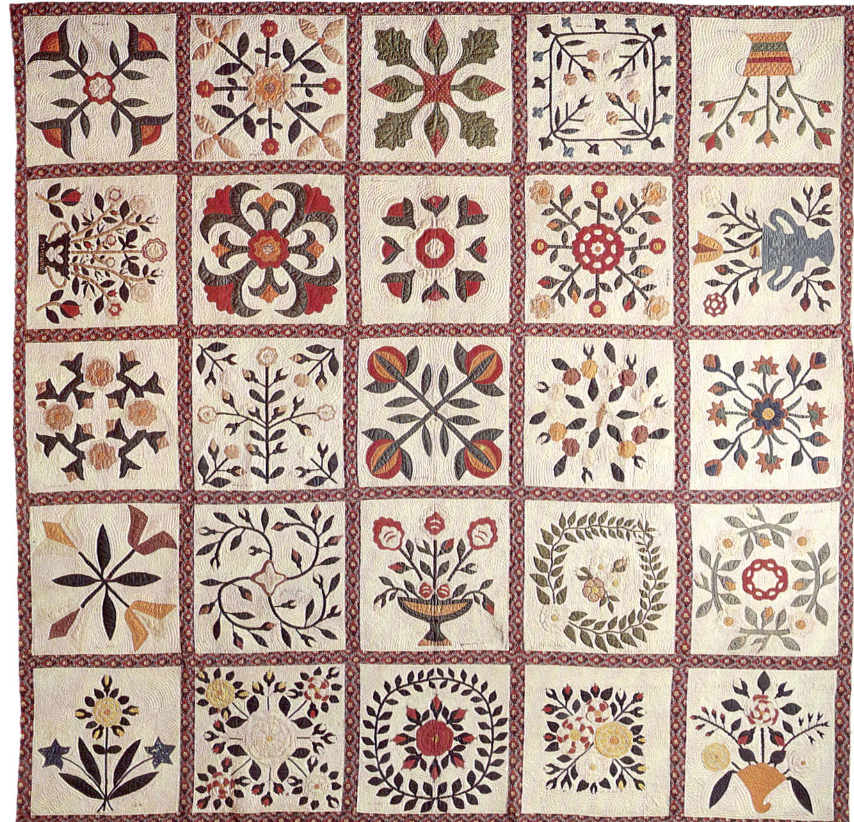

114

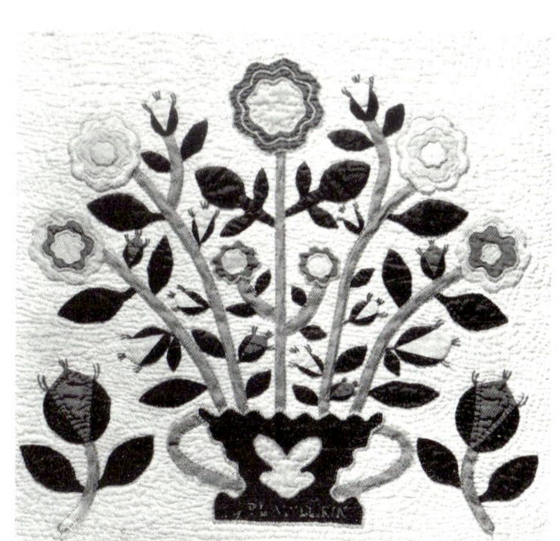

114 detail

Ceramics

On 22 February 1784, the *Empress of China* sailed from New York to Canton, China, and returned with a cargo of porcelain. The America-China trade thrived throughout the Federal period, and chinaware was readily available in a myriad of forms, from chocolate pots and tureens to 300-piece desert services. Ceramics had been imported into Savannah since the eighteenth century. *The Georgia Gazette* on 13 November 1788, for example, listed "Welsh Earthen War [sic] in Crates on Hogg & Currie's Wharf." By 1803, Chinese exports as well as Staffordshireware had replaced imported earthenware and could easily be purchased:

> Something for the Ladies
> The Subscriber has received via Philadelphia 12 sets of Kingto-Chin porcelain, each containing 62 pieces (*Columbian Museum and Savannah Advertiser*, 22 June 1803).

Some local potters persevered, despite the "China, Crockery, and Glass Ware of the Newest Fashion" (*Columbian Museum and Savannah Advertiser*, 24 December 1802) sold by most Georgia merchants. In 1801, Nathaniel Durkee, whose "Manufactory" was "at the old Academy, on the river bank" in Augusta, explained some of the inconveniences particular to his craft:

> He has been at a very considerable expense in establishing this business, as it required time to find out the temperatire [sic] of the different clays in this climate, he flatters himself that now he can furnish as good ware as any on the continent, if not better, as he has found out clay of a superior quality (*Augusta Chronicle and Gazette of the State*, 8 August 1801).

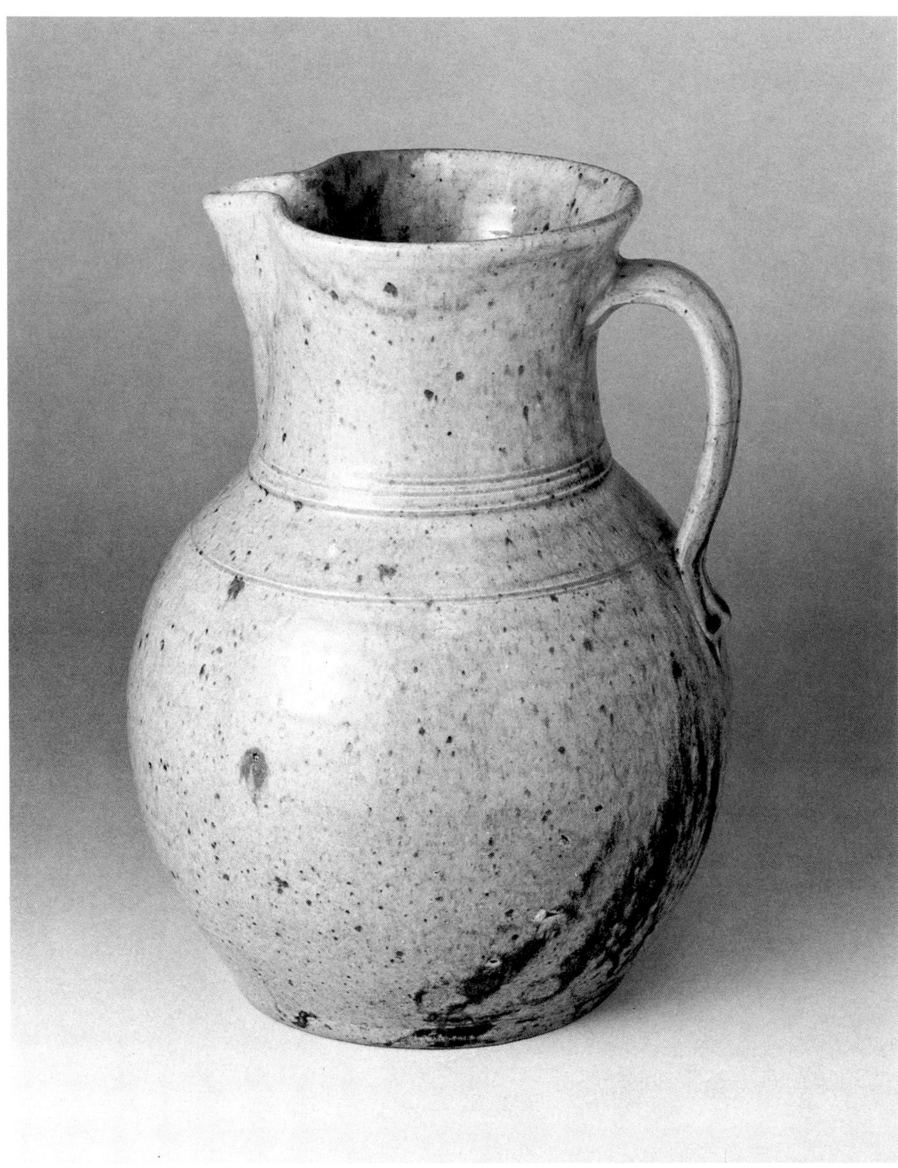

115

Durkee continues to list the primarily utilitarian kitchen wares commonly supplied by the local potter often to supplement the imported porcelain in wealthier homes: "jugs of different sizes, milk pans, pickle potts, sweat meat jars, butter pots, bowls, mugs, flour pots, pitchers of all sizes." The 1820 Census of Manufacturers in Georgia describes practices of a Stone-Ware Manufactory on the Little Ogeechee River

> whose ware was equal to any in the Southern States . . . they make a waggon load which one of them takes and carrys through the Country untill it is sold and when that is disposed of they return and make another . . . .

This might have been the firm of Cyrus Cogburn, "Stone Ware manufacturer" making "Jugs, Jars, etc., etc.," to the amount of $3,000 annually (*1820 Census of Manufacturers in Georgia*, Washington County).

In the 1830s, potters from North Carolina and the Edgefield District of South Carolina relocated in Georgia and brought with them stylistic traditions. Many second generation potters established "jug towns" across the state: Eastern Crawford County, Upson/Pike Counties, Barrow County; and Mossy Creek, White County. However, few examples of pre-Civil War Georgia pottery, characteristically bulbous in shape with sharply collared necks, have been positively identified.

"Form follows function" is the key to these jars and jugs. They were ritually removed from the kiln in autumn, when storage jars were most needed to "put up" recently harvested food. While most forms are derived from English ceramic precedents, their uses were distinctly southern. Molasses or syrup jugs [117, 118] stored the sweetener until it was poured into smaller pitchers for table use. Many pottery forms were shaped specifically for milk processing activities: clay churns with a clay or wooden lid, cream risers, butter bowls and molds, and buttermilk pitchers [115].

In the mid-nineteenth century, vessels were thrown on wheels and ear-like [116] or strap handles were applied after the drying had begun. Although examples of salt-glazed stoneware, so popular in northern states, have been found, alkaline glazes predominated and appear to be uniquely southern. This glaze depends on an alkaline substance (wood ashes or lime) which melts under high firing temperatures and bonds with a silica-bearing sand and clay with some iron content. Variety in surface texture and color, usually green or brown, can be achieved by increasing the iron factor or by adding salt to the glaze.

Ceramic traditions have continued in Georgia often in the form of popular face jugs, made by southern potters before the Civil War and presently produced by the Meaders family of Mossy Creek, Georgia. Buoyed by family heritage, the folk potters survived the surge of industrialization that virtually destroyed most other nineteenth-century crafts.

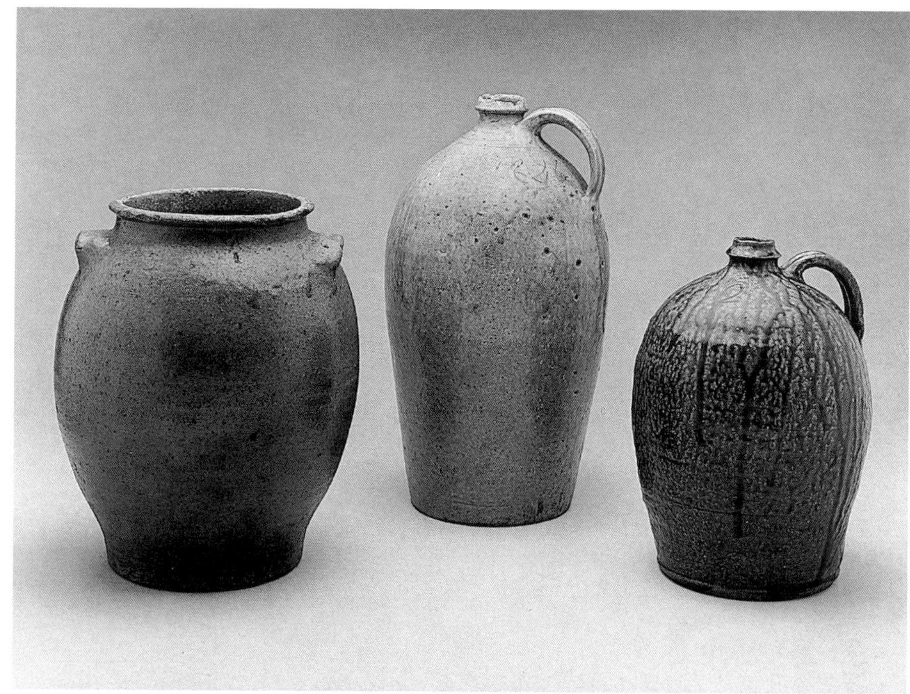

116, 117, 118

115 *Pitcher*, ca. 1850

Eastern Georgia

Stoneware, alkaline glaze

H. 11¼″, Diam. 8½″

Description: Wheel-turned bulbous shaped pitcher; vertical strap handle, incised lines at neck; alkaline glaze probably lime

Collection of Mr. and Mrs. Billy F. Allen

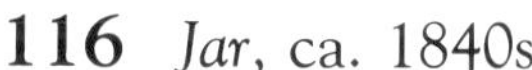

116 *Jar*, ca. 1840s

Possibly White County

Stoneware, alkaline glaze

H. 12⅞″, Diam. 9¼″

Description: Three-gallon food storage jar, with light green lime alkaline glaze showing some blue on one slab handle produced by the presence of rutile (titanium dioxide); bulbous shape indicative of early date

History: Purchased in Blairsville, Union County; possibly made in Mossy Creek, White County

Collection of Dr. John A. Burrison

117 *Jug*, 1846

White County

Stoneware, alkaline glaze

H. 16¼″, Diam. 8″ (8¼″ at widest point)

Incised under glaze on wall near handle: 1846

Description: Elongated, one-handled, three-gallon syrup jug; green alkaline glaze, probably lime; vertical strap handle; sharply collared mouth typical of pre–1860 period; handle side of wall pocked by shot

History: This jug was discovered in a smokehouse in White County; the potter was possibly working at the Mossy Creek pottery center.

Collection of Dr. John A. Burrison

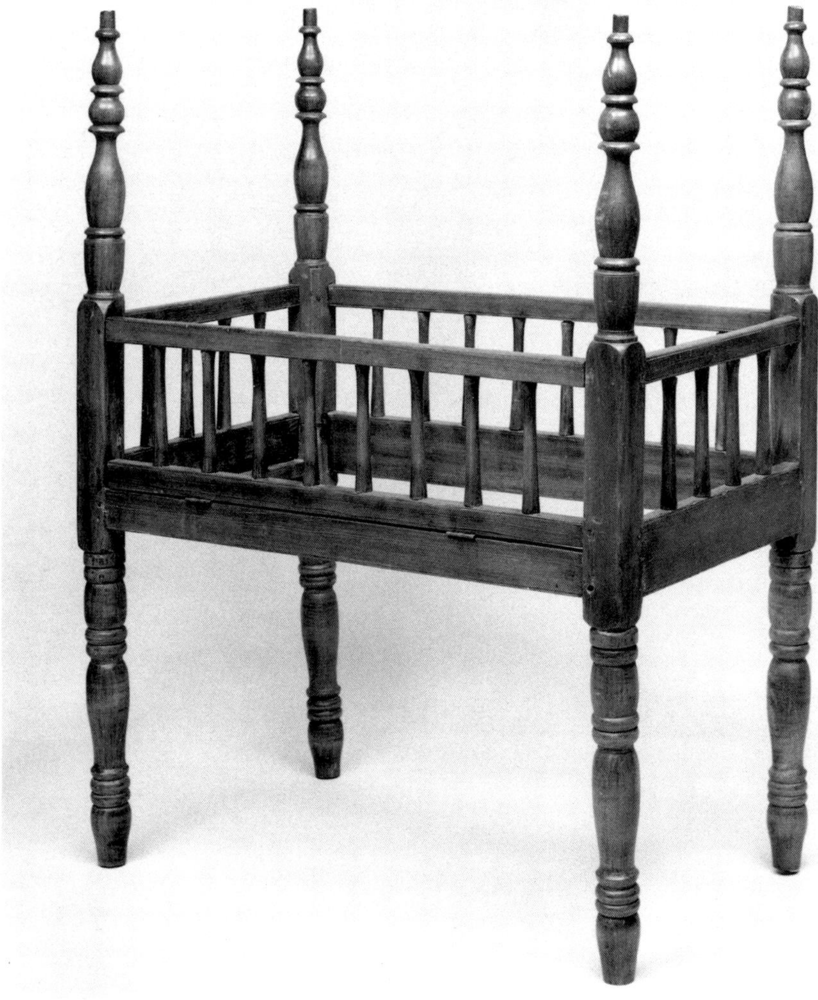

119

118 *Jug*, ca. 1850

North Georgia, possibly Jackson (now Barrow) County

Stoneware, alkaline glaze

H. 11⅞", Diam. 7"

Incised near mouth on handle wall: 2

Description: Two gallon jug with olive-green drippy ash glaze; rimmed foot, and bulbous body with sharp neck collar; vertical strap handle

History: This large jug was possibly made in a "jug factory" in what was then Jackson County.

References: Burrison, *Brothers in Clay*, 248.

Collection of Dr. John A. Burrison

Revival Styles in Georgia

As Georgia became economically solid, the affluent upper- and middle-class planters naturally desired to be culturally up-to-date. The influx of northern craftsmen and imports during the first two decades of the nineteenth century had exposed the local artisans to the late Federal and Empire styles, with three-dimensional carving, reeding, and decorative elements with classical precedents. The locals interpreted these styles with occasional successes [69, 70, 72].

In 1837, at the beginning of the Victorian period in America, the neo-classic symbols that had reflected America's national pride were replaced by designs recalling ancient and far-away lands—Greco-Egyptian, Medieval, Gothic, Baroque, and Rococo motifs. These revivals were reflected not only in cabinetmaking but also in architecture, silver, and textiles until the 1870s.

Of these revivals, Georgians enthusiastically adopted the Greek Revival style in architecture, which was based on the classical orders—Doric, Ionic, and Corinthian—in as many ways as possible: porticos, mantels, stairways, and interior plaster and wood work [96]. Vernacular structures were often "templized" by adding a portico of the correct classical proportions, which were described in detail in architectural copy books. The farmhouse turned Greek temple seems to epitomize the economic and cultural freedom of opportunity in antebellum Georgia.

The interiors of these massive structures had high ceilings that would have dwarfed the delicate Federal furniture of the 1800s. Furnishings for these houses needed to be a substantial height. The houses had rooms for all occasions, single and double parlors, dining rooms, kitchens, and plenty of bedrooms. The change in furniture proportions is illustrated by comparing the 39-inch height of the late Federal sideboard of the 1820 period [72] to the 55-inch height of the revival example [120], or that of the 1810 desk-and-bookcase [62] of 83 inches to the 105-inch Charles Platt secretary bookcase [123]. Heavy applied carving of revival ornamentation [122, 123] and bulbous turnings [119, 121], as well as an overall massiveness [120, 122, 123], helped balance the huge room and the piece of furniture.

The secretary bookcase from the shop of Charles A. Platt is a composite of Victorian revival styles. It runs the gamut from the Moorish ogee arched glass panelled doors to the Georgia state seal inlaid on the prospect door. Two-dimensional light and dark inlay work and crotched veneers compete with three-dimensional applied scroll-work and bands of undulating rosewood elements. Jonathan Fairbanks describes the Victorian influence in furniture as one of contrasts: "Good-vs-evil, fragile-vs-robust, light-vs-dark are but three of an infinite range of contrasts explored and exploited by all nineteenth century arts . . . " (Fairbanks and Bates, *American Furniture, 1820 to the Present*, 379). These stylistic contrasts echo the dichotomies simultaneously occurring on social, political, and cultural levels in pre–1860 Georgia.

119 *Crib*, ca. 1840–1850

Harris County

Tulip poplar posts and blocks and spindles, yellow pine rails and frame

H. 54⅛", W. 41", D. 32½"

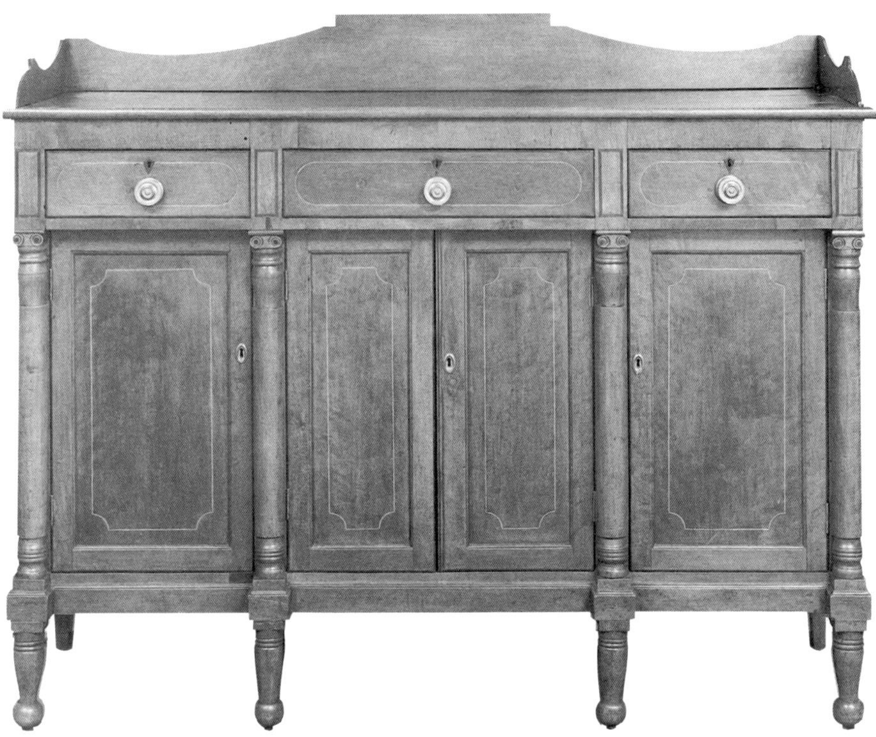

120

Furniture Manufactory and

WARE ROOM.

THE undersigned begs to announce that he has now on hand at his **WARE ROOM,** near the Episcopal Church, an extensive assortment of **Furniture,** of every description.

Connected with the Wore Room is a

CABINET SHOP,

Where he is prepared to make any article of furniture to order, and at short notice, and repair old furniture, do upholstering, &c., &c. He keeps on hand an assortment of

Guilt Moldings, of every variety.

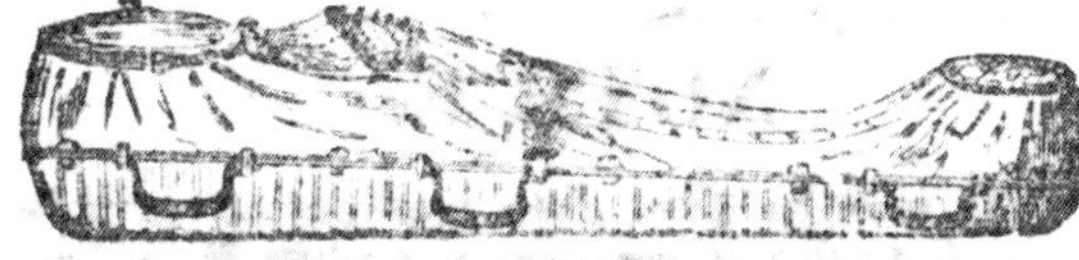

Fisk's Patent Metalic

And other Coffins, constantly on hand.

WILLIAM WOOD.

November 30, 1854.

Figure A

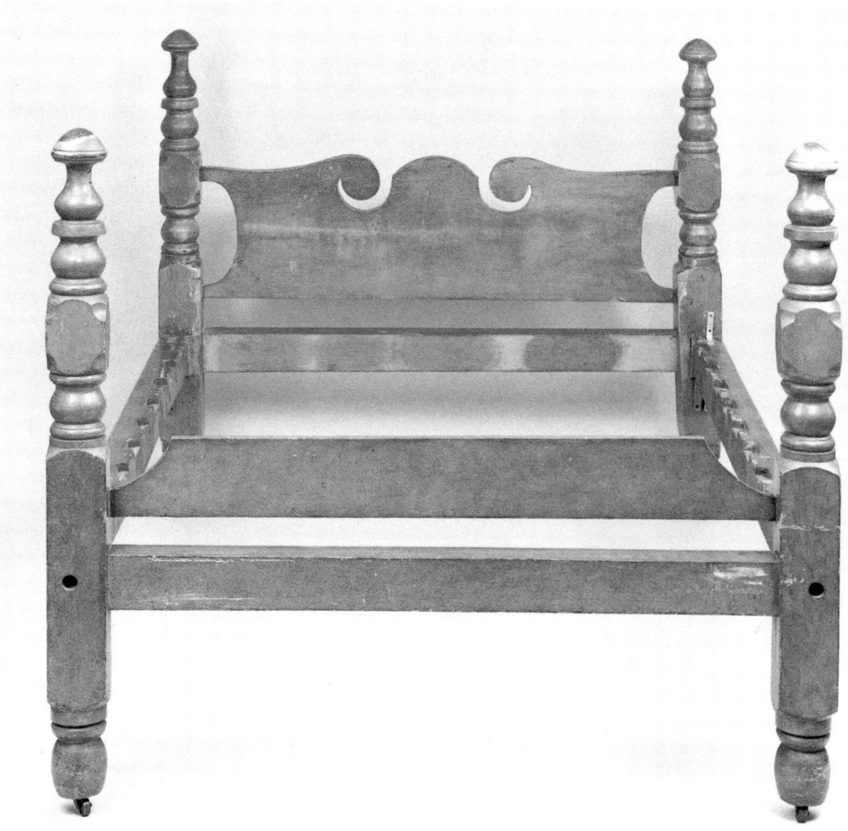

121

Description: Bulbous turnings separated by rings; legs turned separately from crib posts and blocks; spindles taper in the middle; posts extend to provide for a canopy that is not original; hardware on fall side replaced; each end has strip of wood to support slats for mattress.

History: This piece descended in the family of Elvira Amanda Stevens McMichael, who was the fifth child of Hampton and Attalisa Stevens of Harris County.

Private Collection

120 *Sideboard*, ca. 1840–1850

Middle Georgia

Primary woods: yellow birch, light and dark wood inlay; secondary wood: yellow pine

H. 52½", W. 64¾", D. 21½"

Description: Empire and Revival style period characteristics are evident in the recessed side panels, stocky ring-turned legs, shaped splashboard or gallery, four three-quarter round pilasters with classical Ionic voluted capitals; string inlay with hollow-round corners reminiscent of earlier styles [70].

History: Purchased in Houston County

Collection of Mr. and Mrs. William W. Griffin

A woodcut of a sideboard very similar to this one was published in the 30 November 1854 *Southern Banner*, in Athens (figure a). The subscriber was one William Wood, who had a "Ware Room near the Episcopal Church, [with] an extensive assortment of Furniture of every description." Connected to this warehouse was a cabinetmaking shop where he would make "furniture to order, . . . repair old furniture, do upholstering, &c, &c."

121 *Bedstead*, ca. 1830–1850

Walton County

Primary wood: maple head and foot boards; secondary woods: yellow pine and poplar sides and slats

H. 48", W. 52", D. 72"

Description: Boldly turned posts, all matching, with lamb's tongued blocks between sections; headboard is in a reverse scrolled pattern; originally held together by bed bolts, but present hardware is modern

History: Originally belonged to Martha Lumpkin, daughter of Wilson Lumpkin, governor of Georgia from 1831–1835, and for whom Marthasville, now Atlanta, was named before 1843. This piece descended in the family of David Crenshaw Barrow to the present owner.

Collection of Mrs. William Tate

Estate inventories from the piedmont show that beds not only were fairly scarce in most houses but also were often the most valuable possession. While it is difficult to gauge values from these inventories, ones recorded in Morgan County up to 1830 find a "birch bedstead, varnished" worth $18.00, "mahogany bed and furniture" worth $60.00, and "3 bed, steads, and furniture" valued at $160.00. An inventory of Susannah Carlton, also of Morgan County, gives an extensive listing of possible types of "furniture" for beds: "1 bolster, 4 bed quilts, 2 blankets, 5 sheets, 2 pillows, 4 pairs pillowcases, 2 foot valences, 2 sets curtains, 4 white counterpanes." The value of this complete set is not recorded, but a Greene County inventory lists "2 white counterpanes" with needlemarking as being worth $22.

122 *Dressing Bureau*, ca. 1850

Ringgold, Catoosa County

Primary woods: walnut, burl walnut veneer; secondary woods: yellow pine drawer sides and bottom, poplar back

H. 76″ (including mirror, excluding casters), W. 46″, D. 20¾″

Description: Acanthus leaf carving applied to case sides; recessed side panels; ogee-arched bracketed apron; mirror with two drawers with molded fronts is a removable unit attached to bureau top with pegs; a combination of carved rococo scrolls and flowers form a frame on which the mirror can pivot; casters are original on a stepped base

History: Descended in the Yates family

Collection of Mr. and Mrs. Joseph H. Hillsman III

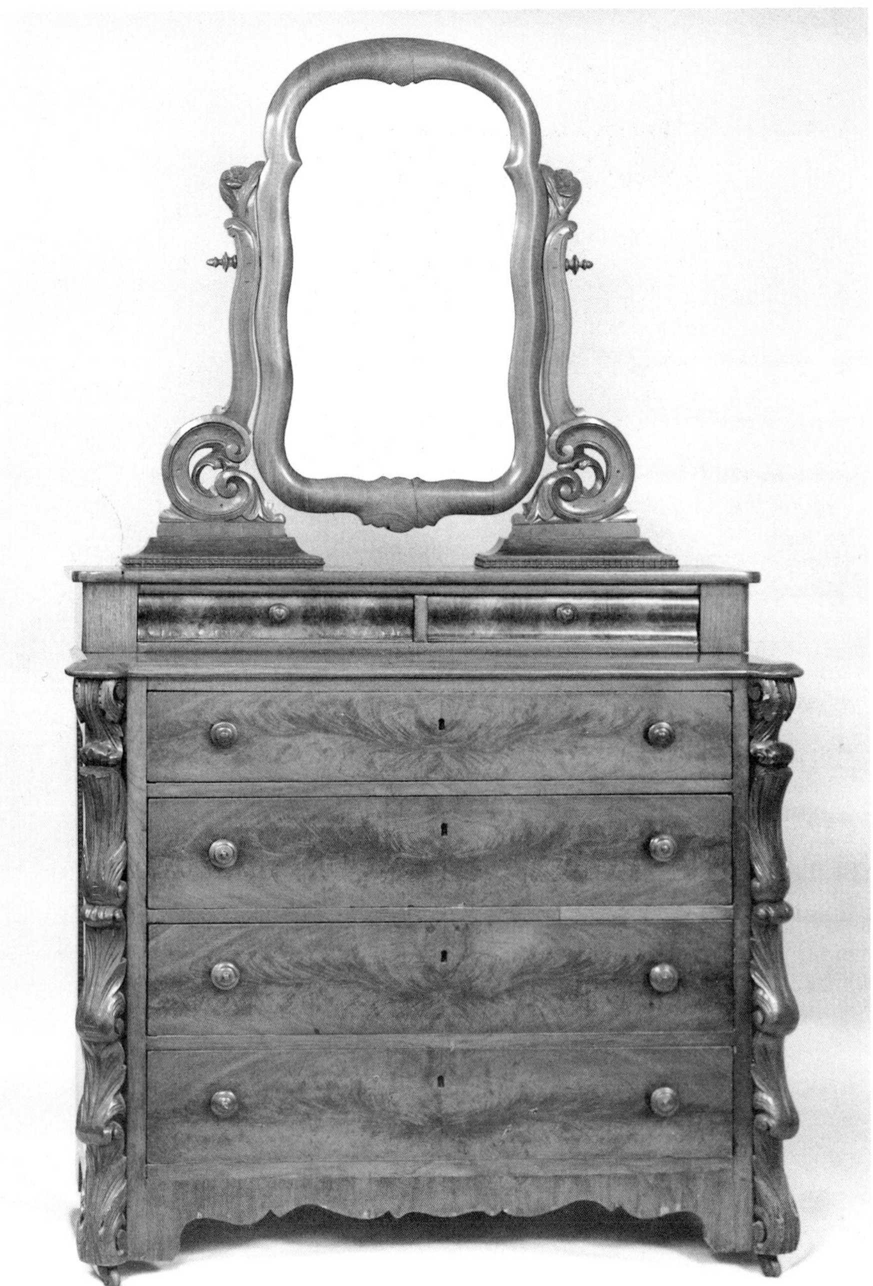

122

123 *Secretary Bookcase*, 1853

Charles A. Platt

Augusta, Richmond County

Primary woods: rosewood veneer, light and dark wood inlay; secondary woods: satin wood bookcase back and smaller interior

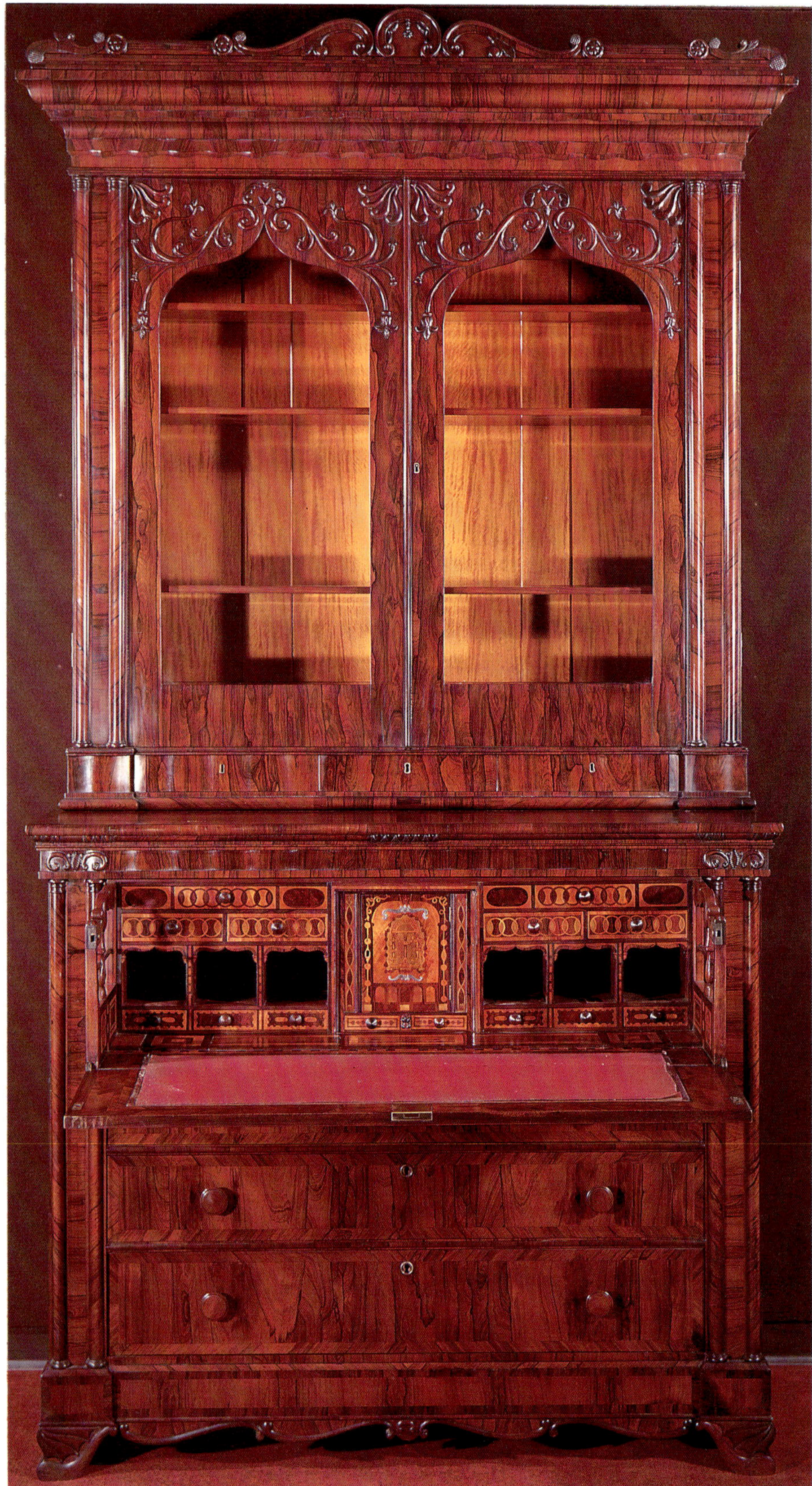
123

drawer sides and bottoms, mahogany interior drawer sides for others; white pine exterior drawer sides and bottoms, white pine desk back; silver swags nailed into prospect door

H. 105¾″, W. 24¼″, 53″

Engraved on silver swags on the prospect door: Manufactured by Charles A. Platt, Augusta, 1853, Geo.

Description: Bookcase has two ogee-arched glass doors with dual half-round pilasters on each side; pilasters repeated on desk front; applied carved rococo scrolls, bell-flowers, fleur-de-lis on crest of bookcase, around doors, on fall drawer, and desk apron; egg-and-dart molding applied beneath overhang of desk top; undulating bands of veneer at entablature, bookcase base, and across front and sides of desk; desk interior has six small drawers and three pigeon holes on each side of prospect door, which is inlaid with the Georgia state seal; three graduated exterior drawers with banded veneer; molded feet

Atlanta Historical Society

Originally from New York, Charles A. Platt advertised an outlet shop in Augusta as early as 1839 (*Georgia Constitutionalist*, 17 December 1839). He was active in Augusta's business community and kept up with the industrial revolution by installing a steam engine in his shop in 1849, just two years after the completion of the Augusta Canal.

While nothing is known about his training in New York, Platt or his shop had some cabinetmaking skills for he won three premiums in the 1853 SCAC state fair. In Augusta, he had a lengthy career, entering into a partnership in 1854 with Jacob B. Platt and Horton B. Aplam; the firm became C. A. Platt & Co. By 1865, the Platt Brothers Furniture Store was established on 710–712 Broad Street in Augusta.

Commemorative Art

At its peak of popularity during the Victorian period, mourning or commemorative art fulfilled aesthetically the spiritual need of a society surrounded by the constant fact of death. Life expectancy was short, and young children were taught not only to accept their own temporal state, but also to eulogize "sleeping" siblings through verse and needlework [108].

The climate in the South exacerbated health problems and increased the death rate. Statewide epidemics of cholera and coastal ones of yellow fever and malaria still plagued Georgia in mid-century. In 1840, life insurance premiums cost one percent more in the southern states (Poesch, *The Art of the Old South*, 264). Despite the fact that medical progress was taking place—the first medical college in the state opened in Augusta in 1828, and Jefferson surgeon Crawford W. Long (1815–1878) initiated the use of ether in 1842—Victorian Georgians continued to be preoccupied with the subject of death.

The iconography of posthumous portraits, ivory miniatures [151], needleworked mourning scenes, jewelry [152, 153], and daguerrotypes (figure 9, p. 79), spoke an understood language to mourners. Pulled drapes, classical urns, flaming torches, sleeping children, and ethereal shafts of light were all emblems signifying the peace and tranquility awaiting one in the afterlife, when the mourner would be reunited with the dead loved one.

124 *Mourning Miniature*, 1789

New England

Watercolor on ivory

H. 1½", W. 1 1/16"

Inscriptions on plinth: Too soon did / Heaven / Assert its / Claim

Telfair Academy of Arts and Sciences, Gift of Mrs. Marjorie Heyward Mingledorff

The classically draped female mourner holds her right hand to her cheek as a sign of virtue and piety. The neo-classical urn with a flame signifying immortality was possibly copied from architectural design books available in America after 1728 (see figures 2, 3, p. 77). Putti direct our attention to the tombstone, the urn of immortality, and to heaven. Framing the scene is the weeping willow, which was a mourning symbol as early as the 1770s.

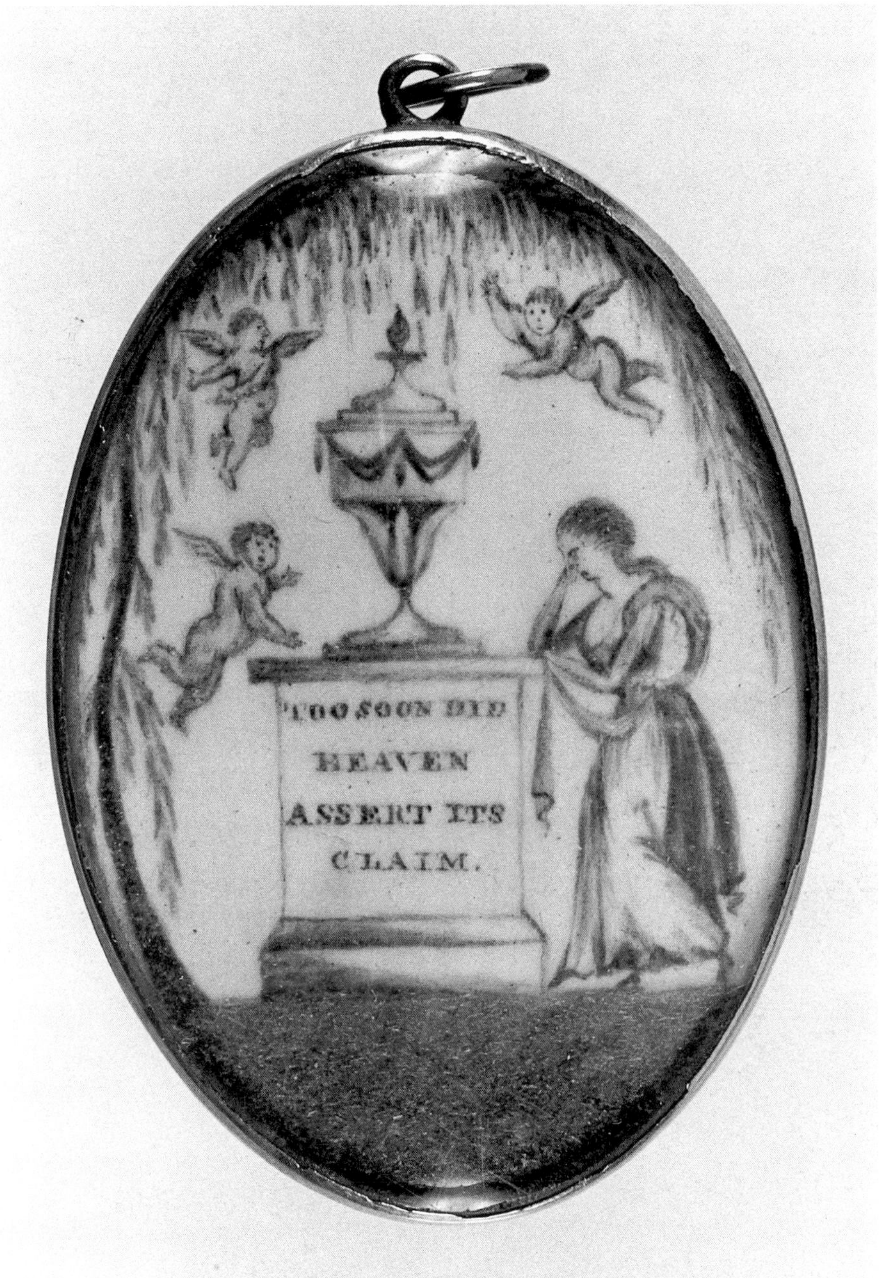

124

125 *Hair Brooch*, 1830s–1850s

Gold and black enamel, hair enclosed in center

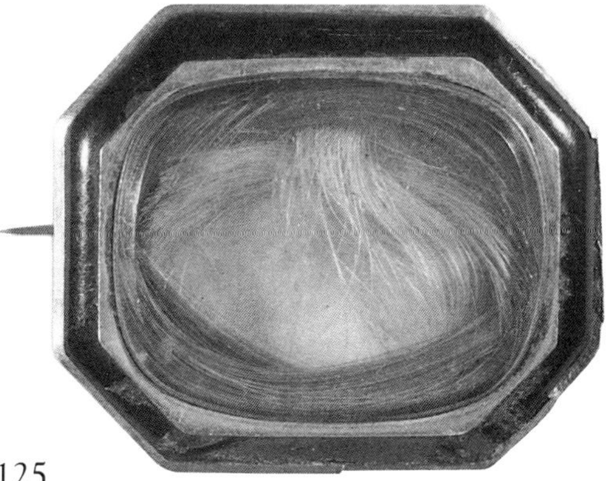

125

L. 1⅜", W. 1¼"

Atlanta Historical Society

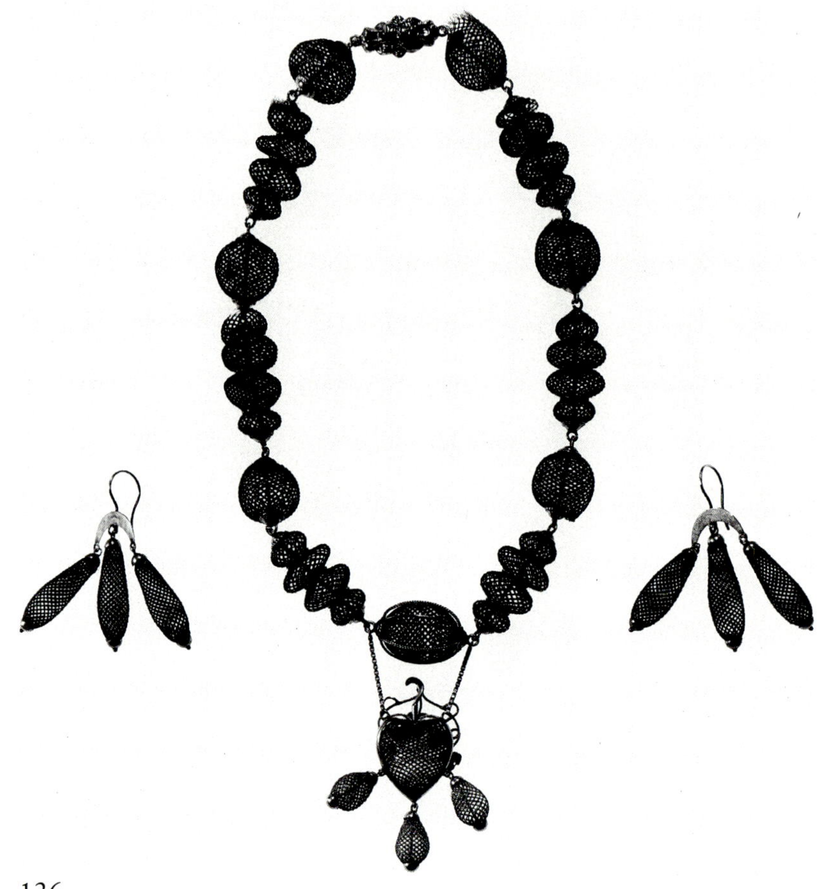

126

126 *Hair Necklace and Earrings*, 1830s–1850s

a. Necklace
   Woven hair and 14K gold
   L. 9"

b. Earrings
   Woven hair and 14K gold
   L. 2"

Description: Suspended from necklace is heart pendant surrounded by grape leaves.

History: Necklace owned by Mrs. William Wirt Clayton, Atlanta, Georgia; earrings, hair of Susan Adelaide Reynolds (Mrs. A. L. Thomas), daughter of Elizy B. Reynolds, post master of Marthasville (Atlanta), Georgia

Atlanta Historical Society

Grape leaves allude to communion wine, which symbolizes the blood of Christ.

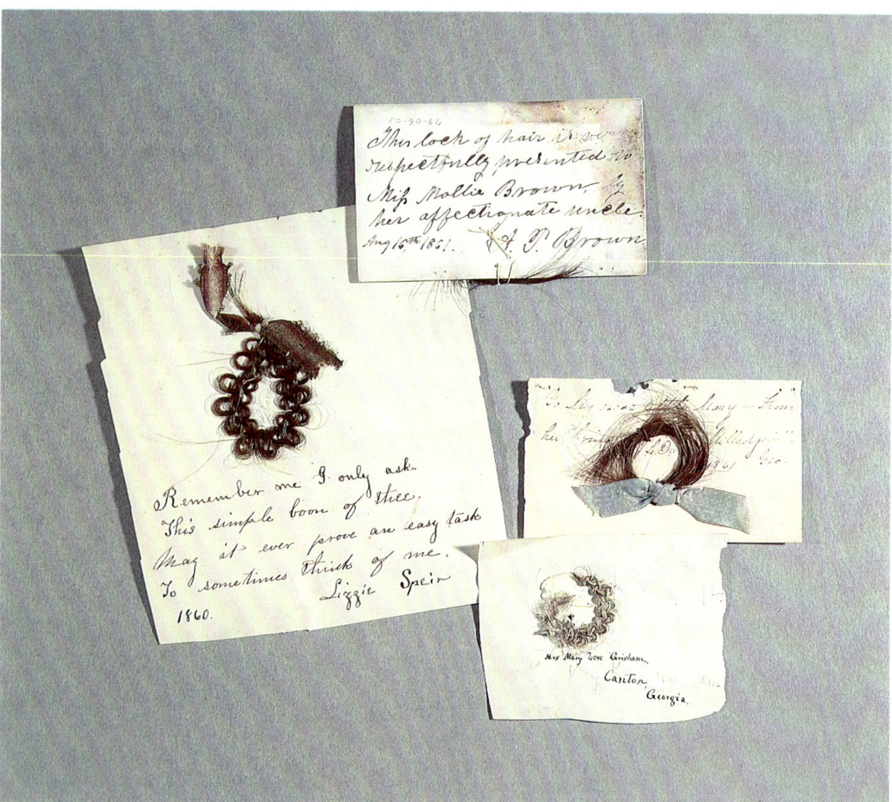

127

127 *Hair cards from Georgia Families Collections*, ca. 1860

Ink on paper, hair and ribbon

Marks:

a) Written in ink under woven hair: Mrs. Mary Love Girsham / Canton / Georgia / 1861
b) Written in pencil within circle of hair: Cousin (underneath) Rember me I only ask / This simple boon of thee / May it ever prove an easy task / To sometimes think of me. / 1860 Lizzy Speir
c) Written in ink: To my dear little Mary from her loving / (inside circle of hair) J. L. Dow / Milledgeville, Ga 1861
d) Written in pencil: This lock of hair is very / Respectfully presented to / Mifs Mollie Brown by / Her affectionate uncle / Aug. 16th, 1861 / A. T. Brown
   Written in pencil on the reverse: Uncle

Atlanta Historical Society

As a keepsake, hair was not always a death or mourning related tradition during the Victorian era. As the verses indicate, the hair cards were exchanged between friends or loved ones while they were alive. Collecting these were typical pastimes for young girls, somewhat like friendship albums, a compilation of signatures of friends and families.

During its height of popularity from 1830 to 1860, hair jewelry was associated with mourning. Besides honoring the dead, the jewelry provided a physical reminder to keep the deceased present, as well as a reminder of one's devotion to friends and family. From a religious standpoint, the hair jewelry represented an eventual reunion in heaven, when mourner and loved one would meet.

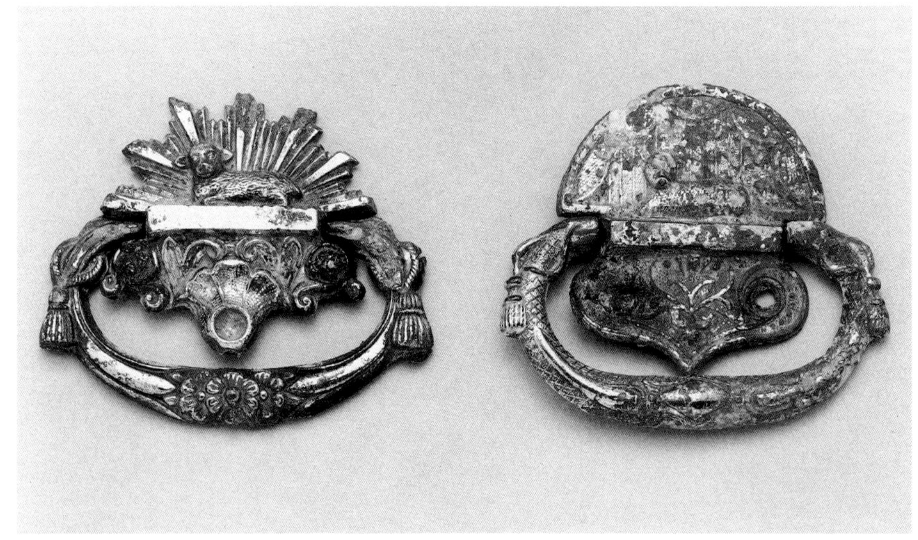

128

128 *Coffin Handles*, 1850s

Silver plated base metal

H. 2¾″, W. 2½″

Description: Handles from children's coffins

Historic Oakland Cemetery, Inc.

The lamb was a popular motif associated with the death of children; it represents innocence, uncorrupted life, the spirit of the innocent child, and Christ Himself, the Lamb of God. Here one lamb is presented within heavenly rays, the other before a slightly raised drapery, a Baroque convention signifying the beginning of life rather than the end.

Tassles have a religious association because of their presence on prayer pillows and can be seen on numerous Victorian funerary markers, where the pillow suggests that death is sleep. Christ refers to death as "falling asleep."

The scalloped shell symbolized the epiphany, the appearance of Christ signifying the promise of resurrection. Floral imagery includes the forget-me-not bloom, a symbol of remembrance.

129 *The Mother's Dream*, 1858–1859

Nathaniel Currier (1813–1888) and James Merritt Ives (1824–1895), working 1857–1880

New York

Lithograph

H. 13½″, W. 9½″

Inscribed: Published by Currier & Ives / 152 Nassau St. NY / THE MOTHER'S DREAM. / The Great Jehovah full of love; / An angel bright did send. / And took my little harmless dove, / To joys that never end.

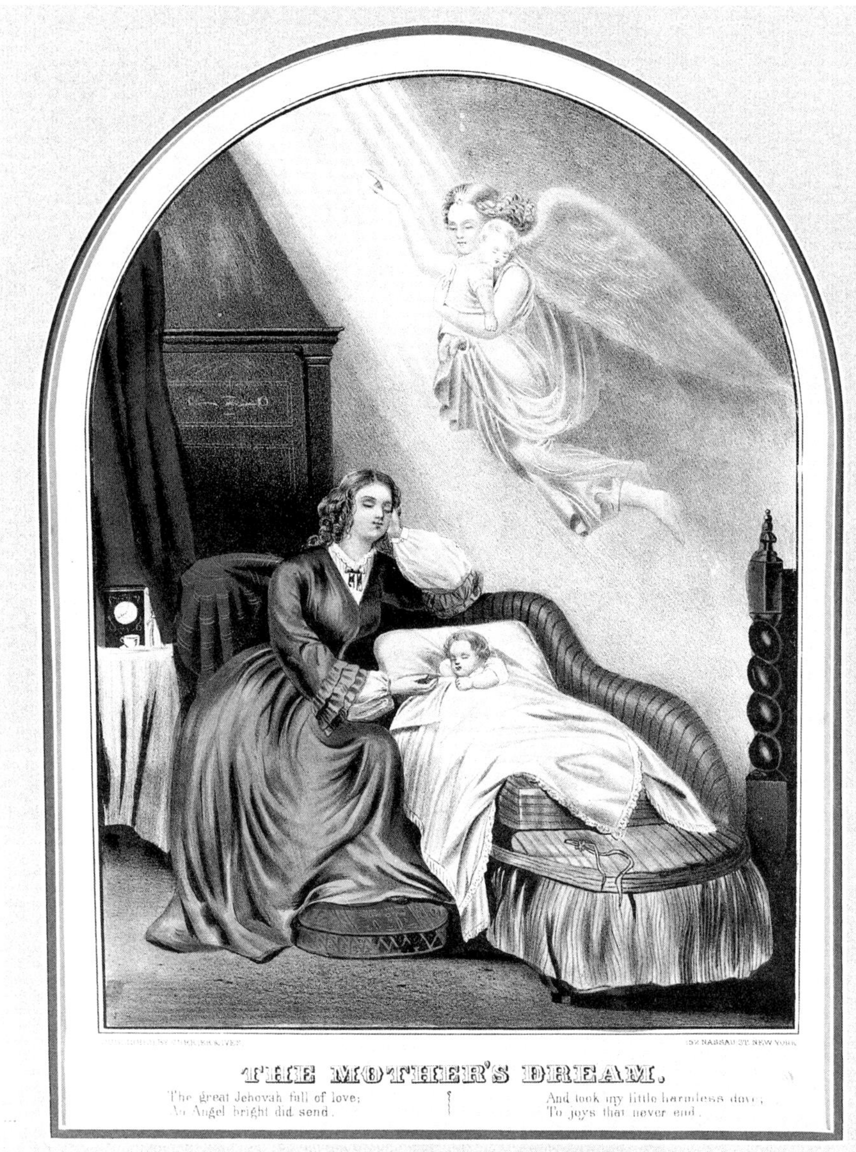

129

History: The original engraving of this was taken from a painting by English artist Thomas Brooks (1818–1891) and published in London by Henry Graves & Company in 1853. A subsequent engraving by Williams & Stephens, first issued in 1853, was the inspiration for the Currier and Ives version.

Collection of Dr. Diana Williams Combs

In this engraving, a mother dreams of her dead child taken to heaven by the emissionary angel pointing heavenward. The eastern or morning star suggests that the faithful will be reborn. The child's soul takes human form and the shaft of light symbolizes the child's salvation. Raised to her cheek, the mother's hand connotes not only piety and virtue but also spiritual reflection.

This domestic scene depicts familial affection between mother and child, in death as in life. The bedroom refers, again, to death as sleep; the headboard and footboard of a bed resemble a funerary marker (figure 4, p. 77); the pulled drape is a dramatization of life and death of the "sleeping" child. The clock on the bed table symbolizes that time has expired for the child.

130 *Cemetery Gate*, 1860s

James Monahan

Savannah, Chatham County

Cast iron

H. 42½", W. 33½", D. 3¾"

Cast inscription, top left of gate: JAMES / MONAHAN

Cast inscription, top right: MAKER / SAVANNAH / GA

Description: Overall cast of floral and C-scrolled acanthus design; fleur-de-lis at base; central harp supported by wings at center; flanked by panels with inverted torches; flowers and leaves support basket of flowers at crest

High Museum of Art, Purchased with funds donated by the Decorative Arts Acquisition Trust

A basket of flowers was associated with mortality, and was often found on gravestones. Forget-me-nots ask that the dead one be remembered. Roses in a basket supported by reversed hanging sprouting grape leaves [126] allude to the wine of communion which symbolizes Salvation through Christ.

A harp symbolizing celestial harmony is supported by a winged hour glass, an emblem of mortality that was popular in English seventeenth-century emblem books. The appearance here of this symbol is an unusual carry-over since it was not frequently seen after the late eighteenth century. Inverted torches are symbols of death, whereas the wreaths that encircle them represent immortality (see figure 11, p. 80).

130

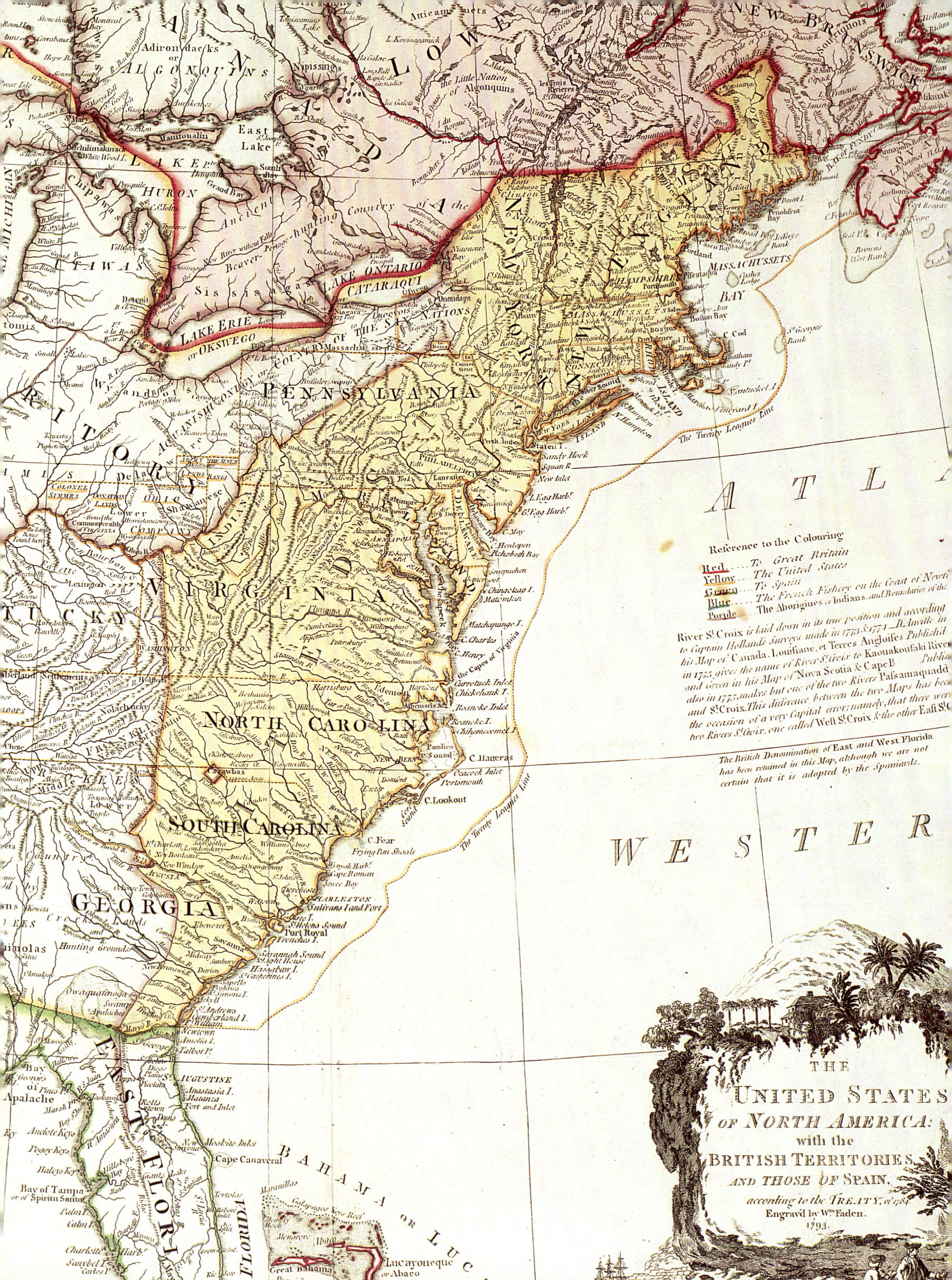
THE
UNITED STATES
OF NORTH AMERICA:
with the
BRITISH TERRITORIES,
AND THOSE OF SPAIN,
according to the TREATY, of 1784
Engrav'd by Wm. Faden.
1793.
Reference to the Colouring
Red.....To Great Britain
Yellow.....The United States
Green.....To Spain
Blue.....The French Fishery on the Coast of Newf
Purple.....The Aborigines or Indians, and Boundaries of the
River St. Croix is laid down in its true position and according
to Captain Hollands Surveys made in 1773 & 1774 _ D. Anville in
his Map of Canada, Louisiane, et Terres Angloises Publish'd
in 1755 gives the name of River St. Croix to Kaouakousaki River
and Green in his Map of Nova Scotia & Cape B Publis
also in 1755, makes but one of the two Rivers Passamaquadd
and St. Croix. This difference between the two Maps has bee
the occasion of a very Capital error; namely, that there wer
two Rivers St. Croix, one called West St. Croix & the other East St. C
The British Denomination of East and West Florida
has been retained in this Map, although we are not
certain that it is adopted by the Spaniards.
ATLA
WESTER
PENNSYLVANIA
VIRGINIA
NORTH CAROLINA
SOUTH CAROLINA
GEORGIA
NEW YORK
MASSACHUSSETS BAY
LAKE HURON
LAKE ERIE
LAKE ONTARIO
The Twenty Leagues Line
BAHAMA OR LUC

Metalworking in Georgia Before 1860

Blacksmithing and silversmithing catered to opposite ends of the economic spectrum: the fundamental, utilitarian wares were produced by the blacksmith and the luxury items by the silversmith. During the earliest years of the settlement, some 15 blacksmiths and locksmiths were known to have been located in Frederica, Ebenezer, and Savannah, while only two silversmiths, William Parker in Savannah (1733) and Frederick William Müller in Ebenezer (1735–1739), established themselves in the new colony.

The logistics of establishing shops were extremely difficult for metalsmiths in Georgia. First of all, the necessary materials were difficult to obtain. Prior to the Revolution, raw materials for American-made silver were produced in other colonies by melting down old English silver or European coins. In Georgia, however, all currency was controlled by the English government and was not easily procurred. Secondly, forges needed specific space requirements. Post–1796 fire laws frequently required that these shops be located outside towns. Michael Germain, a silversmith at the Sign of the Golden Ball in Savannah, complained that he could not establish his business "when he first removed to town" because he was "unable to procure proper assistants, and being disappointed in getting a forge and furnace" (*Columbian Museum and Savannah Advertiser*, 7 February 1800). Even by 1820, James McCliesh, who had been employed by gunsmith Anthony Imfeld in 1811, had "as yet been unable to obtain a shop so as to enable him to erect his brass factory" (*The Daily Georgian*, 29 January 1820). For this reason, a craftsman with metalworking skills often combined many services within his shop. Adrian Loyer, working in Savannah from 1756 to 1781, advertised at one time or another during his long career as a silversmith, clock and watchmaker, gunsmith, and instrument maker; he also sold real estate. Pinkerd & Brown, a 1774 watchmaking partnership at the Sign of the Dial in Savannah, executed "gilding done neatly both in silver and metal" (*Georgia Gazette*, 24 August 1774). In the piedmont, George W. F. de la Huff, a blacksmith in Milledgeville during approximately 1811–15, employed clockmaker James Berry in his shop

Engraved by Young and Dellecker, *Georgia*, ca. 1830. Philadelphia: Anthony Finley. H. 12", W. 9⅞". Special Collections, The University of Georgia Libraries.

(*Georgia Journal*, 20 July 1814). Consequently, craftsmen who called themselves silversmiths or clock and watchmakers most likely repaired imported wares owned by the well-to-do and offered other services that required a forge.

Georgia's period of progress during the years 1790–1830 created a class of planters who could afford silver, but who no longer wanted to import it from England. As in the furniture trade, however, northern-manufactured hollow ware from silver-manufacturing centers such as Philadelphia, New York, and Baltimore flooded Georgia towns with fashionable Empire style silver. Men such as Josiah Penfield and Francis Clarke, who advertised for more than 20 years in Savannah and Augusta papers, surely were capable of supplying silver to the local merchants and planters. Little survives that can be credited to these men, nor do enough examples exist to suggest a unique Georgia style. The hollow ware that does surface with marks of Georgia silversmiths/jewelers leaves questions about whether the pieces were actually made in the silversmith's shop or retailed in the jeweler's store. Spoons with local marks, however, are plentiful.

Newspaper advertisements indicate that seven foundries were located on local creeks and rivers in Jackson, Columbia, Screven, and Wilkes counties before 1820. As the cotton production provided a "raison d'être" for many craftsmen, so it also gave rise to blacksmith shops, which thrived throughout the piedmont selling functional wares needed by planters, such as hardware for securing bales of cotton for shipment, replacement parts for cotton gins, or gins themselves. Few examples of ironwork of any sort, utilitarian or decorative, marked before 1860, have been found. Perhaps ironwork was melted and recycled for military purposes during the Civil War.

Colonial gunsmithing and clock and watchmaking were similar in that parts were imported from England and either assembled or used for repairs. The 1820 Manufacturers Census lists a number of gunsmiths throughout the state. Five from the 1840s–50s are represented in this gallery by sporting rifles. These guns illustrate the engraving skills of the metalworker gunsmith and the southern characteristics of these rifles.

During the decade before the Civil War, accelerated cotton production and a bolstered economy triggered the first semblances of a mature cultural climate. The 1820–50 period was one of compromises for the Georgia craftsman, who saw that steam power and mass-produced goods meant that making a living from individual skills was not only impractical, but also impossible. The lure of northern trade was impossible to resist, especially in the urban environment. These compromises are seen in the blatant practices of the silversmith and gunsmith who sold ready-made imported silver marked by the northern manufacturer and the local jeweler, or rifles marked on the outside by a Georgia gunsmith but assembled with parts bearing New England manufacturers marks. As the nineteenth century progressed, these northern goods were increasingly available and the demand for locally crafted ironwork deteriorated.

Silver

Of all craftsmen, silversmiths and clock and watchmakers trying to make their way in colonial Georgia faced perhaps the toughest circumstances. Because silver was a luxury item, it was not within the reach of the class of settlers brought to the colony by the Trustees. Those who could afford silver most certainly imported it from England or France. This arrangement was not only fashionable, but also convenient for the growing pre-Revolutionary merchant class already in trade relations with the continent. Even after the Revolution, it was apparently advantageous for silversmiths to stress their European background and commercial connections. William Sime [141] and Jacob Moses in Savannah advertised in 1768 as "Goldsmiths and Jewelers from London," and Constantine Hope, watch and clockmaker, included his experience in "both France and England" in an 1807 advertisement (*Georgia Gazette*, 27 April 1768; *Republican and Savannah Evening Ledger*, 26 December 1807).

Throughout the 1820s, clock and watchmaking materials for the most part were imported from Liverpool or Birmingham, England. Men who advertised as "clock and watchmakers" were actually repairers. American dependence upon European silver imports did not continue. In the late seventeenth century, silversmithing traditions had been established in the New England colonies, and by the mid-eighteenth century, Charleston could boast of silversmiths such as Daniel and Thomas You. It is not certain to what extent New England or Charleston silver was imported into Savannah in the eighteenth century. The importance of American manufacturing can be seen in three 1788–89 advertisements by Jeremiah Andrews, who stresses "American manufacture, which may be had as cheap as can be imported" (*Georgia Gazette*, 11 December 1788; Ibid., 15 October 1789; *Georgia State Gazette or Independent Register*, 24 January 1789).

Few examples of Georgia silver from the Federal, or neo-classical, period exist. The sugar tongs marked by William Sime [141] are thought to be the earliest piece of known Georgia silver. Stylistically, the ladle marked PENFIELD has the simple fiddle handle characteristic of the Federal period, but Penfield would not have marked it in this manner until 1815, when he owned his own business.

The history of the silver business bears similarities to the furniture trade in Georgia. For example, in the nineteenth century, New York silver imports became more prevalent. Tea sets, popular since the 1790s, were associated with the New York trade and artisans. Michael Germain in Savannah offered "coffee pots, tea pots, sugar dishes, milk pots, &c. made at this shop by one of the best workmen from New York" (*Georgia Gazette*, 13 November 1788). Huntington & Burrill had "just received from New York three elegant Tea Services" (*Augusta Chronicle*, 29 November 1817).

From 1815 to 1820, the Empire period was at its peak in New York, Philadelphia, and Baltimore. Although dated a bit later, silver found in Georgia displays characteristics of the late Empire period: heavy lobed bodies, decorative milled bands of neo-classic and floral designs, stepped pedestal bases, and cast scrolled handles. The rococo revival of the 1830s and 1840s produced silver with repousséd and chased floral designs. In its earliest stages, the technique was concentrated on the cartouche area. Gradually, it progressed to the front and sides and then to covering the entire piece with three-dimensional ornamentation.

Because all of these characteristics were popular throughout America during the Empire and rococo revival periods, none is particular to Georgia. As a result, decorative art objects made in Georgia are as difficult to identify as are examples of other indigenous crafts. By the second decade of the nineteenth century, silversmiths had become jewelers and engravers, and their businesses were often known as fancy stores which carried everything from watches and jewelry, amulets and sugar tongs, to "silver thimbles, pencil-cases, toothpicks"; even "church service plate [could be] furnished on short notice" (Nathaniel Cornwell, *Darien Gazette*, 18 January 1819). With such a variety of merchandise all marked by the retailer, differentiating between what was actually made by him or merely imported and retailed can be difficult. Occasionally, two marks will occur [137], one of the manufacturer, frequently from New York, and the other of the Georgia retailer.

131 *Teapot*, ca. 1856

Asaph King Childs (1820–1902)

Athens, Clarke County

Silver, Ivory

H. 9″, W. 11¾″, D. 6″

Marked: A. K. CHILDS

Engraved: A Token of / affectionate remembrance / from the Citizens of Athens / to the / Rev. Alonzo Church.DD / 1856

Description: Rococo floral, with repousséd and chased floral pattern and C-scrolls on oval body, spout and lid; beading and applied banding around teapot lip; domed lid with strawberry vine finial; curved cast handle with ivory insulators; four shell and scrolled bracket feet

History: This pot was part of a tea service presented by the citizens of Athens to Dr. Alonzo Church (died 1861), president of The University of Georgia from 1829 to 1859. Early in the twentieth century, the original set was divided among Church descendants and scattered. The teapot, along with reproductions of the six other pieces from the set, was returned to Athens from Mattoon, Illinois, at the death of Alonzo Church III, a fourth generation descendant.

Athens-Clarke Heritage Foundation

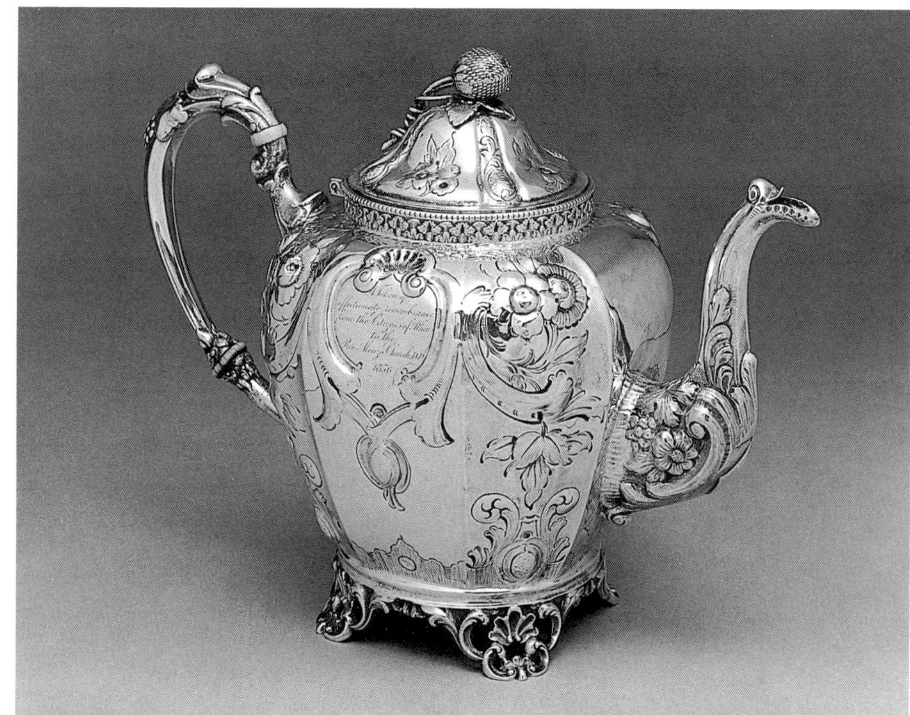
131

A. K. Childs left his native Springfield, Massachusetts, in 1835 to settle in Milledgeville, where his brother Otis (1811–1899) had bought the jewelry and silversmithing business of Jacob Fogle (born 1803). Asaph worked with Otis in Milledgeville until 1846, when he moved to Athens to operate the branch store, located on Broad Street on the first floor of the Franklin House (Cutten, *Silversmiths of Georgia*, 18). In 1847, Asaph became an official partner of the store. The firm marked its wares O.& A.K.CHILDS. This business continued until 1861, when Asaph enlisted in the Confederate Army; it did not reopen when he returned. Childs was active in the 1866 organization of the National Bank of Athens and served as president from 1881 to 1900. He died in Athens in July 1902.

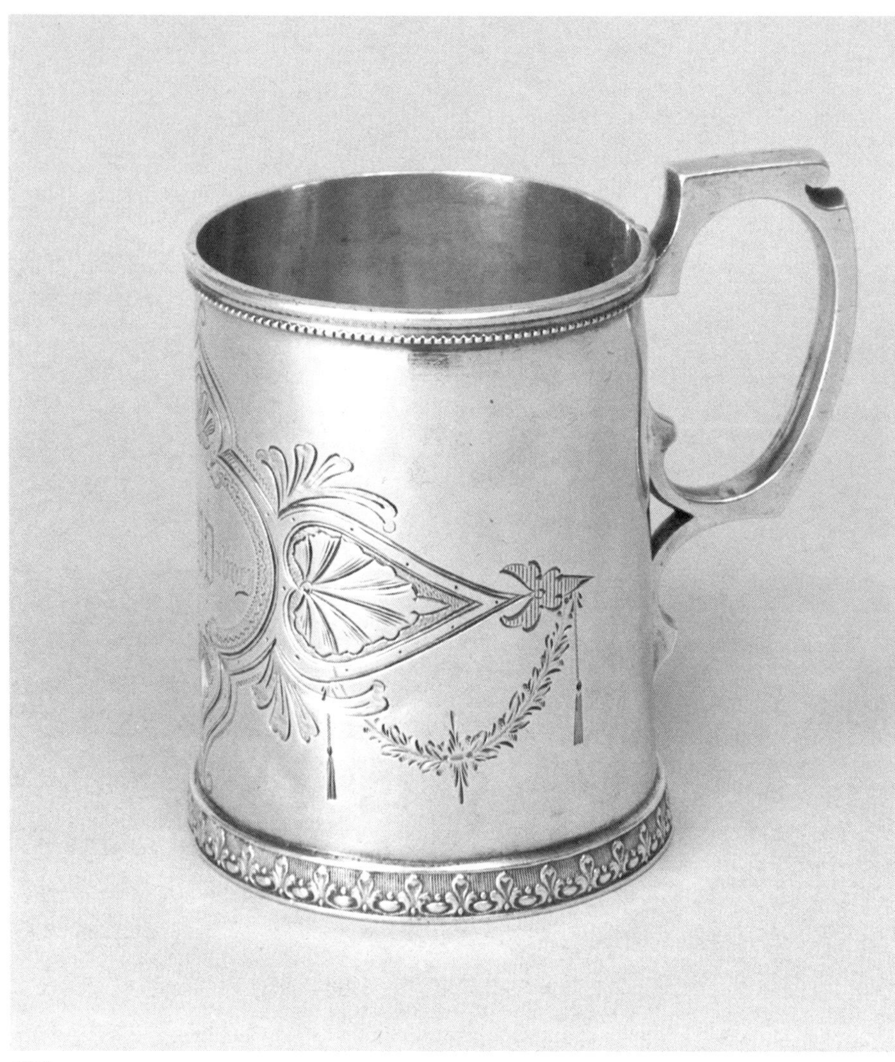

132

132 *Cup*, ca. 1855–1860

E. R. Lawshe (1825–1890s)

Atlanta, DeKalb County (now Fulton County)

Silver

H. 3¼″, Diam. at top 2½″, Diam. at bottom 3 11/15″

Marked: ER LAWSHE

Engraved: Mary D. Dabney

Description: Round bodied cup with straight sides; hollowed scrolled handle in square section; molding and beading around the lip; trefoil stylized floral banding applied around bottom; name possibly added later inside of engraved cartouche of bright-cut shells, swags, and tassles

Collection of Mr. and Mrs. William W. Griffin

E. R. Lawsche may have been Atlanta's first jeweler, watchmaker, optician, and silversmith. He arrived in 1848 and began business in 1850. In 1867, Lawsche employed William A. Haynes as a watchmaker and in 1870 made him a partner. The Lawsche and Haynes firm continued until 1883. While Lawsche possibly had silversmithing skills, his mark is often found with that of another silversmith, retailer, or exporter. This suggests that Lawsche would import a piece from a manufacturer, perhaps Wood & Hughes in New York or W. Carrington & Company in Charleston, stamp it with his mark, and retail it. Lawsche's firm, most likely, merely repaired silver and watches and retailed wares imported from large factories across the United States.

133 *Ewer*, 1850

Clark, Rackett, and Company (1840–1852): Francis Clark (working 1816–1840), Horace Clark (died 1854), and George Rackett (died 1852)

Augusta, Richmond County

Silver

H. 15¾″, Diam. 7¼″

Marked: CLARK, R & C°.

Engraved: Presented by / the City of Augusta. to Henry D. Cumming, / President of the Board of Commissioners of the Augusta Canal / under a resolution of the City Counsel Adopted March 2nd 1850.

Description: Presentation ewer with engraved scene of Augusta Canal Falls on one side; round inverted pear-shaped body with stepped foot; rococo chased floral designs in repoussé; double scrolled handle; molded flared lip; engraving of canal and commemorative inscription possibly added later inside of both cartouches

History: Descended in the family of Henry D. Cumming

Exhibitions: *Georgia Collects American Silver*, High Museum of Art, 1970

References: Farnham and Efird, *Georgia Collects American Silver*, 78; Farnham and Efird, "Early Silversmiths and the Silver Trade in Georgia," *Antiques*, March, 1971, Figure 3, 381.

Private Collection

In 1844, Henry D. Cumming conceived of a canal that would provide water power for future industries in Augusta. The Augusta Canal Company was organized in January 1846, and water flowed through the first three sections by the next November. This ewer is part of a 17-piece silver service presented to Cumming.

The ewer is marked by the local firm of Clark, Rackett, & Company, a wholesale and retail company listed on the corner of Broad and McIntosh Streets. Goblets that accompany the set are marked "W&H," for Jacob Wood and Jasper W. Hughes, a firm operating in New York City during 1840–50. It is possible that the Augusta firm was responsible only for the engraving, and that the piece itself along with the rest of the service was imported from New York.

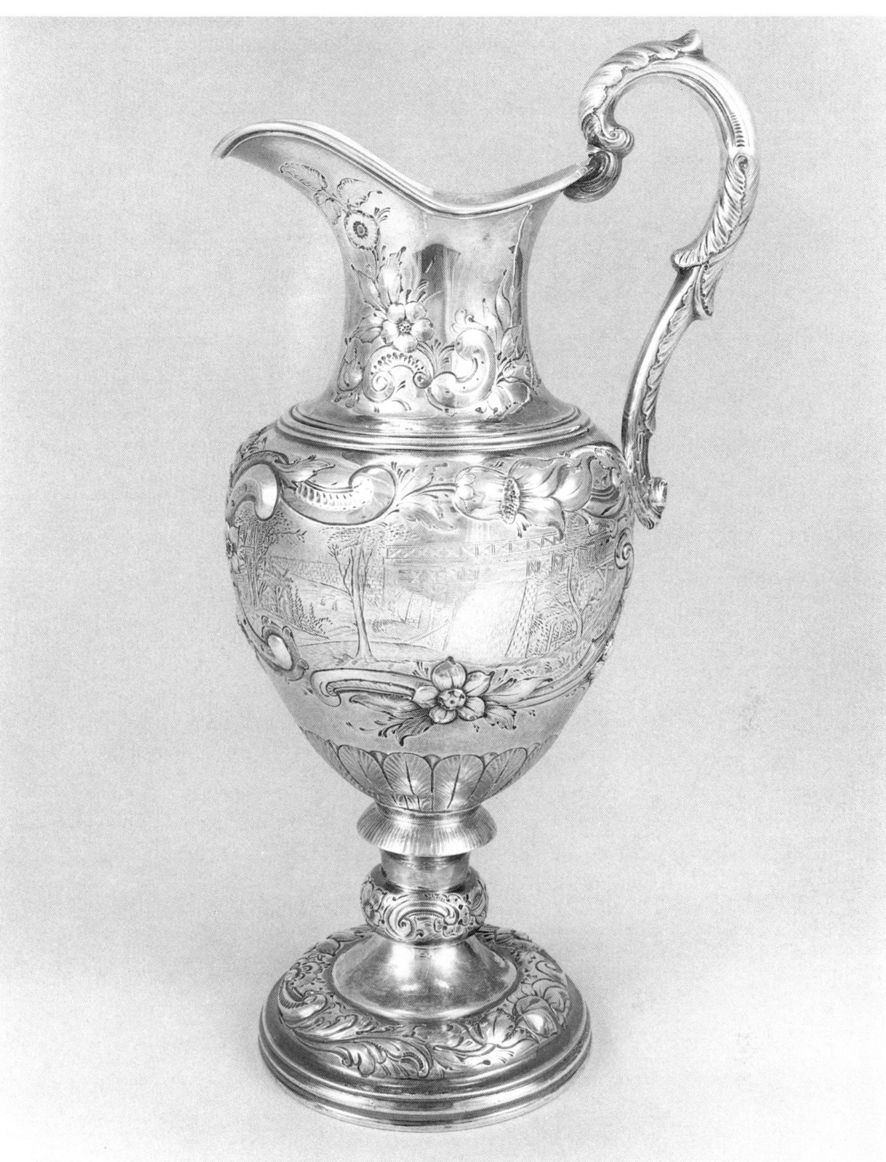

133

134 *Deep Dish*, ca. 1820

Giles Griswold (1775?–1840?)

Augusta, Richmond County

Pewter

H. 1½", Diam. 11⅛"

Marked within double rings with eagle, twice: G. G. / AUGUSTA

Description: Cast dish with molded rim

Henry Francis du Pont Winterthur Museum

Wares made from pewter and other base metals became popular in America during the mid-seventeenth century. This was especially true in less affluent areas or ones inland and less

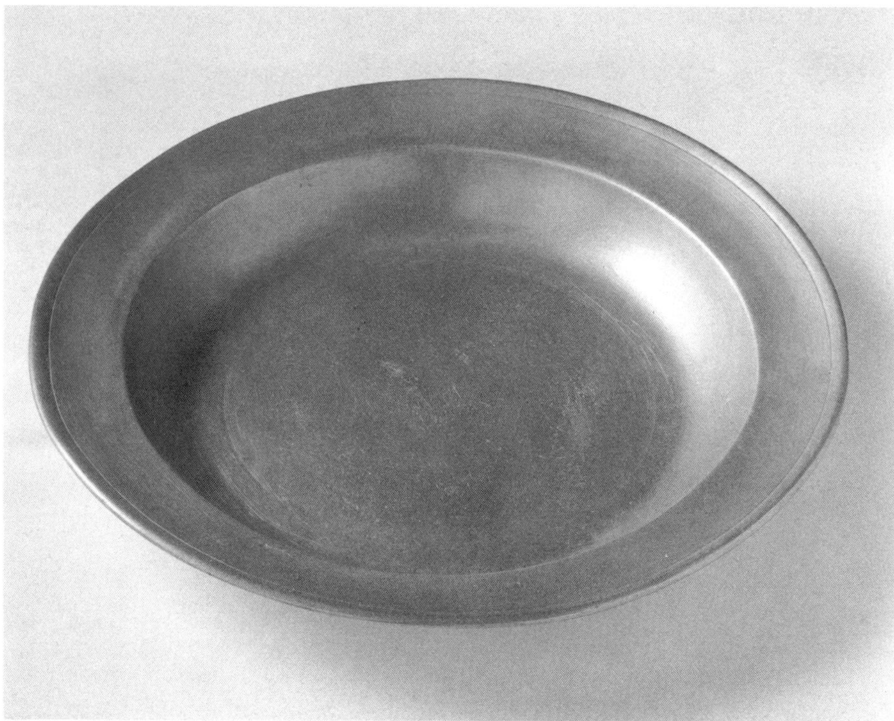

134

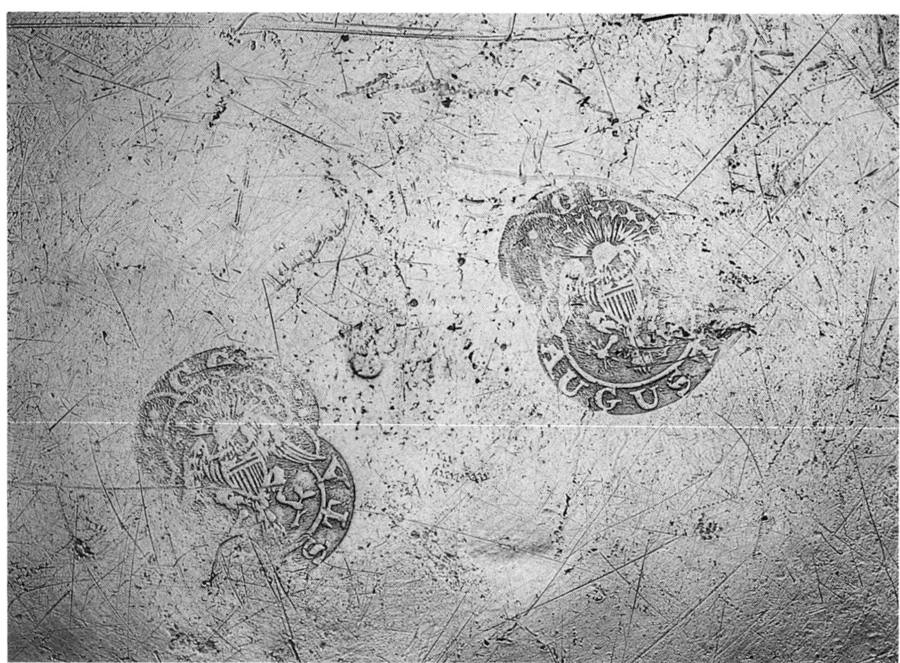

134 detail

familiar with up-to-date fashions likely to be seen in seaport cities. In large cities such as Philadelphia and New York, shops had molds for a wide variety of pewter forms and could compete with the more luxurious silver market. In the 1820s, glass and ceramic tableware was in vogue, and "Britannia ware" was developed in England; it resembled pewter but was harder and could be sold quite inexpensively. This trend, however, was short-lived because the technique of silverplating on top of the base metals made "silver" available to the middle classes.

Pewter, an alloy combining tin with lead, copper, brass, or bismuth, was soft and did not wear well after daily use. Through x-ray analysis, it has been determined that the tin content varied according to the function of the vessel. Tea pots, for example, have a high percentage of tin, while spoons need more bismuth, a hardening antimony.

The deep dish was a common form in American pewter, and its flat-surfaced bottom was easily marked at the time of manufacture. The diameter of the deep dish varied from region to region. Connecticut dishes, for example, had 11- to 13-inch diameters, similar to this one's.

It is believed that Giles Griswold was from Meriden, Connecticut, and that he worked in Augusta during 1816–22. He was listed in Augusta tax digests for the years 1818 and 1820, but not 1823. Thomas Danforth IV, another Connecticut pewterer working in Augusta, referred to Griswold in an 1818 letter to his father: "Giles Griswold is setting the pewter business agoing by horsepower" (Laughlin, *Pewter in America*, 83). He returned to Meriden and died there in 1840.

Griswold's mark is typical of those seen after 1782, when the eagle was named the symbol of the American republic. The use of this motif continued until the 1830s, when a mark of the maker's name inside a rectangle, sometimes serrated, became more common.

135 *Ladle*, ca. 1850

Abram Henry DeWitt (active ca. 1847–1865)

Columbus, Muscogee County

Silver

H. (at bowl) 2⅛", L. 12⅛"

Marked: A.H. DEWITT

Description: Foliate scrolled handle with scallopped, rather shallow bowl

Private Collection

DeWitt purchased the Columbus watch and jewelry store of Henry E. Dibble sometime before December 1847, when DeWitt advertised goods he had purchased on a recent trip to New York. DeWitt continued to advertise from his store on Broad Street until 1865, when he sold his property and moved to Alabama.

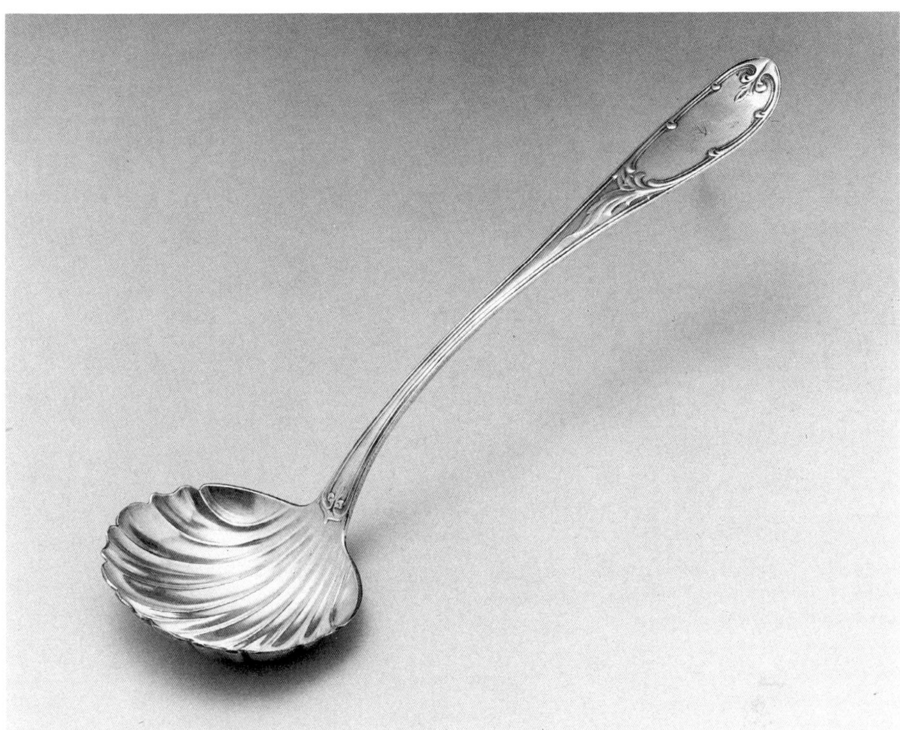

135

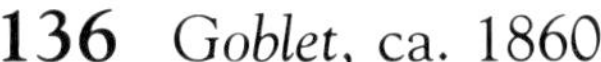

136 *Goblet*, ca. 1860

Possibly Macon, Bibb County

Silver

H. 5⅛", Diam. 2¾"

Marked: CPC / at Macon, Ga. 1860 / to Eagle Factory / for / Rope, Cottonades / & Jeans

Description: Round cupped body on trumpet-shaped stem; stepped base; bright-cut engraving forming cartouche into which dedication was placed later; base has been resilvered, covering mark

Collection of Mrs. William H. Young, Jr., and Mr. William H. Young III

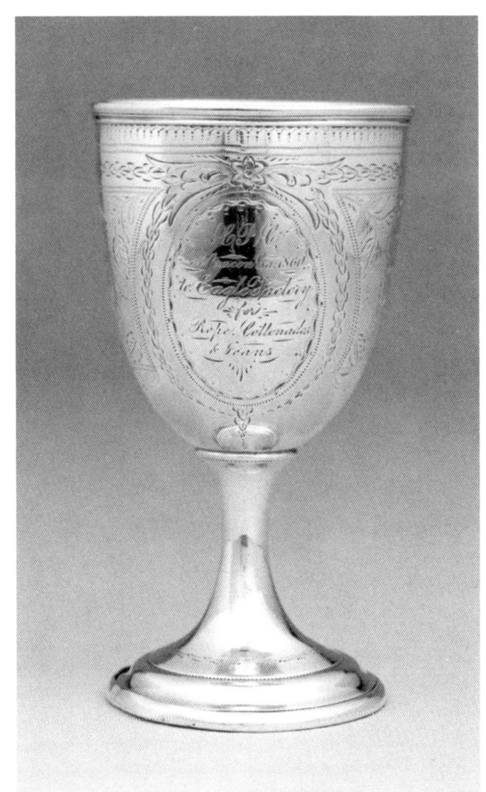

136

Industrialization made steady progress during the 1840s and 1850s; the number of mills handling flour, corn meal, and cotton increased across Georgia. Columbus's location on the Chattahoochee River falls [see 58] provided ample water power needed to make the town a cotton milling center by the 1850s. Before the Civil War, the Eagle Factory, established in 1850, employed 240 workers and used 1500 bales of cotton and 100,000 pounds of wool annually (*The Sunday Ledger-Enquirer*, 16 April 1961).

Founded in 1859, the Georgia Cotton Planters Convention (CPC) was an offshoot of the Southern Central Agricultural Society [see 140]. The CPC was formed by planters who were disgruntled with the SCAC's lack of emphasis on cotton. Howell Cobb was the president.

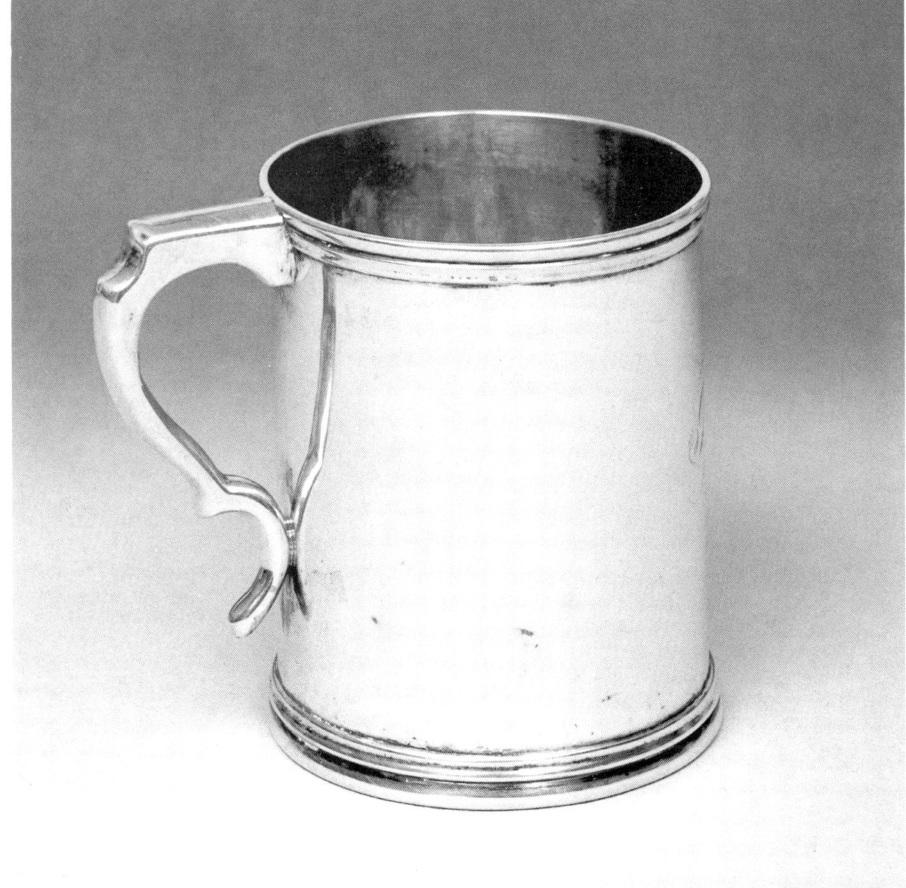

137

137 *Cup*, ca. 1845

Oscar J. H. Dibble (working in Columbus 1843–ca. 1849)

Possibly Columbus, Muscogee County

Silver

H. 3½", W. 4¼" (including handle)

Marked: O.J.H.DIBBLE

Description: Round body with straight sides; scrolled handle in square section; molded lip and base

Private Collection

From 1835 to 1839, Oscar J. H. Dibble served as the agent for D. B. Nichols's watchmaking and jewelry business in Savannah. He bought the business in August 1839, and in 1841 formed a partnership with Pulaski Jacks of New York. This alliance with a New Yorker suggests that Dibble was importing northern wares. He sold Thomas T. Wilmot this Savannah business, which by 1843 employed a watch case maker, silversmith, and a jeweler (Cutten, *The Silversmiths of Georgia*, 111). Wilmot opened another store in Columbus on Broad Street. Dibble operated this store from 1845 until about 1849, when no further mention is made of Dibble in the Columbus newspapers.

138

138 *Sugar Tongs*, ca. 1850

Possibly New York City

Silver

H. 1¼", L. 5¾"

Marked on one arm by an unidentified northern manufacturer, possibly from New York City and on opposite arm: J.VEAL

Description: Scalloped edges and shell terminals

Private Collection

Joseph Veal (active 1848–51) advertised as a silversmith, but a list of his inventory in a 19 August 1848 advertisement in *Madison Family Visitor* suggests that he operated more of a fancy shop with silverware "at Charleston prices" and perfume as well (Cutten, *The Silversmiths of Georgia*, 60). His brother John was a silversmith in Columbia, South Carolina, and also marked his merchandise J. VEAL. Joseph Veal is known also to have imported flatware from Gale and

Hayden, New York, a firm working ca. 1848.

139 *Pitcher*, ca. 1850–1860

Albert Coles (active 1836–1875)

New York City

Silver

H. 6⅜″, W. 5″ (at handle), Diam. 2¾″

Marked in a diamond with eagle in a circle above and head in a circle below: L. H. WING, MACON,GA

Engraved: Georgia / State Agricultural Society / to

Description: Round, pear-shaped body; scrolled handle with acanthus thumb piece; square molding around angular lip; foot on double stepped base; engraved cartouche into which inscription was placed post 1860

Private Collection

This pitcher is the second known hollow ware presentation piece sold in Macon by L. H. Wing. A cup was exhibited at the High Museum of Art in 1970 bearing the identical inscription as this pitcher and the same Wing mark, including the additional mark of Albert Coles who was working in New York during 1836–75. Wing was undoubtedly the engraver of both pieces because the two are identical in format (see *Georgia Collects American Silver, 1780–1870*, Cat. # 292).

As cotton, corn, rice, and livestock became the economic base in Georgia, agricultural societies emerged which advocated improved scientific techniques, such as crop diversification and anti-erosion methods. The first was the Agricultural Society of Georgia, incorporated in Savannah in 1810 but defunct by 1821. The Agricultural Association of Georgia, organized in Milledgeville in 1845, held a state fair there in 1847. The Georgia State Agricultural Society was an 1860 reorganization of the Southern Central Agricultural Society [140]. The engravings on this pitcher and the cup must postdate 1860.

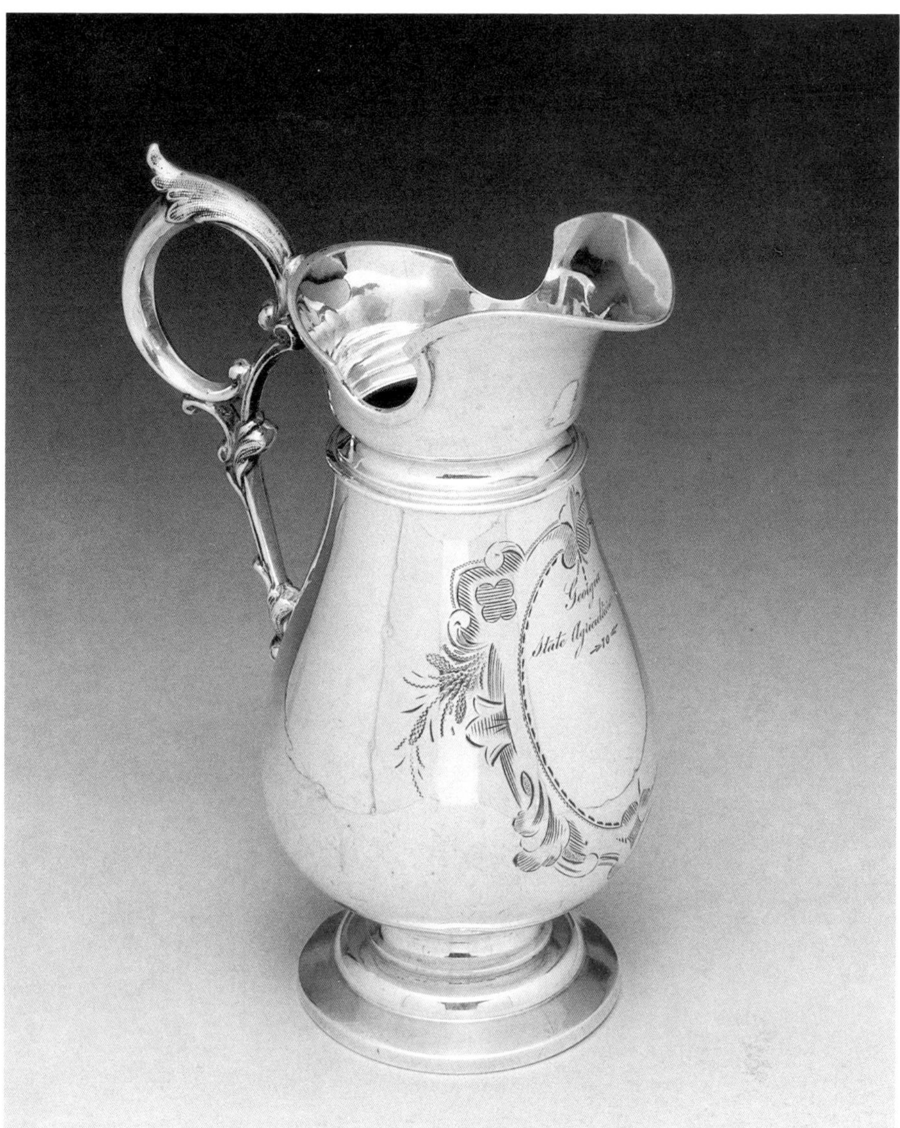

139

140 *Pitcher*, ca. 1852

Edmund J. Johnston (active 1845-ca. 1859)

Macon, Bibb County

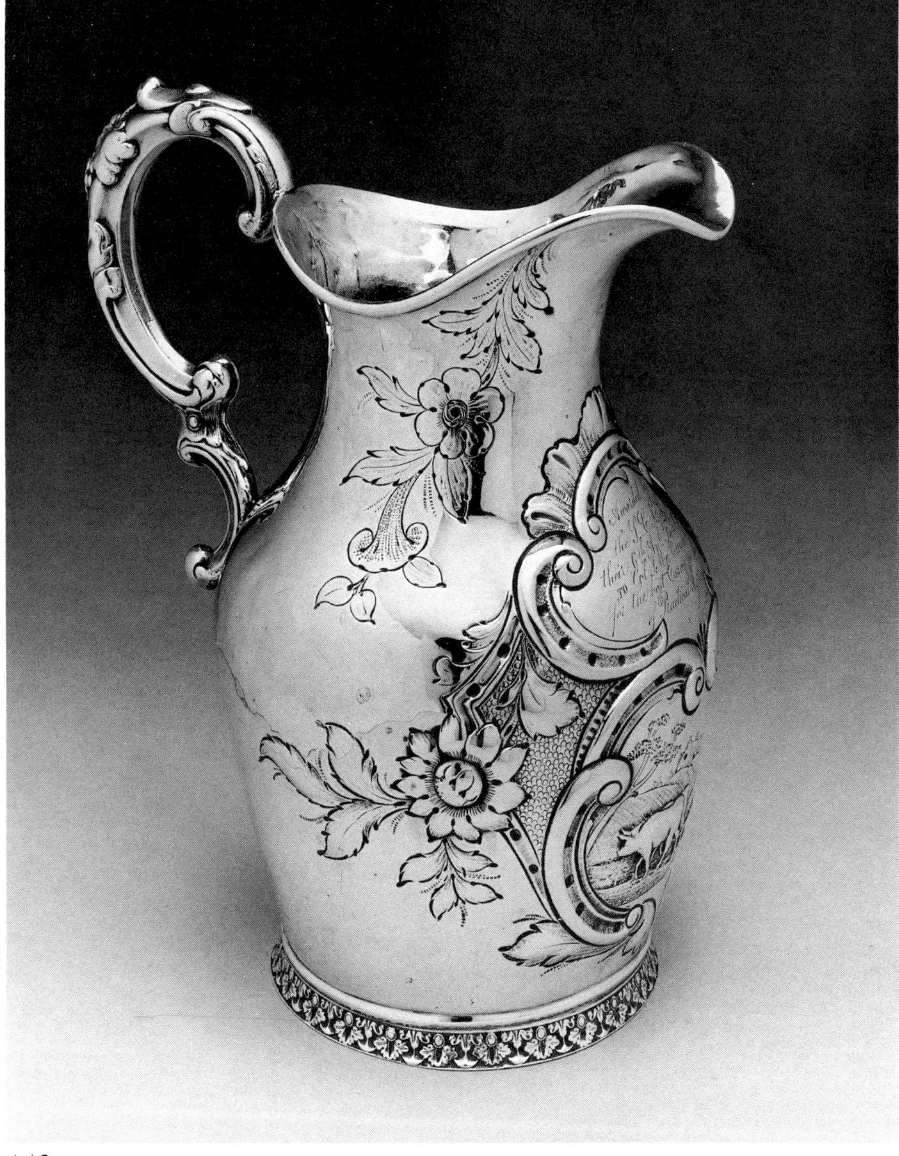

140

Silver

H. 8¾", Diam. 7⅔"

Marked: E. J. JOHNSTON / MACON,GA.

Engraved: Awarded by / the S. C. A. S. at / their 6th An[l]. Fair Oct 1852 / to Col. J. M. Chambers / for the best Essay on the Elements / of Practical Agriculture.

Description: Round, vase-shaped with molded flared lip; stylized floral banding at base; double scrolled handle; rococo repoussé and chased floral designs over front and sides of body; C-scrolls form ruffled cartouche for farming scene in relief and inscription

Collection of William T. Barfield

The Southern Central Agricultural Society, organized in Stone Mountain in 1846, held annual fairs in Stone Mountain, Atlanta, and Macon, respectively. Premiums frequently in the form of silver cups or pitchers were awarded for various competitions involving crafts as well as agriculture. The Atlanta Iron Works was given a $10 premium for "best casting." Silver cups worth $5 were awarded to winners of cabinetmaking contests in Macon in 1851, and E. H. Rogers [150, 151] was given a $10 premium for best rifle and shotgun in the wood and iron category (*Soil of the South*, January 1855, 21). Another presentation cup, also marked by Johnston, is in the collection of the Metropolitan Museum of Art. It is smaller than this pitcher but is similarly decorated with floral designs, C-scrolls, and a repousséd cow; it is engraved as prize for "Best native Heifer" in the 1851 SCAS fair ("Early Silversmiths and the Silver Trade in Georgia," *Antiques*, March 1971, 385).

E. J. Johnston was a member of his brother's watchmaking and jewelry business, W. B. Johnston & Brother, in Macon from 1845 to 1849. He then ventured out on his own and advertised the wholesale and retail business two doors down from the Lanier House. Johnston was most likely a jeweler, as well as an engraver and repairer of clocks and watches.

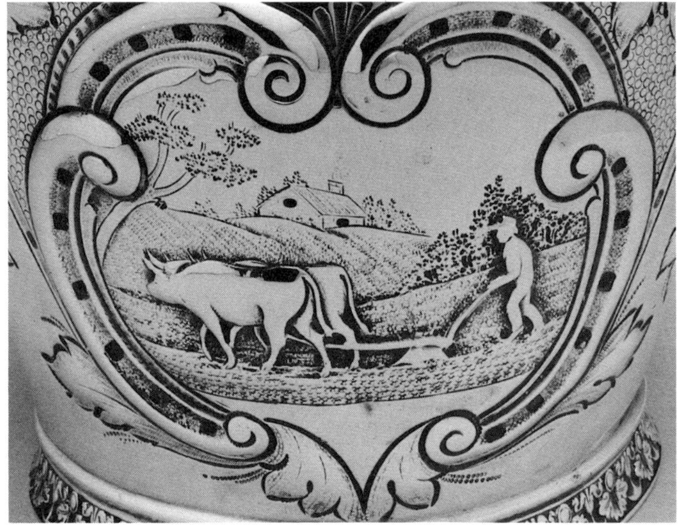

140 detail

141 *Sugar Tongs*, 1769–1773

William Sime (active 1768-ca. 1778)

Savannah, Chatham County

Silver

H. 11/16", L. 6½"

Marked in script on the inside of each arm: W. SIME

Description: Straight-edged shafts that taper to spade-shaped fluted terminals; bright-cut engraving along shaft edges and line engraving around back of "U"

Exhibitions: *Georgia Collects American Silver*, High Museum of Art, 1970

References: Farnham and Efird, *Georgia Collects American Silver*, Cat # 161, 71.

Owens-Thomas House, Telfair Academy of Arts and Sciences, Inc.

In 1768, William Sime and Jacob Moses advertised that they were "Goldsmiths and Jewelers from London," and that "they have brought proper tools for that business" (*Georgia Gazette*, 27 April 1768). By March of the next year, Sime was on his own, and "having practiced in the metropolis of Great-Britain, flatters himself he can do justice to his employer" (*Georgia Gazette*, 1 March 1769). He established another partnership, with William Wright, sometime before January 1774, but dissolved it by April of that same year. Sime had left Georgia by 1778, when the legislature convicted him of treason. Like 100 other people, Sime had signed an oath of loyalty to the Crown in 1774.

This piece is believed to be the oldest example of Georgia-made silver extant. It shows delicate, tapering lines, as well as simple, bright-cut engraving that conforms to the shape of the piece.

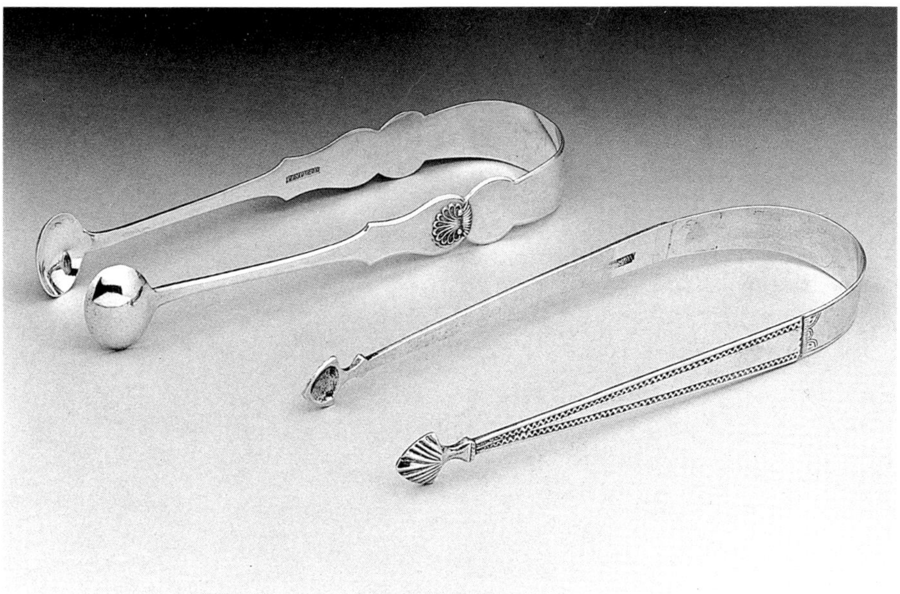

141, 142

142 *Sugar Tongs*, 1815–1820

Josiah Penfield (1785–1828)

Savannah, Chatham County

Silver

H. 13/16", L. 6¼"

Marked inside each arm: PENFIELD

Description: Scallopped shafts that terminate in oval-shaped bowls; applied shell design on sides, known as "King's" pattern

References: Cutten, *The Silversmiths of Georgia*, 128; Farnham and Efird, *Georgia Collects American Silver, 1780–1870*, Cat # 347, 82.

Owens-Thomas House, Telfair Academy of Arts and Sciences, Inc.

[see following entry]

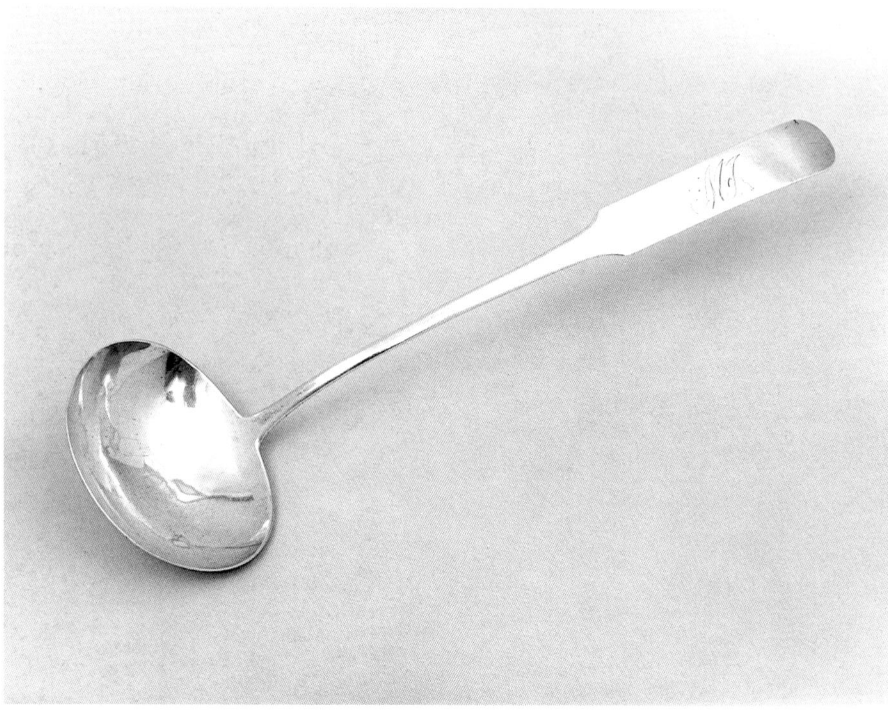

143

143 *Ladle*, 1815–1820

Josiah Penfield (1785–1828)

Savannah, Chatham County

Silver

H. 2″ (at bowl), W. 4″ (at bowl), L. 13¾″

Marked: PENFIELD

Engraved: MJ

Description: Plain fiddle-handled with shoulder and downcurve; large oval bowl; worn engraving is of the period

History: Believed to have descended in the McIntyre family of Thomasville [see 107].

Thomas County Historical Society

Born in Connecticut, Josiah Penfield at the age of 15 came to Savannah and learned the silversmithing trade from his uncle, Isaac Marquand, who had moved there from New York in 1800. By 1810, Penfield was a partner in the firm Marquand (Isaac) & Paulding (Cornelius); Marquand was based in New York after 1803 and Paulding had an import business in New Orleans. Penfield ran the operation in Savannah while Marquand and Paulding took care of importing the wares. As the *Columbian Museum and Savannah Advertiser* reported on 2 July 1810, "One of the partners of Marquand, Paulding and Penfield will embark for Liverpool this week for the purpose of laying in their full supply of goods. Any orders for watches, jewelry, silver plate, or plated goods will be thankfully shipped by the first return vessel to this port" (Cutten, *The Silversmiths of Georgia*, 90). In the 23 December 1815 issue of the *Republican and Savannah Evening Ledger*, Penfield announced that he had "purchased the stock of the late concern of Marquand, Paulding, and Penfield." He continued under his own name until 1820, when he employed his cousin Frederick Marquand, recently from New York, and the firm became J. Penfield and Co. located on Broughton Street. Marquand left in 1826 and Moses Eastman replaced him, but Penfield had developed tuberculosis by this time. He died in 1828 in Rye, New York, at his father's home.

Penfield was a deacon in the Baptist church, and left in his will $2500 to the Georgia Baptist Convention to "create a fund for the education of pious young men for the gospel ministry." This fund was the beginning of Mercer University.

144 *Porringer*, ca. 1826–1830

Frederick Marquand (1799–1882) working Savannah 1820–1826

New York City

Silver

H. 1⅝", W. 7½" (including handle), Diam. (of bowl) 5"

Marked at base of bowl: FM [with pseudo hallmarks of lion passant, male head, and the letter "F"]

Marked beneath handle: F. MARQUAND [with same pseudo hallmarks]

Engraved on handle: ES

Description: Bowl with convex sides and domed bottom; pierced handle with scrolled trefoil design

High Museum of Art

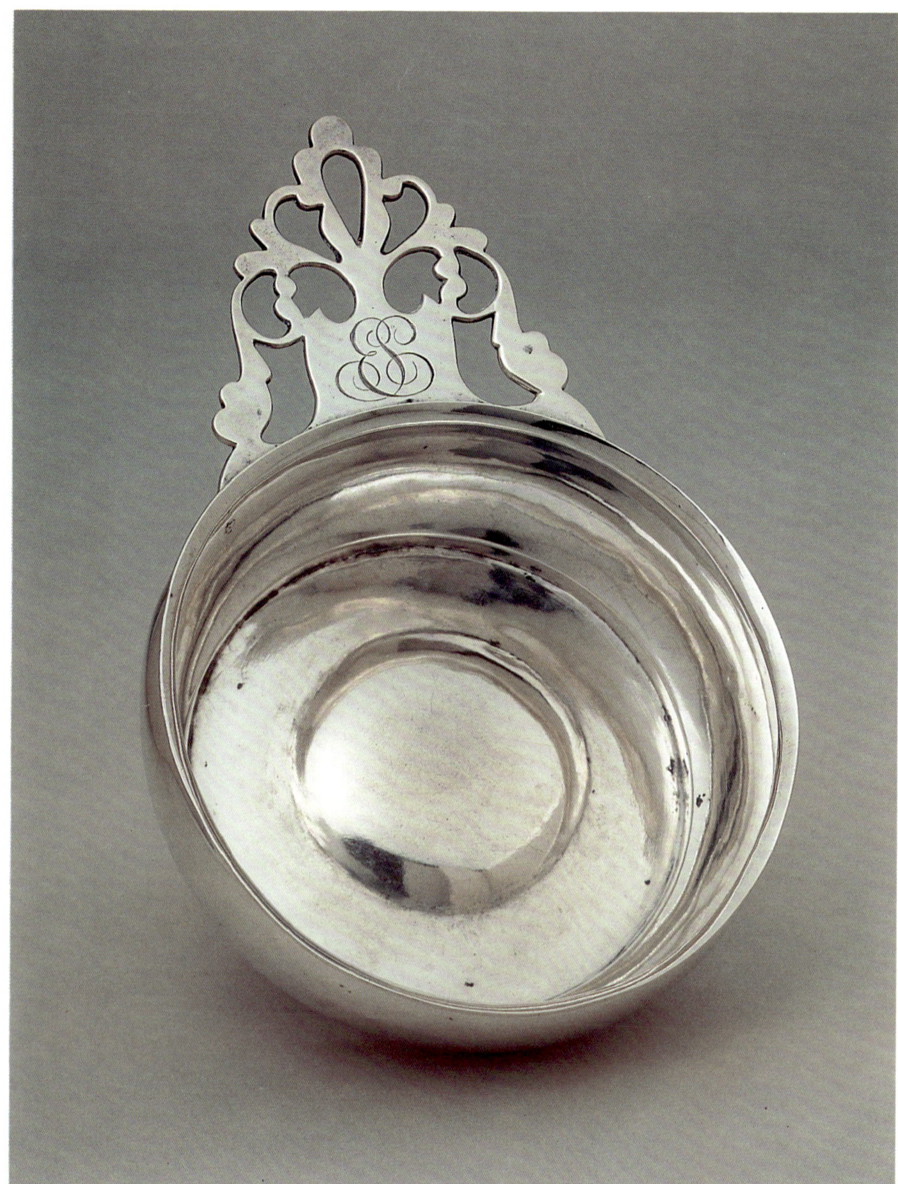

144

Many silversmiths in Georgia had fairly lengthy careers. For example, Edward Griffin worked for more than 20 years in Savannah. However, little hollow ware survives that was marked by any of the numerous men who advertised as silversmiths/clock and watchmakers. A puzzling exception to this is the substantial amount of sophisticated hollow ware marked by Frederick Marquand (1799–1882) who worked in Savannah from 1820 to 1826 in the firm of J. Penfield & Co. Marquand was the son of Isaac Marquand (1766–1838), who was originally from Fairfield, Connecticut. Isaac had apprenticed with his uncle, Jacob Jennings, and had established his own silversmith business by 1787. After a brief period in Edenton, North Carolina, Isaac moved to Savannah and advertised as a "Jeweler and Watchmaker from New York" (*Columbian Museum and Savannah Advertiser*, 21 January 1800). Interestingly, Isaac, who had silversmithing skills, did not open a silversmithing shop in Savannah but worked in aspects of the business that required only engraving and repairing skills. As early as 21 November 1800, Isaac Marquand was receiving merchandise from New York, which he "sold wholesale and retail" (*Columbian Museum and Savannah Advertiser*, 21 November 1800). In 1801, Isaac

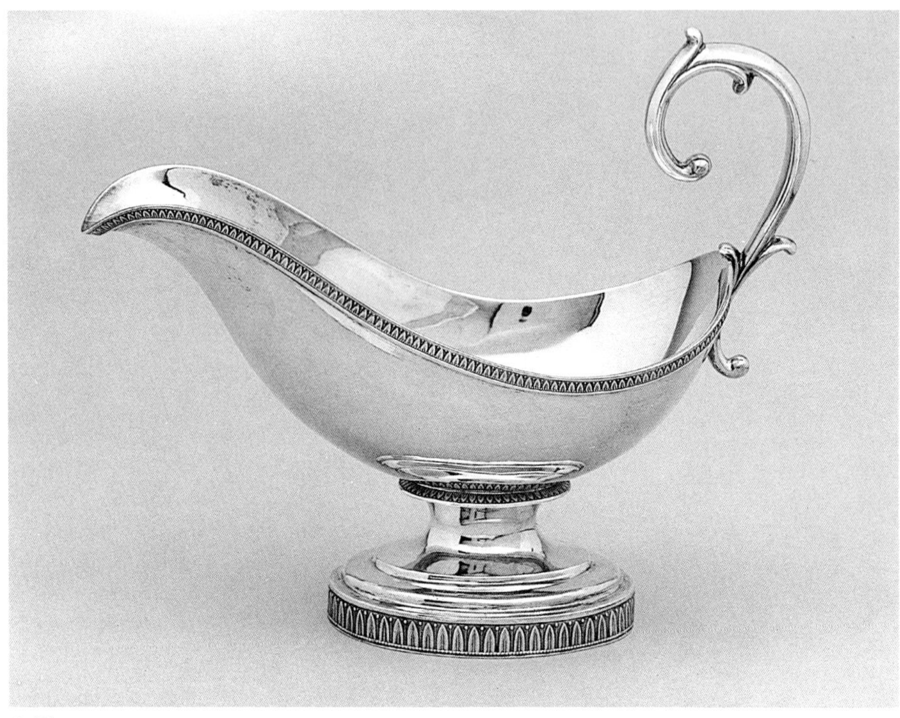

145

Marquand had "taken into co-partnership Mr. C. (Cornelius) Paulding from New York" (*Columbian Museum and Savannah Advertiser*, 10 November 1801). The firm Marquand & Paulding, at the Sign of the Gold Watch, prospered from 1802 to 1809 as an import and consignment house. Marquand spent most of this time between 1803 and 1806 in New York. He is listed in the city directories as a merchant at 166 Broadway (Cutten, *The Silversmiths of Georgia*, 87).

In 1810, Marquand and Paulding employed Josiah Penfield, Marquand's nephew who had been working for his uncle since 1800. In 1815, Penfield "purchased the stock of the late concern of Marquand, Paulding, & Penfield," and worked on his own until 1820 (*Republican & Savannah Evening Ledger*, 23 December 1815).

At this time, Frederick Marquand, having served his apprenticeship under his father's firm in New York, came to Savannah to join his cousin's business, which became J. Penfield & Co. (*The Savannah Daily Republican*, 7 January 1820). Frederick married in 1822 and lived in Savannah until 1826, when he returned to New York (Cutten, *The Silversmiths of Georgia*, 85). Moses Eastman replaced him in Penfield's shop and the name remained J. Penfield and Co. Little else is known about the six years that Frederick Marquand spent in Savannah. He apparently did not advertise under his own name, a common practice when one was working under another man's firm name. It also was not customary to mark silver with one's mark if it was not that of the firm's name. Only during 1826–30 was Frederick Marquand listed by his own name as a jeweler in the New York City directories, at the same address as his father, 166 Broadway. By 1830, his brother had joined him, and the firm was then known and marked as Marquand & Brother. The hollow ware that bears these marks, FM, F. MARQUAND, with or without hallmarks or letters, shows definite New York characteristics and exhibits far superior craftsmanship than do other known silver pieces thought to be of Georgia manufacture. Since the quantity of silver bearing those marks exceeds what one man could produce during a four-year period, it is possible that this silver was purchased from his father Isaac's firm, which by 1830 had become a major import and commissioning business. It was marked and retailed by Frederick.

The porringer, a form of hollow ware popular in seventeenth- and eighteenth-century New England, was rarely made in the South, even in urban centers such as Baltimore or Charleston. So prolifically was the porringer produced in the North that regional differences can be traced through the characteristics of the pierced pattern on the handle.

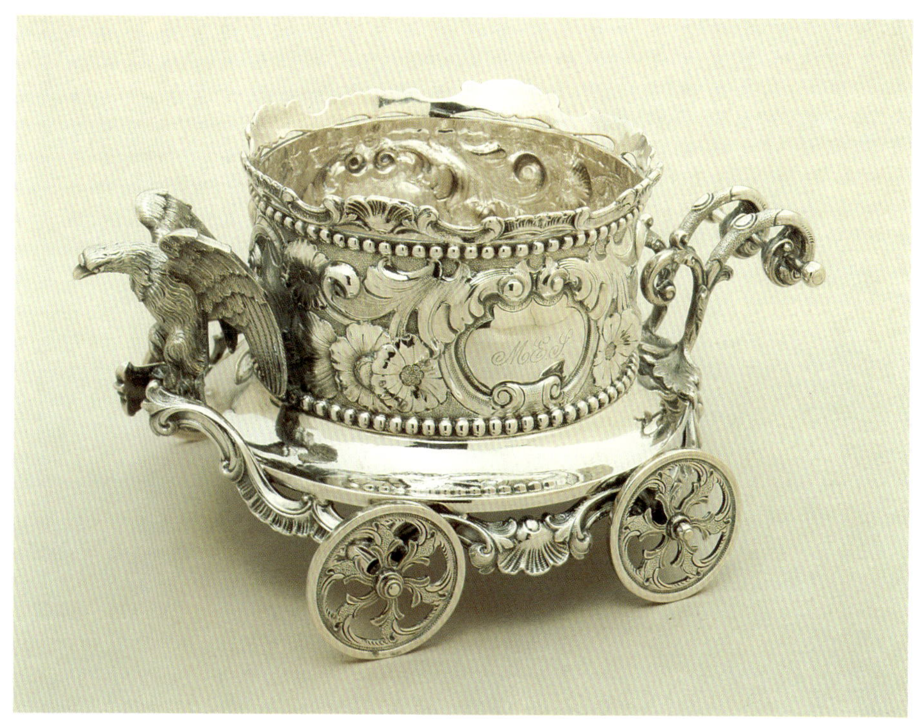

146

145 *Sauce Boat*, ca. 1826–1830

Frederick Marquand (1799–1882)

New York City

Silver

H. 7¾", W. 9⅛", Diam. 4¼"

Marked: MARQUAND

Description: Urn-shaped body with flaring lip; free-standing C-scroll handle; neoclassical beaded-leaf banding around stepped pedestal top, base, and around lip

Historic Savannah, Inc.

146 *Wine Wagon*, ca. 1850

Samuel Wilmot (born 1777; working ca. 1825–1856)

Savannah or Charleston

Silver

H. 5", W. 10", Diam. 6"

Marked: S. WILMOT

Engraved on one side: MES

Description: Rococo repoussé floral design covers the round body with straight sides; cast, free-standing eagle at one end, scrolled double handle at the other; four cast wheels move; repoussé C-scrolls form cartouche

Exhibitions: *Georgia Collects American Silver*, High Museum of Art, 1970

References: Farnham and Efird, *Georgia Collects American Silver, 1780–1870*, 83; Morton, *Southern Antiques & Folk Art*, 97, 247.

High Museum of Art

A Samuel Wilmot who advertised in New Haven, Connecticut, in 1808 might possibly be the same man who

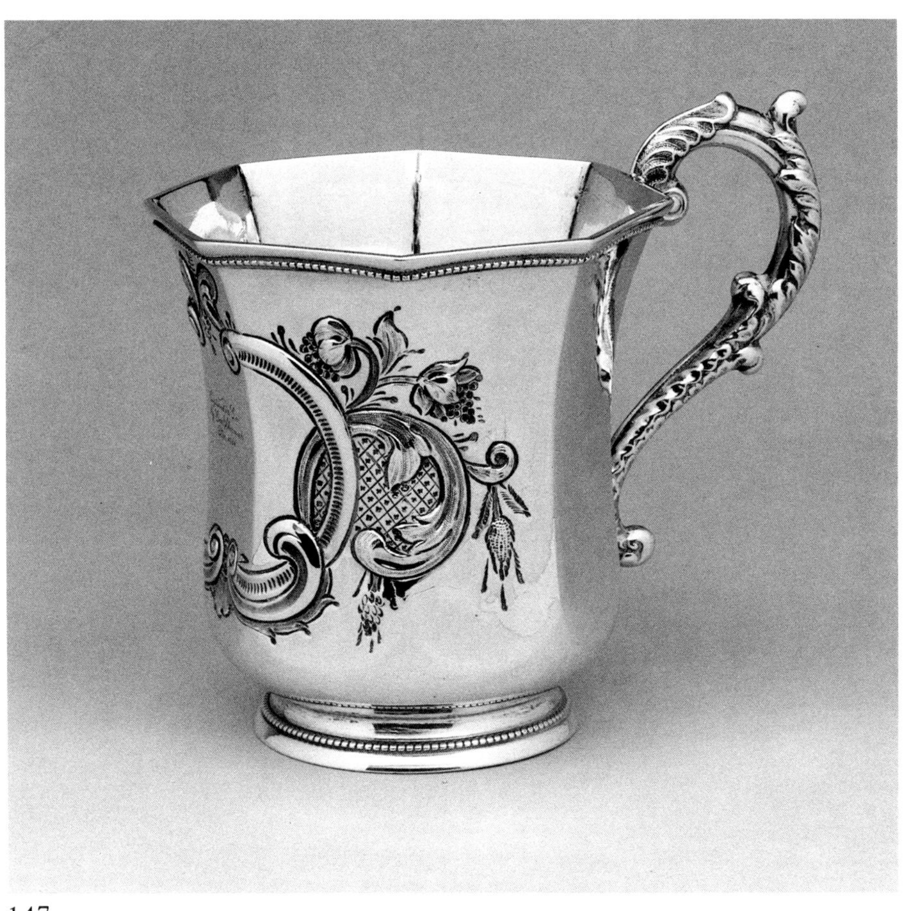

147

was in Georgetown, South Carolina, by 1825. He advertised as a gold and silversmith there until 1835. By 1837, he had moved to Charleston and gone into business with Thomas T. Wilmot, who may or may not have been his brother. Until 1840, S. and T. T. Wilmot were listed in Charleston directories as jewelers at 267 King Street. Thomas Wilmot advertised in Savannah as early as 1843. Samuel did not appear until 1850, but he used the same address as Thomas: No. 1 Market Square. Samuel continued to advertise watches, jewelry, and silverware in Savannah, and formed a partnership with Henry A. Richmond in 1856. How long this relationship lasted is uncertain, but in 1868, Wilmot had sold his land in Savannah and moved to Bridgeport, Connecticut.

The concentrated repoussé designs filling the body of the wagon are typical of the later period of the rococo influences in American silver during 1850–80. If Wilmot did in fact make this highly sophisticated piece, he could have been in Savannah by mid-century. It is not known whether he continued the silversmith/jewelry business after he returned to Connecticut.

147 *Cup*, 1850–1856

H. P. Horton and Rikeman (first name unknown) (working ca. 1850–1856)

Savannah

Silver

H. 4⅝", W. 5" (including handle), Diam. 3 11/16"

Marked: HORTON & RIKEMAN

Engraved: Captured in Georgia / by Gen. Sherman / Dec. 1864

Description: Octagonal body with flaring lip; beading around lip and foot; C-scrolled handle with acanthus thumb piece; repousséd C-scrolls form cartouche and floral designs and diapering on front and sides of body; engraving added later

Exhibitions: *Southern Silver*, The Museum of Fine Arts, Houston, Texas, 1968

References: Cutten, *The Silversmiths of Georgia*, frontispiece, and 4; Williams, "Savannah Silver and Silversmiths," *Antiques*, March 1967, 349; Warren, *Southern Silver*, Cat # D-2-A.

Owens-Thomas House, Telfair Academy of Arts and Sciences, Inc.

This cup was found in the 1950s in a Maine farm house. The owners were descendants of a watchmaker and jeweler, Amasa W. Hall, who had come to Atlanta in 1852 and had conducted his business there. To escape the Civil War, Hall and his family left Atlanta and were eventually reunited in Lewiston, Maine. This cup was transported north with the Halls then, not captured by General Sherman as the engraving suggests.

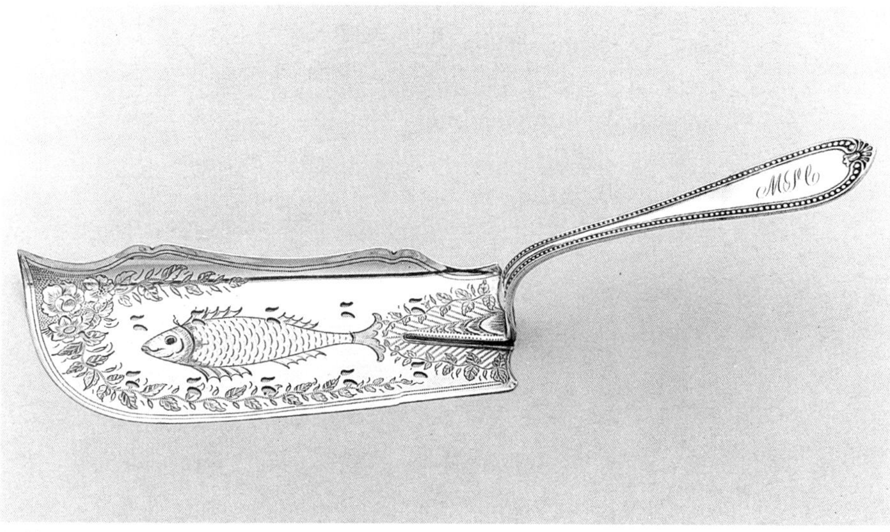
148

148 *Fish Slice*, ca. 1850

H. P. Horton (working ca. 1850)

Savannah, Chatham County

Silver

H. 3″ (to handle), W. 11½″, L. 2⅝″

Marked on back of handle: H.P.HORTON

Inscribed: MSC

Description: Upturned beaded handle; flat pierced blade with upturned scalloped edge; bright-cut fish with floral design engraving surrounding

Exhibitions: *Southern Silver*, Museum of Fine Arts, Houston, Texas, 1968

References: Williams, "Savannah Silver and Silversmiths," *Antiques*, March 1967, 348; Warren, *Southern Silver*, Cat # D–2-B.

Owens-Thomas House, Telfair Academy of Arts and Sciences, Inc.

The fish slice, or knife, belonged to Maria Sophia Champion, and was most likely retailed by Horton possibly after his partnership with Rikeman broke up. Marks that are incised are often those of a retailer rather than a maker.

Little is known about the watchmaking, silversmithing, and jewelry firm of Horton & Rikeman except that it commenced business at 116 Broughton Street in 1850 and continued until 1 February 1856. Flatware with individual marks of both men are extant.

Gunsmithing in Georgia Before 1860

The introduction of firearms into the state of Georgia probably occurred

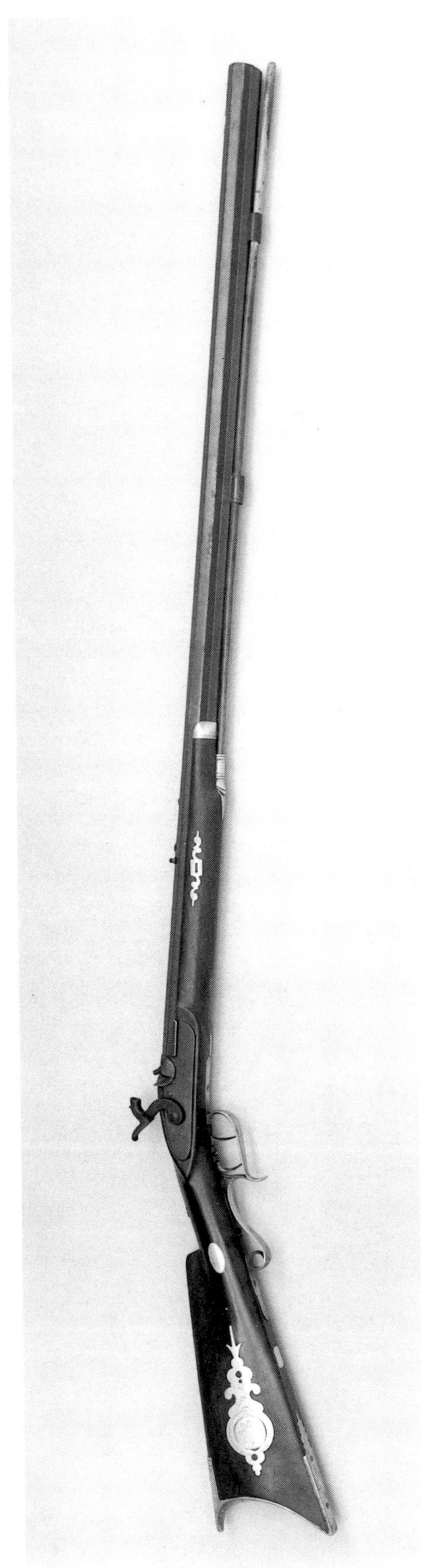

149

when the Spanish came through in 1540 under the leadership of Hernando deSoto. Before 1733, gun powder, lead, flints, and inexpensive muskets had been traded between the Indians in Georgia and Europeans in Charleston. When Georgia became a British colony, the flint lock system of ignition became prevalent and remained so until the 1830s. It was replaced by the more modern percussion cap system of ignition.

During the colonial period, firearms were primarily for military use, but the game that abounded along the marshes and woodlands of the Georgia coast brought a demand for sporting guns. Much like Charleston, Savannah became famous as a dueling city. Although later outlawed in the state, duels were fought across the Savannah River on an island that was either neutral or part of South Carolina.

Since good quality firearms could be easily imported from England, there was little need for gunmakers in pre-revolutionary America, but many gunsmiths nevertheless established businesses. These craftsmen repaired or sold British firearms with flint lock ignitions. No Georgia-marked examples survive, however.

By the 1830s, the gunsmithing industry had slowly begun to prosper, and the earliest guns marked by Georgia gunsmiths date from the 1840s.

The five rifles exhibited show several stylistic similarities, especially in the type of hardware used for the lower flammer thimble (all similar), the trigger guard [151, 152], or cartouches on side of barrel [149, 151]. An ad in the 1784 *Gazette of the State* announcing "an assortment of ready-made gun work and brass mounting, handy for country smiths" is an especially early bit of evidence that these elements of a firearm were available to be purchased and assembled by the gunsmith (John Richards, *Gazette of the State*, 8 April 1784). The barrel on the Jones rifle [153] is marked by a New England manufacturer. There is no doubt that in port towns like Savannah gun parts somewhat like clock making materials were readily available.

149 *Half-Stock Sporting Rifle*, ca. 1850

Henning D. Murden (1815–1903)

Crawfordville, Taliaferro County

Walnut stock; hickory ramrod; silver inlay; steel patch box

L. 51¼″, L. of barrel 36″

Marked on underside of stock: H.D.MURDEN / CRAWFORDVILLE, GA

Description: .45 caliber; percussion ignition; octagonal barrel; single set cheek piece stock; double set trigger; housing plate engraved with fowling scene of pheasants

Alexander H. Stephens State Park, Department of Natural Resources, Parks and Historic Sites

Henning D. Murden lived in Robinson, Georgia, but his rifles are marked "Crawfordville," the closest town of any size. This rifle is typical of Murden's work, of which several examples are known, in that it is a half-stock sporting rifle. The sophistication of its design and decoration suggests it may have been made-to-order.

150 *Half-Stock Sporting Rifle*, ca. 1845

Elisha H. Rogers and Robert Abbey (working 1842–1860)

Augusta, Richmond County

Walnut stock; hickory ramrod; iron and gold furniture; silver nose cap

L. 50⅛″, L. of barrel 33½″

Marked on top of the barrel: ROGERS & ABBEY / AUGUSTA / N°. 9

Engraved on gold plate on lock plate: 1847 Geo G McWhorter / from his / father

Description: .36 caliber; percussion ignition; octagonal barrel with alternating flat and round surfaces; double cheek piece on stock; single set trigger; flat English style checkering; false muzzle; peep site; lock plate engraved with floral design

Exhibition: National Rifle Association Exhibition, Atlanta, 1974, silver medal winner

Collection of Robert Berryman

[see following entry]

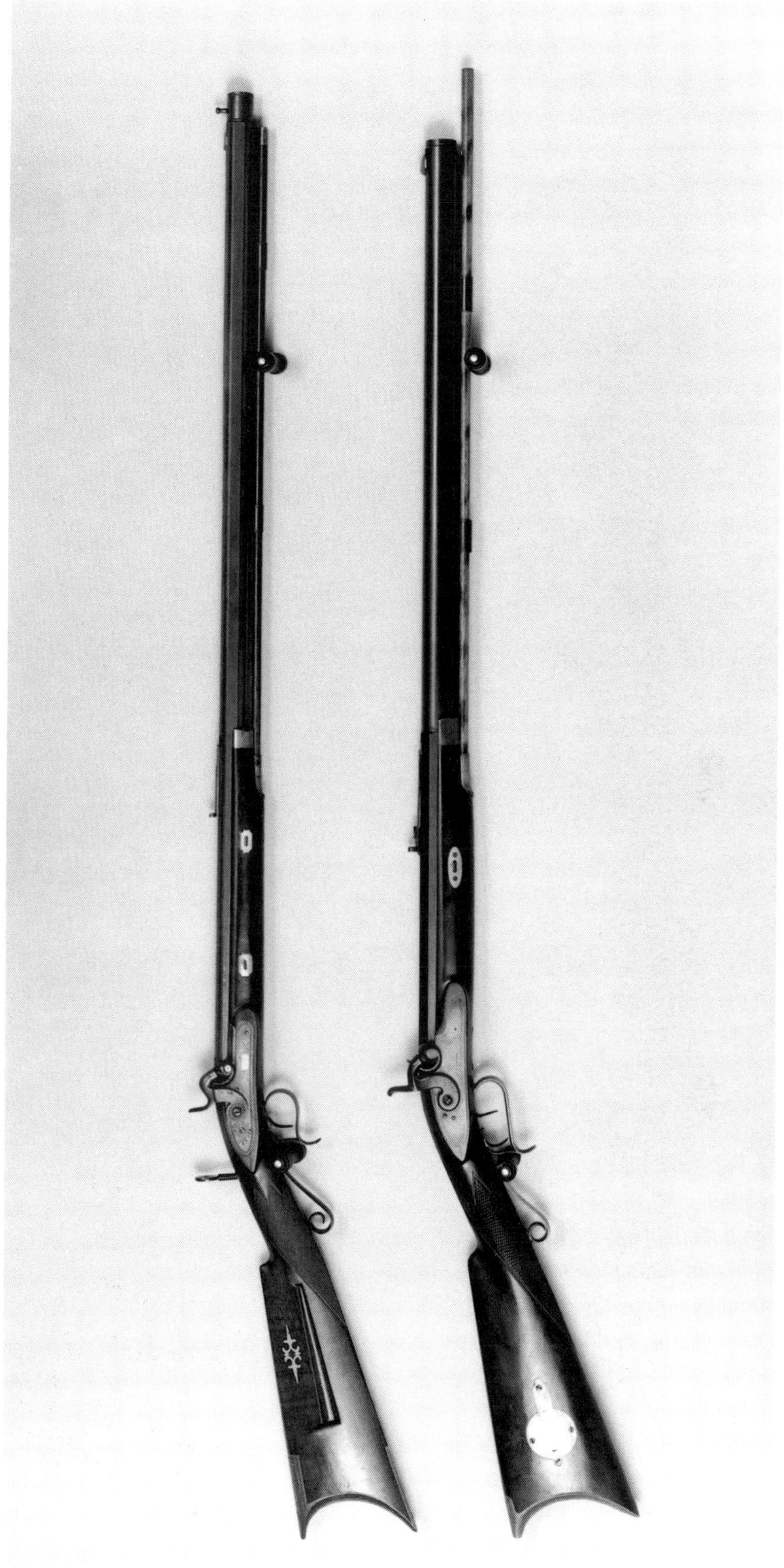

150, 151

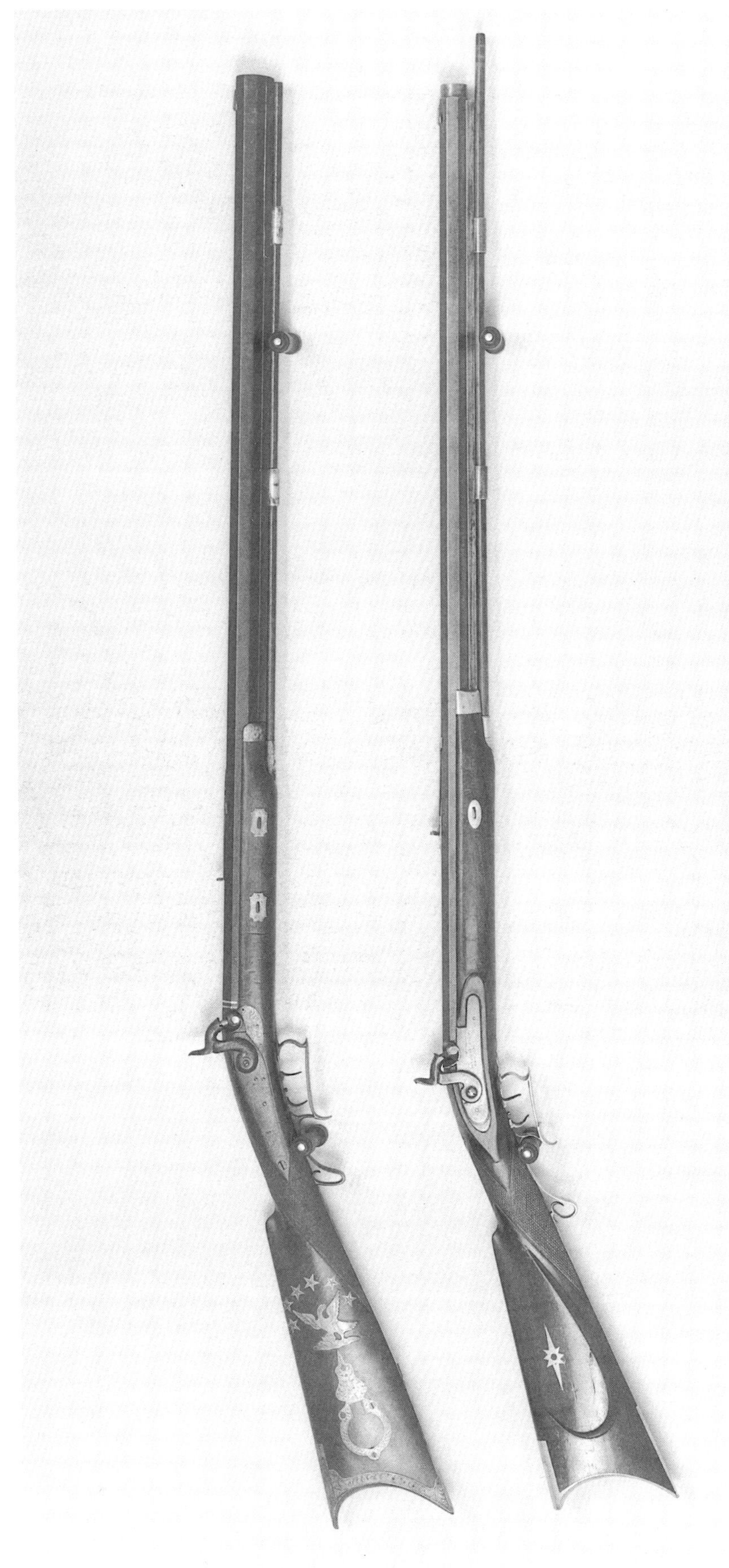

152, 153

151 *Half-Stock Sporting Rifle*, ca. 1845

E. H. Rogers (ca. 1813–1891)

Augusta, Richmond County

Walnut stock; German silver patch box; pewter nose cap; ramrod

L. 48½", L. of barrel 31⅞"

Marked on lock plate: E H ROGERS / AUGUSTA GA / CAST STEEL

Marked on top of barrel: E H ROGERS

Description: .45 caliber; percussion ignition; part octagonal/part round barrel, which is finished in brown; checkering at stock wrist; double set triggers; single screw lock

Exhibitions: American Society of Arms Collectors Meeting, New Orleans, 1979, Atlanta, 1982; National Rifle Association Meeting, Atlanta, 1974

Collection of Richard N. Kennedy, Jr.

Originally from New York, Elisha H. Rogers first moved to Savannah before establishing himself in Augusta by the 1840s. His partnership with Robert Abbey lasted 18 years, but he produced firearms under his own name. He won a $10 premium for a shotgun and a rifle he entered in the 1855 annual fair of the Southern Central Agricultural Society for the category of wood and iron working.

152 *Half-Stock Sporting Rifle*, ca. 1854

Jacob T. Trumpler (working ca. 1850)

Madison, Morgan County

Walnut stock; hickory ramrod; silver furniture; gold banding at breech and gold cartouche and ribbon

L. 49⅞", L. of barrel 32⅞"

Inscribed: "J T Trumpler / Madison, Geo" on ribbon; "PLURIBUS UNUM" on eagle's swag; "CONSTITUTION" on arch of the Georgia seal

Engraved on cartouche on top of barrel: "FLR"

Description: .40 caliber; percussion ignition; full octagonal barrel; double set triggers; single cheek piece; single screw lock plate; back action lock plate; engraving on lock plate; originally had a blue finish

Exhibitions: National Rifle Association Convention, Atlanta, 1974, medal for 5th best rifle in the world

Collection of Cecil W. Anderson

Jacob Trumpler is first found in Savannah in the 1850 census records. It is not known when he moved to Morgan County, for his name does not appear in any subsequent census records for that county. This rifle must have been made to order for an important official of the state, or possibly as a presentation piece. It is believed that Trumpler did execute the engraving. Trumpler is not as well known for his work in Georgia as for his rifles and Derringer pistols made in Little Rock, Arkansas, from 1855 to 1885.

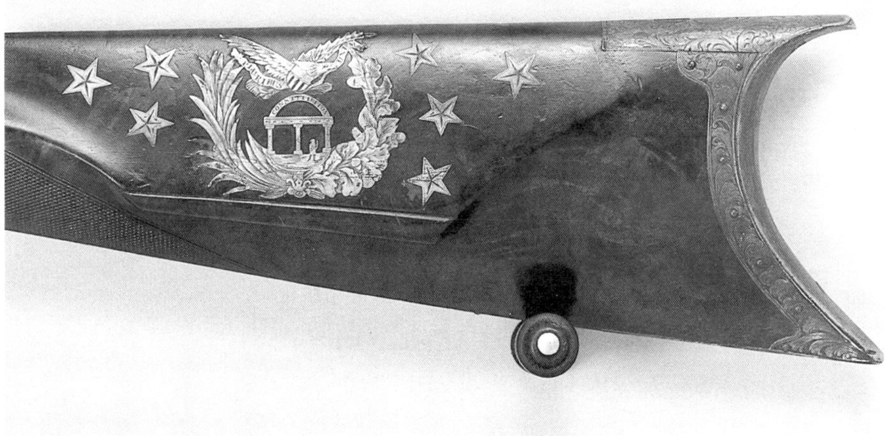

152 detail

153 *Half-Stock Sporting Rifle*, ca. 1850

John T. Jones (working 1846–1860)

Savannah, Chatham County

Walnut stock; hickory ramrod; German silver furniture; pewter nose cap

L. 50", L. of barrel 33½"

Marked on lock plate and top of barrel: J.T.JONES / SAV GA

Description: .40 caliber; percussion ignition; full octagonal barrel turned around ½ inch at muzzle; original brown finish; stock sheckered at wrist; double cheek piece; double set triggers; single screw lock; imported English pistol lock; originally had peep site

Exhibitions: American Society of Arms Collectors Meeting, New Orleans, 1979, Atlanta, 1982

Collection of Richard N. Kennedy

John T. Jones was born in 1824 in New Jersey, but he was in Savannah in a partnership with C. W. Rogers by 1846. This partnership ended in 1847, but he worked in Savannah until 1860.

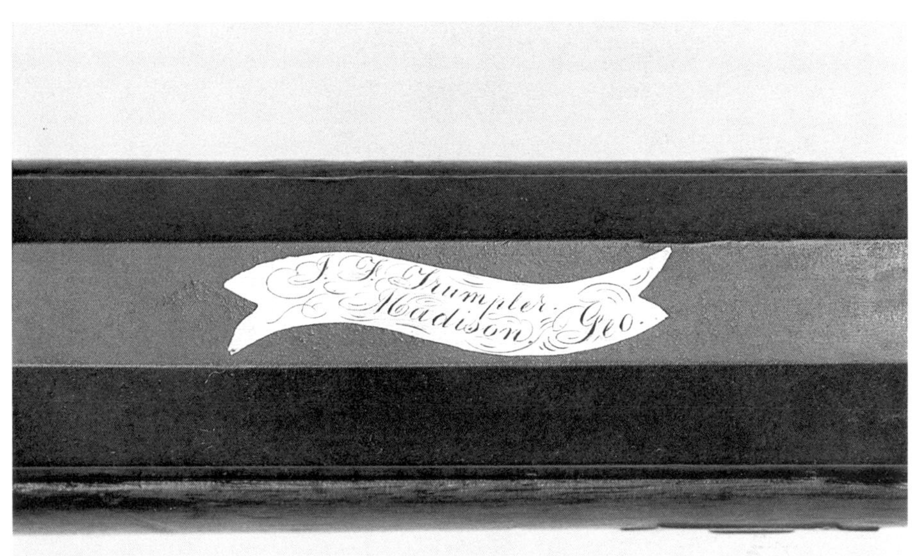

152 detail

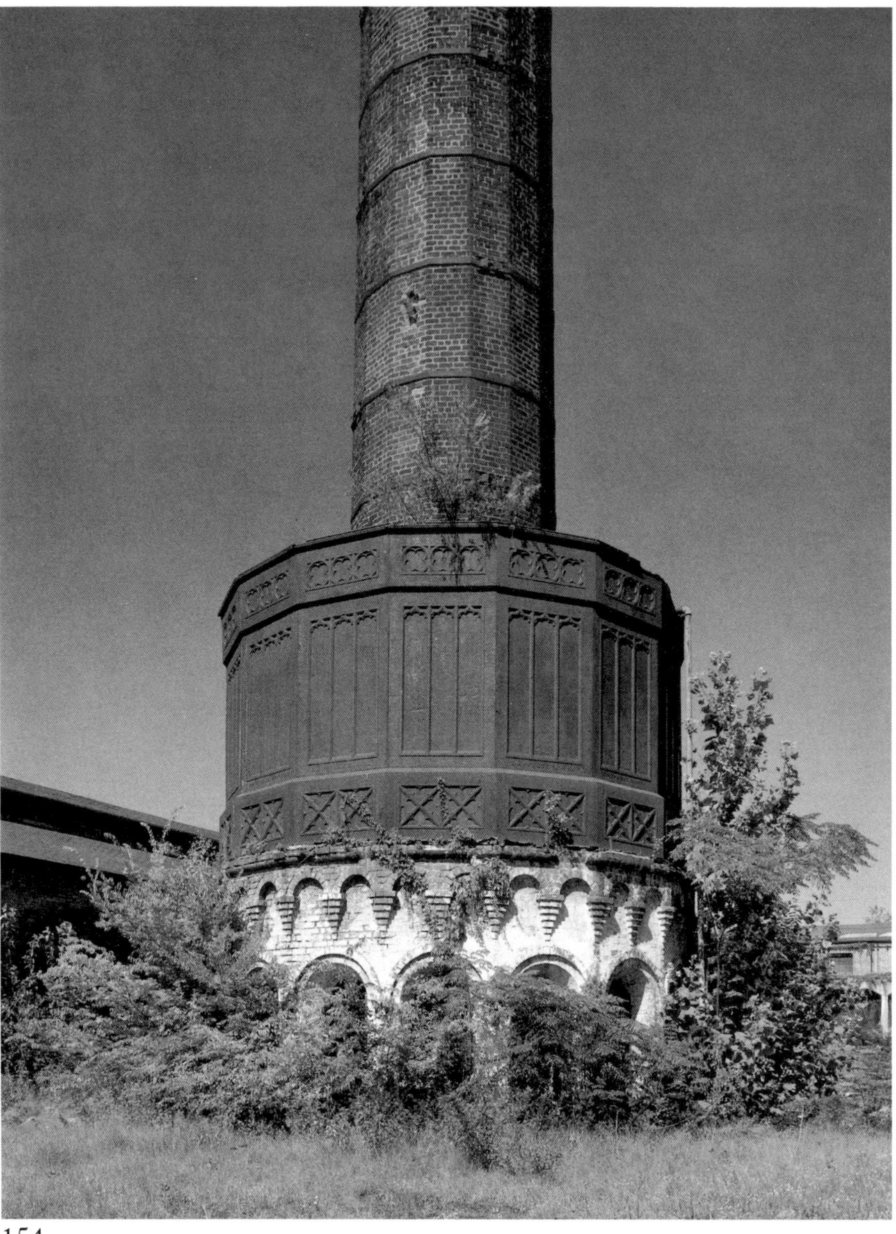

154

154 *Water Tank*, 1853

David and William Rose (active ca. 1850–1865)

Savannah, Chatham County

Cast iron

Marked on each of the 16 sides of the tank: D & W^{m}. Rose, Sav^{h}. GA

Description: Combined with smokestack and privies; chimney 123 feet high; brick barrel vaults form arches behind which were privies and changing rooms; polygonal cast iron tank embossed with quartrefoils, ogee arched panels, and other Gothic revival designs

References: John Linley, *The Georgia Catalog*, 136–39.

City of Savannah

The paucity of documented cast or wrought iron work in Georgia dating before 1860 is puzzling. There were several foundries "in blast" throughout the state before 1820: Robinson's Iron Works, near Richmond County, 1792; Sweetwater Iron Works, Columbia County, 1796–1811; Files' Iron Works, Jackson County, 1797–98; Adullam Furnace, Jackson County, 1797; Providence Iron Works, Columbia County, 1800–17; Bird & Hemp, Shoals of the Ogeechee, Screven County, 1796–97. Advertisements from these foundries indicate that substantial amounts of iron were being manufactured. For example, Bird & Hemp in 1797 made "1500–2000 lbs. of bar iron a week, of a quality equal to any made on the Continent" (*Augusta Chronical and Gazette of the State*, 7 October 1797).

After the 1820 fire in Savannah, where most of the local architectural ironwork should exist, architect William Jay advocated the use of iron in future buildings in Savannah because of its fireproof qualities. Henry McAlpin (died 1851), who already had a brickmaking business on his plantation, the Hermitage, outside Savannah, also started an iron foundry "where castings of all descriptions are done in the neatest manner . . . elegant railings, balconies or platforms, and likewise for tombs or fences cast from newest patterns-Backs of chimneys" (*The Daily Georgian*, 11 June 1821). Northern competition persisted, however, and again, before the 1860s, it is impossible without a stamp to distinguish the local products from those imported, particularly from the New York manufacturies of John B. Wickersham and the James Beebee Company, working during 1851.

Trained as machinists in Lancastershire, England, David and William Rose opened a foundry on Indian Street in Savannah. They advertised in 1854 "iron and brass castings . . . at Northern Prices" (Hartridge, "Architectural Trends in Savannah," *Antiques*, March 1967, 330). They were listed in the first Savannah City Directory in 1859. Many of the mid-nineteenth century cemeteries in Savannah—Laurel Grove, Bonaventure, and Vincent de Paul—have gates bearing the Rose stamp. The gate of the Owens-Thomas House also has their stamp. The Roses continued in business on the canal, between West Broad and Fahm Street, until the Civil War, when the Confederacy used their foundry.

The entire complex of the Central of Georgia Railroad is a study of Gothic and Romanesque Revival architecture styles usually associated with ecclesiastical or domestic buildings. However, in the true spirit of the revival, materials are used "to the maximum advantage of their structural qualities, which were to be expressed visually" (Linley, *The Georgia Catalog*, 135). Unfortunately, unlike the airy temple structures characterizing the Greek Revival, the complicated roof lines and delicate exterior decorations of Gothic Revival were not well suited to the hot, humid Georgia climate. Soon the roofs leaked and the finials and trim rotted.

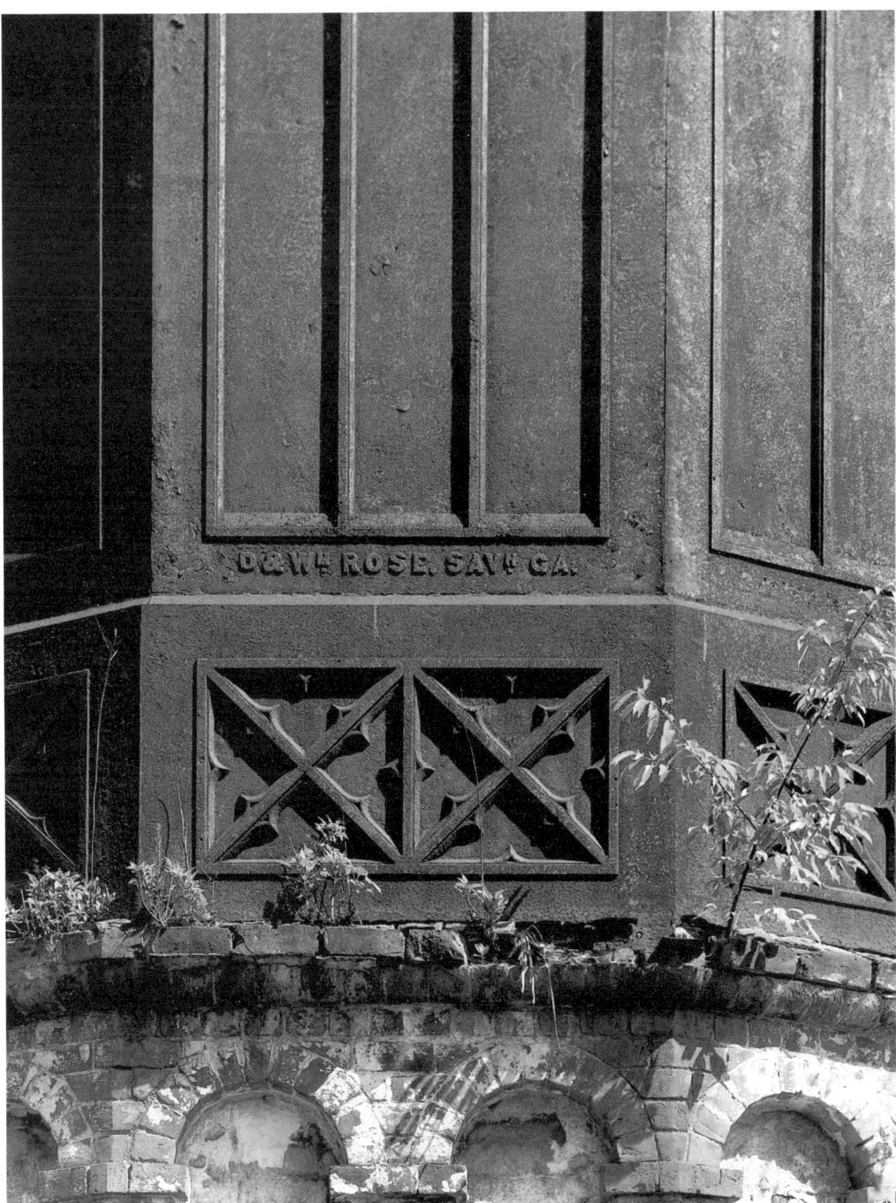

154 detail

BIBLIOGRAPHY

Primary Sources

Anderson, Hugh, and David Douglas. *A True and Historical Narrative of the Colony of Georgia.* Charleston, 1741.

Catalogue of the Teachers, Pupils, and Patrons of the LaGrange Female Insititute, for the Scholastic Year Commencing Jan. 15th, ending Nov. 1st 1848. New York: Joseph H. Jennings, 1848.

Catesby, Mark. *The Natural History of Carolina, Florida, and the Bahama Islands: Containing the Figures of Birds, Beasts, Fishes, Serpents, Insects, and Plants.* London: Printed for Benjamin White, at Horace's Head, in Fleetstreet, 1771.

Georgia Historical Society. *The Letters of Honorable James Habersham, 1756–1775.* Savannah, Ga.: The Savannah Morning News Print. 1904.

Hall, Capt. Basil. *Forty Etchings from Sketches made with the Camera Lucida in North America in 1827 and 1828.* London: Moon, Boys and Graves, 1849.

Hepplewhite, Alice. *The Cabinet-Maker and Upholsterer's Guide; or, Repository of designs for every article of household furniture . . . From drawings by A. Hepplewhite and Co. . . .* 3d ed. London: Printed for I. and J. Taylor, 1794.

McKinney, William L., and James Hall. *History of the Northern Tribes of North America.* Vol. 1. Philadelphia: E. C. Biddle, 1833.

Nicholson, Peter. *The Carpenter's New Guide: being a complete book of lines for carpentry and joinery.* 2d. ed. London: Printed for I. and J. Taylor, 1792.

Shaw, Joshua. *Picturesque Views of American Scenery.* Philadelphia: Mathew Carey & Sons, 1820.

Trimmings, Thomas, et al. *The Philadelphia Cabinet and Chair-Makers' Book of Prices.* Philadelphia: Federal Society of Cabinet and Chair-Makers, 1794.

Urlsperger, Samuel, ed. *Ausführliche Nachrichten.* 12 vols. Halle, Germany: Waisenhaus, 1735 ff.

Watkins, George, and Robert Watkins. *A Digest of the Laws of the State of Georgia, from its Establishment as a British Province Down to the Year 1798 Inclusive.* Philadelphia: R. Aiken, 1800.

White, George. *Statistics of the State of Georgia.* Savannah: W. Thorne Williams, 1849.

Records of the 1820 Census of Manufacturers in Georgia: Wilkes, Richmond, Jones, and Jackson counties.

Wills and Estate Inventories from Greene County, Georgia, 1814–1830.

Wills and Estate Inventories from Hancock County, Georgia, 1809–1830.

Wills and Estate Inventories from Morgan County, Georgia, 1826–1830.

Newspapers

American Beacon and Norfolk and Portsmouth Daily Advertiser, Virginia

Augusta Chronicle and Gazette of the State

Augusta Herald

City Gazette and The Daily Advertiser, Charleston, South Carolina

Columbian Herald, Charleston, South Carolina

Columbian Museum and Savannah Advertiser

Columbian Museum and Savannah Daily Gazette

Columbian Weekly Enquirer, Savannah

Daily Georgian

Gazette of the State of Savannah

Georgia Constitutionalist

Georgia Express, Athens

Georgia Gazette, Savannah

Georgia Journal, Milledgeville

Georgia Messenger, Macon

Georgia Republican and State Intelligencer, Savannah

Louisville Public Advertiser, Kentucky

Mirror of the Times, Augusta

Pennsylvania Mercury, Philadelphia

Republican and Saturday Evening Ledger

Republican Star and General Advertiser, Easton, Maryland

Savannah Republican

South Carolina Gazette, Charleston, South Carolina

Southern Banner, Athens

Virginia Gazette and General Advertiser

Virginia Gazette and Petersburg Intelligencer

Virginia Gazette and Weekly Advertiser

Exhibition Catalogues

Chambers, Bruce W. *American Paintings in the High Museum, a Bicentennial Catalogue.* Atlanta: High Museum of Art, 1975.

Dickens, Roy S., Jr. *Of Sky and Earth.* Atlanta: High Museum of Art, 1982.

Farnham, Katherine Gross, and Callie Huger Efird. *Georgia Collects American Silver, 1780–1870.* Atlanta: High Museum of Art, 1971.

Goldsborough, Jennifer Faulds. *Silver in Maryland.* Baltimore: Museum and Library of Maryland History, Maryland Historical Society, 1983.

Green, Henry D. *Furniture of the Georgia Piedmont Before 1830.* Atlanta: High Museum of Art, 1976.

Griffin, William W., et al. *Neat Pieces: The Plain-Style Furniture of 19th Century Georgia.* Atlanta: Atlanta Historical Society, 1983.

Horton, Frank L., and Jan Garrett Hind. *The Museum of Early Southern Decorative Arts.* Winston-Salem, N.C.: Museum of Early Southern Decorative Arts, 1979.

McBride, Walter. *Our Heritage in Weaving.* Grand Rapids, Michigan: Grand Rapids Art Museum, 1976.

Powers, Deborah S. *Revolutionary America: An Exhibition.* Bloomington: The Lilly Library, Indiana University, 1976.

Reynolds, Elizabeth P. *Southern Comfort.* Atlanta: Atlanta Historical Society, 1978.

Rogers-Price, Vivian. *John Abbot in Georgia: The Vision of a Naturalist Artist.* Madison: Madison-Morgan Cultural Center, 1983.

Stewart, Robert. *Henry Benbridge, American Portrait Painter.* Washington, D.C.: National Portrait Gallery, Smithsonian Institution, 1971.

Vlach, John Michael. *The Afro-American Tradition in Decorative Arts.* Cleveland, Ohio: The Cleveland Museum of Art, 1978.

Wadsworth, Anna, et al. *Missing Pieces: Georgia Folk Art, 1770–1976.* Atlanta: Atlanta Historical Society, 1976.

Ward, Barbara McLean, and Gerald W. R. Ward. *Silver in American Life.* New Haven: Yale University Art Gallery, 1979.

Warren, David B. *Southern Silver.* Houston: The Museum of Fine Arts, 1968.

Periodicals

"An Account of the City of Charles-Town, Metropolis of the Province of South-Carolina, with an Exact and Beautiful Prospect Thereof." *The London Magazine* 31 (June 1762), 296.

Banks, William Nathaniel. "George Cooke, Painter of the American Scene." *Antiques* 102 (September 1972), 448–54.

Coatney, G. Robert, and Robert G. Scholtens. "Georgia-Made Clocks." *Bulletin of the National Association of Watch and Clock Collectors, Inc.* 17 (October 1975), 454–77.

Comstock, Helen. "Furniture of Virginia, North Carolina, Georgia, and Kentucky." *Antiques* 61 (January 1952), 58–99.

Couch, Dale L. "John Riley Hopkins: A Nineteenth Century Georgia Cabinetmaker." *Atlanta Historical Society Journal* 28 (Summer 1984), 43–55.

Cumming, William P. "Mapping of the Southeast: The First Two Centuries." *The Southeastern Geographer* 16 (1966), 3–19.

"Description of Frederica." *The London Magazine* 14 (August 1745), 395–96.

Estes, Rosemary Niner. "Daniel Cannon: A Revolutionary 'Mechanick' in Charleston." *Journal of Early Southern Decorative Arts* 9 (May 1983), 1–31.

Farnham, Katharine Gross, and Callie Huger Efird. "Early Silversmiths and the Silver Trade in Georgia." *Antiques* 99 (March 1971), 380–85.

Green, Henry D. "Furniture of the Georgia Piedmont Before 1820." *Art and Antiques* 5 (January-February 1982), 80–87.

———. "Georgia's Early Governor's Mansion at Milledgeville, 1838–1868." *Antiques* 94 (December 1968), 864–67.

"Georgia Prehistory: An Overview in Time and Space, Symposium Papers presented at the Georgia Academy of Science, Atlanta, 1972." *Early Georgia* 3 (June 1975), 1–63.

Hartridge, Walter Charlton. "Architectural Trends in Savannah." *Antiques* 91 (March 1967), 324–30.

Hunter, Anna C. "The Bay: Savannah's Water Front." *Antiques* 91 (March 1967), 332–33.

Johnson, Marilyn A. "John Hewitt, Cabinetmaker." *Winterthur Portfolio* 4 (1968), 185–205.

Jones, George Fenwick, ed. "The Secret Diary of Paston Johann Martin Bolzius." *Georgia Historical Quarterly* 53 (March 1969), 78–110.

Jones, Grant D. "The Ethnohistory of the Guale Coast Through 1684." *The Anthropology of Saint Catherines Island, Natural and Cultural History* 55 (1978), 178–210.

Rauschenberg, Bradford L. "The Mysterious Duché." *Luminary* (Winter 1983), 6.

Ristow, Walter W. "State Maps of the Southeast to 1833." *The Southeastern Geographer* 16 (1966), 33–40.

Rogers-Price, Vivian and William W. Griffin. "John Abbot: Pioneer Artist-Naturalist in Georgia." *The Magazine Antiques* 124 (October 1983), 768–73.

Saye, Albert B. "Was Georgia a Debtor Colony?" *Georgia Historical Quarterly* 24 (December 1940), 323–32.

Spalding, Phinizy B. "The Return of John Milledge." *Columns* 17 (Fall 1971), 7.

Swan, Mabel Munson. "Coastwise Cargoes of Venture Furniture." *Antiques* 55 (April 1949), 278–80.

Theus, Mrs. Charlton M. "Furniture in Savannah." *Antiques* 91 (March 1967), 364–67.

Williams, James A. "Savannah Silver and Silversmiths." *Antiques* 91 (March 1967), 347–49.

Additional Sources

Baillie, G. H.; C. Clutton; and C. A. Ilbert. *Britten's Old Clocks and Watches and Their Makers*. New York: Bonanza Books, 1956.

Bishop, Robert. *Folk Painters of America*. New York: E. P. Dutton, 1979.

Burrison, John A. *Brothers in Clay, the Story of Georgia Folk Pottery*. Athens: University of Georgia Press, 1983.

Burroughs, Paul H. *Southern Antiques*. Richmond: Garrett & Massie, Inc., 1931.

Caldwell, Joseph R. *Irene Mound Site, Chatham County, Georgia*. Athens: University of Georgia Press, 1941.

Cashin, Edward J. *The Story of Augusta*. Augusta: The Richmond County Board of Education, 1980.

Clarke, William Bordley. *Freemasonry in Georgia*. Macon: Masonic Educational and Historical Commission of the Grand Lodge of Georgia, 1933.

Coleman, Kenneth, ed. *A History of Georgia*. Athens: University of Georgia Press, 1977.

Coleman, Kenneth, and Charles Stephen Carr, eds. *Dictionary of Georgia Biography*. 2 vols. Athens: University of Georgia Press, 1983.

Cooper, Wendy A. *In Praise of America*. New York: Alfred A. Knopf, 1980.

Coulter, E. Merton. *College Life in the Old South*. New York: MacMillan, 1928.

Coulter, E. Merton, and Albert B. Saye, eds. *Georgia's Disputed Ruins*. Chapel Hill: University of North Carolina Press, 1937.

———. *Old Petersburg and the Broad River Valley of Georgia*. Athens: University of Georgia Press, 1965.

———. *The Journal of Peter Gordon, 1732–1735*. Athens: University of Georgia Press, 1963.

———. *Thomas Spalding of Sapelo*. University, La.: Louisiana State University Press, 1940.

Cumming, William P. *British Maps of Colonial America*. Chicago: University of Chicago Press, 1974.

———. *The Exploration of North America 1630–1776*. New York: G. P. Putnam's Sons, 1974.

———. *The Southeast in Early Maps*. Chapel Hill: University of North Carolina Press, 1962.

Cutten, George Barton. *The Silversmiths of Georgia*. Savannah: Pigeonhole Press, 1958.

Davis, Harold E. *The Pledging Province, Social and Cultural Life in Colonial Georgia, 1733–1776*. Chapel Hill: University of North Carolina Press, 1976.

Dickens, Roy S., Jr., and James L. McKinley. *Frontiers in the Soil: The Archaeology of Georgia*. Atlanta: Frontiers Publishing Company, 1979.

Fairbanks, Jonathan L., and Elizabeth Bidwell Bates. *American Furniture, 1620 to the Present*. New York: Richard Marek Publishers, 1981.

Garrett, Franklin M. *Yesterday's Atlanta*. Miami: E. A. Seemann, Inc., 1977.

Gnann, Pearl Rahn. *Georgia Salzburgers and Allied Families*. Macon: 1956.

Gritzner, Janet B. "Tabby in the Coastal Southeast: The Culture of an American Building Material." Ph.D. dissertation. Louisiana State University, 1978.

Gross, Katharine Wood. "The Sources of Furniture Sold in Savannah, 1789–1815." Master's thesis. University of Delaware, 1967.

Guthorn, Peter J. *British Maps of the American Revolution*. Monmouth Beach, N.J.: Philip Freneau Press, 1972.

Halley, David J. "The Mississippi Period." *Early Georgia*, edited by Marilyn Pennington. Athens: Society for Georgia Archaeology, 1975.

Handbook. Savannah: Solomon's Lodge Number 1, Free and Accepted Masons, 1972.

Hollis, John Hudson, IV. *Mapping Georgia's Growth, 1750–1900*. Atlanta: Miller Hudson, Inc., 1982.

Honan, James D. *The McKinney-Hall Portrait Gallery of American Indians*. New York: Crown Publishers, Inc., 1972.

Hudson, Charles. *The Southeastern Indian*. Knoxville: University of Tennessee Press, 1976.

Hvidt, Kristian, ed. *Von Reck's Voyage, Drawings and Journal of Philip Georg Friedrich von Reck*. Savannah: The Beehive Press, 1980.

Jackson, Harvey H., and Phinizy B. Spalding, eds. *Forty Years of Diversity, Essays on Colonial Georgia*. Athens: University of Georgia Press, 1984.

Jeffries, Richard W. *The Tunacunnhee Site: Evidence of Hopewell Interaction in Northwest Georgia*. Athens: University of Georgia Press, 1976.

Johnson, Edith Duncan. *The Houstouns of Georgia*. Athens: University of Georgia Press, ca. 1950.

Jones, George Fenwick. *Henry Newman's Salzburger Notebooks*. Athens: University of Georgia Press, 1966.

———. *The Salzburger Saga*. Athens: University of Georgia Press, 1984.

Kemble, Frances Anne. *Journal of a Residence on a Georgia Plantation, 1838–1839*. New York: Alfred A. Knopf, 1970.

Koch, Mary Levin. "A History of the Arts in Augusta, Macon, and Columbus, Georgia, 1800–1860." Master's thesis. University of Georgia, 1983.

Kovell, Ralph M., and Terry H. Kovell. *A Dictionary of American Silver and Pewter and Silver Plate*. New York: Crown Publishing Inc., 1968.

Lane, Mills B., ed. *A Rambler in Georgia*. Savannah: The Beehive Press, 1973.

Lanning, John Tate. *The Diplomatic History of Georgia*. Chapel Hill: University of North Carolina Press, 1936.

———. *The Spanish Missions of Georgia*. Chapel Hill: University of North Carolina Press, 1935.

Levy, B. H. *Savannah's Old Jewish Community Cemeteries*. Macon: Mercer University Press, 1983.

Lewis, Bessie, and Mildred Huie. *Patriarchial Plantations of Saint Simons Island*. Darien, Georgia: 1974.

Linley, John. *The Georgia Catalog, Historic American Buildings Survey*. Athens: University of Georgia Press, 1982.

Lister, Raymond. *Antique Maps and Their Cartographers*. Hamden, Conn.: Arahon Books, 1970.

Lorant, Stephan. *The Glorious Burden: The American Presidency*. New York: Harper & Row, 1968.

Lunny, Robert M. *Early Maps of North America*. Newark, N.J.: The New Jersey Historical Society, 1961.

Martin, Van Jones, and William R. Mitchell, Jr. *Landmark Homes of Georgia, 1733–1983*. Savannah: Golden Coast Publishing Company, 1982.

McCullar, Bernice. *This is Your Georgia*. Montgomery: Viewpoint Publications, Inc., 1972.

McPherson, Robert G., ed. *The Journal of the Earl of Egmont*. Athens: University of Georgia Press, 1962.

Mitchell, George. *In Celebration of a Legacy, the Traditional Arts of the Lower Chattahoochee Valley*. Columbus: Columbus Museum of Arts and Sciences, 1981.

Mitchell, William R., Jr. *Landmarks: The Architecture of Thomasville and Thomas County, Georgia.* Thomasville: Thomasville Landmarks, 1980.

Montgomery, Charles F. *American Furniture: The Federal Period, 1788–1825.* New York: The Viking Press, 1966.

———. *A History of American Pewter.* New York: Prager Publisher, 1973.

Mooney, Chase Curran. *William H. Crawford, 1772–1834.* Lexington: University Press of Kentucky, 1974.

Most Worshipful Grand Lodge of Ancient Free and Accepted Masons of the Commonwealth of Virginia. *Freemasonry: What is it?* Supreme Council 33°, Ancient and Accepted Scottish Rite, Southern Jurisdiction, 1980.

Moye, Sue McLendon. *Inventory of Early Stewart County Furniture, Decorative Styles, and Accessories.* Stewart County: Lower Chattahoochee Area Planning and Development Commission, 1978.

Myers, Robert Manson, ed. *The Children of Pride.* New Haven: Yale University Press, 1972.

National Society of the Colonial Dames of America in Georgia. *Early Georgia Portraits, 1715–1870.* Compiled by the Historical Activities Committee. Marion Converse Bright, State Chairman. Athens: University of Georgia Press, 1975.

Nichols, Frederick Doveton. *The Architecture of Georgia.* Savannah: The Beehive Press, 1976.

———. *The Early Architecture of Georgia.* Chapel Hill: University of North Carolina Press, 1957.

Poesch, Jesse. *The Art of the Old South.* New York: Alfred A. Knopf, 1983.

Pope, G. D., Jr. *Ocmulgee.* Washington, D.C.: United States Department of the Interior, National Park Service, 1956.

Ramsey, L. G. G., ed. *The Complete Encyclopedia of Antiques.* New York: Hawthorn Books, Inc., 1962.

Rauschenberg, Bradford L. *Andrew Duché: A Potter . . . a Little Too Much Addicted to Politics.* Winston-Salem: Museum of Early Southern Decorative Arts, 1985.

Richardson, Edgar P.; Brooke Hindle; and Lillian B. Miller. *Charles Willson Peale and His World.* New York: Harry N. Abrams, Inc., 1982.

Roberts, Kenneth D. *The Contributions of Joseph Ives to Connecticut Clock Technology, 1810–1862.* Bristol, Conn.: American Clock and Watch Museum, Inc., 1970.

Rubin, Saul Jacob. *Third to None.* Savannah: S. J. Rubin, 1983.

Sawyer, Elizabeth, and Jane F. Matthews. *The Old in New Atlanta.* Atlanta: JEMS Publications, 1976.

Schiffer, Margaret Berwind. *Furniture and its Makers of Chester County, Pennsylvania.* Philadelphia: University of Pennsylvania Press, 1966.

Schiffer, Nancy, and Herbert Schiffer. *Woods We Live With.* Exton, Penn.: Schiffer, Ltd., 1977.

Schwartz, Seymour I., and Ralph E. Ehrenberg. *The Mapping of America.* New York: Harry N. Abrams, Inc., 1980.

Sears, William H. *Excavations at Kolomoki, Final Report.* Athens: University of Georgia Press, 1956.

Sellars, Charles Coleman. *Charles Willson Peale.* New York: Scribner Sons, 1969.

———. *Portraits and Miniatures by Charles Willson Peale.* Philadelphia: American Philosophical Society, 1952.

Sheftall, John McKay. *Germans in the Southeastern United States of America, an Historic Overview.* Bonn, Germany: Consulate General of the Federal Republic of Germany, 1982.

Shirley, Rodney W. *The Mapping of the World: Early Printed World Maps 1472–1700.* London: The Holland Press, 1983.

Spalding, Phinizy B. *Oglethorpe in America.* Chicago: University of Chicago Press, 1977.

———. "South Carolina and Georgia during the Oglethorpe period, 1732–1743." Phd. dissertation. University of North Carolina, 1963.

Theus, Mrs. Charlton M. *Savannah Furniture, 1735–1825.* Savannah: 1967.

Thomas, Cyrus. "Report on the Mound Exploration." *12th Annual Report, Bureau of American Ethnology, 1890–1891.* Washington, D.C.: Smithsonian Institution, 1891.

Tooley, R. V. *The Mapping of America.* London: The Holland Press, 1980.

———. *Maps and Map Makers.* New York: Crown Publishers, 1952.

Tyler, Moses Colt. *A History of American Literature,* edited and abridged, Archie H. Jones. Chicago: University of Chicago Press, 1967.

Ver Steeg, Clarence L., ed. *A True and Historical Narrative of the Colony of Georgia.* Athens: University of Georgia Press, 1960.

Wheat, James Clements, and Christian F. Brun. *Maps and Charts Published in America Before 1800, Bibliography.* New Haven: Yale University Press, 1969.

Williams, Stephen, ed. *The Waring Papers: The Collected Works of Antonio J. Waring, Jr.* Cambridge: The Peabody Museum, 1965.

Wilson, Thomas. "Prehistoric Art." *Report of the United States National Museum for the Year Ending June 30, 1896.* Washington, D.C.: U.S. Government Printing Office, 1898.

Worsely, Etta Blanchard. *Columbus on the Chattahoochee.* Columbus: Columbus Office Supply Company, 1951.